Members of the Advisory Board are instrumental in the final selection of articles for each edition of ANNUAL EDITIONS. Their review of articles for content, level, currentness, and appropriateness provides critical direction to the editor and staff. We think that you will find their careful consideration well reflected in this volume.

## Editors/Advisory Board

### EDITOR

**Fred H. Maidment**
*Park College*

### ADVISORY BOARD

**Lawrence S. Audler**
*University of New Orleans*

**Larry Brandt**
*Nova Southeastern University*

**Donna K. Cooke**
*Florida Atlantic University*

**John L. Daly**
*University of South Florida*

**Daniel A. Emenheiser**
*University of North Texas*

**Raymond L. Hilgert**
*Washington University*

**Daniel O. Lybrook**
*Purdue University*

**Faten Moussa**
*SUNY at Plattsburgh*

**Robert K. Prescott**
*Eckerd College*

**Margaret A. Rechter**
*University of Pittsburgh*

**Joseph F. Salamone**
*SUNY at Buffalo*

**Sheldon C. Snow**
*Pepperdine University*

**Rieann Spence-Gale**
*Northern Virginia Community College*

**Harold Strauss**
*University of Miami*

**Larry Theye**
*University of Nebraska Kearney*

**Richard J. Wagner**
*University of Wisconsin Whitewater*

**Ann C. Wendt**
*Wright State University*

## Staff

### EDITORIAL STAFF

**Ian A. Nielsen,** Publisher
**Roberta Monaco,** Senior Developmental Editor
**Dorothy Fink,** Associate Developmental Editor
**Addie Raucci,** Senior Administrative Editor
**Cheryl Greenleaf,** Permissions Editor
**Joseph Offredi,** Permissions/Editorial Assistant
**Diane Barker,** Proofreader
**Lisa Holmes-Doebrick,** Program Coordinator

### PRODUCTION STAFF

**Brenda S. Filley,** Production Manager
**Charles Vitelli,** Designer
**Lara M. Johnson,** Design/ Advertising Coordinator
**Laura Levine,** Graphics
**Mike Campbell,** Graphics
**Tom Goddard,** Graphics
**Eldis Lima,** Graphics
**Juliana Arbo,** Typesetting Supervisor
**Marie Lazauskas,** Typesetter
**Kathleen D'Amico,** Typesetter
**Larry Killian,** Copier Coordinator

iii

# To the Reader

In publishing ANNUAL EDITIONS we recognize the enormous role played by the magazines, newspapers, and journals of the public press in providing current, first-rate educational information in a broad spectrum of interest areas. Many of these articles are appropriate for students, researchers, and professionals seeking accurate, current material to help bridge the gap between principles and theories and the real world. These articles, however, become more useful for study when those of lasting value are carefully collected, organized, indexed, and reproduced in a low-cost format, which provides easy and permanent access when the material is needed. That is the role played by ANNUAL EDITIONS.

New to ANNUAL EDITIONS is the inclusion of related World Wide Web sites. These sites have been selected by our editorial staff to represent some of the best resources found on the World Wide Web today. Through our carefully developed topic guide, we have linked these Web resources to the articles covered in this ANNUAL EDITIONS reader. We think that you will find this volume useful, and we hope that you will take a moment to visit us on the Web at **http://www.dushkin.com** to tell us what you think.

The practice of human resource management is evolving into an exciting and highly diverse profession. Changes in the economic, social, and political forces in countries all over the world have made the study and practice of human resource management a key factor in the success of any organization.

Management must respond to these forces in many ways, not the least of which is the effort to keep current with the various developments in the field. The 43 articles that have been chosen for *Annual Editions: Human Resources 00/01* reflect an outstanding cross section of the current articles in the field. The volume addresses the various component parts of HRM (human resource management) from compensation, training, and discipline to international implications for the worker and the employer. Articles have been chosen from leading business magazines such as *The Harvard Business Review* and journals such as *Workforce* to provide a wide sampling of the latest thinking in the field of human resources.

*Annual Editions: Human Resources 00/01* contains a number of features designed to be useful for people interested in human resource management. These features include a *topic guide* to locate articles on specific subjects, selected *World Wide Web* sites, which are cross-referenced by number in the topic guide and can be referenced to explore further the article topics, and a *table of contents* with abstracts that summarize each article with bold italicized key ideas. The volume is organized into seven units, each dealing with specific interrelated topics in human resources. Every unit begins with an overview that provides background information for the articles in the section. This will enable the reader to place the selection in the context of the larger issues concerning human resources. Important topics are emphasized and key points and questions are presented to address major unit themes. In addition, World Wide Web sites that pertain to each unit are listed.

This is the tenth edition of *Annual Editions: Human Resources*. It is hoped that many more will follow addressing these important issues. We believe that the collection is the most complete and useful compilation of current material available to the human resource management student. We would like to have your response to this volume, for we are interested in your opinions and recommendations. Please take a few minutes to complete and return the postage-paid *article rating form* at the back of the volume. Any book can be improved, and we need your help to continue to improve *Annual Editions: Human Resources.*

Fred Maidment

Fred Maidment
*Editor*

iv

# Contents

## UNIT 1

## Human Resource Management in Perspective

Ten selections examine the current environment of human resource management with special emphasis on corporate strategy, the Americans with Disabilities Act, and sexual harassment.

The concepts in bold italics are developed in the article. For further expansion please refer to the Topic Guide and the Index.

v

## UNIT 2

# Meeting Human Resource Requirements

Five articles discuss the dynamics of human resource job requirements, planning, selection, recruitment and information systems.

The concepts in bold italics are developed in the article. For further expansion please refer to the Topic Guide and the Index.

UNIT 3

## Creating a Productive Work Environment

Five selections examine how to
increase productivity in the workplace by motivating employees,
developing effective communication channels, and providing
good leadership and direction.

UNIT 4

## Developing Effective Human Resources

Four articles discuss how to develop
human resources through employee
training and career development.

The concepts in bold italics are developed in the article. For further expansion please refer to the Topic Guide and the Index.

**UNIT 5**

# Implementing Compensation, Benefits, and Workplace Safety

Ten articles discuss employee compensation, incentive arrangements, executive pay, and safety and health considerations.

**UNIT 6**

## Fostering Employee/ Management Relationships

Five selections examine the dynamics of labor relations, collective bargaining, disciplinary action, temporary employees, and workplace ethics.

The concepts in bold italics are developed in the article. For further expansion please refer to the Topic Guide and the Index.

**UNIT 7**

# International Human Resource Management

Four articles discuss the increasing globalization of human resource management.

# Topic Guide

This topic guide suggests how the selections and World Wide Web sites found in the next section of this book relate to topics of traditional concern to human resources students and professionals. It is useful for locating interrelated articles and Web sites for reading and research. The guide is arranged alphabetically according to topic.

The relevant Web sites, which are numbered and annotated on pages 4 and 5, are easily identified by the Web icon ( ◎ ) under the topic articles. By linking the articles and the Web sites by topic, this ANNUAL EDITIONS reader becomes a powerful learning and research tool.

| TOPIC AREA | TREATED IN | TOPIC AREA | TREATED IN |
|---|---|---|---|
| **Benefits** | 1. HR Comes of Age<br>3. New Mandate for Human Resources<br>17. Remedy Cures Work Doldrums<br>18. Practical Lessons<br>21. Sharpening the Leading Edge<br>30. Overload<br>32. They Want More Support<br>33. Health Care on the Home Front<br>34. Hands-On Health Care Benefits<br>38. Temp Firms Turn Up the Heat<br>40. Impact of 'Inpats'<br>◎ **4, 25, 27, 28** | | 28. Challenging Behaviorist Dogma<br>29. Six Dangerous Myths<br>34. Hands-On Health Care Benefits<br>38. Temp Firms Turn Up the Heat<br>40. Impact of 'Inpats'<br>41. Don't Get Burned by Hot New Markets<br>◎ **4, 8, 9, 18, 26, 31** |
| **Blue-Collar Workforce** | 1. HR Comes of Age<br>2. Profitable Personnel<br>11. There Is No Future for the Workplace<br>13. Is Anybody Out There?<br>17. Remedy Cures Work Doldrums<br>27. Let the Evidence Speak<br>28. Challenging Behaviorist Dogma<br>30. Overload<br>31. Dealing with the Dark Side<br>32. They Want More Support<br>33. Health Care on the Home Front<br>35. Unions: New Activism or Old Adversarial Approach?<br>36. Workers Are Not the Usual Suspects<br>37. Values-Based Discipline<br>38. Temp Firms Turn Up the Heat<br>◎ **1, 2, 4, 5, 6, 9, 11, 13, 17, 20, 24, 25, 27, 28** | **Corporate Strategy and Human Resources** | 2. Profitable Personnel<br>3. New Mandate for Human Resources<br>4. HR Side of Sears' Comeback<br>5. Taking Your Seat 'At the Table'<br>6. HR 2008<br>12. In Defense of Preference<br>13. Is Anybody Out There?<br>14. Job-Hunting Professionals Are Looking for Respect<br>15. Start Your Web Research<br>16. Memory Bankers<br>17. Remedy Cures Work Doldrums<br>18. Practical Lessons<br>19. True Tales and Tall Tales<br>20. Show Them Where You're Headed<br>22. Aligning Training with Business Objectives<br>26. New Thinking on How to Link Executive Pay with Performance<br>27. Let the Evidence Speak<br>28. Challenging Behaviorist Dogma<br>29. Six Dangerous Myths<br>39. Cutting Off the Supply Side<br>40. Impact of 'Inpats'<br>42. Why HR Managers Need to Think Globally<br>◎ **3, 4, 8, 9, 13, 16, 17, 18, 19, 20, 21, 24, 30** |
| **Career Development** | 3. New Mandate for Human Resources<br>6. HR 2008<br>12. In Defense of Preference<br>13. Is Anybody Out There?<br>14. Job-Hunting Professionals Are Looking for Respect<br>20. Show Them Where You're Headed<br>21. Sharpening the Leading Edge<br>22. Aligning Training with Business Objectives<br>23. Use the Web<br>32. They Want More Support<br>40. Impact of 'Inpats'<br>42. Why HR Managers Need to Think Globally<br>◎ **3, 4, 8, 13, 14, 18, 19** | **Education and Training** | 1. HR Comes of Age<br>2. Profitable Personnel<br>3. New Mandate for Human Resources<br>6. HR 2008<br>8. Sexual Harassment<br>9. Workplace Harassment<br>10. What You're Liable for Now<br>15. Start Your Web Research<br>21. Sharpening the Leading Edge<br>22. Aligning Training with Business Objectives<br>38. Temp Firms Turn Up the Heat<br>40. Impact of 'Inpats'<br>43. Interviewing in Japan<br>◎ **4, 5, 8, 18, 20, 22** |
| **Compensation** | 13. Is Anybody Out There?<br>14. Job-Hunting Professionals Are Looking for Respect<br>17. Remedy Cures Work Doldrums<br>18. Practical Lessons<br>25. Pros & Cons of Pay for Performance<br>26. New Thinking on How to Link Executive Pay with Performance<br>27. Let the Evidence Speak | **Employee Stress** | 2. Profitable Personnel<br>7. ADA: The Law Meets Medicine<br>8. Sexual Harassment<br>9. Workplace Harassment<br>10. What You're Liable for Now<br>11. There Is No Future for the Workplace |

3

# ● AE: Human Resources

The following World Wide Web sites have been carefully researched and selected to support the articles found in this reader. If you are interested in learning more about specific topics found in this book, these Web sites are a good place to start. The sites are cross-referenced by number and appear in the topic guide on the previous two pages. Also, you can link to these Web sites through our DUSHKIN ONLINE support site at *http://www.dushkin.com/online/*.

**The following sites were available at the time of publication. Visit our Web site—we update DUSHKIN ONLINE regularly to reflect any changes.**

## General Sites and Statistics

### 1. Bureau of Labor Statistics
*http://stats.bls.gov:80*
The home page of the BLS, an agency of the U.S. Department of Labor, offers Data, Economy at a Glance, Keyword Searches, Surveys and Programs, other statistical sites, and more.

### 2. Economics Statistics Briefing Room
*http://www.whitehouse.gov/fsbr/esbr.html*
Easy access to current federal economic indicators is available at this site, which provides links to information produced by a number of federal agencies. Subjects are Output, Income, Employment, Unemployment, Earnings, Production and Business Activity, Prices and Money, Credits and Securities Markets, Transportation, and International Statistics.

### 3. Human Resource Professional's Gateway to the Internet
*http://www.hrisolutions.com/index2.html*
This up-to-date Web site offers links to other human relations locations, recruiting related Web sites, human resources–related companies, as well as search tools.

### 4. HVL HR Internet Resources
*http://www.hvl.net/hr_res.htm*
Ranging from Al Doran's HRM and Payroll on the Internet list through Eric Wilson's HR Professional's Gateway to the Internet to Ray's List of HRM Connections, this Web site covers Associations, Benefits & Compensation; Salary Information; Government Information Sources; Labor Relations; Occupational Health & Safety; Recruiting; and Training among its many topics.

### 5. In the Workplace
*http://www.ilr.cornell.edu/workplace.html*
The Cornell School of Industrial and Labor Relations offers this site on the Net. It consists of a useful Work Index; a list of Centers, Institutes, and Affiliated Groups; and an Electronic Archive that covers full-text documents on the glass ceiling, child labor, and more.

### 6. Labor Force, Employment, and Unemployment
*http://www.cris.com/%7Enetlink/bci/2BCIlst.html*
Here is helpful statistical information about the civilian labor force. The site covers job vacancies, marginal employment adjustments, employment, diffusion indexes of employees on private nonagricultural payrolls, unemployment, the labor force, and civilian labor force participation rates.

### 7. NBER Home Page
*http://www.nber.org*
The National Bureau of Economic Research engages in specialized research projects on every aspect of economics. The thirteen programs include asset pricing, economics of aging, labor studies, and productivity.

### 8. Voice of the Shuttle: Postindustrial Business Theory Page
*http://humanitas.ucsb.edu/shuttle/commerce.html*

Information on many subjects includes Restructuring, Reengineering, Downsizing, Flattening, Outsourcing, Business & Globalism, Human Resources Management, Labor Relations, Statistics & History, and resources on job searches, careers, working from home, and business startups.

### 9. Wages, Labor Costs, and Productivity
*http://www.globalexposure.com/09bcilst.html*
Useful statistics covering wages and compensation, unit labor costs, and productivity are offered here by Global Exposure, Inc. Includes many indexes and links.

## Human Resource Management in Perspective

### 10. Counsel Quest: Employment and Labor Law
*http://www.counselquest.com/z-employ.htm*
This site offers wide-ranging Web resources covering age discrimination in employment, all of the civil rights legislation, the glass ceiling commission, Americans with Disabilities statutes, the Fair Labor Standards Act, whistleblowing support, unions today, and employment law, to name just a few topics covered by this annotated list.

### 11. Entrants to the Labor Force
*http://stats.bls.gov/emptab3.htm*
The Bureau of Labor Statistics provides interesting figures here about entrants to the labor force by sex, race, and Hispanic origin for the years 1982, 1993, and 1994, and projected for 2005.

### 12. Law at Work
*http://www.lawatwork.com*
From this site you can not only look at current labor laws, such as OSHA, but consider drug testing at work, violence in the workplace, unemployment questions, sexual harassment issues, affirmative action, and much more.

## Meeting Human Resource Requirements

### 13. America's Job Bank
*http://www.ajb.dni.us*
You can find employers or job seekers and lots of job market information from this site. Employers can register job openings, update them, and request employment service recruitment.

### 14. AmericanRecruitment
*http://www.americanrecruitment.com*
This is the Web site of the nation's "leading producer of Sales, Retail, & Management Career Fairs." There is both candidate and company information available here.

### 15. Labor Consultants of America
*http://www.laborconsultants.com/index.htm*
At this site learn about workplace-related issues, and link to federal government sites such as the National Labor Relations Board, the Lawyer's Committee for Civil Rights Under Law, and LaborNet's Guide to Internet Resources on Labor.

### 16. National Center for the Workplace
*http://socs.berkeley.edu/~iir/ncw/execsum.html*

Through interdisciplinary research, information sharing, and policy analysis and development, the NCW addresses the problems created by the convergence of broad economic, social, cultural, political, and technological changes in the workplace. It describes its grant projects here.

## Creating a Productive Work Environment

**17. The Downsizing of America**
*http://www.nytimes.com/specials/downsize/glance.html*
The complete 7-week series on downsizing in America is printed on the Web by the *New York Times*, in which it appeared.

**18. Employee Incentives and Career Development**
*http://www.snc.edu/socsci/chair/336/group1.htm*
This site states that effective employee compensation and career development is an effective tool in obtaining, maintaining, and retaining a productive workforce. There are links to Pay-for-Knowledge, Incentive Systems, Career Development, Wage & Salary Compensation, and more.

**19. Empowerment, Employee Ownership, and Employee Motivation**
*http://www.ualberta.ca/~slis/guides/humanres/EEE.htm*
Access the Foundation for Enterprise Development files at this site. Their mission is to foster the development of competitive enterprises based on the premise that sharing company ownership and meaningful involvement with employees are effective ways of motivating the workforce in order to achieve business goals.

**20. The Future of Worker-Management Relations**
*http://www.ualberta.ca/~slis/guides/humanres/FWM.htm*
The report of the U.S. Federal Commission on the Future of Worker-Management Relations, which covers many issues, including enhancement of workplace productivity, changes in collective bargaining practices, and intervention in workplace problems by government agencies, may be found here.

## Developing Effective Human Resources

**21. Employment Interviews**
*http://www.snc.edu/socsci/chair/336/group3.htm*
The importance of proper interview techniques to the building of a workforce is discussed here. The page has links to related sites and refers to a book by Alder and Elmhorst, *Communicating at Work: Principles and Practices for Business and the Professionals.*

**22. Feminist Majority Foundation**
*http://www.feminist.org*
This site houses the Feminist Career Center, an Affirmative Action page, and information of interest to women.

**23. How to Do an Employee Appraisal**
*http://www.visitorinfo.com/gallery/howapp.htm*
At this site learn online how to do an annual performance review appraisal and read a "horror story" of a badly done one.

**24. Human Resource Management**
*http://www.ozemail.com.au/~cyberwlf/3UB/main2.html*
This site leads to Employee Training facts, Human Resource Planning steps, plus Recruitment Information and a Selection Process outline.

## Implementing Compensation, Benefits, and Workplace Safety

**25. BenefitsLink: The National Employee Benefits Web Site**
*http://www.benefitslink.com/index.shtml*
This link offers facts and services for employers sponsoring employee benefit plans and for participating workers.

**26. Executive Pay Watch**
*http://www.paywatch.org/paywatch/index.htm*
While keeping an eye on the issue of executive salaries, bonuses, and perks in CEO compensation packages, this labor union site offers suggestions to working families on what can be done to curb exorbitant pay schemes.

**27. Social Security Administration**
*http://www.ssa.gov*
Here is the official Web site of the Social Security Administration.

**28. WorkPlace Injury and Illness Statistics**
*http://www.osha.gov/oshstats/bls/index1.html*
The Bureau of Labor Statistics Web presence links to many issues of occupational injury and illness and offers much statistical information.

## Fostering Employee/Management Relationships

**29. Eastman on Defending Your Employee Rights**
*http://www.users.nac.net/thelaw/rights/employ.htm*
This current article is a discussion of protecting your employee rights from abuse, discrimination, exploitation, and fraudulent and wrongful terminations.

**30. Fair Measures: Legal Training for Managers**
*http://www.fairmeasures.com/asklawyer/archive/*
All the questions in this Ask the Lawyer Archive are answered by Rita Risser, an employment law attorney. They cover a range of employee/management relations and are aimed at fostering out-of-court solutions to problems.

## International Human Resource Management

**31. Globalization and Human Resource Management**
*gopher://hoshi.cic.sfu.ca:70/00/dlam/business/ forum/asia/adler/*
Dr. Nancy J. Adler, a faculty member at McGill University, discusses strategic international human resource development in this thorough summary for the Internet.

**32. Labor Relations and the National Labor Relations Board**
*http://www.snc.edu/socsci/chair/336/group2.htm*
From this site you can explore labor relations in today's international marketplace.

**We highly recommend that you review our Web site for expanded information and our other product lines. We are continually updating and adding links to our Web site in order to offer you the most usable and useful information that will support and expand the value of your Annual Editions. You can reach us at:**
*http://www.dushkin.com/annualeditions/.*

**www.dushkin.com/online/**

## Unit Selections

## Key Points to Consider

❖ What social and economic trends do you feel are the most significant? Has downsizing gone too far? How will these trends impact on the labor force as it enters the twenty-first century? How can human resource management make a difference? Does it make a difference?

❖ What are some of the ways that firms can better utilize the skills and talents of their employees? How can small businesses benefit from better human resource management?

❖ What were the most important changes for the American worker in the twentieth century, and what changes do you see as likely in the next 20 years? How is human resources' role likely to change?

❖ What are the implications of the Americans with Disabilities Act?

❖ Sexual harassment is a very important area of concern for most organizations. What do you think organizations can and should do about it? Should it also be applied to customers?

 **Links**

## www.dushkin.com/online/

These sites are annotated on pages 4 and 5.

The only constant is change. Industrial society is dynamic, a great engine that has brought about many of the most significant changes in the history of the human race. Since the start of the industrial revolution in England over 200 years ago, industrialized society has transformed Western civilization in a multitude of ways. Many great inventions of the last 200 years have significantly altered the way people live and the way they see the world.

At the time of the Declaration of Independence, the 13 colonies comprised an overwhelmingly agricultural society that clung to the Atlantic coast of North America. Now at the beginning of the twenty-first century, the United States is a continental nation with the world's largest industrial base and perhaps the smallest percentage of farmers of any major industrialized country. These changes did not happen overnight, but were both the result and the cause of the technological innovations of the industrial revolution. The technological marvels of today, such as television, radio, computers, airplanes, and automobiles, did not exist until after the industrial revolution, and a disproportionate number of them did not exist until after the start of the twentieth century.

With technological changes have come changes in the ways people earn their living. When Thomas Jefferson authored the Declaration of Independence in 1776, he envisioned a nation of small, independent farmers, but that is not what later developed. Factories, mass production, and economies of scale have been the watchwords of industrial development. Industrial development changed not only the economy but also the society. Most Americans are no longer independent farmers but are, for the most part, wage earners, making their living working for someone else.

Changes in the American labor force include the increase in women and minorities working next to white males. The nature of most jobs has changed from those directly associated with production to those providing services in the white-collar economy. Many other changes are developing in the economy and society that will be reflected in the workforce. For the first time since the early days of the republic, international trade represents a significant part of the American economy, having increased greatly in the past 20 years. The economic reality is that the GM autoworker competes not only with Ford and Chrysler, but also with Toyota and Volkswagen.

Society, the economy, and the workforce have changed. Americans today live in a much different world than they did 200 years ago. It is a highly diverse, heterogeneous world—one full of paradox. When people think of American industry, they tend to think of giant companies like IBM and General Electric, but, in fact, most people work for small firms. The relative importance of the *Fortune* 500 companies in terms of employment in the economy has been declining both in real and percentage terms. Small organizations are where economic growth is today.

Change has brought not only a different society, but a more complex one. Numerous rules and regulations must be followed that did not exist 200 years ago. The human element in any organization has been critical to its success, and foreknowing what the human resource needs of the organization are going to be 1, 5, or even 10 years into the future is a key element for continuing success.

Individual lives have also changed. In the first part of the twentieth century, it was common for a worker to spend his or her entire life with one organization, doing one particular job. Now the worker can expect to do many different jobs, probably with a number of different organizations in different industries. Mergers, technological change, and economic fluctuations all put a premium on individual adaptability in a changing work environment for individual economic survival.

The changes in industrial society have often come at a faster rate than most people were willing to either accept or adapt to. Many old customs and prejudices have been retained from prior times, and while progress has been made with regard to certain groups—no American employer today would dare to end an employment notice with the letters "NINA" (No Irish Need Apply), as was common at one time—for other groups, the progress has been slow at best. Women represent about half of American workers, but they are paid only about 70 percent of what men earn. African Americans, other minorities, and people with disabilities have been discriminated against for centuries in American society, to the point where the federal government has been forced to step in and legislate equal opportunity, both on and off the job. Finally, the clash of differing cultures seems ever more pronounced in our society. America has traditionally viewed itself as a melting pot, but it is clear that certain groups have historically "melted" more easily than others, a situation that is reflected in the workplace.

Human resource management plays an important role in industrial America. Business leaders recognize the value of their employees to the future of their organizations. Increasingly, competition in world markets is becoming based on the skills and abilities of people, not machines. Indeed, among major competitors, virtually everyone has essentially the same equipment. The difference is often what the people in the organization do with the equipment.

Society, the workplace, and the way they are viewed have all undergone major changes. Frederick W. Taylor and Elton Mayo, early writers in management, held certain views about industry at the beginning of the twentieth century, while Peter Drucker, Thomas Peters, and others have different ideas now, at the beginning of the twenty-first century. The American society and economy, as well as the very life of the average American worker, are different from what they were 200 or even 100 years ago, and both the workers and the organizations that employ them must respond to those changes.

# Human Resource Management in Perspective

# HR

# Comes of Age

The human resource profession has matured from an administrative support role to a key strategic function in successful organizations. The evolution has been intimately tied to changing workplace values, economic conditions, technological innovations and many other factors.

BY MICHAEL LOSEY

**W**orkforce management has become increasingly complex. The heritage and growth of the human resource management profession is closely linked to people's attitudes about work, the evolution of employment-related laws and sociological trends. The HR field today recognizes the dynamic relationship between strategy, people, technology and the processes that drive organizations. Although this dynamic relationship appears obvious now, the evolution of the profession has often been slow.

One could argue that the HR field dates back to the first working arrangements between master craftspeople and their apprentices. Before the Industrial Revolution, working arrangements involved close relationships between mentors and apprentices dedicated to learning a particular trade. Apprentices were often required to live in the shop or home of the master craftsperson. If an apprentice was injured or sick, the master's family was responsible for restoring the young worker's health and welfare. Master and apprentice shared in good times and bad, in profit and in loss.

The usefulness of this age-old relationship came to an abrupt end with the advent of the Industrial Age. In one powerful stroke, the notion of work moved from guilds and home shops to steam-driven factories. The introduction of the assembly line brought a need for low-skilled employees capable of performing repetitive tasks. Management philosophy at the turn of the century was epitomized by Henry Ford, who often wondered why workers brought their heads to work when all he really needed was their hands and feet.

Assembly line production required that large numbers of people come together for work, but these workers were interchangeable and, to some extent, expendable, because few skills were required for most factory jobs. Employers' attentions focused on consumer demands, the speed at which new machines produced goods and the processes that drove production—concerns that were sometimes placed well ahead of the needs of employees.

## The personnel administration movement

By the late 1800s, people problems were a very real concern in the workplace. For the average blue-collar worker, most jobs were low-paying, monotonous and unsafe. Some industries experienced difficulty recruiting and retaining employees because of the poor working conditions workers were exposed to. As the means of production continued to shift from farmlands and guilds to city factories, concerns grew about wages, safety, child labor and 12-hour workdays. Workers began to band together in unions to protect their interests and improve living standards. Government stepped in to provide basic rights and protections for workers.

Forward-thinking employers recognized that productivity was connected to worker satisfaction and involvement and realized they could not meet production schedules with bands of disgruntled employees. In the late 1800s and early 1900s, the personnel profession that grew out of concerns about employee absenteeism and high turnover attempted to solve worker problems with such basic personnel management functions as employee selection, training and compensation.

It's believed that the first personnel management department began at the National Cash Register Co. (NCR). NCR faced a major strike at the turn of the century but eventually defeated the union after a lockout in 1901. After this difficult union battle, company President John H. Patterson decided to improve worker relations by organizing a personnel department to handle grievances, discharges, safety and other employee issues. The depart-

ment also kept track of pending legislation and court decisions and these first personnel managers provided training for supervisors on new laws and practices.

NCR was not alone in its efforts to address employee grievances. Other employers were looking for management solutions that would alleviate employee disenchantment. Many attempted to ease labor unrest by increasing wages. For example, Ford experienced employee turnover ratios of 380 percent in 1913; in 1914, the company doubled the daily salaries for line workers from $2.50 to $5, even though $2.50 was a fair wage at that time.

Although industrial giants were beginning to understand that they had to do more than just hire and fire if they were going to meet consumer demands for products, most of the objectives of early personnel professionals were one-sided. Business leaders still viewed the work itself as infinitely more important than the people doing it, and production rates remained the top concern. Because employers believed employees would accept more rigid standards if they received extra pay and benefits, most employer-sponsored business solutions were aimed at making employees more efficient. From this mind-set grew scientific management approaches based on the work of Frederick W. Taylor and other experts whose goal was to get people to perform as efficiently as machines.

Of course, such approaches did little to improve worker morale or improve working environments. To counter the growing strength of the labor movement, some employers hired strikebreakers or kept blacklists of union members. Others made workers sign "yellow-dog" contracts—agreements that they would not join unions. Still others attempted to protect their interests by creating company unions to preempt the influence of outside union activities.

Government stepped up to help those who were less fortunate through reforms of work hours, new laws governing the work of children and workers' compensation laws aimed at protecting employees injured on the job. In 1913, Congress created the U.S. Department of Labor "to foster, promote and develop the welfare of working people, to improve their working conditions and to enhance their opportunities for profitable employment."

(Continued on page 14)

| | HISTORY/<br>TECHNOLOGY | SHRM<br>HISTORY | HR<br>HISTORY | LEGISLATIVE/<br>LEGAL |
|---|---|---|---|---|
| 1947 | | Volunteers with National Association of Personnel Directors (NAPD) create advisory committee to review association activities and reorganization options. | | Congress passes the Taft-Hartley Act (Labor-Management Relations Act) after a veto by President Truman. The Wagner Act of 1935 (National Labor Relations Act) had guaranteed employees the right to organize and participate in union activities. The Taft-Hartley Act was enacted to balance labor management relations by protecting employers from unfair union practices such as closed shops, featherbedding and refusal to bargain. The law also permits the president to intervene in strikes for national emergency and other reasons. |
| 1948 | Harry S. Truman defeats Thomas E. Dewey in the presidential election | NAPD Advisory Committee recommends dissolving the association and creating a new national organization--the American Society for Personnel Administration (ASPA). | General Motors Corp. and the United Automobile Workers sign the first major contract with an "escalator" clause, providing for wage increases based on the Consumer Price Index. | |
| 1949 | NATO is established. | 67 people attend ASPA's first national conference in Cleveland. | Child labor is directly prohibited for the first time by an amendment to the Fair Labor Standards Act of 1938. | |
| 1950 | President Truman orders Army to seize all railroads to prevent a general strike. The railroads return to their owners in 1952. U.S. sends 35 military advisers to South Vietnamese government to fight communist forces. | ASPA begins publishing *Personnel News.* | | |
| 1951 | In the first transcontinental television broadcast, President Truman addresses the Japanese Peace Treaty Conference in San Francisco. Levittown, N.Y., started in 1946, is completed. These 17,000 homes represent the prototype for many suburban communities. | | Coalmine disaster claims 119 lives in West Frankfurt, Ill. | |
| 1952 | First hydrogen bomb explodes Nov. 1 at Eniwetok Atoli in Pacific Oceans. | ASPA establishes working office at Marquette University in Milwaukee. | | |
| 1953 | | ASPA formalizes chapter network. Chapters in New York and Philadelphia become first to affiliate. | | |
| 1954 | In *Brown v. Board of Education,* U.S. Supreme Court unanimously rules that racial segregation in public schools is unconstitutional. | ASPA begins publishing *Journal for Personnel Administration.* Membership tops 500. | Peter Drucker's encyclopedia *The Practice of Management* lays out five basic managerial roles: setting objectives, organizing, motivating and communicating, measuring, and developing people. The book introduces the popular technique "Management by Objectives." | Federal minimum wage is 75 cents an hour. |
| 1955 | Rosa Parks refuses to yield her seat on a Montgomery, Ala., bus to a white man, leading to a boycott and court ruling against bus segregation ordinance. | | American Federation of Labor and the Congress of Industrial Organizations merge to form the AFL-CIO, representing about 15 million workers. Union membership peaks at one of every three private-sector workers. | |
| 1956 | Federal Aid Highway Act launches interstate highway system. First transatlantic telephone cable begins operation. | ASPA's *Personnel News* becomes *Personnel Administrator.* | William Whyte's *The Organization Man* describes the mundanity of work life in the offices and bureaucracies of large corporations. | Federal minimum wage rises to $1 an hour. |
| 1957 | President Eisenhower sends federal troops to Little Rock, Ark., to enforce court order admitting black students to Central High School. Soviet Union's launch of the first satellite, Sputnik, spurs U.S. spending on science education. | ASPA establishes new offices at Michigan State University. Professor Paul L. Moore named executive vice president. Membership reaches 1,212. | | |
| 1958 | First U.S. satellite, Explorer I, discovers Van Allen radiation belt encircling Earth. National Airlines flies first domestic passenger jet between New York and Miami. | ASPA office at Marquette University closes. Operations move to East Lansing, Mich. | Welfare and Pension Plans Disclosure Act requires administrators of health, insurance, pension and supplementary unemployment compensation plans to file descriptions and annual financial reports. | |

| | HISTORY/<br>TECHNOLOGY | SHRM<br>HISTORY | HR<br>HISTORY | LEGISLATIVE/<br>LEGAL |
|---|---|---|---|---|
| **1959** | Alaska and Hawaii admitted as states. | ASPA membership dues increase from $18 to $25. | | Landrum-Griffin Act (Labor Management Reporting and Disclosure Act) protects employees from union abuses, guaranteeing the rights to vote by secret ballot for union representatives, to sue unions and to have fair hearings for disciplinary measures. |
| **1960** | Four black college students refuse to move from a Woolworth lunch counter in Greensboro, N.C., inspiring the tactic of "sit-ins." By year-end, more than 70,000 students participate in sit-ins. | ASPA membership passes 2,000. | About one-third of married women are employed. | |
| **1961** | Mercury astronaut Alan Shepard Jr. completes United States' first sub-orbital space flight. | | Amendments to the Fair Labor Standards Act extend coverage to an additional 3.6 million workers, mostly in retain trade and construction, and raise minimum wage. | Federal minimum wage rises to $1.15 an hour. |
| **1962** | John Glenn Jr. becomes first U.S. astronaut to orbit Earth. First U.S. communications satellite launched. James Meredith enters University of Mississippi after federal troops quell riots. President Kennedy orders blockade of Cuba after aerial photos reveal Soviet missile installations. | ASPA charters its 50th chapter, the Central Florida Personnel Association in Orlando. | | |
| **1963** | Dr. Martin Luther King Jr. delivers "I Have a Dream" speech to 200,000 civil rights supporters in Washington, D.C. President Kennedy assassinated in Dallas. More than 15,000 U.S. troops are serving in South Vietnam by year-end. U.S. aid exceeds $500 million for the year. | ASPA membership reaches 3,000. | Federal minimum wage rises to $1.25 an hour. | The Equal Pay Act attempts to eliminate sex discrimination in pay. |
| **1964** | First of the 80 million baby boomers (born 1946 to 1964) turn 18. | ASPA hires Leonard Brice as first full-time, salaried executive vice president. First formal offices open in Berea, Ohio. | | Civil Rights Act of 1964 bans workplace discrimination on the basis of race, color, religion, sex and national origin and creates the Equal Employment Opportunity Commission for enforcement. |
| **1965** | Voting Rights Act eliminates poll taxes, literacy tests and other bars to voting. Rioting in Los Angeles' Watts neighborhood kills 34 and causes $200 million in damage. U.S. forces in South Vietnam reach 184,000 by year-end. | *ASPA Action*, forerunner to *HR News*, is first published. | The McNamara-O'Hara Service Contract Act provides wage standards for employees performing work on federal service contracts. | President Johnson signs Executive Order 11246, outlining affirmative action requirements for federal contractors. Enforced by the Office of Federal Contract Compliance Programs, the order requires employees to compare their workforce with the available labor market and establish goals to remedy under-representation of women and minorities. |
| **1966** | Medicare, one of President Johnson's "Great Society" programs, begins to pay part of medical expenses for citizens over age 65. | ASPA Foundation created. | | Amendments to the Fair Labor Standards Act, the most far-reaching so far, extend minimum wage protections to 10 million workers previously excluded from coverage. |
| **1967** | Thurgood Marshall becomes first black U.S. Supreme Court justice. Carl Stokes in Cleveland and Richard Hatcher in Gary, Ind., are first blacks elected mayors of major cities. By year-end, 475,000 troops are serving in South Vietnam. | ASPA membership tops 4,000. | Federal minimum wage rises to $1.40 an hour. | The Age Discrimination in Employment Act prohibits discrimination against individuals between the ages of 40 and 65. In 1978, it is extended to age 70. In later years, the age cap is abolished for most jobs. |
| **1968** | Dr. Martin Luther King Jr. is assassinated in Memphis while supporting striking sanitation workers. Sen. Robert Kennedy of New York is assassinated in Los Angeles after winning California presidential primary. French students spark a nationwide strike of 10 million workers. | ASPA charters 100th chapter in Seattle, Wash. Membership reaches 5,400. | Women make up 15 percent of all managers. | Federal minimum wage rises to $1.60 an hour. |
| **1969** | U.S. forces in South Vietnam peak at 543,000 in April. Anti-war demonstrations climax with march of 250,000 in Washington, D.C. Neil Armstrong and Edwin Aldrin Jr. become first astronauts to walk on the moon. | ASPA dues increase from $25 to $30. Membership tops 6,600. | Lawrence Peter and Raymond Hull's *The Peter Principle* popularizes tongue-in-cheek theory that good workers are promoted until they reach their level of incompetence. | |

| | HISTORY/<br>TECHNOLOGY | SHRM<br>HISTORY | HR<br>HISTORY | LEGISLATIVE/<br>LEGAL |
|---|---|---|---|---|
| 1970 | First Earth Day celebrated. Japan's exports reach $20 billion, punctuating its postwar rise to a world economic power. | San Francisco hosts more than 1,150 HR professionals at ASPA's annual conference, the first to exceed 1,000 in attendance. | | Occupational Safety and Health Act establishes safety rules for workplaces, enforced by the Occupational Safety and Health Administration. At the time, it was estimated that workplace accidents disabled more than 2 million workers a year and killed almost 15,000. |
| 1971 | U.S. forces in Vietnam decline to 140,000. | ASPA charters 150th chapter, the Lehigh Valley Personnel Association in Bethlehem, Pa. | | In *Griggs v. Duke-Power*, the U.S. Supreme Court articulates the principle of adverse impact, in which a selection process or procedure discriminates by having a disproportionate effect on a protected group. |
| 1972 | US. combat troops leave Vietnam in August, although bombing of North Vietnam continues. Five men are arrested June 17 for breaking into Democratic Party offices in Watergate complex in Washington, D.C. | ASPA membership tops 10,000. | | Vietnam Era Veterans Readjustment Act requires federal contractors to undertake affirmative-action programs for veterans. |
| 1973 | Last U.S. troops leave Vietnam March 29. OPEC oil embargo sparks energy shortages and long lines at gas stations. | | Rehabilitation Act prohibits government employers and businesses with federal contracts from discriminating against people with disabilities. U.S. Supreme Court's *McDonnell-Douglas v. Green* decision outlines elaborate three-step process for determining hiring and promotion discrimination under the concept of disparate treatment. | |
| 1974 | President Nixon resigns in the wake of the Watergate scandal. | ASPA charters 200th chapter in Anchorage, Alaska. Membership reaches 14,000. | Federal minimum wage rises to $2 an hour. | The Employee Retirement Income Security Act establishes pension plan reporting and disclosure rules, fiduciary standards, funding, participation and vesting rules, and plan termination insurance through the Pension Benefit Guaranty Corp. |
| 1975 | | ASPA Accreditation Institute is incorporated. Membership dues increase to $40. | Federal minimum wage rises to 2.10 an hour. | |
| 1976 | America celebrates its bicentennial. Viking II lands on Mars. | ASPA becomes charter member of new World Federation of Personnel Management Associations. ASPA Accreditation Institute administers its first exams. | Federal minimum wage rises to $2.30 an hour. | |
| 1977 | President Carter pardons Vietnam War draft evaders. | ASPA opens full-time Washington, D.C. office. | | |
| 1978 | | ASPA membership tops 20,000. | Federal minimum wage rises to $2.65 an hour. | Pregnancy Discrimination Act establishes protections and standards for maternity leaves. |
| 1979 | Federal government guarantees $1.5 billion in loans to aid third-largest automaker, Chrysler Corp. Ninety people, including 63 Americans, are taken hostage in Iran by militant followers of Ayatollah Khomeini. | ASPA Accreditation Institute is renamed the Personnel Accreditation Institute. | Federal minimum wage rises to $2.90 an hour. | Lane Kirkland is elected president of the AFL-CIO. |
| 1980 | U.S. boycotts summer Olympics in Moscow. Mt. Saint Helens erupts; John Lennon is shot and killed. | ASPA executive vice president Leonard Brice retires. Ronald C. Pilenzo hired as president. Reorganization transfers chief executive officer responsibilities from president to chairman of the board of directors. | NBC's documentary "If Japan Can, Why Can't We?" publicizes W. Edwards Deming's gospel of total quality management, which he taught Japanese Industry after World War II. | Federal minimum wage rises to $3.10 an hour. |
| 1981 | President Reagan dismisses most of 13,000 striking federal air traffic controllers who defied a back-to-work order. Reagan survives an attempted assassination by John Hinckley Jr. | ASPA publishes first hardbound book, *Uniform Guidelines*. | William Quchi's *Theory Z* examines the Japanese practices of lifetime employment and company values. First 401(k) defined contribution pension plans introduced. Women make up 27 percent of managers but only 1 percent of senior executives. | Federal minimum wage rises to $3.35 an hour. |

| | HISTORY/ TECHNOLOGY | SHRM HISTORY | HR HISTORY | LEGISLATIVE/ LEGAL |
|---|---|---|---|---|
| 1982 | 13-year lawsuit against AT&T ends with agreement to spin off 22 Bell System telephone companies in return for being allowed to expand into previously prohibited areas of telecommunications and computer industries. | ASPA board decides to relocate headquarters to Washington, D.C., area. Membership tops 30,000. *Resource* newspaper commences publication. | Tom Peters and Robert Waterman publish *In Search of Excellence*, the all-time best-selling business book, with global sales now near 6 million. The book identifies lessons from 62 successful companies. Unemployment rate hits 10.8 percent in November, highest rate since 1940. | IRA participation is extended to all workers. |
| 1983 | Sally K. Ride becomes the first woman to go into space. U.S. invades Grenada. | | | |
| 1984 | Ronald Reagan becomes the first president to serve two full consecutive terms since Dwight Eisenhower. | ASPA headquarters relocates to Alexandria, Va. | | |
| 1985 | | | Average weekly earnings for U.S. production workers reaches $299.09. | The Consolidated Omnibus Budget Reconciliation Act (COBRA) requires companies to offer continuing health insurance coverage to participants who lose eligibility. |
| 1986 | U.S. officials record 21,517 cases of AIDS and 11,713 deaths from the disease, and warn that the numbers will increase tenfold in the next five years. | First ASPA leadership conference. ASPA hosts World Congress on Human Resource Management in Washington, D.C. | *Working Mother* magazine publishes its first annual list of companies that help parents balance work and family life. | In *Meritor Savings Bank v. Vinson*, the U.S. Supreme Court identifies "hostile environment" as a type of sexual harassment. The Immigration Reform and Control Act requires employers to verify citizenship status of new hires. |
| 1987 | ASPA purchases headquarters building at 606 N. Washington St. in Alexandria, Va. | | | |
| 1988 | Unemployment rate drops to 5.3 percent at year-end, a 14-year low. | | | Worker Adjustment and Retraining Notification Act requires larger employers to give 60 days' notice or 60 days' pay for worksite closings or major layoffs. U.S. Department of Transportation publishes drug-testing regulations for workers in the transportation industry. Drug-Free Workplace Act requires some employers to certify that they provide a drug-free environment. Employee Polygraph Protection Act prohibits requiring lie detector tests as a condition of employment. |
| 1989 | | ASPA changes name to Society for Human Resource Management after members ratify change by 8-to-1 margin. Publications change names to *HRMagazine* and *HR News*. | | |
| 1990 | Unemployment rate reaches three-year high of 6.1 percent. | Michael R. Losey leaves Unisys to become SHRM president and CEO at retirement of Ronald Pilenzo. Personnel Accreditation Institute changes name to Human Resource Certification Institute. | Federal minimum wage rises to $3.85 an hour. About 70 percent of married women are employed, more than double the 1960 rate. | The Americans with Disabilities Act prohibits discrimination against people with physical and mental disabilities in public accommodations, transportation and employment. The workplace provisions, including requirements to make "reasonable accommodations" take effect in 1992. |
| 1991 | Unemployment rate reaches five-year high of 7 percent in June. President Bush approves recommendation of a commission to close 34 domestic military installations because of federal budget crunch and end of the Cold War. | Institute for International Human Resources created. Federal minimum wage rises to $4.25 an hour. | Women make up 41 percent of managers and 3 percent of senior executives. Lotus Development Corp. becomes first publicly traded company to offer benefits to employees' gay domestic partners. | The Civil Rights Act of 1991 makes it easier for employees and applicants to win lawsuits and punitive damages; prohibits use of different norms based on race or sex for scoring tests; permits use of jury trials; and expands coverage of discrimination laws to U.S. citizens working for U.S. corporations in other countries. |
| 1992 | Unemployment rate reaches eight-year high of 7.8 percent in June. After trimming 40,000 employees in 1992, IBM says it will cut 25,000 more jobs in 1993. | SHRM named secretariat (headquarters) of the World Federation of Personnel Management Association. Headquarters building renovated and mortgage paid off. | | National Labor Relations Boards (NLRB) ruling that employee involvement teams at Electromation Inc. in Elkhart, Ind., are company-dominated unions creates doubt about legal issues concerning the increasing use of teams in the workplace. |

| | HISTORY/<br>TECHNOLOGY | SHRM<br>HISTORY | HR<br>HISTORY | LEGISLATIVE/<br>LEGAL |
|---|---|---|---|---|
| **1993** | Terrorists' bombing of World Trade Center in New York kills six people and injures hundreds. | Newspaper Personnel Relations Association becomes Society's first Professional Emphasis Group (PEG). Diversity and Education Initiatives introduced. Six thousand attended annual conference in Washington, D.C. Membership reaches 57,000. | Nationally televised address by President Clinton urges Congress to adopt sweeping health care reforms and provide universal coverage. | The Family and Medical Leave Act, twice vetoed by former President Bush, is passed again by Congress and becomes the first law signed by President Clinton. The law guarantees 12 weeks of unpaid leave to employees for birth or adoption of a child or for their own serious illness or that of a child, spouse or parent. |
| **1994** | Republicans capture both houses of Congress for the first time in decades. | SHRM establishes first online presence on Prodigy. | | |
| **1995** | Domestic terrorists' bombing of federal office building in Oklahoma City, Okla., kills 169, prompting heightened security precautions at workplaces nationwide. | World Wide Web site launched at http://www.shrm.org. Headquarters space needs are studied, and new building is authorized. | Three unions—United Auto Workers (UAW), United Steelworkers (USW) and International Association of Machinists (IAM)—announce plans to unify by the year 2000, creating North America's largest union with 2 million members. | Congress passes Congressional Accountability Act, obligating itself to comply with private-sector employment laws. In *NLRB v. Town and Country Electric*, the U.S. Supreme Court rules employers may not discriminate against paid union organizers seeking jobs. |
| **1996** | Oldest of the 80 million U.S. baby boomers turn 50. | SHRM joins with University of Michigan and Wiley and Sons to publish the quarterly journal *Human Resource Management.* Ground broken for new headquarters in Alexandria, Va. Consultants Forum PEG starts. Employment Management Association votes to merge with SHRM as a PEG. | Resolving some issues in a national debate over health care, Congress passes incremental reform legislation limiting coverage exclusions for pre-existing conditions, enhancing workers' ability to retain health benefits when switching jobs, and mandating parity of mental health benefits. | Federal appeals court strikes down President Clinton's executive order to cancel contracts of federal contractors that hire permanent replacements for strikers. President Clinton vetoes the TEAM Act, which was passed to clarify limits on employee teams. |
| **1997** | Federal minimum wage rises to $5.15 an hour. Unemployment rate drops to 24-year low of 4.7 percent. | SHRM moves into new 80,000-square foot headquarters in Alexandria, Va. Membership exceeds 85,000. | Contingent workforce issues play a major role in two-week strike of 180,000 International Brotherhood of Teamsters drivers, package sorters and other workers against United Parcel Service. The company eventually agrees to move 10,000 part-time workers to full-time. | California adopts the first state ergonomics regulation, aimed at stemming the burgeoning number of cumulative trauma disorders in a variety of industries. |
| **1998** | | SHRM celebrates 50th anniversary, creates new Professional Emphasis Group, the SHRM High-Tech Net. | | |

*Sources: The Ultimate Business Library: 50 Books that Shaped Management Thinking.* Stuart Crainer. AMACOM, 1997.
*Human Resource Management: A Practical Approach.* Michael Harris, Dryden Press, 1997.
*Employment Law 101 Deskbook.* David Copus, National Employment Law Institute, 1996.
*The World Almanac and Book of Facts, 1994.* Funk and Wagnalls, 1993.

(Continued from page 9)

The Labor Department grew rapidly during World War I as the war effort became a national priority. By the war's end, the Labor Department—through the War Labor Administration (WLA)—had set numerous policies to ensure that wage, hour or working condition problems did not hinder the war effort and industrial growth. WLA initiatives were model programs but frequently fell short of business needs. They could not meet the challenges that would soon stop the industrial explosion in its tracks.

In 1929, the onset of the Great Depression drastically changed the rules of business. With profits dwindling, employers first eliminated voluntary welfare programs, then jobs. The government, led by President Franklin Roosevelt, provided some assistance by creating jobs ranging from road building to painting murals on government buildings through the Civil Works Administration and later the more extensive Works Progress Administration. New social programs, including old-age pensions, labor standards and minimum wages for some industries, were developed.

With dreams of the good life fading for most workers, unions established strong roots in many industries and gathered political clout with Congress. The Norris-LaGuardia Act changed the rules of the game in labor-management relations by making "yellow-dog" contracts unenforceable and severely restricting the use of federal court injunctions in labor disputes. Union organizations grew in power after passage of the National Labor Relations Act (NLRA) in 1935, also known as the Wagner Act.

The NLRA signaled a change in the federal government's role in labor-management relations, giving employees the right to organize unions and bargain collectively, while prohibiting employers from engaging in certain unfair labor practices. The act also created the National Labor Relations Board (NLRB), which continues to establish procedures for conducting union organizing and election campaigns and has authority to investigate unfair labor practices.

As employers began to understand the need for professionals who could play a middle role between employees and employers, the personnel manager's role emerged. It was during this first movement that employers began to truly understand that employees were more than machines with interchangeable faces. The personnel managers of this period did not have all the answers, but the developing practices and concerns of the era set the stage for continuing study and investment in the role of effective human resource management.

## Human relations movement

The field of human relations—or industrial and personnel relations—that emerged in the 1920s provided a new focus for the profession. In an effort to increase productivity, personnel programs expanded to include medical aid and sick benefits, vaccinations, holidays, housing allowances and other new benefits. New personnel roles emerged as unions began challenging the fairness and validity of Taylor's scientific management theories.

The human relations movement provided new insights derived from studies that linked improved productivity to management philosophies emphasizing employee communications, cooperation and involvement. This new thinking about employee cooperation grew from the works of Elton Mayo—known as the Father of Human Relations—and from the Hawthorne Studies, an important series of illumination experiments conducted between 1924 and 1932.

Conducted at the Hawthorne Works of AT&T's Western Electric Plant near Chicago, the Hawthorne Studies were the first to question Taylorism's behavioral assumptions. Mayo, who conducted the studies to explore how changes in working environments affected productivity, was surprised by the results.

Although the study began as an effort to quantify the levels of lighting and other physical conditions that would maximize employee productivity, Mayo and his researchers soon found a much greater link between employee productivity and the level of attention managers paid to employees and their behavior. The studies concluded that, in motivating workers, human factors were often more important than physical conditions. For the first time, productivity research put forth the controversial proposition that workers' feelings were important. Mayo's work propelled further developments in HR management.

The concept of employee motivation increased in importance in the 1940s. When World War II ended the nation's economic drought and brought full production and full employment to the industrial giants, labor was again in short supply. As men were called to serve their country, shortages emerged, and women and teens were called on to keep the engines of industry rolling. For the first time, people of color took jobs previously not open to them. Expanded job growth also meant expanded roles for the personnel manager—recruiting, testing, training, mediating, and keeping an eye on employee morale and production efficiency.

As the 1940s moved forward, Mayo's work and real-world business experiences launched a greater understanding of the dynamics of work groups and the social needs of employees. Business leaders began to appreciate the production that resulted when managers acted less like taskmasters and more like good leaders, counselors and facilitators. Nonmonetary rewards became an important supplement to monetary rewards for motivating employees. New theories on the benefits of improving the relationships between management and employees abounded.

But many Americans awoke to harsh realities after World War II. Returning war veterans were ill equipped to meet the technological demands of the new workplace. The federal government responded with measures such as the GI Bill of Rights, which guaranteed university-level educational assistance to returning veterans and was instrumental in developing new leaders and a powerful new workforce for the United States.

After the war, the country was also rocked by severe inflation and labor unrest. After enduring wage freezes imposed during the war, unions sought to make up for lost time. Union membership had grown from about 6 percent when the NLRA was passed to about 23 percent in 1947. Strikes became more frequent and union tactics, in some cases, more militant.

A strong anti-union sentiment emerged and against this backdrop Congress overrode President Truman's veto of the 1947 Labor-Management Relations Act, better known as the Taft-Hartley Act. The new law banned the use of "closed shops," which required workers to join the union to be hired, and placed government in the role of mediating union and management disagreements. But as the turbulent 1940s came to an end, a new turbulence was brewing in the Far East. Once again, the country mobilized for war production with the outbreak of the Korean War.

## Human resource movement

After the Korean War, a new class of college-educated managers emerged with a greater sense of social responsibility than their predecessors. Throughout the second half of the 20th century, social well-being coupled with social upheaval—best exemplified by the struggle for desegregation—changed the thinking of employees in the United States.

As the 1960s and 1970s unfolded, a more personable group of managers emerged, and their interests in people and feelings influenced all facets of business, including the growth of market research, communications and public relations. This group of managers emphasized the relationship between employers and employees, rather than scientific management. Programs to increase wages and fringe benefits continued to be developed. New studies linked greater productivity to management philosophies that encouraged worker ideas and initiatives.

The new laws of the Great Society sprouted from this social foundation—laws that protected employees from unsafe jobs and from violations of basic civil rights. Personnel and human relations managers were now responsible for motivating people and helping their organizations navigate a maze of regulations, executive orders and court decisions.

As time progressed, the nature of work continued to change. A well-educated group of baby boomers began to take new theories to heart. Boomers placed human rights and ideas of self-fulfillment at the forefront of their workplace concerns. These people wanted more than an occupation; they wanted jobs that were challenging and interesting. Employees of this era began to view themselves as stakeholders in their companys' enterprises.

In contrast to the attitude of the early 1900s—where workers were considered cogs in the industrial machine—many of the highly skilled knowledge workers of today actually control the machines, carrying the power and ability to make decisions to satisfy customers needs. In looking for ways to increase productivity, baby boomers are also heavily influenced by psychology and other behavioral sciences. Dedicated to making work meaningful, enriching the work environment, communicating and managing by objectives, this generation seeks to tie the goals of individuals with the goals of the organization. Most businesses have been happy to go along with the new programs, since their efforts are tied to increased productivity.

As bottom-line results improve and more competitive advantages are tied to human resource innovations, the power of human resource management has begun to extend beyond the domain of human resource departments. Organizations have recognized the importance of human resource considerations in long-range strategic planning. Today, the human resource professional is charged with optimizing employee skills, matching people to jobs and maximizing the potential of employees as valuable resources.

## Poised for the future

Many challenges remain for the HR profession. Companies must maintain ethical standards to match heightened social mores and the greater attention given to the ways they behave and communicate. The diverse composition of the workforce means employers must work to ensure that they reward effort, not prejudices against sex, race, age, national origin, religion or other global differences.

Many companies still have not made their human resource professionals key participants in strategic business decisions. And top management still resists sharing decision-making power with employees, who must be given such power if they are to add value to products and services.

While maintaining the special body of HR knowledge, professionals in human resource management must also be generalists who understand economics, politics, social and cultural trends, technological innovations, changing work values, skill shortages, government mandates in labor laws, affirmative action, health care management, privacy concerns, international trends, and myriad other issues. For HR professionals, the challenge of today's business environment is to understand and manage the important interaction of technology, work flow, organizational strategies and, most important, people.

The human resource profession has come a long way since the early days of Henry Ford and other industrial giants who believed they needed little more than able bodies to keep production lines running. In our new age of technology and rapid product innovation, unleashing the minds and creative souls of tomorrow's workforce is the factor most likely to propel businesses and the HR profession into the future.

---

Michael R. Losey, SPHR, CAE, is president and chief executive officer of the Society for Human Resource Management.

**Feature** HR and the bottom line

# Profitable personnel

For many practitioners, it's an article of faith that people management is the most important factor in determining profitability. But now an in-depth study of manufacturing firms has produced hard evidence to confirm it. **Michael West** and **Malcolm Patterson** describe its findings

Michael Hammer, co-architect of business process re-engineering, once stated that "the biggest lie told by most organisations is that 'people are our most important assets'. Total fabrication: they treat people like raw material. If we're serious about treating people as an asset, we're looking at a dramatic increase in investment in them."

Our most recent study, commissioned by the IPD, suggests that Hammer's observation is bitingly accurate when directed towards medium-sized manufacturing firms in the UK. Yet the research, based on an intensive examination of more than 100 such employers over seven years, reveals that people management is not only critical to business performance: it also far outstrips emphasis on quality, technology, competitive strategy or research and development in its influence on the bottom line.

Companies whose attitude surveys reported high levels of job satisfaction and commitment among staff showed improving financial performance. Furthermore, HR practices explained nearly one-fifth of the variation between companies in productivity and profitability. The results strongly support the link between effective people management and strong business performance.

The study, known as the Sheffield effectiveness programme, was conducted at the University of Sheffield's Institute of Work Psychology and the Centre for Economic Performance at the London School of Economics. It shows that half of the firms have no individual in charge of HR, and that more than two-thirds have no written personnel strategy. Managers described the approach to training as reactive, with only 6 per cent of them reporting organised training strategies. Planned job rotations, high-flyer schemes and formal career planning are rare, while one-quarter of firms reported no progress in achieving single status and harmonisation.

These patterns run counter to the considerable emphasis placed by managers on quality, new technology and competitive strategy. Yet our research suggests that these areas explain only a small amount of the differences in financial performance.

What is perplexing about this anomaly is that there is a growing consensus in the media that personnel policies can provide a source of competitive advantage. Although there are

*Michael West is professor of work and organisational psychology at the Institute of Work Psychology, University of Sheffield. Malcolm Patterson is project manager of the Sheffield effectiveness programme at the Institute of Work Psychology.*

differences as to what constitutes good practice, many analysts believe that it can improve productivity and, consequently, performance by enhancing skills, promoting positive attitudes and giving people more responsibility so that they can make the fullest use of those skills.

From this model we can specify appropriate HR practices. For example, employees' skills are best acquired by effective recruitment and selection; best enhanced by strategic training and appraisals; and best employed in jobs designed to promote employee autonomy, flexibility and problem-solving. Positive employee attitudes and motivation may be sustained and developed by favourable reward systems, harmonisation and involvement.

Our findings generally support these links. As well as confirming strong ties between attitudes and performance, they show that two forms of HR practice are related to improvements in profitability and productivity: acquisition and development of skills (as assessed by the sophistication of induction, training, selection and appraisal practices); and job design (as assessed by the degree of job variety, responsibility, skill flexibility and teamwork).

Zotefoams (see "An effervescent culture"), a foam manufacturer based in Croydon, Surrey, provides an excellent example of a company that enhances skills and designs jobs to encourage the optimum use of those skills. A notable aspect is that it is one of very few organisations to encourage its shopfloor employees to draw on their experience to create innovative solutions to issues of cost, quality and efficiency.

Another exception is SP Systems, a manufacturer of resins for racing yachts. The firm, based on the Isle of Wight, attempted a radical approach to encouraging innovation. When production staff were asked to suggest possible improvements to work practices, a proposal to move dirty materials to a storage area was met with the offer of a budget and time off from production to design and build a new facility. The production team did just that, well under budget and ahead of the deadline.

That led to the development of further ideas and innovation within the company. It provides a better example of developing creativity and innovation than any number of vacuous mission statements. And it is no coincidence that SP Systems has also shown one of the most remarkable increases in productivity of all the firms involved in our study.

The lesson is simple: if two employees from competing firms are equally skilled and creative, the one who uses more of these skills and creativity is more valuable to their employer. Yet in many companies the average job cycle time is so short and employees' roles so

# An effervescent culture

Zotefoams enjoys the highest profits and labour productivity of all the companies taking part in the Sheffield effectiveness programme. The firm is also one of the most enlightened when it comes to unlocking the potential of its employees.

The company has invested heavily in producing a skilled, flexible and motivated workforce. Shopfloor employees operate in teams and are able to perform a variety of tasks. They also have expanded responsibilities, including dealing with quality problems and determining work priorities.

The aim was to locate know-how and information access at the lower levels of the hierarchy. With the expertise to manage their own work, recognise problems and generate solutions—three-quarters of Zotefoams' workforce have received training in group problem-solving skills—fewer issues need to be resolved by managers and the firm is able to respond to situations with greater flexibility and speed.

Training plays a key role in achieving this level of empowerment. All shopfloor employees, supervisors and managers undergo NVQ training, from levels 2 to 5, and a number of staff are trained to teach colleagues relevant skills.

Reward systems support this enlightened approach. The company pays its shopfloor staff well above the average rate for the industry and it has also adopted skill-based pay to motivate and reward skill development.

Zotefoams also promotes a team ethos by breaking down traditional shopfloor-management boundaries. There is a single salary structure for all staff, employee share options and profit-sharing (the percentage being the same for everyone) throughout the company. The directors have no special privileges.

constrained that it suggests that their managers' commitment is to monotony, skill impoverishment and demotivation, rather than their valuable opposites.

### Demand satisfaction

One of the most exciting results from the study is that the satisfaction of the workforce is such an important predictor of future productivity. The measure of satisfaction covered many aspects of working life, from pay and conditions through to "softer" issues such as recognition for good work, attention paid to suggestions and relationships with team members and supervisors.

The results suggest that people management is not just about traditional HR practices such as recruitment, appraisal and training. It is important to take account of the whole person and address the satisfaction of all employees across a range of areas. The most enlightened organisations consider many aspects of employee satisfaction, including their needs for growth and development, their sense of security, relationships with colleagues

# Just the ticket

Simpson Label Co, with a workforce of around 90 people, has been achieving consistent growth. Measured against its UK competitors, its profitability places it in the top quartile.

A commitment to employee development is a strong element of Simpson's culture. One of its key aims is to foster "involvement and co-operation to maximise everyone's autonomy and responsibility for their own work". It has invested in employees through comprehensive and strategic training, biannual appraisals and teamworking throughout the company. Shopfloor employees have been given considerable scope to manage themselves.

Communication takes the form of monthly face-to-face team briefings for all staff, a quarterly internal newsletter and regular employee attitude surveys. Company performance is imparted through a review of annual trading results.

These practices have proved extremely effective. Results from the attitude surveys show that Simpson staff are highly committed to their company. For example, 81 per cent of them said they were satisfied with the "way the firm is managed", compared with an average of 56 per cent in other companies we surveyed.

The Sheffield effectiveness programme also assessed employees' views of 20 aspects of their work environment—for instance, quality, training and interdepartmental relations. Across the 54 companies we surveyed, shopfloor staff had a significantly less positive view of their organisation on 17 of the 20 dimensions than their managerial and professional colleagues. This was in marked contrast to Simpson. Survey results showed differences on only three dimensions, indicating that the company is successfully implementing a team culture and breaking down hierarchical boundaries.

and supervisors, the balance between home and work, and even physical fitness.

For example, a wire and cable manufacturer we studied, Raychem, has comprehensive HR strategies in place that set out in detail what people can expect in relation to almost all aspects of employment conditions. The firm, based in Swindon, Wiltshire, offers opportunities for development, both in the workplace in the form of enriched jobs, but also outside the workplace—for instance, its

provision of sports facilities and even children's parties.

How employees see their company as a community is an equally important predictor of productivity and profitability. In particular, the "human relations" climate of the organisation appears to have a significant influence upon performance. A concern for welfare, good communication, high-quality training, broad autonomy and respect for employees collectively create a community climate.

### Exclusion zone

Company climates can be either supportive or negligent, depending on the commitment and ingenuity of managers. In one firm we visited in the south-west of England, the decision has been taken to de-skill the workforce, to have all jobs on a cycle time of three minutes and to ignore current rhetoric about enlightened HR management. There is a minimum commitment to creating a community, and the sense of mutual indifference and disrespect between managers and employees is almost tangible. It is perhaps no coincidence that the firm is facing economic instability.

Simpson Label Co (see "Just the ticket") represents the other end of the enlightenment scale. It involves all of its employees through continuous communication, removing status barriers, promoting autonomy and encouraging teamwork.

Similarly, John McGavigan & Co in Glasgow, a supplier to the automotive industry, has made a sustained commitment to building a sense of community. Teamwork is central to this strategy. Autonomous teams give presentations to managers about their projects and make videos about their successes for other workers. Interdepartmental cooperation and communication are nurtured. Teams identify and solve problems and are part of a vibrant community where vigorous debate and innovation are valued. The contribution to financial savings has been directly identifiable.

What is most striking is the pervasive sense of inclusion of all members of the workforce in relevant decision-making. At McGavigan's, drawing on the knowledge and experience of all employees is central to its strategy of building a sense of community.

Our experience in these companies has led us to believe that good people management is not simply about selection, appraisal and so on. It is about the development of whole communities in which people feel socially included, rather than alienated, by the experience of work.

It is this notion of involvement and community that may help to explain an interesting aspect of our findings. The results reveal that it is the overall satisfaction of staff, accumulated across different areas of work experience and averaged across all employees in the company, that affects business performance. What makes this particularly interesting is that job satisfaction of individuals is typically a poor predictor of individual job performance. This leads us to speculate that the overall level of satisfaction across all employees can create a climate in which they are motivated to co-operate and collaborate beyond mere job expectations.

Unfortunately, too many organisations have only a nominal commitment to HR practices. One company we worked with in the oil and gas industry is managed by a group of experienced oil industry executives who are highly qualified technically. They appointed a recent graduate to manage HR and report to the production manager, but the production manager and many of his colleagues view concepts such as HR management as merely the tinsel rather than the trunk of their "organisational tree". The task of their recruit is simply unmanageable in this context.

In companies such as Raychem, however, people management practices are seen as central. Here, people management is the lifeblood of the organisation rather than a condescension to current popular practice.

The old jibe often directed towards HR managers—"big hat, no cattle"—is blunted by our findings, which indicate that people management accounts for 19 per cent of the variation in profitability and 18 per cent of the variation in productivity. While R&D emphasis can account for a respectable 8 per cent, emphasis on quality, new technology and competitive strategy barely creep about 1 per cent in terms of their contribution.

### Fear of an unknown quantity

Managing the "whole person", developing skills and ownership, managing the organisational community and fostering creativity are vital. The mystery is: why are managers so slow to implement such practices? One reason, perhaps, is that the ambiguity of managing people is daunting in comparison with managing quality via statistical process control, technology via the purchase of a new machine, or the delineation of a new competitive strategy based on cost reduction.

People are unpredictable and their needs are diverse. But the task of good management is to recognise that organisations consist of individuals with different requirements. Economic success depends on the management's ability to respond to such diversity.

What, then, are the essential ingredients for creating an organisation that views investment in people as a source of competitive advantage? We believe that the role of senior managers is crucial. They need to be convinced about the use of effective people management. Hopefully, our research and similar US studies will provide the reason for senior managers to shift their attention to the key business issues that face them: creatively and effectively managing the whole person, skills acquisition and development, the community of their organisation and the well of innovation from which they must draw to survive.

Among the companies we have been working with, it is those in which the managers have eagerly addressed these challenges that have experienced rapid improvements in financial performance. Such innovation requires courage and commitment, but it will pay off.

### Further Reading
Malcolm Patterson, Michael West, Rebecca Lawthorn and Stephen Nickell, **The Impact of People Management Practices on Business Performance**, IPD, 1997.

*HR should be defined not by what
it does but by what it delivers.*

# A New Mandate for
# Human Resources

## by Dave Ulrich

SHOULD WE do away with HR? In recent years, a number of people who study and write about business—along with many who run businesses—have been debating that question. The debate arises out of serious and widespread doubts about HR's contribution to organizational performance. And as much as I like HR people—I have been working in the field as a researcher, professor, and consultant for 20 years—I must agree that there is good reason for HR's beleaguered reputation. It is often ineffective, incompetent, and costly; in a phrase, it is value sapping. Indeed, if HR were to remain configured as it is today in many companies, I would have to answer the question above with a resounding "Yes—abolish the thing!"

But the truth is, HR has never been more necessary. The competitive forces that managers face today and will continue to confront in the future demand organizational excellence. The efforts to achieve such excellence—through a focus on learning, quality, teamwork, and reengineering—are driven by the way organizations get things done and how they treat their people. Those are fundamental HR issues. To state it plainly: achieving organizational excellence must be the work of HR.

The question for senior managers, then, is not Should we do away with HR? but What should we do with HR? The answer is: create an entirely new role and agenda for the field that focuses it not on traditional HR activities, such as staffing and compensation, but on outcomes. HR should not be defined by what it does but by what it delivers—results that enrich the organization's value to customers, investors, and employees.

More specifically, HR can help deliver organizational excellence in the following four ways:

*Dave Ulrich is a professor at the University of Michigan's School of Business in Ann Arbor. He is the author of* Human Resource Champions: The Next Agenda for Adding Value and Delivering Results *(Harvard Business School Press, 1997).*

■ First, HR should become a partner with senior and line managers in strategy execution, helping to move planning from the conference room to the marketplace.

■ Second, it should become an expert in the way work is organized and executed, delivering administrative efficiency to ensure that costs are reduced while quality is maintained.

■ Third, it should become a champion for employees, vigorously representing their concerns to senior management and at the same time working to increase employee contribution; that is, employees' commitment to the organization and their ability to deliver results.

■ And finally, HR should become an agent of continuous transformation, shaping processes and a culture that together improve an organization's capacity for change.

Make no mistake: this new agenda for HR is a radical departure from the status quo. In most companies today, HR is sanctioned mainly to play policy police and regulatory watchdog. It handles the paperwork involved in hiring and firing, manages the bureaucratic aspects of benefits, and administers compensation decisions made by others. When it is more empowered by senior management, it might oversee recruiting, manage training and development programs, or design initiatives to increase workplace diversity. But the fact remains: the activities of HR appear to be—and often are—disconnected from the real work of the organization. The new agenda, however, would mean that every one of HR's activities would in some concrete way help the company better serve its customers or otherwise increase shareholder value.

Can HR transform itself alone? Absolutely not. In fact, the primary responsibility for transforming the role of HR belongs to the CEO and to every line manager who must achieve business goals. The reason? Line managers have ultimate responsibility for both the processes and the outcomes of the company. They are answerable to shareholders for creating economic value, to customers for creating product or service value, and to employees for creating workplace value. It follows that they should lead the way in fully integrating HR into the company's real work. Indeed, to do so, they must become HR champions themselves. They must acknowledge that competitive success is a function of organizational excellence. More important, they must hold HR accountable for delivering it.

Of course, the line should not *impose* the new agenda on the HR staff. Rather, operating managers and HR managers must form a partnership to quickly and completely reconceive and reconfigure the function—to overhaul it from one devoted to activities to one committed to outcomes. The process will be different in every organization, but the result will be the same: a business era in which the question Should we do away with HR? will be considered utterly ridiculous.

---

## HR's activities appear to be—and often are—disconnected from the real work of an organization.

---

### Why HR Matters Now More Than Ever

Regardless of their industry, size, or location, companies today face five critical business challenges. Collectively, these challenges require organizations to build new capabilities. Who is currently responsible for developing those capabilities? Everyone—and no one. That vacuum is HR's opportunity to play a leadership role in enabling organizations to meet the following competitive challenges:

**Globalization.** Gone are the days when companies created products at home and shipped them abroad "as is." With the rapid expansion of global markets, managers are struggling to balance the paradoxical demand to think globally and act locally. That imperative requires them to move people, ideas, products, and information around the world to meet local needs. They must add new and important ingredients to the mix when making strategy: volatile political situations, contentious global trade issues, fluctuating exchange rates, and unfamiliar cultures. They must be more literate in the ways of international customers, commerce, and competition than ever before. In short, globalization requires that organizations increase their ability to learn and collaborate and to manage diversity, complexity, and ambiguity.

**Profitability Through Growth.** During the past decade, most Western companies have been clearing debris, using downsizing, reengineering, delayering, and consolidation to increase efficiency and cut costs. The gains of such yard work, however, have largely been realized, and executives will now have to pay attention to the other part of the profitability equation: revenue growth.

The drive for revenue growth, needless to say, puts unique demands on an organization. Companies seeking

to acquire new customers and develop new products must be creative and innovative, and must encourage the free flow of information and shared learning among employees. They must also become more market focused—more in touch with the fast changing and disparate needs of their customers. And companies seeking growth through mergers, acquisitions, or joint ventures require other capabilities, such as the finely honed skills needed to integrate different organizations' work processes and cultures.

**Technology.** From videoconferencing to the Internet, technology has made our world smaller and faster. Ideas and massive amounts of information are in constant movement. The challenge for managers is to make sense and good use of what technology offers. Not all technology adds value. But technology can and will affect how and where work gets done. In the coming years, managers will need to figure out how to make technology a viable, productive part of the work setting. They will need to stay ahead of the information curve and learn to leverage information for business results. Otherwise, they risk being swallowed by a tidal wave of data—not ideas.

**Intellectual Capital.** Knowledge has become a direct competitive advantage for companies selling ideas and relationships (think of professional service, software, and technology-driven companies) and an indirect competitive advantage for all companies attempting to differentiate themselves by how they serve customers. From now on, successful companies will be the ones that are the most adept at attracting, developing, and retaining individuals who can drive a global organization that is responsive to both its customers and the burgeoning opportunities of technology. Thus the challenge for organizations is making sure they have the capability to find, assimilate, develop, compensate, and retain such talented individuals.

**Change, Change, and More Change.** Perhaps the greatest competitive challenge companies face is adjusting to—indeed, embracing—nonstop change. They must be able to learn rapidly and continuously, innovate ceaselessly, and take on new strategic imperatives faster and more comfortably. Constant change means organizations must create a healthy discomfort with the status quo, an ability to detect emerging trends quicker than the competition, an ability to make rapid decisions, and the agility to seek new ways of doing business. To thrive, in other words, companies will need to be in a never-ending state of transformation, perpetually creating fundamental, enduring change.

### HR's New Role

The five challenges described above have one overarching implication for business: the only competitive weapon left is organization. Sooner or later, traditional forms of competitiveness—cost, technology, distribution, manufacturing, and product features—can be copied. They have become table stakes. You must have them to be a player, but they do not guarantee you will be a winner.

In the new economy, winning will spring from organizational capabilities such as speed, responsiveness, agility, learning capacity, and employee competence. Successful organizations will be those that are able to quickly turn strategy into action; to manage processes intelligently and efficiently; to maximize employee contribution and commitment; and to create the conditions for seamless change. The need to develop those capabilities brings us back to the mandate for HR set forth at the beginning of this article. Let's take a closer look at each HR imperative in turn.

**Becoming a Partner in Strategy Execution.** I'm not going to argue that HR should make strategy. Strategy is the responsibility of a company's executive team—of which HR is a member. To be full-fledged strategic partners with senior management, however, HR executives should impel and guide serious discussion of how the company should be organized to carry out its strategy. Creating the conditions for this discussion involves four steps.

First, HR should be held responsible for defining an organizational architecture. In other words, it should identify the underlying model of the company's way of doing business. Several well-established frameworks can be used in this process. Jay Galbraith's star model, for example, identifies five essential organizational components: strategy, structure, rewards, processes, and people. The well-known 7-S framework created by McKinsey & Company distinguishes seven components in a company's architecture: strategy, structure, systems, staff, style, skills, and shared values.

It's relatively unimportant which framework the HR staff uses to define the company's architecture, as long as it's robust. What matters more is that an architecture be articulated explicitly. Without such clarity, managers can become myopic about how the company runs—and thus about what drives strategy implementation and what stands in its way. They might think only of structure as the driving force behind actions and decisions, and neglect systems or skills. Or they might understand the company primarily in terms of its values and pay inadequate attention to the influence of systems on how work—that is, strategy execution—actually gets accomplished.

Senior management should ask HR to play the role of an architect called into an already-constructed building to draw up its plans. The architect makes measurements; calculates dimensions; notes windows, doors, and staircases; and examines the plumbing and heating infrastructures. The result is a comprehensive set of blueprints that contains all the building's parts and shows how they work together.

Next, HR must be accountable for conducting an organizational audit. Blueprints can illuminate the places in a house that require immediate improvement; organizational-architecture plans can be similarly useful. They are critical in helping managers identify which components of the company must change in order to facilitate strategy execution. Again, HR's role is to shepherd the dialogue about the company's blueprints.

Consider a company in which HR defined the organization's architecture in terms of its culture, competencies, rewards, governance, work processes, and leadership. The HR staff was able to use that model to guide management through a rigorous discussion of "fit"—did the company's culture fit its strategic goals, did its competencies, and so forth. When the answer was no, HR was able to guide a discussion of how to obtain or develop what was missing. (For an example of the questions asked in this discussion, see the chart "From Architecture to Audit.")

The third role for HR as a strategic partner is to identify methods for renovating the parts of the organizational architecture that need it. In other words, HR managers should be assigned to take the lead in proposing, creating, and debating best practices in culture change programs, for example, or in appraisal and reward systems. Similarly, if strategy implementation requires, say, a team-based organizational structure, HR would be responsible for bringing state-of-the-art approaches for creating this structure to senior management's attention.

Fourth and finally, HR must take stock of its own work and set clear priorities. At any given moment, the HR staff might have a dozen initiatives in its sights, such as pay-for-performance, global teamwork, and action-learning development experiences. But to be truly tied to business outcomes, HR needs to join forces with operating managers to systematically assess the impact and importance of each one of these initiatives. Which ones are really aligned with strategy implementation? Which ones should receive attention immediately, and which can wait? Which ones, in short, are truly linked to business results?

---

## Decreasing costs and improving efficiency will help HR become a partner in executing strategy.

---

Because becoming a strategic partner means an entirely new role for HR, it may have to acquire new skills and capabilities. Its staff may need more education in order to perform the kind of in-depth analysis an organizational audit involves, for example. Ultimately, such new knowledge will allow HR to add value to the executive team with confidence. In time, the concept of HR as a strategic partner will make business sense.

**Becoming an Administrative Expert.** For decades, HR professionals have been tagged as administrators. In their new role as administrative experts, however, they will need to shed their traditional image of rule-making policy police, while still making sure that all the required routine work in companies is done well. In order to move from their old role as administrators into their new role, HR

# FROM ARCHITECTURE TO AUDIT

After HR has determined the company's underlying architecture, it can use a framework like the one below to guide the organization through the discussion and debate of the audit process.

| | Question | Rating (1–10) | Description of best practice | Gap between company's current practice and best practice |
|---|---|---|---|---|
| SHARED MIND-SET | To what extent does our company have the right culture to reach its goals? | | | |
| COMPETENCE | To what extent does our company have the required knowledge, skills, and abilities? | | | |
| CONSEQUENCE | To what extent does our company have the appropriate measures, rewards, and incentives? | | | |
| GOVERNANCE | To what extent does our company have the right organizational structure, communications systems, and policies? | | | |
| CAPACITY FOR CHANGE | To what extent does our company have the ability to improve work processes, to change, and to learn? | | | |
| LEADERSHIP | To what extent does our company have the leadership to achieve its goals? | | | |

staff will have to improve the efficiency of both their own function and the entire organization.

Within the HR function are dozens of processes that can be done better, faster, and cheaper. Finding and fixing those processes is part of the work of the new HR. Some companies have already embraced these tasks, and the results are impressive. One company has created a fully automated and flexible benefits program that employees can manage without paperwork; another has used technology to screen résumés and reduce the cycle time for hiring new candidates; and a third has created an electronic bulletin board that allows employees to communicate with senior executives. In all three cases, the quality of HR work improved and costs were lowered, generally removing steps or leveraging technology.

But decreased costs aren't the only benefit of HR's becoming the organization's administrative expert. Improving efficiency will build HR's credibility, which, in turn, will open the door for it to become a partner in executing strategy. Consider the case of a CEO who held a very low opinion of the company's HR staff after they sent a letter to a job candidate offering a salary figure with the decimal point in the wrong place. (The candidate called the CEO and joked that she didn't realize the job would make her a millionaire.) It was only after the HR staff proved they could streamline the organization's systems and proce-

dures and deliver flawless administrative service that the CEO finally felt comfortable giving HR a seat at the strategy table.

HR executives can also prove their value as administrative experts by rethinking how work is done throughout the organization. For example, they can design and implement a system that allows departments to share administrative services. At Amoco, for instance, HR helped create a shared-service organization that encompassed 14 business units. HR can also create centers of expertise that gather, coordinate, and disseminate vital information about market trends, for instance, or organizational processes. Such groups can act as internal consultants, not only saving the company money but also improving its competitive situation.

**Becoming an Employee Champion.** Work today is more demanding than ever—employees are continually being asked to do more with less. And as companies withdraw the old employment contract, which was based on security and predictable promotions, and replace it with faint promises of trust, employees respond in kind. Their relationship with the organization becomes transactional. They give their time but not much more.

That kind of curtailed contribution is a recipe for organizational failure. Companies cannot thrive unless their employees are engaged fully. Engaged employees—that is, employees who believe they are valued—share ideas, work harder than the necessary minimum, and relate better to customers, to name just three benefits.

In their new role, HR professionals must be held accountable for ensuring that employees are engaged—that they feel committed to the organization and contribute fully. In the past, HR sought that commitment by attending to the social needs of employees—picnics, parties, United Way campaigns, and so on. While those activities must still be organized, HR's new agenda supersedes them. HR must now take responsibility for orienting and training line management about the importance of high employee morale and how to achieve it. In addition, the new HR should be the employees' voice in management discussions; offer employees opportunities for personal and professional growth; and provide resources that help employees meet the demands put on them.

Orienting and training line management about how to achieve high employee morale can be accomplished using several tools, such as workshops, written reports, and employee surveys. Such tools can help managers understand the sources of low morale within the organization—not just specifically, but conceptually. For instance, HR might inform the line that 82% of employees feel demoralized because of a recent downsizing. That's useful. But more than that, HR should be responsible for educating the line about the causes of low employee morale. For instance, it is generally agreed by organizational behavior experts that employee morale decreases when people believe the demands put upon them exceed the resources available to meet those demands. Morale also drops when goals are unclear, priorities are unfocused, or performance measurement is ambiguous. HR serves an important role in holding a mirror in front of senior executives.

HR can play a critical role in recommending ways to ameliorate morale problems. Recommendations can be as simple as urging the hiring of additional support staff or as complex as suggesting that reengineering be considered for certain tasks. The new role for HR might also involve suggesting that more teams be used on some projects or that employees be given more control over their own work schedules. It may mean suggesting that line executives pay attention to the possibility that some employees are being asked to do boring or repetitive work. HR at Baxter Healthcare, for example, identified boring work as a problem and then helped to solve it by redesigning work processes to connect employees more directly with customers.

Along with educating operating managers about morale, HR staff must also be an advocate for employees—they must represent the employees to management and be their voice in management discussions. Employees should have confidence that when decisions are made that affect them (such as a plant closing), HR's involvement in the decision-making process clearly represents employees' views and supports their rights. Such advocacy cannot be invisible. Employees must know that HR is their

voice before they will communicate their opinions to HR managers.

**Becoming a Change Agent.** To adapt a phrase, Change happens. And the pace of change today, because of globalization, technological innovation, and information access, is both dizzying and dazzling. That said, the primary difference between winners and losers in business will be the ability to respond to the pace of change. Winners will be able to adapt, learn, and act quickly. Losers will spend time trying to control and master change.

The new HR has as its fourth responsibility the job of building the organization's capacity to embrace and capitalize on change. It will make sure that change initiatives that are focused on creating high-performing teams, reducing cycle time for innovation, or implementing new technology are defined, developed, and delivered in a timely way. The new HR can also make sure that broad vision statements (such as, We will be the global leader in our markets) get transformed into specific behaviors by helping employees figure out what work they can stop, start, and keep doing to make the vision real. At Hewlett-Packard, HR has helped make sure that the company's value of treating employees with trust, dignity, and respect translates into practices that, for example, give employees more control over when and where they work.

Change has a way of scaring people—scaring them into inaction. HR's role as a change agent is to replace resis-

---

## HR must now train line management in methods of achieving high employee morale.

---

tance with resolve, planning with results, and fear of change with excitement about its possibilities. How? The answer lies in the creation and use of a change model. (For an example of a very effective change model, developed with and used extensively by GE, see the chart "Change Begins by Asking Who, Why, What, and How.") HR professionals must introduce such a model to their organizations and guide executive teams through it—that is, steer the conversation and debate that answers the multitude of questions it raises. The model, in short, must be a managerial tool championed by HR. It helps an organization identify the key success factors for change and assess the organization's strengths and weaknesses regarding each factor. The process can be arduous, but it is one of the most valuable roles HR can play. As change agents, HR professionals do not themselves execute change—but they make sure that it is carried out.

Consider the case of a company whose senior management team announced that "valuing diversity" was a top priority in 1996. Six months into the year, the team ac-

# PROFILE OF A CHANGE INITIATIVE IN DISTRESS

One company's HR professionals used this chart to help senior management
understand why a high-profile diversity initiative was going nowhere.

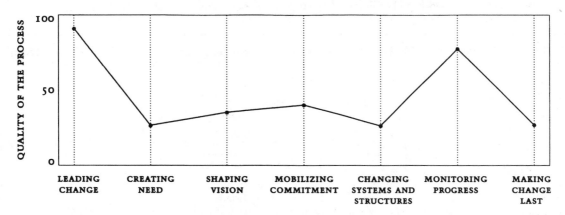

knowledged that the diversity initiative had received more rhetoric than action. The company's HR professionals asked the team to spend several hours profiling the diversity initiative using a change model. (See the graph "Profile of a Change Initiative in Distress.") The resulting analysis revealed that the diversity initiative would fail unless the senior management team explored several critical questions, among them: Why are we seeking diversity? What will be the benefit to the business and its customers? What is the ideal form of diversity for this organization? Who needs to be supportive and involved to make the initiative come to life?

HR leaders spent several more hours with the management team guiding a conversation that answered those questions. Shortly afterward, they were able to present the team with an action plan for moving the diversity initiative forward. Thus HR did not decide what changes the organization was going to embrace, but it did lead the process to make them explicit.

Perhaps the hardest and most important challenge facing many companies in this era of flux is changing their culture. In helping to bring about a new culture, HR must follow a four-step process:

■ First, it must define and clarify the concept of culture change.

■ Second, it must articulate why culture change is central to business success.

■ Third, it must define a process for assessing the current culture and the desired new culture, as well as for measuring the gap between the two.

■ And fourth, it must identify alternative approaches to creating culture change.

HR played an important part in changing the culture at Sears, which underwent a transformation of its business beginning in 1994. In facilitating that change, HR first took on the task of getting the organization to define and clarify the concept of culture. It helped lead the top 100

managers through discussions and debates of the questions, What are the top three things we want to be known for by our customers? and What do we do that is world class in those things? Ultimately, those conversations led to a consensus that Sears would define its culture as "the identity of the company in the minds of the best customers." In addition, HR at Sears took on the responsibility of making the business case for a transformation of the company's culture. It compiled data showing that even a small increase in employee commitment led to a measurable increase in customer commitment and store profitability. The data illustrate conclusively that Sears's transformation affected employees, customers, and investors.

HR at Sears guided the company's culture change in numerous other ways.[1] The specific details, however, are not nearly as important as their implications. HR can be the architect of new cultures, but to do so, its purpose must be redefined. Virtually every imperative of the new mandate for HR requires such a redefinition. And for it to happen, senior managers must lead the way.

## Four Changes for the Line

The new mandate for HR requires dramatic changes in how HR professionals think and behave. But perhaps more important, it also requires that senior executives change what they expect from HR and how they behave toward the HR staff. The following are four ways senior operating managers can create an era in which HR is focused on outcomes instead of activities:

**Communicate to the organization that the "soft stuff" matters.** At Hewlett-Packard, managing people was one of the two *hoshin* (major objectives) of the CEO for 1997. At General Electric, CEO Jack Welch claims he spends 40% of his time on people issues. At Southern Company, senior managers are working to create an empowered organization to ensure faster and better decision making.

# CHANGE BEGINS BY ASKING WHO, WHY, WHAT, AND HOW

HR staff at GE used this change model to guide a transformation process at the company.

| Key Success Factors for Change | Questions to Assess and Accomplish The Key Success Factors for Change |
|---|---|
| Leading change (Who is responsible?) | Do we have a leader . . . <br> who owns and champions the change? <br> who publicly commits to making it happen? <br> who will garner the resources necessary to sustain it? <br> who will put in the personal time and attention needed to follow through? |
| Creating a shared need (Why do it?) | Do employees . . . <br> see the reason for the change? <br> understand why it is important? <br> see how it will help them and the business in the short term and long term? |
| Shaping a vision (What will it look like when we are done?) | Do employees . . . <br> see the outcomes of the change in behavioral terms <br> (that is, in terms of what they will do differently <br> as a result of the change)? <br> get excited about the results of accomplishing the change? <br> understand how it will benefit customers and other stakeholders? |
| Mobilizing commitment (Who else needs to be involved?) | Do the sponsors of the change . . . <br> recognize who else needs to be committed to the change <br> to make it happen? <br> know how to build a coalition of support for the change? <br> have the ability to enlist support of key individuals in <br> the organization? <br> have the ability to build a responsibility matrix to make <br> the change happen? |
| Modifying systems and structures (How will it be institutionalized?) | Do the sponsors of the change . . . <br> understand how to link it to other HR systems such as <br> staffing, training, appraisal, rewards, structure, and <br> communication? <br> recognize the systems implications of the change? |
| Monitoring progress, (How will it be measured?) | Do the sponsors of the change . . . <br> have a means of measuring its success? <br> plan to benchmark progress against both the results of the <br> change and the process of implementing it? |
| Making it last, (How will it get started and last?) | Do the sponsors of the change . . . <br> recognize the first steps in getting started? <br> have a short-term and long-term plan to keep attention <br> focused on the change? <br> have a plan to adapt the change over time? |

The point? For HR to be taken seriously, senior managers must demonstrate that they believe typical HR issues—the soft stuff like culture change and intellectual capital—are critical to business success.

Operating managers can signal this belief in several ways. They can talk seriously about how organizational capabilities create value for investors, customers, and employees. They can invest the time needed to make sure organizational changes are debated and implemented. They can include HR professionals in strategy discussions and state explicitly that without the collaboration of HR, strategies are more hopes than realities, promises than acts, and concepts than results.

**Explicitly define the deliverables from HR, and hold HR accountable for results.** It is one thing to tell HR that it is responsible for employee contribution and quite another to set a specific goal—say, a 10% increase in employee morale as measured by a survey. And once such specific goals are set, consequences must follow if they are missed.

The new mandate for HR is like any other business initiative in this way. A company has a much better chance of achieving its goals if senior managers state specifically what they expect from HR and then track, measure, and reward performance.

**Invest in innovative HR practices.** Like every other area of business, HR gets its share of new technologies and practices, and senior line executives should be always on the lookout for such practices. Conferences and management literature are always good places to hear of new ways of approaching HR, but senior managers should also be aware of innovative HR practices going on at other companies and of new practices that are being advocated by respected consultants.

Investing in new HR practices is another way to signal to the organization that HR is worthy of the company's money and attention. It is also a way to make sure that HR has the tools, information, and processes that it needs to execute its new mandate.

---

# When more is expected of the HR function, a higher quality of HR professional must be found.

---

As new practices are identified, line managers should expect HR to adapt to them, not adopt them. Too often, after learning about an innovative idea, HR immediately tries to copy it wholesale. Such efforts often fail, and at a high emotional cost. Instead, investment in new HR practices should focus on learning not only what works elsewhere but also how a new practice should work in the company's unique competitive situation.

**Upgrade HR professionals.** Finally, the hardest but perhaps most important thing senior managers can do to drive forward the new mandate for HR is to improve the quality of the HR staff itself. Too often, HR departments are like computers made up of used parts. While the individual

parts may work, they don't work well together. When more is expected of HR, a higher quality of HR professional must be found. Companies need people who know the business, understand the theory and practice of HR, can manage culture and make change happen, and have personal credibility. Sometimes, such individuals already exist within the HR function but need additional training. Other times, they have to be brought in from other parts of the company. In still other cases, they must be hired from outside.

Regardless, HR cannot expand its role in an organization without the requisite expertise. Becoming a strategic partner demands a degree of knowledge about strategy, markets, and the economy. Becoming an administrative expert demands some knowledge of reengineering, as well as the intricacies of what the line actually does. If HR is to effect real change, it must be made up of people who have the skills they need to work from a base of confidence and earn what too often it lacks—respect.

## Hard Work Ahead

To meet the increased expectations of their organizations, HR professionals must begin to act professionally. They must focus more on the deliverables of their work and less on just getting their work done. They must articulate their role in terms of the value they create. They must create mechanisms so that business results quickly follow. They must measure their effectiveness in terms of business competitiveness rather than employee comfort and lead cultural transformation rather than consolidate, reengineer, or downsize in order to turn a company around.

Senior executives who recognize the economic value and the benefit to their customers of intellectual capital and organizational capability need to demand more of the HR function. They need to invest in HR as if it were a business. And they must get beyond the stereotype of HR professionals as incompetent value-sapping support staff. It's time to destroy that stereotype and unleash HR's full potential.

## Note

1. For more on the transformation of Sears, see The Employee-Customer-Profit Chain at Sears, by Anthony J. Rucci, Steven P. Kirn, and Richard T. Quinn, HBR, January/February 1998.

# The HR Side of Sears' Comeback

*At least one-third of Sears' dramatic financial and cultural transformation has been HR-driven.*

## By Jennifer Laabs

One Saturday morning in March 1994, one hundred of Sears, Roebuck and Co.'s most senior executives met for one purpose: to continue strategizing the details of an organizational transformation plan they'd started back in 1992. The group had already accomplished much—in only two years, after a prior 10-year slump, the firm had pulled itself back into the black from having a net loss of $3.9 billion on sales of $52.3 billion (in 1992 alone), most of which was from the merchandising group.

But the agenda for this particular day was different than usual. Each executive had to pretend he or she was a news reporter, and had to arrive prepared to read aloud the first few sentences of an article they each had written about what they envisioned the Hoffman Estates, Illinois-based company would be in 1999 and how it got there.

"We spent five hours that day having our top 100 executives, one at a time, stand up and read his or her two paragraphs," recalls Anthony J. Rucci, Sears' former executive VP of administration, who left the post in 1998 to become the dean of the business school at University of Illinois at Chicago. "People's ideas were all over the ballpark. Some people had us opening motorcycle dealerships in China and all kinds of innovative, if somewhat crazy, things," Rucci recalls.

From that process and through several other steps, Sears' senior management team gelled its firm's new vision into a simple, but powerful vision statement: "To make Sears, Roebuck and Co. a compelling place to shop, work and invest." A big part of achieving that strategy was to transform Sears' solid 113-year culture into a vibrant, modern, customer-driven one. After some analysis, Sears realized its customers were primarily (70 percent) women. This inspired "the softer side of Sears" approach and store facelifts that included installing wider aisles, softer lighting and fancier displays to mimic more expensive department stores.

Sears also narrowed its focus. After having seen other more-focused retailers like Wal-Mart and Target take significant market share away from the long-established retailer, the company's new chairman and CEO, Arthur C. Martinez, was determined to see Sears not only regain its position, but to lead the market. To achieve market leadership, Martinez folded the company's longstanding catalog operations and refocused the company by divesting it of its insurance and real estate subsidiaries—The Allstate Corp. and The Homart Development Co. In 1996, the company marked its first year of operations focused exclusively on retailing since 1931.

Over the past seven years, Sears' drive toward financial and cultural transformation has involved unwavering effort from the entire senior management team and every Sears associate. But it has also been a drive that wouldn't have been accomplished without the efforts of Sears' HR team, first led by Rucci, and now headed by John T. Sloan, Sears' senior vice president of human resources who succeeded Rucci in March 1998.

Achieving the initial financial turnaround by 1994 and coming up with a compelling mission statement were big steps in the right direction. But for HR, it was only the beginning of a long road to implementing the transformation of HR's own processes and the entire company's culture. HR was not only up to the challenge, it has exceeded expectations and has become a model for the retail industry—and others—to follow.

*Jennifer Laabs is the associate managing editor for WORK-FORCE. E-mail laabsj@workforcemag.com to comment.*

## Transforming Sears' HR group.

While the rest of the company was immersed in a transformation effort, Sears' HR department was undergoing its own metamorphosis. Back in late 1993, shortly after Rucci came on board at Sears, he challenged his senior HR team to take six months and come back with a redesign of the HR function. The design *had* to be radical, and it *had* to treat the internal organization as if it were the customer.

That meant they had to go out and identify the requirements of the customer before they could figure out what the HR function ought to look like to meet those requirements. They extensively surveyed their customers—finding out what they liked and what they didn't like based on a specific set of questions, such as: "How do you think the comp and rewards side of HR is functioning? How about selection and college recruiting? And what about HR information systems and support?"

Based on data derived from surveying, the HR transformation team went back and completely changed the HR function. It reassessed everyone in the HR function with these new standards of customer service orientation, responsiveness and so on. Then it completely restaffed the department using a "zero-based" staffing approach. In addition, Rucci changed the reporting relationships of HR people—rather than reporting to him, he had them report to the businesses they supported. Moving HR back to the line, so to speak, is an idea that is now only just beginning to take hold for most HR departments, and helps move HR into strategic business partner status.

"We asked a lot of all of our HR people," says Rucci. "On one hand, people responded marvelously. We couldn't ask them to do any more than they did. On the other hand, change, if not done well—even under the best circumstances—creates a certain degree of anxiety for people." Rucci explains that having a clear vision early on about what excellence was supposed to look like in the transformation process paid huge dividends later on. "When we came back and asked people to make these changes, at least they knew what the end vision looked like," says Rucci. "We spent an enormous amount of time communicating and getting people at all levels involved in the change process."

Today, having transformed the HR operations and processes, Sears' 650 HR people spend most of their time continuously helping associates align with the company's new vision. Adds Sloan: "Although HR at Sears is vitally linked to all three aspects of the vision of the company, we spend the bulk of our time on making Sears a compelling place to work." That has translated into a host of training, development and rewards strategies.

## Employees learn new ways of working.

By 1994, Sears had done a good job of transforming senior managers' ideas around Sears vision, but the average associate still wasn't fully engaged in the process. The new mission statement was rolled out, but it needed legs to help employees understand what it meant for them. With 838 full-line department stores, more than 2,700 off-the-mall stores and more than 300,000 employees, Sears needed to embark on a companywide plan to spread the word.

"One of the things we discovered—and it's sort of a fundamental principle of organizational change—is that change is much more effective if people understand why you're asking them to change rather than just saying 'do it,'" explains Steve Kirn, Sears' vice president of organizational learning and development. "You have to give them a framework for why particular kinds of changes are important."

Sears' learning chiefs figured out a powerful way to *show* employees why the transformation was necessary, rather than just *tell* them by using Learning Maps™ (Learning Map™ is a trademark of Perrysburg, Ohio-based Root Learning® Inc.) and town hall meetings. Learning Maps provide information and encourage employees to think about the industry and the company they work in. At Sears, groups of roughly 10 employees at a time "walk through" each map aided by a written guide and questions. For example, the first Learning Map Sears associates (employees) walked through was called "A New Day on Retail Street." It takes people on a time-capsule journey from the '50s through the '90s and shows people how the retail environment has changed, how demographics have changed—from the country's ethnic makeup to the number of working women—and how much free time people have on their hands to go shopping.

During these sessions, employees learned that the number of visits the average shopper made to a shopping center per month was 12 in 1980, but only four in 1990. "So the group looks at that number and ends up saying, 'Whoa, we don't have as many opportunities to see our customers as we used to. We'd better make shopping easy for them because it looks like they're shopping with a greater eye toward convenience,'" says Kirn. At town hall meetings, larger groups of employees who had been through the Learning Maps process came together to talk about what changes they could make in their individual stores to help Sears reach its overall goals. Employees were asked to figure out one thing they could do, could stop doing or could simplify when they returned to work the next day to improve Sears' competitive position. Because they were local improvements, headquarters didn't have to approve the changes.

In general, Sears associates get much more training now than before the transformation began. Over the past four years, Sears has spent the equivalent of millions of dollars on training its associates about Sears' new goals and in world-class retailing skills.

The good news for Sears is that all the training around Sears' new vision has stuck firmly in the minds of its associates. "The impact now is the sense of ownership that associates feel," says Gale Book, Sears' store trainer in

Pensacola, Florida. "It's no longer just a small group of people who have an impact on assignments. It now comes from all different areas of the store."

Whereas some companies initiate turnaround projects and get their initial goals met, Sears has built a platform on which to root its long-term business planning. Employees use the company's three C's (compelling place to shop, work and invest) to test management decisions in day-to-day business. They also learned about the beliefs that senior managers had identified are important to Sears for the future, the three P's—"a passion for the customer, the belief that Sears' people add value to the enterprise and an uncompromising belief in performance leadership."

For example, though no formal orientation existed before, now there's an eight-week orientation process. And management education, which had been virtually nonexistent before the turnaround because of severe cost-cutting measures, is a high priority. Some of that learning takes place in person at Sears University (SU) which was established in 1995. Since SU opened, more than 40,000 Sears managers have been trained through the program. They also operate a strategic-retail-management program, which more than 250 senior executives have attended in groups of approximately 30 at a time.

Other learning takes place through desktop or distance learning courses. Employees can borrow audio or videotapes to brush up on everything from selling techniques to strategic planning. And employees can demonstrate their mastery of courses or modules they've taken through Sears Training Tracking System (STTS—an interactive voice-response testing system. Today, more than 20,000 Sears employees a year are in learning programs that range from one to six days a shot.

"The really important message is: There's no magic bullet when it comes to how you deal with people," says Kirn. "You create cultural transformation by doing things in an array of business areas. The trick is to make them all interlock, and not to compete with one another."

## Measuring the return on investment.

As the former head of human resources, Rucci led the transition team—sanctioned by Martinez, organized by Rucci and made up of 16 line executives—that was responsible for implementing the culture change Martinez envisioned. The transformation team figured it wasn't enough to just have a vision, they had to determine exactly how to put that vision into action. They set out to come up with an econometric model that would show people how to add true value to their retail operation.

They postulated a theory that a company's financial performance—rather than an obvious sign of how a company is doing—actually is a lagging indicator. This means that by the time Sears (or any company for that matter) publishes its annual report, it's too late to do anything about financial performance—especially if it isn't favorable. They figured there had to be some "leading indica-

tors" that would help predict later financial performance. For Sears, those turned out to be something that may seem rather obvious to most business people, but few, if any, companies have made the link as directly as Sears. They theorized that things like employee attitudes and whether customers see their stores as fun places to shop were directly linked to financial performance, and they've actually proved it.

By culling many taskforce suggestions and through much of their own work, the transformation team arrived at a business model that would track success in many areas including management behavior, employee attitudes, customer satisfaction and financial performance. To track and measure the outcomes of the business model, they developed a highly effective and world-class performance index called the *employee-customer-profit model*. It comprises six measurements: one measure for a compelling place to work, two for a compelling place to shop and three for a compelling place to invest. By means of an ongoing process of data collection, analysis, modeling and experimentation, the Total Performance Indicators (TPI) show Sears how well it's doing with customers, employees and investors.

In an elaborate 800-store study of employee attitudes recently conducted by Sears, researchers found there's a direct correlation between employee satisfaction and profitability. Sears found that if positive employee attitudes on 10 essential factors—including workload, treatment by bosses and so forth—increase by 5 percent, then customer satisfaction will jump 1.3 percent, leading to a one-half percentage-point rise in revenue.

Sears' customer satisfaction ratings began creeping upward in 1993 measured against their leading competitors. A *Fortune* magazine survey published in February 1997 showed Sears' customer satisfaction jumped 5.6 percent from 1995 to 1996, more than twice as much as any other retailer surveyed. In '96 and '97, its customer satisfaction scores rose two more percentage points, placing it at parity with its target competition. Since March 1997, Sears cash registers have been randomly kicking out receipts that ask customers to call an automated toll-free number and respond to questions. The survey results are then compiled into a statistically significant customer satisfaction score— a number that has risen several points since 1996.

Associate satisfaction scores also increased during that period. The employee satisfaction score is now 69.5, and has risen 1.5 percent in the past year and a half alone. "It's extremely difficult to move up a quarter of a point, so every move up really is a significant move in the right direction," says Sloan. "And what we've found is the stores that have higher scores basically perform better financially than those with lower scores." So the firm knows where to focus its energy and attention.

Another measure of employee satisfaction is the fact that the company's turnover rate has plummeted from 100 percent turnover when the transformation project started to 66 percent—the bulk of the turnover being in the part-time hourly ranks. For salaried personnel, turnover is about 20 percent. "Our largest area of opportunity is continuing to address our part-time, hourly workforce," says Sloan. "But that has dropped significantly since we started the transformation, and continues to drop."

The increase in employee satisfaction scores and drop in turnover further indicate there's alignment inside the organization with the firm's strategy and direction. For Sears—with annual revenues of approximately $44 billion—this increase amounts to more than $200 million in additional revenues for the company each year. That alignment and performance needs to be rewarded.

## Transforming rewards and compensation.

When Sears redirected its vision, it also needed to drastically change the way it paid and rewarded people. "Too often, companies attempt to change employee behavior by changing pay and incentive practices," said Martinez in an interview with the *ACA Journal* (Autumn 1997). "Over the long term, people change their behavior not because of pay practices, but because they relate to the organization's vision and strategy. Pay practices then need to reinforce that strategy."

On January 1, 1996, Sears' senior management took the bold step of placing a substantial portion of the company's 200 top executives' long-term incentive compensation at risk based on the TPI: being a compelling place to shop, work and invest. This means executive incentives are based on non-financial as well as financial performance—divided equally between customer measures, employee measures and investor measures. "That puts the retailer on the corporate world's cutting edge in using a 'balanced scorecard' that includes non-financial factors," commented Bob Duncan, professor of leadership and change at the J. L. Kellogg Graduate School of Management at Northwestern University in a *Chicago Tribune* article last year.

Putting executive pay on the line is the hot compensation trend of the '90s, but it's a radical departure for the once-paternalistic Sears, where paychecks were steady and benefits were better than average. Now all of Sears' 19,000 salaried managers have pay tied to financial performance of their business units and company performance. Six years ago, 90 percent of a Sears manager's pay, on average, came in the form of salary. Now it's closer to 80 percent, and it's even lower for top execs whose bonuses can exceed their salary. It's all in an effort to move away from entitlement mentality, and toward a focus on what drives financial rewards: the customer.

## Turnabout is fair play.

Financially speaking, the market value of Sears increased by nearly $15 billion from 1992 through the end of 1997, adjusting for the effects of spinoffs (exact final figures for 1998 weren't available at press time). "We didn't have a great year in '98," admits Jan Drummond, a Sears spokesperson. "However, we're on the right course." Sears has come a long way. She explains that Sears' revenue back in 1993 was $29 billion when Sears Merchandise Group was the retail arm of Sears and included Allstate and other service businesses. "The revenue now for us as a stand-alone retail organization is going to be in the neighborhood of $43 to $45 billion in 1998," adds Drummond. Even Wall Street analysts are impressed by Sears' comeback, even if some think Sears' retailing strategy still seems fuzzy. Sears managers admit they still have work to do.

Said Martinez in the firm's 1996 annual report: "While we have made good financial progress and have solid growth plans, we have not yet achieved fully the kind of transformation that we seek for the business. Transformation requires a workforce, from top to bottom, who is committed to embracing and fostering change. Associates must think like owners if we're to keep the process of continuous reinvention alive inside the company."

Still, Sears' human resources efforts in nurturing the company to where it is today are no less than heroic, and have earned much notice by the media, HR analysts, consultants and academicians. "Sears has been creative in both the theory and practice of HR. The company recognized early that employee commitment predicted and affected customer commitment," says Dave Ulrich, a professor at the University of Michigan Business School where he co-directs the Human Resource Executive Education Program, and has been a consultant with Sears' HR executives during the transformation process. "As a result, it focused HR practices on enhancing employee commitment." Just about everything HR could change to help add value to the organization, it did change with a high level of excellence.

Perhaps it's cliché to say that Sears is a true Diehard. With a 113-year history, that may be obvious. The ultimate compliment is that a company with such a long history can figure out how the eldest player on retail street can still be a wise player. Certainly, the fact that Sears has determined its human resources are a key to playing the game effectively is noteworthy. While we await the fully transformed Sears, we applaud the HR side of Sears for its world-class efforts thus far. It's a compelling HR example to follow.

## General Excellence

*The* WORKFORCE *Magazine Optimas Award for General Excellence is given to a department that meets the standards established for at least six of the other nine Optimas categories: Competitive Advantage, Financial Impact, Global Outlook, Innovation, Managing Change, Partnership, Quality of Life, Service and Vision.*

# Taking Your Seat 'At the Table'

*By Lin Grensing-Pophal*

*You'll need to strategize to move into the strategic planning process.*

### How Strategic Has HR Become?

When asked "is HR a major part of your company's strategic process?" 155 senior human resource executives provided the following responses:

| | |
|---|---|
| Always | 37% |
| Sometimes | 42% |
| Rarely | 19% |
| Never | 2% |

Source: HR Leaders Poll, The Conference Board, October 1998.

BrandonMaddox

**M**any HR professionals treasure the idea of taking a seat at the corporate table. While some have gained established seats that are comfortable and worn, others have yet to earn even a peek into the boardroom.

According to a recent survey, more than a third of responding senior HR professionals say they are always involved in strategic planning; more than 40 percent are sometimes involved. But nearly 25 percent of the respondents are rarely or never involved in strategy. (See the chart at left.)

What is getting in the way? Part of the problem is that HR has not traditionally been viewed in a strategic role—it has been considered a support service department. Many professionals groomed in this environment have a difficult time moving into a different role.

But the time is ripe for change, say experts.

"In the past, HR was largely transactional," says Brian Becker, Ph.D., a professor of organization and human resources at the University of Buffalo School of Management. But, Becker points out, the business environment has changed—and altered HR's role along with it. "Compared to earlier periods in our economic history, intellectual capital—

for the first time—has a great deal of value," he says.

William Bliss, president of Bliss & Associates in Brewster, N.Y., says that competition for capable and talented employees has elevated the role of HR in many organizations. Like Becker, he ties this trend to a new appreciation for "human capital." He sees opportunities for HR executives to work with CFOs and CEOs to develop solid models to evaluate human capital.

Brenda Vander Meulen, who operates an organizational development and strategic planning company, River Hills Consulting, in Holland, Mich., believes that HR professionals are in a position to vastly improve their value to the organizations they serve. "I think HR needs to begin to see itself as holding the key to the critical resource of the company," she says.

## What's Holding Us Back?

Too many HR professionals are complacent, says Bliss. "They may be great recruiters, or great benefits people or great trainers," he says, "but if they don't understand what the business is doing, why the competition is better than they are, it's inevitable that they'll be gone in a matter of time."

Vander Meulen sees "an awful lot of HR people out there who see their job as primarily maintenance. They need to start seeing themselves in what I think is a more correct role—as a partner."

Diana Lewis, vice president of HR at EcoLab, in St. Paul, Minn., a $2.5 billion cleaning and sanitation company that employs 15,000 people worldwide, concedes that it can be difficult to make the transition to strategic partner. "There are so many day-to-day operational issues that need attention that our tendency is to fight those battles and not create the time to work on some of the strategic issues that really require more reflection, more analysis and more time."

But, she warns, "When you're so involved in those more operational HR issues, that's the way management sees you, and those are the things they involve you in. In some ways, momentum keeps you where you are."

Bliss recommends that HR professionals critically evaluate how they spend their time. "A lot of HR people today, especially those who were brought up in the bureaucracy, don't think in terms of adding value," he says. "They'll spend 10 hours of company time on something that will save $100." He advises HR professionals to ask themselves what is truly important.

Another barrier is focusing too much on HR issues, instead of developing a broader understanding of general business and industry-specific issues. During Vander Meulen's tenure with a former employer, she served as strategic business partner for the company's operations—an area that employed 3,000 people. She credits her ability to become a credible member of the leadership team, in large part, to her experience in diverse areas of the company.

"I worked 11 years around the company before I went into HR," she says. "Too often I think HR people spend their entire careers in HR, and they really don't know what's going on in the organization. They need to get out of HR; that builds incredible credibility."

Lewis agrees. "I think it's true that you need to do everything you can to expand your business knowledge," she says. In addition to the traditional paths of education, training or reading trade journals, she recommends developing relationships with business partners within the organization.

And partners, says Vander Meulen, share information with each other. They listen to each other. They gather perspectives from many sources. "Partners don't just say, 'You can't do that—that's not our policy.'"

Partnering with other business units was part of the organizational structure at the company where Vander Meulen worked. But even if partnering isn't a formal process in your organization, you can still take the initiative to align the HR function more closely with other areas of the company.

## Getting Started

Where should HR professionals focus their energies if they want to get involved in strategic planning?

"HR people first get involved in strategic planning in areas that are most closely aligned with HR issues," Lewis says. "I always think the most typical one is around succession planning or development planning. That piece of HR is really a strategic process."

Bliss agrees that retention and succession planning are key issues that can provide the opportunity to participate in strategic planning. "Take a look at what the organization is going to look like two, three or five years out," he says. "What kinds of skills are going to be required? What kinds of businesses is the company going to be in? Where will these businesses be located?"

Lewis says there are any number of natural inroads that allow HR professionals to move into strategic planning. She recommends starting in areas where you already have responsibility and taking that responsibility to a new, more strategic, level.

For instance, suppose you have high turnover in a certain area and are doing a lot of staffing. "You might take the time to say, 'This is costing us a lot of money and detracting from our productivity,'" Lewis says. "You could quantify it. You could look at ways to better align your staffing strategies with business needs.

"If I have a recurring operational problem, I think, 'Maybe there's an issue here that has some implications beyond the short-term'—something that has some strategic piece. I already have the responsibility for fixing those short-term issues, and I can expand on that responsibility."

Becker says HR professionals "need to think of the HR area as an entire system that is designed to implement strategy." That system must be aligned with the organization's overall strategy. To do this you must understand the business' problems, he says. That requires moving outside the narrow confines of what has been traditionally considered "HR's role."

Vander Meulen stresses the importance of developing solid relationships throughout the organization. These relationships can serve to expand awareness of critical business issues and to enhance credibility. "You begin to ask questions like: 'How well does the compensation plan work for you? Does it support your objectives or does it get in your way? In what ways? Tell me more.'"

Becker agrees. "HR professionals have to have an understanding of how value is created in the organization. They have to understand the business problems facing line managers as well as line managers do." HR professionals need this understanding not because they will advise line managers on solutions to their business problems, but because they have to understand what Becker calls "the human capital impediments to successfully solving those business problems."

And there are direct benefits to expanding your involvement in the strategic aspects of managing human capital. Lewis points out that success breeds success. If you show you can perform well in one aspect of strategic planning, you are more likely to be involved in other projects.

"A lot of HR managers want to have a seat at the table when strategy is being developed," Becker says, "and that's fine. But, strategic concepts are cheap. The challenge, and what differentiates the successful and less successful companies a lot of times, is the ability to implement the strategy." It is the people in an organization who implement strategy, Becker adds, so HR is in a position to play a critical role in this process.

*Lin Grensing-Pophal, SPHR, is a Wisconsin-based business journalist with HR consulting experience in employee communication, training and management issues. She is the author of* A Small Business Guide to Employee Selection *and* Motivating Today's Workforce: When the Carrot Can't Always Be Cash *(Self-Counsel Press, 1991).*

**Future Trends**

## HR's role *will* change.
## The question is *how*.

# HR 2008

## A Forecast Based on
## Our Exclusive Study

By Floyd Kemske

**WORKFORCE commissioned a special six-month study to determine the direction of the HR profession and the workplace in the next 10 years. Here, we present the 60 top predictions by 10 of HR's leading workforce directors and consultants that will impact how you view and conduct HR right now.**

January is always a time when human resources professionals think about the future. It's a time to plan, envision, prioritize and set goals for the new year. Although management, by its very nature, demands that HR professionals look ahead, it can be difficult, if not downright daunting, to see beyond the veil of 1998 and into the years beyond.

So we set out to help you do just that—get a picture of what the workplace, HR and jobs themselves will look like 10 years from now. Earlier this year, we handpicked 10 leading HR directors, vice presidents and consultants (see "Distinguished Members of the 'HR 2008' Panel" for profiles of the panelists), and invited each of them to make some educated guesses in six specific areas of WORKFORCE editors thought would undergo the most upheaval over the next 10 years: workplace flexibility, global business, work and society, workforce development, the definition of jobs, and last, but not least, the strategic role of HR.

The process went like this: WORKFORCE determined through a strategic analysis of HR and the workplace what the six areas of greatest change might be in the next 10 years. Then we painstakingly selected 10 panelists who were former WORKFORCE Magazine Optimas Award winners or who've been leading consultants to the HR profession.

Once we selected the panel, we asked them to brainstorm individually what developments they think will occur in these six areas. Next, we asked them to rank the importance of these developments. Then we fed the rankings back to them for more ranking. Finally, we chose their top-60 predictions to report to you.

This process is what futurists call a Delphi study. Futurists, however, use the technique of iterative polling to generate discussion and critical examination. WORKFORCE has used it here to create a consensus, to get a feeling for what this particular profession anticipates for itself in the next decade.

The result is a picture of HR and the work environment in the year 2008 that's decidedly upbeat and confident in the status and influence of HR professionals. Perhaps we might have expected that, given the status of our panelists. But their predictions are by no means "pre-

# This is a picture of HR and the work environment in the year 2008 that's decidedly confident in the status of HR.

dictable." Although they collectively paint a picture of HR moving further along already established HR paths in some areas, our panelists forecast some completely unexpected twists and turns in other areas, such as envisioning the end of job descriptions and job titles, and the advent of HR professionals as organizational performance experts. Their suggestions are compelling.

But this study isn't so much about predicting the future as it is about surfacing the assumptions that will guide the behavior and decisions of HR professionals over the next decade. WORKFORCE predicts you'll think about this year, and indeed the next 10, with a new perspective. (You'll find the complete list of predictions on the next 2 pages.) Here, we discuss the highlights and give you insight about how the predictions might affect you, your workforce and your organization by the year 2008.

**Workplace Flexibility: Collaborative work in a virtual office.** Our panelists believe the future workplace will be characterized by creative, flexible work arrangements. Specified work hours and schedules will have little or no importance, and information technology will even free the employee from a specified work location. Work will become much more collaborative, and the government will support the flexibility by increasing benefits portability.

According to panelist Evelyne Steward, senior vice president of HR for the Calvert Group in Bethesda, Maryland, organizations don't have very much choice about this. "We need to change our business paradigm," she says. "The employee is in the driver's seat. We need to meet employee needs if we're going to have a competent workforce."

Several panelists said they thought the study's predictions about workplace flexibility confirmed their personal beliefs. "I have always thought the hours of work would become less important and there would be increasing emphasis on performance and results," says panelist Bonnie Hathcock, vice president of HR and development for US Airways in Arlington, Virginia. "What we're seeing is the elimination of the traditional command-and-control structure and the creation of the virtual workplace."

According to panelist Tharon Greene, director of HR for the City of Hampton, Virginia, employees are [able to meet the challenges and] demands that will be made on them by the massive redesign of work. "Employees respond to their jobs," she says. "Design a big job, you get big work."

The No. 1 prediction in this area emphasized "collaborative cultures," so we contacted futurist and consultant Joyce L. Gioia. She suggests this trend is well under way. "We've been seeing more managers who spend nearly all their time managing work teams. These are self-created and self-sustaining cross-functional teams that take their objectives from management but work with a great deal of autonomy. They recruit their own members and plan their own strategies. They may even have virtual structures, communicating via e-mail and teleconferencing." Gioia is president of Herman Associates Inc., a Greensboro, North Carolina-based firm that offers strategic consulting and training to help organizations handle HR issues and prepare for the future.

It may sound paradoxical that jobs are going to be both more autonomous and collaborative. But if you've ever participated in a chat group on the Web or on one of the online services, then you know it's possible to create and maintain a community or a team even across time zones. Chat groups are fairly primitive compared to some of the software (known as *groupware*), such as Lotus *Notes*, that facilitates teamwork.

If there's a single, large implication from our panelists' 10 predictions in the area of workplace flexibility, it's that we can all expect to attend fewer meetings in the future. It's true we can have face time through videoconferencing, but millions of self-employed people and telecommuters function perfectly well (and productively) without them. Their example suggests that offsite workers (who some studies say eventually will be two-thirds of an organization's workforce in the next century) will likely spend far less time in videoconferences than they spend with their e-mail.

Can you shape employee behavior without face-to-face meetings? For that matter, can you sustain a corporate culture without the thousands of subtle signals that reinforce it in an office "neighborhood"? These are particularly important questions for HR professionals, who in many organizations are the cultivators and keepers of corporate culture. But the experience of successful intercompany task forces and standards committees (not to mention virtual organizations) shows that you may not need a full-blown culture to establish values. HR professionals should be studying the employees their companies assign to intercompany work groups, as well as telecommuters and other offsite workers, so they can understand the most important variables in independent work arrangements, because these will be more the rule than the exception in the near future.

Incidentally, we may not regain all the time that may be wasted in meetings. Human nature is surprisingly constant in different arenas and media. Anecdotal evidence suggests many groupware users waste time prettying preliminary and interim work products because it's visible to other group members. Team leaders will have to learn how to manage this tendency the way they have always had to learn how to contain grandstanding and preening at meetings.

There are some things that must or ought to be done in person—counseling, performance reviews, company softball games—and there probably always will be a small core of employees who habitually work at a central office, a core that may include at least some HR professionals. Perhaps this also suggests we'll move further and further toward the decentralization model of human resources organizations that we've been moving to in the past several years.

At the very least in the future, most of us probably will see our Federal Express couriers more often than we see our supervisors. And how human resources professionals will help manage that eventuality will be necessary to address.

**Global Business: Borderless business requires a global workforce.** As could be expected, our panelists see major growth in world trade, the world marketplace and the development of an international workforce. Because of this, they see organizations relying on HR professionals as the facilitators of work across borders and among different cultures.

But panelist Russ Campanello, an independent HR strategy consultant in Arlington, Massachusetts, said this prediction is just part of the picture. "Globalization is a given," he says. "But we haven't said much about the implications of that. Globalization, for example, means that business goes on 24 hours a day. This has profound implications for the way work is done. Look at the Internet commerce company Verifone, which has attempted to design the work to be handed off from time zone to time zone, so that it follows the daylight around the globe. What does something like that do to the organization's acquisition and location of talent?"

WORKFORCE sought the advice of the Washington, D.C.-based Institute for International Economics, where Visiting Fellow J. David Richardson (author of "Why Exports Really Matter!" and "Why Exports Really Matter More!"; National Association of Manufacturers 1995) confirmed that globalization means the world won't work in the old way. "Cross-cultural adaptation is becoming more necessary," he says. "I can tell you that as an educator, I see changes in the

# 60 HR Predictions For 2008

## Workplace Flexibility

1. Collaborative cultures will be the workplace model.

2. Creative employment contracts will support more time off, flexibility in hours and work location, technological job aids and more pay at risk with significant upside potential.

3. Company intranets will become a major tool for communication, training and benefits administration; HR will play a leading role in developing this important tool.

4. Intelligence through knowledge transfer capability will separate the best employees from the rest.

5. Employees will have more and more choices about work arrangements, allowing them to meet their individual needs.

6. Work hours scheduling will become less important as organizations focus on performance and results.

7. Company facilities will become "virtual" through work-at-home, telecommuting and outsourcing.

8. The workweek will be less structured—employees will still work 40-plus hours, but at varied times and places other than the office.

9. Legislation will lead to greater portability of health, welfare and retirement benefits.

10. Free-lance teams of generic problem solvers will market themselves as alternatives to permanent workers or individual temps.

## Global Business

1. The role of corporate HR will change to that of creator of overall values and direction, and will be implemented by local HR departments in different countries.

2. Technology, especially the Internet, will enable more businesses to enter the global marketplace.

3. HR professionals will have advanced acumen in international business practices, international labor laws, multicultural sensitivities and multiple languages.

4. HR professionals will need to be knowledgeable of other cultures, languages and business practices to help their companies find and enter more markets.

5. HR people will have to understand other cultures and help people work with, and transfer among, various cultures.

6. Megaglobal business alliances will grow in number and scope, requiring great finesse on the part of the HR professional.

7. There will be an explosive growth of companies doing business across borders, and it will be the most significant change for the economy in modern times.

8. Cultural understanding and sensitivity will become much more important for the HR professional of the future, whereas multiple language ability isn't going to become a necessary competency.

9. The continued emergence of a world marketplace will require development of an international workforce.

10. Small teams of HR professionals will focus on providing performance improvement consulting services to a variety of locations around the world.

## Work and Society

1. Family and life interests will play a more prevalent role in people's lives and a greater factor in people's choices about work— there will be more of a "work to live" than a "live to work" mentality.

2. Employees will demand increases in workplace flexibility to pursue life interests.

3. Dual-career couples will refuse to make the sacrifices required today in their family lives and more people (not just women) will opt out of traditional careers.

4. Families will return to the center of society; work will serve as a source of cultural connections and peripheral friendships.

5. Workers will continue to struggle with their need for work/life balance, and it will get worse.

6. Integration of work with quality-of-life initiatives will create solutions to problems formerly seen as the responsibility of government.

7. Community involvement and social responsibility will become part of an organization's business vision.

8. "Cocooning" will become more popular as workers look to their homes for refuge from the pressures of a more competitive workplace and depersonalized society.

9. Just as defined-contribution plans have begun to take over from Social Security, companies will take on responsibility for elder care, long-term care and other social needs through cafeteria-style benefits programs.

10. Those people who refuse or are unable to adapt to new technologies will find they're working harder and accomplishing less.

---

relative values of different kinds of preparation for students. We'll see more emphasis on language, history and geography and less on natural science. You can hire science." Richardson, who's also a professor of economics at the Maxwell School of Citizenship and Public Affairs at Syracuse, New York-based Syracuse University, sees an interesting effect of globalization among his master's degree students. "Other things being equal," he says, "the students who are most successful in finding jobs are the ones from cross-cultural families or who have some kind of experience with another culture in their backgrounds."

Richardson didn't quite like the wording of prediction No. 6 ("Megaglobal business alliances will grow in number and scope, requiring great finesse on the part of the HR professional"), saying that "mega-alliances"

have very little to do with the growth of global business. "There's a great deal of growth in international business among small firms in the form of international supply chains, representation deals and a lot of creative arrangements," he says. "When you look at the number of American firms that have become exporters over the past 20 years, there has been almost no growth among those with 500 or more employees. But among smaller firms, the number of exporters has grown 20 percent."

Is Richardson hopeful about the role of HR in global business? "I think most people have a stereotype of HR people," he says. "They are thought to be maintainers—they maintain peace, mental health, employee career momentum and so on. Looking to the future, they need to be adventurers rather than maintainers. That's not the stereotype,

but that's who will succeed in HR in the global marketplace."

If you have any doubts about the need to prepare for globalization, they can easily be dismissed by a glance at current headlines. Last fall, real estate lending in Thailand led to a financial crisis in Hong Kong, which caused the Dow Jones average to plummet. This globe-circling shock wave alone is enough to show us that national economies are becoming increasingly irrelevant. There's only one economy, and it spans the world. But the picture of a great, booming world economy that emerges from our panelists' predictions may be a little too rosy. The Hong Kong stock market crash and its aftermath are proof that adjusting to globalization may not always be easy.

Nevertheless, it's increasingly unlikely that American business can or will turn back

We asked our panelists to make their predictions in each of the six areas. All tabulations and rankings were done within these areas. Here we present the top-10 predictions for each area, ranked by order of importance within the area, with the most important first.

## Workforce Development

1. Lifelong learning will be a requirement.
2. The focus of training/learning activities will be on performance improvement and not just on skill building.
3. Employees with varied skills and competencies will be valued more highly than those with a depth of expertise in a single area.
4. Problem solving and decision making will become a required curriculum with practical work problems as the training medium.
5. Training will be delivered "just in time," wherever people need it, using a variety of technologies.
6. Companies will demand constant personal growth, and employees will respond positively to higher expectations.
7. It will not be possible to survive in the workplace without basic computer skills.
8. People who can learn new skills/competencies quickly will be highly valued in a faster changing world.
9. Team projects and special assignments will be a major factor in personal development.
10. As the computer-savvy generation is more assimilated into the workforce, employees will become much more productive in complex tasks and less dependent on other people and departments.

## Definition of Jobs

1. Organizations won't pay for the value of the job but for the value of the person.
2. Versatility will be the key factor in determining employee value with strategic thinking, leadership, problem solving, technology and people skills close behind.
3. Compensation systems will be linked to business outcomes.
4. All jobs will require higher levels of computer skills.
5. Positions will be organized in teams focused on a task, not organized around a hierarchy.
6. Positions will be defined by the competencies needed to be performed.
7. Employees will be more independent, moving from project to project within their organizations.
8. Many jobs will be redesigned to be much broader in scope, especially in management positions, resulting in leaner head counts.
9. Employees will be increasingly measured by how much value they contribute to the business, not by whether they fulfilled predetermined objectives.
10. Work will be more challenging, and jobs will become increasingly complex.

## Strategic Role of HR

1. Successful HR departments will focus on organizational performance.
2. HR's value will be to have the right people ready at the right time: recruiting leaders to join the company's mix of talent and keeping the "bench" full of enabled, competent workers.
3. The focus of the HR function will be human capital development and organizational productivity; HR may be renamed to reflect this.
4. HR will evolve from strategic business partnership to strategic business leadership (driving change and results, not just monitoring them).
5. A key HR role in the future will be multidisciplinary consulting around individual, team, business unit and corporate performance.
6. Managers will grow to depend more and more on HR professionals as they realize that good people management can be the strategic advantage in the next decade.
7. Leading change will become HR's greatest contribution to the corporation.
8. More and more businesses will use HR as a strategic partner.
9. HR will have a "seat at the table" as part of the top management team and report directly to the CEO in most companies.
10. A key HR role will be managing increasingly scarce human and intellectual capital.

from the rush to globalize. If most companies maintain a presence in other countries, either through local branches or international business alliances, they cannot leave the intercultural work issues to chance, and our panelists suggest it's the HR function that will manage this beat.

At the most mundane level, this may mean support services in obtaining visas for border-crossing employees. At the deeper levels, however, someone will need to maintain written and unwritten corporate policies for transportability to other cultures. It's clear that our panelists think HR professionals will have to step up their global skills and competencies in the next 10 years.

But we must not assume that human resources professionals' roles will just be another exercise in managing multicultural diversity. The global landscape is littered with companies that have been forcibly ejected (or decamped in disgrace) from countries that found their work offensive. Manage your domestic diversity badly and you may get a morale problem or a lawsuit. Manage your affairs in another country badly and you'll have a market disappear or employees taken hostage.

The first order of business is to keep top management informed of the costs of not paying attention to the transnational issues.

Our panelists suggest that corporate HR will keep in touch with local HR departments in different countries. It will maintain a corporate culture that works for both the domestic company and its international presence. This will require an understanding of foreign cultures. Local human resources departments can help with that, but communicating clearly with them (in both directions) will be corporate's responsibility. Our panelists may be whistling in the dark when they suggest human resources professionals will not need to learn foreign languages. They will certainly have to have foreign language speakers on staff.

The proposition that small teams of human resources professionals will take performance improvement consulting services to different global locations is one of the most exciting propositions to come out of the study. Although human resources managers might not have to know local languages in depth, it's unlikely you could be on such a team without understanding the

language of those whose performance needs to be improved. The members of these teams will have to be steeped in the values and assumptions of the other culture before they enter it. There may be a role for corporate anthropologists in this arena. Not only will human resources directors have to think outside the box in determining how they deal with global workforce issues, they'll have to make sure they remember the proverbial business box is getting increasingly bigger and more complex.

**Work and Society: Working to live, not living to work.** In this area, our panelists foresee a workplace that will free up employees to pursue life interests and family obligations. They also anticipate a growing involvement in the community by business organizations, which will take increasing responsibility for social needs.

"We're starting to see signs that people are questioning how much of their lives must be dedicated to work," says panelist Dave Pylipow, director of employee relations for Hallmark Cards Inc. in Kansas City, Missouri. "Companies need to consider the fact

# Distinguished Members of the "HR 2008" Panel

**Dennis J. Blair**
**Vice President of HR**
**GTE Technology and Systems**
**Needham, MA**

Prior to his current position, Blair served as vice president of HR at GTE Airfone in Oak Brook, Illinois. He served on the board of directors of the Wisconsin State Telephone Association and its executive committee. He also has been a board member for the Greater Madison Chamber of Commerce and the Business and Education Partnership. He's a past member of GTE's HR Council, a group of GTE's senior HR officers, that sets the HR direction for the firm.

**Russell J. Campanello**
**Independent HR Strategy Consultant**
**Arlington, MA**

Campanello's current clients are business leaders who are repositioning the HR function by introducing a new support model and technology infrastructure, and are focusing on the work of human development and organizational productivity. He was most recently at Cambridge, Massachusetts-based Nets Inc., an Internet commerce company, where he oversaw people, technology and facilities strategies. Prior to that, he spent nine years as vice president of HR at Lotus Development Corp. in Cambridge, Massachusetts. WORKFORCE magazine recently named him one of the 25 most important workplace visionaries of the past 75 years (January 1997).

**Jac Fitz-enz**
**Founder and President**
**Saratoga Institute**
**Santa Clara, CA**

Fitz-enz is the acknowledged father of staff benchmarking and performance evaluation and was the first to explain the service-quality-productivity link that's currently the subject of worldwide discussion and analysis. The institute publishes international benchmarks on human financial performance, best practices and staff customer satisfaction. He's the author of "How to Measure Human Resource Management," (McGraw Hill 1995), "Benchmarking Staff Performance," (Jossey-Bass Publishers 1993) and "Human Value Management," (Jossey-Bass Publishers 1990).

**Tharon Greene**
**Director of Human Resources**
**City of Hampton, VA**

Greene has held her current position since 1981. The Hampton HR department has been recognized nationally and inter-nationally for innovation in HR management. In 1995, it won the WORKFORCE Magazine Optimas Award for *General Excellence* in HR management. It also received the 1990 International Personnel Management Association Agency Award of Excellence and recognition by Public Technology Inc. for the department's self-managing team structure, workforce literacy program and Hampton Employee Teletips, an HR information system for city employees.

**Bonnie C. Hathcock**
**Vice President of HR and Development**
**US Airways**
**Arlington, VA**

At US Airways, Hathcock is charged with influencing a winning corporate culture, building employee competencies that have value to customers and transforming the HR/development organization into a strategic leadership department with effective business processes. Before joining US Airways, she was vice president of HR with Siemens Business Communications Inc. in Santa Clara, California, where she and her HR team won the 1996 WORKFORCE Magazine Optimas Award for *Managing Change.*

**Bob Peixotto**
**Vice President<R Total Quality and HR**
**L.L. Bean Inc.**
**Freeport, ME**

In 15 years at L.L. Bean, Peixotto has held a variety of positions in HR, strategic planning and finance. He's a member of the company's Executive Committee. Divisions of L.L. Bean have won the Margaret Chase Smith Maine State Quality Award and the Productivity Management Association's North American Leadership Award. His department received the 1994 WORKFORCE Magazine Optimas Award for excellence in *Managing Change.*

**Dave Pylipow**
**Director of Employee Relations**
**Hallmark Cards Inc.**
**Kansas City, MO**

At Hallmark, Pylipow is responsible for corporate employee relations policy development and interpretation; medical services; and employee relations services. He also works with HR directors throughout the company to ensure the consistent application of corporate HR policy and manages the HR functions that support Hallmark's Canadian operation. Hallmark won the 1996 WORKFORCE Magazine Optimas Award in the *Quality of Life* category.

**Eelyne S. Steward**
**Senior Vice President of HR**
**Calvert Group**
**Bethesda, MD**

Steward is a member of the firm's leadership team and is responsible for creating an environment that allows employees to reach their potential and molding a socially responsible culture. Under her leadership, Calvert Group has been selected (five years in a row) by *Working Mother* as one of the 100 Best Companies for working mothers. *Business Week's* September 15, 1997, special report on family-friendly corporate policies listed Calvert Group as No. 3 of the top non-*Standard & Poor's 500* companies. In 1995, Calvert received the WORKFORCE Magazine Optimas Award in the *Quality of Life* category. The company also received the 1996 Points of Light Award from the Points of Light Foundation for excellence in corporate community service.

**Dave Ulrich**
**Professor of Business Administration**
**The University of Michigan**
**Ann Arbor, MI**

Ulrich is on the core faculty of the Michigan Executive Program, and is codirector of both Michigan's HR executive and the advanced HR executive program. He has authored: "Learning Capability: Generating * Generalizing Ideas with Impact" (Oxford 1998), "Tomorrow's (HR) Management: Thirty-Seven Thought Leaders Call for Change" (Wiley & Sons 1997) and "Human Resource Champions: The Next Agenda for Adding Value and Delivering Results" (Harvard Business Press 1997).

**Bob Wilner**
**Department Director/HR**
**McDonald's Corp.**
**Oak Brook, IL**

Wilner's department is responsible for executive succession planning, development and executive compensation for McDonald's officers and country managers globally. Wilner has more than 25 years of operations and HR experience with McDonald's. He also has consulting responsibility for all aspects of HR for operations in China, Hong Kong and Taiwan. He's a GLOBAL WORKFORCE Magazine advisory director, as well. McDonald's was the 1996 *General Excellence* award winner of the WORKFORCE Magazine Optimas Award.

# Our panelists clearly believe work is going to occupy a smaller part of people's emotional lives in the future.

that this questioning is going on if they want to remain competitive."

Says panelists Greene: "The issues in this section struck a responsive chord with me, not just around child care, but around elder care as well. In our office of nine, we have four people dealing with this. It must be the same all over. These are tough issues, and they have changed a lot even in just the past five years."

As with the global business area, panelist Campanello thought the predictions on work and society didn't go far enough. "It looks to me like the focus is on 1980s and 1990s backlash," he says. "It sounds like we've all decided we're done killing ourselves with work. That's true, but I was disappointed that the real possibilities didn't show up here. I think telecommuting may spark a resurgence of home and community that's even more powerful than what we suggest here. People may begin sharing information in communities, for example, the way we now do in organizations."

Panelist Bob Peixotto, vice president of total quality and HR at L.L. Bean Inc. in Freeport, Maine, pointed out that the first four predictions, which emphasize how employees will realize more fulfillment in their personal lives, are at odds with the fifth prediction, which says that the struggle to balance life and work will get worse. "I think prediction No. 5 is more realistic," he says. "While I'd like to see [predictions] one through four come true (these forecasts all involve families and workers' personal lives taking on a greater role and work itself taking on a lesser role), this trend could reduce U.S. competitiveness. As long as people in other world economies are willing to invest in education and work harder for less pay, we'll have a difficult time unilaterally working less. This pressure may be equally strong for both blue-collar and white-collar workers."

The emphasis on families prompted us to call the Families and Work Institute in New York City and speak with Research Associate Jennifer Swanberg, who's on "The National Study of the Changing Workforce." She confirmed that the nation is enjoying an increased focus on family life. "There appears to be an attitude shift under way," she says, "and it's showing up in how people spend their time. Since 1977, we've seen an increase in the amount of time men spend on home chores and on child care. Among women, we've seen a decrease in the amount of time spent on chores and no change in the amount of time spent on child care." But the institute's research also seems to underline Peixotto's remarks about the struggle to

attain balance. "Both men and women are spending less time on themselves," she says.

Our panelists clearly believe work is going to occupy a smaller part of people's emotional lives in the future. Some people will adjust to this easily, because they already have family and life interests standing ready to fill in the gap. But others will doubtless feel a little lost, which may cause them to demand more support from their employers or lead them to bring more of their personal and life interests—such as family, community or even spirituality—into the workplace. Of course, if they are working at home, they may not have very far to go.

"HR 2008" panelists say the prevailing attitude of "live to work" will shift over toward one of "work to live" as people devote more attention to family and life interests. But are people fleeing the workplace to pursue personal interests, or are they simply finding that new patterns of work allow them to attend to those interests more closely? The rise in self-employment and telecommuting is allowing people to decompartmentalize and integrate their lives. When workers' offices are in a corner of their bedrooms or right off their family living rooms, work becomes just another thing they do rather than another world they travel to. In the future, work will be more like an ongoing transaction and less like participation in a culture.

In any case, modern industrial culture separates people's work lives from their personal lives fairly rigidly, and anything that pierces the barrier between them is bound to impact human resources management significantly. Does this mean you will have to deal with employees on a much more personal level than you're used to? Not necessarily. Although employees will be integrating their personal and family lives into their work more, it's difficult to imagine our ideas of workplace privacy changing significantly. Nor will employees necessarily seek more support from their employers for personal problems, since they'll have access to this support from their communities. But they will expect greater flexibility from their employers regrading personal issues, and this may affect the way managers (with human resources' directors' instructions) do evaluations, performance reviews and career planning.

## Workforce Development: Constant learning in a just-in-time format.
Our panel foresees a world in which employees will learn constantly, and the nimbleness with which they learn will set their value to their organizations. They will have basic computer skills, and they will use technologies

as training vehicles, acquiring both skills and learning only when they need them. The firms they work for will train them for performance, not for skill building.

According to panelist Pylipow, the ability of employees to learn quickly and repeatedly has implications beyond training and will affect other areas in the purview of human resources management, namely recruiting and HR planning. "It's the critical piece in talent sourcing," he says, "the ability to learn over and over again."

We sought advice in this area from the American Society for Training and Development (ASTD), based in Alexandria, Virginia. "Your predictions seem consistent with what we're seeing," says ASTD President Curtis Plott, "but I think there's an area you've missed—that intellectual capital is no longer just something to talk about. Wall Street has discovered it. Recently, Smith Barney, and Montgomery Securities have developed investment lines in training and education, and the interest has been so high that they're oversubscribed."

A new focus on performance measurement is shifting emphasis away from skill building. Our predictions picked this up, and Plott says it will alter the structure of the training industry. ASTD's research indicates the companies will transform into learning organizations—one of the 10 major trends the organization says its members need to understand.

Plott says prediction No. 5 falls slightly short in not mentioning learner control (a major issue in just-in-time, technology-delivered training) and prediction No. 3 ("Employees with varied skills and competencies will be valued more highly than those with a depth of experience in a single area") seems to sell expertise short. "Varied skills and depth of expertise may be valued equally in the future," he says.

Another implication the study didn't surface in workforce development, according to futurist Gioia, is the learning an organization's managers will have to undergo. She thinks most work will be accomplished by teams that will require more leadership than management. "The leaders of such teams need first to have a high level of trust," she says. "Second, they need to ensure that the required skills and abilities are present. And third, they need to know how to appreciate individual team members. It's going to be up to HR people to help managers learn to behave this way, because for many of them it's not natural."

Our panelists' prediction No. 5 ("Training will be delivered just in time, wherever you need it, using a variety of technologies")

# Our panelists see a growing importance for the human resources profession and HR professionals over the next 10 years.

suggests that future workers might never have to go to a class again. But there's already a movement afoot to make training virtually unnecessary. Given the ubiquity of powerful desktop computers with multimedia capabilities, it's theoretically possible to build into the applications employees use whatever they need (training, guidance, advice) to get a job done. The example that partisans of this approach, known as electronic performance support (EPS) systems, like to point to is the applications software *Quicken*™. The manufacturer says if you know how to write a check, you know how to use *Quicken,* and it's pretty much true. If all our systems at work could be made to function in an intuitive, user-friendly way, it could eliminate a great deal of training burden for corporations.

That EPS systems are possible, however, is no guarantee they'll happen on a broad scale. They face enormous political problems because their development is interdisciplinary—involving information systems, training, documentation and line functions. There are questions of ownership and control that are seemingly insurmountable in many organizations. HR undoubtedly will have to be involved in sorting out the issues and implementing solutions.

**Definition of Jobs: Jobs get bigger and broader.**    The predictions show our panelists believe that as organizations become more flexible, employees will have to be more flexible as well. Their jobs will be broad, generalized, challenging and independent. They'll be required to produce results rather than just put in time, and they'll be prized for their versatility and for skills that are more generic than specialized. The panelists felt this area of the study had the strongest consensus. "The commonality was remarkable," says Campanello. "It's good to know there's consensus in the field about these issues."

Over the two centuries of the Industrial Revolution, both employers and employees have come to rely on the job description. But if work goals change constantly, and work-group membership shifts from assignment to assignment, a formal job description becomes more of a hindrance than a tool. In the next 10 years, job descriptions, even job titles, may go the way of bureaucratic hierarchies. Companies will continue to shed the trappings of military-style command-and-control mechanisms and become much more collegial.

If jobs have fewer specifically defined responsibilities and there's less emphasis on specific technical skills, it will doubtless af-

fect personnel planning. It may be that organizations will recruit less for particular skills and more for organizational fit. The idea of a finite job description is rooted deeply in our culture, and many organizations will have a great deal of difficulty adjusting to the ambiguity of tomorrow's jobs. This certainly has implications for employment law, given the fact that it's difficult to measure work for hire, if that work is a moving target. We can probably expect a great deal of litigation between now and then. The HR profession should be mounting a formal effort to educate the rest of society on the flexible jobs of the future and how to prepare for them.

This need for preparation is true for more than just the managerial and professional jobs. Blue-collar jobs are increasingly being automated, and the people in them often have to be "up-skilled." The factory worker of the future (or even the present) isn't simply expected to master a set of steps required to run a machine, but must grasp the workings of a system in a way that was never expected in the past.

We've learned that computerization doesn't dumb-down jobs. It makes them increasingly complex, and it requires greater judgment, discrimination and even imagination on the part of the worker. In short, the worker increasingly will define the job, rather than the other way around.

**Strategic Role of HR: Becoming leaders, not just partners.**    Our panelists see a growing importance for the human resources profession and HR professionals over the next 10 years. HR will focus on organizational performance, and it will move into a leadership position as organizations come to understand how much they depend on it.

This area, understandably, generated some of the greatest excitement among our panelists. "The nature of HR is changing," says Steward. "We're finally getting a seat at the table. The reason is simple, really: People are important."

Says Peixotto: "The focus on organizational performance and human capital development is critical. I see it as a move away from a service role and toward a consulting role." He adds, "I think we're approaching a time when HR people who don't understand the organization's business will have a hard time succeeding."

WORKFORCE editors think that many predictions in this area will be realized in our panelists' organizations, because our panelists are among the foremost practitioners and activists in the profession. However these new roles and responsibilities won't be

handed to HR professionals on silver platters. No function in an organization gains new responsibilities without first gaining influence. As the changes outlined in the first five areas of our study take place, HR leaders will have to watch for opportunities to acquire influence within their organizations and to make people understand that the importance of human capital isn't just a slogan; it's a competitive advantage. In many firms there will be a great deal of inertia to overcome.

How do you spot the opportunities to make yourself more strategic to your company? An important first step, as Peixotto's comment implies, is to understand your company's business. The top prediction in this area is that "successful HR departments will focus on organizational performance." Such a focus requires a knowledge of your company's industry that's deeper than many HR professionals are used to. What are the principal issues your company faces in the areas of materials supply, production, quality control, distribution and sales? Find out. Then address the workforce capability gaps.

Note that Peixotto's position combines responsibilities for both HR and total quality assurance. It's an arrangement that seems prescient, given our discussion about job flexibility and redesign. It also foretells HR's increasingly collaborative role, just like every other job in the workplace. It means HR pros' core competencies will need to change along with their roles.

**The Value of Predicting: Having a vision and a way to achieve it.**    We have put some of the best minds we could find to work on creating a vision of HR a decade from now, but we can't say for sure all their predictions will come true. Even such intelligent and well-informed people give us a description of the future that is, at best, secondhand. Like the rest of us, our panelists can visit the future only in their imagination. No one crosses the moving line of the present, which means there must always be uncertainty on the other side.

Yet HR professionals have an enormous opportunity to influence the future of jobs, the workplace and the human resources profession. If you can see it (as the saying goes) even in your mind's eye, you can achieve it. HR leadership is all about envisioning and engaging the power of a creative, capable, global workforce. If you see something in the future that doesn't look right, change it now. You'll be 10 years ahead of the pack.

---

*Floyd Kemske is a free-lance writer and novelist based in Pepperrell, Massachusetts.*

# ADA: The Law Meets Medicine

*By Timothy S. Bland*

*Are employees protected if they can control their conditions with medication?*

One of your managers needs your advice: He wants to fire an employee for repeated absenteeism and wants to make sure he is legally entitled to do so.

The employee in question suffers from depression but is able to control this condition with medication. As a result, you determine that he is not disabled, is not protected by the Americans With Disabilities Act (ADA) and is not entitled to accommodation for his attendance problem.

That's right, isn't it?

Yes, that decision is perfectly legal—in some federal circuits. (For an explanation of the federal circuit courts, see *HR Magazine*'s December 1998 month's Legal Trends column.) In other circuits, however, it is dead wrong.

Here's why.

Some federal circuits have decided that they will determine if a condition is a disability (and therefore protected by the ADA) by considering it in its unmedicated state. For example, a diabetic would be considered disabled even if she could control her condition by taking insulin at regular intervals.

Other federal circuits have decided to consider conditions in their medicated state. According to this view, the same diabetic would not be considered disabled because she is able to function without significant limitation when she takes her medication.

Other circuits have yet to decide this issue at all.

The stakes in this legal debate are enormous. By extending the protection of the ADA to individuals who can control their conditions with medication, courts increase the number of employees to whom HR professionals must offer accommodation. Courts that do not offer ADA protection to these individuals limit the number of employees who can demand accommodation. Either view affects HR professionals dramatically.

Because the courts are in disagreement, the issue will likely be decided by the Supreme Court at some point, and it is hoped that all employers will have a single, clear standard to follow. Until then, however, you will need to understand how the law works in your jurisdiction.

## Background

Every ADA case involves a primary question: Is the individual bringing the suit disabled within the meaning of the statute?

According to the language of the law, the ADA protects individuals who:

• Have a history of impairment. (Some conditions flare up from time to time, then subside. People who suffer from such conditions are protected, even when the condition is not active.)

• Do not suffer from a condition that is covered by the law but are treated—or "regarded by" employers—as if they do.

• Suffer from a physical or mental impairment that substantially limits one or more major life activities.

The ADA does not define "major life activities." However, regulations published by the Equal Employment Opportunity Commission (EEOC) define the phrase as "those basic life activities that the average person in the general population can perform with little or no difficulty," including "caring for oneself, performing manual tasks, walking, seeing, hearing, breathing, learning and working."

Individuals are substantially limited if they cannot perform an activity in the same manner, under the same conditions or for the same length of time as an average person in the general population.

According to the EEOC regulations, whether an impairment is substantially limiting depends on factors such as:

• The nature and severity of the impairment.

• The duration, or expected duration, of the impairment.

• The actual or expected long-term impact of the impairment.

Individuals are considered substantially limited in the activity of working only if they are significantly restricted in their ability to perform a class or broad range of jobs, as compared to an average, similarly situated person. An inability to perform a single, particular job is not a substantial limitation and does not qualify for ADA protection.

## The Contradictions

Although the ADA has a fairly comprehensive scheme for determining if individuals are disabled, the law does not clearly state if this determination is supposed to be made with or without regard to mitigating measures, such as medications.

Even the ADA's legislative history appears inconsistent on this issue. In some ways, it seems that Congress intended that disability be determined without regard to mitigating measures. For example, the House Judiciary Report states that when determining disability, "[t]he impairment should be assessed without considering whether mitigating measures, such as auxiliary aids or reasonable accommodations, would result in a less-than-substantial limitation."

On the other hand, at least one Senate Report indicates that in determining the existence of a disability, the focus should be on an impairment's effects on the individual, not on the impairment's qualities.

To further complicate matters, the EEOC's regulatory guidelines also are inconsistent. Portions of the guidelines state that the existence of an impairment should be determined "without regard to mitigating measures such as medicines, or assistive or prosthetic devices." The guidelines further state that "an individual with epilepsy would be considered to have an impairment even if the symptoms of the disorder were completely controlled by medicine."

But another section of the guidelines takes the opposite view. Specifically, that portion states that someone with the condition of high blood pressure controlled by medication may not have a disability but may be regarded as having one.

This is important because the "regarded as" provision—by the EEOC's own definition—protects only those individuals who are not actually disabled but who are treated as if they are. (See the legal definition [under "Background."]) That means the individual in the above example who can control his or her condition with medication cannot—by definition—be considered disabled under the law.

Without the "regarded as" provision, employers could discriminate against someone they believed to be disabled, then win a lawsuit on a technicality when they learned the individual was not actually disabled.

## Disability in the Medicated State

Several federal courts, including the 6th and 10th Circuits of the U.S. Court of Appeals, consider an individual's condition in the medicated state.

The case of *Murphy v. United Parcel Service, Inc.* (946 F. Supp. 872 D. Kan. 1996), decided by a federal district court in Kansas, demonstrates the legal reasoning used in these cases. In the case, a truck mechanic (Murphy) alleged that his employer (UPS) discharged him due to his disability—hypertension.

In an unmedicated condition, Murphy's blood pressure was approximately 250/160. Murphy, who had successfully worked as a mechanic for 22 years for other employers, alleged that this high blood pressure limited him in numerous major life activities. But as long as he took medication, his only limitation was that he could not hold a job requiring repetitive lifting of 200 pounds.

Unlike at Murphy's previous employers, however, UPS drivers must meet U.S. Department of Transportation regulations. These regulations require individuals to maintain a blood pressure lower than or equal to 160/90. Murphy's physician testified that—even with medication—Murphy's blood pressure would always be higher than 160/90. As a result, UPS discharged Murphy.

In determining whether Murphy was disabled, the court looked at his condition in its medicated state. Because his only physical limitation—in the medicated state—was that he could not hold a job that required repetitive lifting of 200 pounds, the court ruled that he was not substantially limited in any major life activity and was therefore not disabled.

The 6th and 10th Circuits also have found that the ADA guidelines published by the EEOC directly conflict with the ADA's requirement that plaintiffs prove that an impairment substantially limits their lives. For example, if diabetics can control their condition with insulin, they cannot argue that their lives are substantially limited by the condition.

Further, saying that an individual is disabled if he or she needs insulin removes from the ADA's definition of disability the requirement that only those persons are disabled who are substantially limited in major life activities. Although the word "limited" may convey different shades of meaning, it cannot be meaningless, as acceptance of the EEOC's interpretation would render it. Thus, because the EEOC's interpretive guidance conflicts with the ADA's statutory provisions, the guidance must be rejected, these courts have reasoned.

These courts also decline to follow the ADA's legislative history. According to them, the language of the statute is not ambiguous, so the legislative history and congressional intent need not be considered.

When medication partially—but not completely—controls an individual's condi-

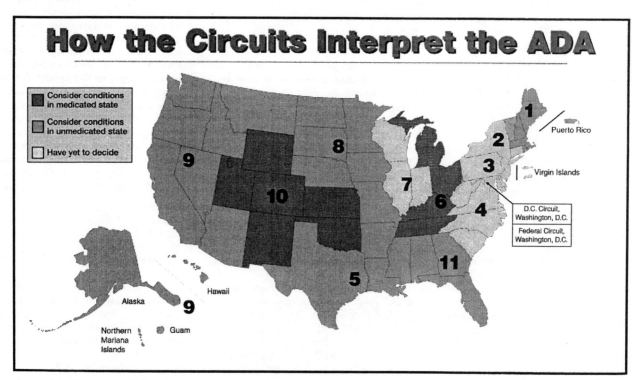

tion, it becomes extremely difficult to determine if the individual is disabled. For example, if an epileptic can reduce her number of seizures with medication—but cannot completely eliminate them—would she be protected by the ADA?

Unfortunately, there is no easy answer. In this example, it depends on whether the individual—despite medication—still suffers enough seizures to render her substantially limited in a major life activity. The answer will vary from one case to the next. HR professionals faced with such a situation should consult with experienced legal and medical advisers to help them properly make this determination.

## Disability Determined in Unmitigated State

Numerous other federal courts, including the 1st, 8th, 9th and 11th Circuits of the Court of Appeals, have taken the position that disability must be determined without regard to mitigating measures. Most recently, in September 1998, the 5th Circuit ruled that serious impairments analogous to those mentioned in the EEOC's guidelines and the ADA's legislative history must be considered in their unmitigated state.

Some courts point out that the ADA's definition of "disability" is similar to the one used in the Rehabilitation Act, and that several cases decided under the Rehabilitation Act determined that disability should be decided without regard to mitigating measures. Congress was aware of these court rulings when it passed the ADA, so it must have agreed with them; otherwise, it would have used a different definition of disability.

The courts holding this position also consider the EEOC's interpretive guidance to be persuasive. They find nothing inherently illogical in determining whether an impairment substantially limits a major life activity without regard to mitigating measures.

Likewise, they find that nothing in the language of the statute rules out this approach. The statute does not say "impairment plus treatment" or "impairment after treatment" or "treated impairment." It just says impairment.

Furthermore, according to these courts, the EEOC's interpretative guidance does not ignore the statute's "substantially limits" requirement. Rather, the interpretation relates "substantially limits" to the untreated impairment.

Under this view, courts and employers must still determine whether the untreated impairment substantially limits a major life activity for the untreated impairment to constitute a disability under the ADA.

This interpretation of the law poses problems for human resource professionals: When making disability determinations, they may be forced to speculate as to the nature and extent of an employee's condition in the absence of medication.

For example, consider individuals with chronically recurring depression. If these individuals control their condition with medication, their depression will never result in the substantial limitation of a major life activity.

Without medication, they may suffer depressive episodes of varying degrees from time to time. However, it would be impossible to predict when a depressive episode may occur, or its length or severity. Anyone attempting to assess whether or when the individual would be disabled in the absence of medication would be resigned to speculation.

To help you make such decisions, and to give those decisions some legal credence, seek competent medical advice. Don't rely on your own guesses about what employees may or not experience. Always get medical experts to provide documented analysis and estimates of the potential limitations employees are likely to experience in an unmedicated state.

Before talking to a medical professional about an employee, get the employee to sign a medical authorization allowing the company to do so.

In seeking medical advice, the most important thing an HR professional can do is make sure the employee is examined and diagnosed by a qualified, conservative physician. Where do you find such physicians? Go to HR professionals who are extensively involved in handling workers' compensation claims for their companies and ask them to provide you with referrals.

If the employee is being treated by a physician of the employee's own choosing, the company may need to pay for the employee to be examined and diagnosed by a physician of its choosing. At the very least, the company may need to have a physician of its choosing examine all relevant records, test results and other diagnostic procedures performed by the employee's physician to determine if that physician's diagnosis and prescribed treatment are reasonable and necessary.

## Undecided Circuits

The 2nd, 3rd, 4th and 7th Circuits have yet to decide this issue. What should employers in those circuits do?

At the very least, HR professionals in these circuits have a vested interest in following the development of this issue within their jurisdictions. Make sure you keep track of any upcoming ADA cases that would resolve this issue at the circuit court level.

If there are no cases at the circuit court level, then look for decisions within your district that indicate the trend in your jurisdiction.

If no decisions exist at the district court level, you have two options.

You can play it safe by considering employees' conditions in their unmedicated states—which would follow the lead set by the majority of circuit courts that have decided this issue—and offer reasonable accommodation where appropriate.

The other option is to carefully consult with legal counsel about the possible consequences of making the disability determination in the medicated condition. This choice ultimately boils down to a business decision of how much risk your company is willing to incur. Most companies will probably determine that taking the more cautious approach makes the most sense.

*Timothy S. Bland, PHR, is a labor and employment attorney with McKnight Hudson Ford & Harrison in Memphis, where his practice is limited to representing management. He is a magna cum laude graduate of the University of Illinois College of Law.*

# SEXUAL HARASSMENT:
# New Rules, New Behavior

Justice Clarence Thomas, former U.S. Senator Bob Packwood, President Clinton and various business leaders have all helped propel sexual harassment into the headlines. But beyond headlines, the bigger story is the rise in the number of large and small businesses being hit with sexual harassment suits.

According to a recent report in the *Wall Street Journal,* "Bias claims are escalating in the face of employers' attempts to head them off." The report continues, "Despite 'extensive' training of supervisors, discrimination complaints filed with the Equal Employment Opportunity Commission keep climbing. Philadelphia labor lawyer Stephen Cabot expects to see more than 16,000 sexual-harassment cases in 1998, up from 6,883 in 1991." Other attorneys agree, noting that once the courts got involved, the rules changed.

"The June 1997 Supreme Court ruling said, in part, that 'an employer is absolutely liable for quid pro quo' [a favor for a favor] and that in the absence of no tangible admissions, the courts will deal with 'hostile environment' as an issue," says New York City attorney Bob Nobile, of Winston & Strawn.

Other court cases have contributed to a changed corporate landscape. Two recent landmark Supreme Court rulings put every company on notice when they made it easier for employees to sue by holding companies responsible for supervisors who participate in or allow sexually harassing behavior, even if the employee did not suffer any adverse consequences or the company knew nothing about the behavior.

Most notably, both bias suits involved sexual misconduct of supervisors that was not reported until after the employees resigned and subsequently filed suit. On the bright side, the courts also held that for employers to prevail, they must show they "exercised reasonable care to prevent or correct promptly any sexually harassing behavior" and that "the employee unreasonably failed to take advantage of any preventive or corrective opportunities provided by the employer or to avoid harm otherwise."

## PREEMPTIVE ACTION

What this means for CEOs on down is that all employers—both large and small—must have a sexual harassment policy in place. They must train all employees on the policy. They must have clear procedures for reporting such behavior—including allowing employees access to management other than their supervisor. And they must communicate the policy effectively and openly.

Clearly, a company can never be certain it will not be hit with a sexual har-assment claim, but it is prudent to be aware of and prepared for the possibility. To do this a company must have in place a good sexual harassment policy that is backed up with training and a working open-door policy.

To be effective, a training program should involve employees companywide and include more than a human resource manager telling employees the "do's" and "don'ts." Increasingly aware of the consequences, more businesses are taking sexual harassment seriously, training employees through role-playing and allowing them to discuss "real life" situations. All this helps employers and employees understand that sexual harassment is real and affects everyone.

Experts who counsel on sexual harassment issues maintain that apart from a company's having a clear, well-communicated sexual harassment policy in place, avoidance of problems is likely to further involve behavior modification throughout the organization.

Darlene Orlov, president of Orlov Resources for Business Inc., a New York City human resource training and consulting firm, coaches CEOs and says that basically her work entails changing behavior. "Most of the people I work with—who generally have already had one bad experience—want to change their behavior because they realize that next time they may lose their job. Also, people are taking this issue very seriously because they realize it is something that is not going to go away."

Orlov takes a practical approach to training, using traditional learning tools such as role playing, exercises and discussion. In working with top management, Orlov prescribes a three-part

---

These days, no one is safe from charges of sexual harassment. The best you can do is have a policy in place and enforce it.

---

checklist that employers can adhere to. It clearly defines what sexual harassment is and, if followed, ideally will prevent any charges of sexual misconduct at any level in an organization:

- Stay away from sex-related topics in the workplace.
- Do not engage in any form of sexually oriented behavior, including touching another employee other than a professional handshake.
- Never intimate or suggest that a person could receive or lose a job benefit based on granting or denying a sexual favor.

Orlov notes that she is aware of generational differences and says, "When a person has grown up with a certain sexual orientation of dealing with the opposite sex they often bring that behavior to the workplace, even if it is not appropriate in today's environment."

Winston & Strawn's Nobile agrees. "There are three things I always tell CEOs: One, have a well-defined policy in place. Two, focus on training, training, training—for both supervisors and employees. And three, ask yourself if you would enact your behavior toward

employees in front of your children or your spouse.'"

## COSTLY (BUT PREVENTABLE) BEHAVIOR

These days, no one is exempt from charges of sexual harassment. Texaco, Lockheed Martin, Mitsubishi, Home Depot, Smith Barney and Wal-Mart are all industry titans, but also companies with poor track records in the employment liability wars sweeping the country.

Last summer, Mitsubishi Motor Manufacturing of America shelled out $34 million to settle a sexual harassment case brought by the EEOC on behalf of more than 300 female employees. Among their complaints: being groped, gestured to, urged to reveal their sexual preferences and exposed to sexually explicit pictures. Last year, Home Depot agreed to pay $65 million to more than 6,000 current and former female employees and job applicants in 10 states to settle a class-action sex discrimination suit.

## DELUXE DOES IT RIGHT

Although it may be too soon for business journals to report on "The 100 Best Anti-Harassment Companies," at least one U.S. company has gotten the attention of the courts—and the media. Deluxe Specialty Manufacturing Co. in Hutchinson, Kan., was in the spotlight recently when a federal district court in Wichita dismissed a sexual harassment suit brought by two female employees against the fuel-tank producer. The court credits Deluxe's "good anti-harassment policy." HR Manager David Perry says the firm's anti-harassment policy has been in place for eons.

"Deluxe has been around for a very long time and so has its policy," says Perry. "Then, when the company changed ownership last April, I looked at the policy, tweaked it, and—along with the full support of top management—made sure these messages reached all employees. The first thing we did was to start from day one—at orientation—to let staffers know that

---

## DEFINING SEXUAL HARASSMENT: A SAMPLE POLICY

Sexual harassment is a form of sexual discrimination. Sexual harassment negatively affects job performance, productivity, morale and employment opportunities. Sexual harassment negatively affects [your company's] goodwill, community standing and profitability. Sexual harassment is offensive, inappropriate and illegal. [Your company] prohibits the sexual harassment of its employees by management, coworkers, independent contractors, non-employees, vendors and visitors. Sexual harassment will not be tolerated. Violators of our sexual harassment policy will be subject to disciplinary action, up to and including discharge. Sexual harassment includes unwelcome sexual advances, requests for sexual favors, and other verbal and physical conduct of a sexual nature. Sexual harassment includes conduct that is based on a person's sex and alters the terms and conditions of that person's employment. Sexual harassment includes inappropriate conduct irrespective of whether the harasser and the person harassed are of different sexes or are of the same sex.

Examples of sexual harassment include:

- Employment decisions that are based on the submission to or the rejection of unwelcome sexual advances or requests for sexual favors.
- Conduct of a sexual nature that unreasonably interferes with work performance.
- Conduct of a sexual nature that creates an intimidating, hostile or offensive work environment, including: unwelcome verbal comments, jokes, suggestions or derogatory remarks based on sex; unwelcome leering, whistling, physical touching, pats, squeezes, repeated brushing against or the impeding or blocking of one's movement.
- References regarding an individual's sex life or comments about an individual's sexual activities, deficiencies or prowess.
- Unwelcome visual harassment, sexually suggestive or derogatory pictures, drawings or cartoons; and unwelcome communications, notes, phone calls and e-mail.

*Note: This policy should be followed with a posting encouraging employees to take action when sexual harassment occurs. It should include detailed guidelines instructing employees how to take action (including freedom to bypass supervisors), as well as notification that individuals who knowingly make false claims may be subject to appropriate disciplinary action.*

*Source: United Insurance Co. Ltd. of Bermuda*

harassment, in any form, would not be tolerated. We also posted the policy in the plant in full view of all employees and several times a year we discuss it in meetings. The policy addresses not only sexual harassment, but racial, ethnic and handicap harassment, as well. Basically, what it says is that all forms of harassment will not be tolerated at Deluxe."

Deluxe's policy also goes the distance and informs employees that they can report a complaint to any member of the company, including the general manager or owner, assuring employees that all complaints will be taken seriously and investigated without delay.

Another reason Deluxe Specialty Manufacturing Co. gets top kudos is what Perry points to as a key element of the firm's policy. "We make it very clear to employees that sexual harass-

ment complaints don't have to be major in nature: At Deluxe, even the most minor infractions are investigated."

## GOOD MANAGEMENT ENTAILS TRAINING

Has the plethora of high-profile media attention and recent court rulings changed the face of corporate America? If it hasn't as yet, it will in the near future. Clearly, employers have been put on notice that certain behavior will not be tolerated and employees are now free to demand a "harassment-free" workplace—or sue. If that means that supervisors need to tread overcautiously then perhaps that is not such a bad thing.

Attorney Louis Pechman, labor and employment law specialist with Berke-Weiss & Pechman, LLP, New York City, says it all boils down to good versus bad

management. "When we do sexual harassment training, what we end up talking about is 'what is good management' because a lot of the sexual harassment cases evolve out of what is really bad management." Pechman further adds, "If a company has good management and there's more time and attention paid to getting the work done, and the focus is on the job description rather than external personality issues, then that by itself reduces sexual harassment issues and discrimination. This is not just a New York City view; I see this as a global [reality]."

---

*JOANNE COLE is a New York City-based business writer and president of Cole Communications & PR Marketing.*

# Workplace Harassment: Employees vs. Customers

## R. Bruce McAfee, Diana L. Deadrick, and Scott W. Kezman

In recent years, the issue of sexual harassment has received considerable attention. The impeachment trial of President Clinton, the Senate's confirmation hearings for Clarence Thomas, and the Navy's "Tailhook" scandal, among others, have piqued nearly everyone's interest in the topic. But though much has been said and written about this type of harassment, the issue of employees being harassed by customers has been almost completely ignored. This form of harassment is likely to be an area of growing concern for employers because of several current workplace trends. We are witnessing significant growth in service sector jobs, coupled with an increased emphasis on service quality and customer satisfaction. Organizational goals that espouse "customers for life" and "the customer is always right" could lead to situations in which employees are reluctant to report incidents of customers harassing them.

Moreover, employees receive less supervision and more responsibility for customer service because of trends toward telecommuting and self-management. Because many employees work in isolation to various degrees, their employers have less knowledge about and control over the workplace environment.

The legal issues surrounding employer liability for harassment by customers have not yet been clarified by the courts. As a result, employers are left in the awkward position of not knowing their potential liability. Unfortunately, in the legal arena there is no such thing as taking "no action." Doing nothing can have deep legal consequences.

### EMPLOYER LIABILITY

According to the Equal Employment Opportunity Commission, a company may be responsible for customer harassment of its employees if it fails to take corrective action within its control once it knows or has reason to know of the customer's conduct. Interestingly, the EEOC took this position in 1980 when it disseminated the Guidelines on Sexual Harassment. Even though the Guidelines do not constitute "the law," courts have historically relied on them for clarification and have adopted some of their definitions and standards in formulating decisions on workplace harassment. When faced with the novel issue of sexual harassment by customers, several courts have specifically identified the Guidelines as the "authority" for imposing liability on an employer. One federal district court stated:

> Because Title VII affords employees the right to work in an environment free from discriminatory intimidation, ridicule, and insult, this Court holds that, in the appropriate case, an employer could be liable for the sexual harassment of employees by nonemployees, including its customers. (*Powell v. Las Vegas Hilton Corp.*, 1992)

More recently, the Ninth Circuit Court of Appeals stated:

> We now hold that an employer may be held liable for sexual harassment on the part of a private individual, such as the casino patron, where the employer either ratifies or acquiesces in the harassment by not taking immediate and/or corrective action when it knows or should have known of the conduct. (*Folkerson v. Circus Circus Enterprises, Inc.*, 1997)

Given that the courts have also applied the Guidelines to cases of "nonsexual" harassment (such as race or religion), the scope of employer liability for harassment by customers will likely include instances of nonsexual as well as sexual harassment.

The EEOC Guidelines list three key factors to be evaluated when determining employer liability: (1) whether the employer knows or should have known

Reprinted with permission from *Business Horizons*, March/April 1999, pp. 79-84. © 1999 by Indiana University Kelley School of Business.

about the conduct; (2) whether the employer takes immediate and appropriate corrective action; and (3) the extent of the employer's control and legal responsibility for the nonemployee harasser. Although it will be up to the courts to apply and further define these factors in the context of harassment by customers, past court decisions regarding harassment among employees provide a basis for predicting how the courts might interpret the first two factors. However, the third factor is unique to the situation of harassment by nonemployees and raises questions that have yet to be fully answered by either the courts or the EEOC.

## Employer Knowledge

In terms of the first factor, employer knowledge, the courts are likely to hold an employer liable for harassment by customers if: (1) the employee complains of harassment and those complaints are ignored; (2) a supervisor or manager knows about the harassment and takes no steps to remedy the situation, even though the employee does not complain; or (3) the harassment is so severe and pervasive that it is reasonable to conclude the employer should have known of it. When harassment by a customer crosses the line from "grin and bear it" to "severe and pervasive" is an open question. The line may depend on such factors as the type of business and/or the employer's relationship with the customers involved.

## Corrective Action

With regard to the second factor, corrective action, the courts have generally held that in cases of harassment by fellow employees, firms must do more than merely require harassers to apologize or request that they desist. But in the case of customer harassment, will the courts deem an apology by the customer and/or a request by the employer to desist sufficient? What constitutes an "appropriate" response when it comes to harassment by customers?

Six court cases can shed some light on this issue. Three of them found that organizations can be held liable for failing to take prompt corrective action to eliminate reported incidents of harassment by customers. In a fourth, an employer was ordered to pay more than $200,000 to an aggrieved employee. And two cases were decided in favor of the employers, who, the courts said, had taken appropriate corrective action to stop the reported harassing behavior.

In the first case, EEOC Decision #84-3 (1984), four of a restaurant's "regular" male customers directed jokes and comments of a sexual nature toward a waitress. The waitress responded angrily, walked away, asked another employee to wait on them, and reported the incident to the restaurant owner. The owner excused the conduct as drunken behavior and commented that such conduct was to be expected.

The waitress later said she would prefer not to wait on these men again and would refuse to tolerate such behavior; the manager responded that she might not be able to continue her employment with him. Subsequently terminated, the waitress filed a charge with the EEOC, which found that the customers' behavior created an intimidating, hostile, or offensive work environment and that the employer knew about the conduct but failed to take immediate and appropriate action. It added that the firm was in an especially advantageous position to address the waitress's complaint by either telling the harassing customers that such behavior would not be tolerated in the future, or relieving the waitress of any duty to wait on them in the future.

In *EEOC v. Sage Realty Corporation* (1981), a lobby attendant at a large office building in New York City was required to wear a uniform that was revealing in nature and resulted in her being subjected to repeated sexual propositions, lewd comments, and gestures. Ultimately, the attendant refused to wear the uniform, but was told she must either wear it or leave the floor. She again refused, and was offered a "layoff letter" that stated she had lost her job because of lack of work. The U.S. District Court of New York found that the employer had failed to take prompt action designed to stop the harassment. Specifically, the employer's requirement that the attendant wear the uniform, when it knew that wearing it subjected her to sexual harassment, could constitute sex discrimination. Further, the court added that wearing a sexually revealing uniform is not a bona fide occupational qualification; indeed, it actually interfered with the attendant's ability to perform her job.

In the third case, *EEOC v. Federal Express* (1995), a foot courier for FedEx reported that she was harassed by a customer living in one of the buildings on her delivery route. His behavior ranged from asking her out on dates and weekend jaunts to publicly proclaiming that she looked better with her clothes off than on. She complained to her immediate supervisor on two occasions, and FedEx wrote a letter to the customer requesting that he refrain from "any future conduct that could be perceived as offensive or intimidating." The tenant stopped speaking to the courier, but continued to harass her by allegedly waiting for her in the lobby. The customer also threatened to sue FedEx, which subsequently eliminated the entire building from the courier's route. However, the courier was not given a replacement building, so a loss of pay resulted.

Several important issues were brought to light in this case. FedEx argued that it was different from previous cases because the employee was harassed outside the workplace—not inside, such as when a waitress is harassed by a restaurant patron. The U.S. District Court of Washington concluded that this was a distinction without a difference because the alleged harassment was instigated by a FedEx customer and directed at a FedEx employee during the course and scope of her employment. According to the court, "Title VII affords employees the right to work in an environment free from discriminatory intimidation, ridicule, and insult." FedEx also argued that it took appropriate corrective action, considering its limited ability to control a nonemployee who is not on company premises. The Court countered that, by stripping the courier of an entire building on her route, the firm in effect punished her for complaining. Instead, FedEx could simply have chosen to stop serving the tenant. The Court concluded that whether these actions were in fact reasonable should be determined by a jury.

In the most recent case to address this issue, *Lockard v. Pizza Hut, Inc., et al.* (1998), a jury awarded $200,000 in compensatory damages and $37,000 in attorneys' fees to a waitress at a Pizza Hut franchise, based on the conduct of two male customers she had been ordered to wait on. The waitress testified she told her manager when the customers arrived that she was uncomfortable waiting on them because of past experiences she had had while serving them. With no inquiry as to why she did not want to wait on the customers, the shift manager ordered her to serve them anyway. After being seated, one of the men then grabbed the waitress's hair. She reported this to the manager and asked that he assign someone else to serve the men. But the manager refused (even though several male waiters were working) and told the waitress, "You were hired to be a waitress. You waitress." When she returned to the customers' table with a pitcher of beer, one of them pulled her to him by the hair, grabbed her breast, and put his mouth on her breast. The waitress then quit and left the restaurant.

In upholding the jury's verdict that the waitress's employer, the Pizza Hut franchisee, was properly held liable, the Tenth Circuit Court of Appeals stated:

> Prior to the sexual assault, [the waitress] had informed [the shift manager] of the hair pulling incident and had also told him ... that she did not wish to serve these customers. We hold that this information was sufficient to place [the manger] on notice that these customers were likely to sexually harass [the waitress]. Accordingly, once [she] reported this information to [the manager], [the franchisee's] obligation to respond adequately and promptly was triggered. Instead of following the guidelines set forth in Pizza Hut's policy manual [i.e., ask the customer to leave and eject if the customer persists], [the manager] ordered [the waitress] to continue waiting on the customers. . . .
> [He] placed [her] in an abusive and potentially dangerous situation, although he clearly had both

the means and authority to avoid doing so by directing a male waiter to serve these men, waiting on them himself, or asking them to leave the restaurant. [The waitress], under the instruction of [the manager], returned to their table and was again subjected to sexually abusive conduct. Because [the manager] had notice of the customers' harassing conduct and failed to remedy or prevent the hostile work environment, [the franchisee] is liable for [his] failure.

In contrast to the above, the courts found in two other cases that the firms involved did take appropriate corrective action to stop reported incidents of harassment. In *Hallberg v. Eat 'N Park* (1996), a customer placed his hand on a waitress's arm and made an obscene sexual remark. The waitress immediately reported the incident, and the restaurant manager confronted the customer the next time she saw him enter the restaurant, only two days after the initial report. The manager told the offender that he would be barred from the restaurant if there were any further complaints. The U.S. District Court of Western Pennsylvania concluded that the restaurant was not liable for any damages because the firm had taken prompt action designed to stop the harassment. It added that a remedy need only be "reasonably calculated to stop harassment" in order to relieve an employer from liability.

In *Mart v. Dr. Pepper* (1996), an account sales representative employed by Dr. Pepper claimed to have been harassed by one of her customers, an on-premises manager of a Pepsi facility. The sales rep contended that the manager made inappropriate comments on several occasions involving sexual connotations and offensive language directed at the plaintiff as well as at other women. Eventually, the plaintiff reported the incident to her boss; an investigation was conducted, and a written reprimand was issued to the defendant. The U.S. District Court of Kansas ruled that the defendant's offensive language was not sufficiently severe or pervasive to alter the conditions of employment and create an abusive working environment. Further, the court held that Dr. Pepper was not liable because, upon learning of the alleged harassment, it took prompt, adequate, and effective action to remedy the situation.

One might ask why these latter two cases were brought to court at all, given the employers' prompt and remedial actions. Specifically, did the plaintiffs continue to experience problems with the customers after their employers took action? Did the plaintiffs believe their employers could have and should have done more in the way of corrective action? In both cases, no further incidents of harassment had occurred. In *Hallberg*, the plaintiff did not return to work, so it is unclear whether the remedial action was effective. In *Mart v. Dr. Pepper*, no further incidents occurred between the time the plaintiff complained to her employer and the time she resigned.

Regarding the question of "appropriate" action, a definitive answer is beyond the scope of the court records. However, in *Hallberg*, the court noted that the plaintiff wanted the customer banned from the restaurant immediately, but was unable to cite any authority that suggests a plaintiff may dictate the remedy an employer chooses as a means of stopping harassment. In *Mart v. Dr. Pepper*, the court noted that although the plaintiff had been an excellent performer and had been offered other positions with the company in other states after she resigned, she did not accept either position, nor did she specify reasons for her resignation.

## Employer Control

The third factor, employer control, is unique to the situation of harassment by customers, so it is more difficult to say what standards the court will develop. The EEOC and the courts are slowly defining these standards; in fact, three of the previously discussed cases—EEOC Decision #84-3, *EEOC v. Federal Express*, and *Lockard v. Pizza Hut, Inc. et al.*—pertain to this issue. In the first, the EEOC found that the customers' conduct was within the employer's control because the harassers were not "strangers" to the employer; in fact, he had a friendly personal relationship with them. In light of such circumstances, the Commission concluded that the employer had some degree of control over the customers and was in an "advantageous position" to remedy the situation.

In the FedEx case, the company argued that it had taken appropriate corrective action given its limited ability to control a customer not on company premises. But the U.S. District Court contended that it could have chosen to decline to serve the tenant, and concluded that whether the firm's action was reasonable should be decided by a jury.

In the Pizza Hut case, the court maintained that several actions could have been taken by the employer—from assigning a male waiter to the harassing customers to ejecting them from the restaurant. However, because the employer did nothing, liability for the customers' behavior was appropriate.

Finally, in *Grist v. Focus Homes, Inc.* (1997), a sixteen-year-old male who functioned at the level of a two- to five-year-old repeatedly harassed female employees of a firm that operated programs for individuals with developmental disabilities. The Eighth Circuit Court of Appeals held that a trial was required to determine whether the firm had acted appropriately. The court stated:

While we recognize that [the employer] faced multiple obstacles in immediately preventing [the resident] from acting out... that does not end the inquiry. [The employer] clearly controlled the environment in which [the resident] resided, and it had the ability to alter those conditions to a substantial degree.

It is too soon to say exactly what circumstances will be evaluated when determining the amount of control an employer has over customers. Nevertheless, the more regular and persistent the contact between the employer and harassing customer is, the more likely it is that the courts will find some type of control on the part of the employer.

## IMPLICATIONS FOR HUMAN RESOURCE MANAGEMENT

Based on the preceding court cases, two areas in human resource management appear particularly relevant to reducing employer liability for customer harassment of workers. Employee training programs are one preventive approach to the problem. And employee surveys coupled with performance reviews represent a monitoring approach to identifying potential or real problem situations.

## Employee Training

According to the EEOC Guidelines, the best way to eliminate harassment is through such preventive measures as affirmatively raising the subject, expressing strong disapproval, informing employees of their rights to raise the issue, and developing methods to sensitize all concerned. The key to prevention is taking actions that create an environment free of harassment by anyone, including customers.

One method for informing and educating employees is to develop training programs that include conflict management skills, which can be used to combat harassment when it occurs. Given that employees often work alone or beyond the watchful eye of a supervisor, they need to learn how to confront offensive customers directly. If a company teaches employees to handle such situations when they occur, it will be in a better position to prevent the harassment from becoming severe or pervasive. If an employer is already providing customer service training to employees, it should be relatively easy to incorporate these or other similar conflict resolution techniques into the training program.

Managers also need to be trained to confront abusive customers. Such training could parallel the instruction given to nonsupervisory employees and focus on resolving various types of customer harassment situations, ranging from mild to severe forms.

Because the approach to be taken is highly situational, each firm may want to seek legal counsel when addressing this issue.

## Employee Surveys and Performance Reviews

If companies want to become aware of the frequency and severity of harassment by customers, they need to develop information-gathering procedures that are specific to this problem. Such information can be used for fact-finding as well as problem-solving purposes. A questionnaire or "audit" could be given to a sample of employees or to a particularly vulnerable group to determine whether harassment by customers is a problem and where the behavior is most pronounced. At the same time, other information could also be obtained: Are employees aware that customer harassment is illegal? To what extent do employees understand the firm's harassment policy as it relates to the behavior of customers? To what extent do they understand which behaviors constitute harassment? Do employees know how to file a harassment complaint within the firm, and do they know how to handle the offenders?

Likewise, managers could be surveyed to determine their answers to similar questions and the extent to which they are aware of any problems. For those firms that have employees who are supervised from a distance (self-managed work teams, employees in field offices, traveling salespeople), an audit could be a particularly effective means of identifying potential problems before they become legal cases.

In addition to conducting audits, companies may also want to use formal and informal performance evaluation and review meetings with employees. Supervisors could be encouraged to use a "management by walking around" approach to determine whether vulnerable employees are being harassed and to talk directly with them about any such problems they are having. Moreover, companies should encourage regular input and feedback from employees to identify and resolve situations of harassment by customers. As a result, employers will become better informed about potential thorny situations, and workers are more likely to believe employers are serious about eradicating the problem and maintaining a harassment-free work environment.

Although all the issues surrounding employer liability for harassment by customers have not yet been fully clarified by the courts, employers need to heed the EEOC Guidelines and take an active approach to eliminating the problem. Indeed, such an approach is consistent with today's trends toward employee empowerment and total quality management, both of which rely on a culture of perceived fairness and mutual respect. A culture like this requires that companies "enable" employees to recognize and deal with harassment by customers when it occurs. Moreover, they need to assure employees that their right to a harassment-free workplace is protected and that any such conduct by customers will not be allowed. By taking actions to prevent, monitor, and rectify these situations, a culture of mutual respect between "internal" and "external" customers is more likely to develop.

## References

EEOC Decision No. 84-3 (1984), C.C.H. EEOC Decisions 6841.

EEOC Guidelines, 29 C.F.R. 1604.11 (1992).

*EEOC v. Federal Express Corporation*, 1995 WL 569446 (W.D.Wash., 1995).

*EEOC v. Sage Realty Corporation*, 507 F.Supp. 599 (F.D.N.Y., 1981).

*Folkerson v. Circus Circus Enterprises, Inc.*, 107 F.3d 745 9th Cir. 1997 at 756.

*Grist v. Focus Homes, Inc.*, 112 F.3d 1107 at 111-2 (8th Cir. 1997).

*Hallberg v. Eat 'N Park*, 1996 U.S. Dist. Lexis 3573 (W.D.PA, 1996).

*Lockard v. Pizza Hut, Inc., et al.*, Nos. 97-7027 and 7078 (10th Cir., Dec. 14, 1998).

*Mart v. Dr. Pepper Company, Pepsi-Cola General Bottlers*, 1996 WL 226067 (D.Kn., 1996).

*Meritor Savings Bank v. Vinson*, 477 US 57 (1986).

*Powell v. Las Vegas Hilton Corp.*, 841 F.Supp. 1024 (D.Nev., 1992).

**R. Bruce McAfee** is a professor of business administration at Old Dominion University, Norfolk, Virginia, where **Diana L. Deadrick** is an associate professor of management. **Scott W. Kezman** is an attorney and a member of the Labor and Employment Section at Kaufman and Canoles, P.C., also in Norfolk.

# What You're Liable For Now

*The Supreme Court clarified the law with decisions in three sexual harassment cases this year. Will you need to tweak your policy or prepare big changes?*

By Jennifer Laabs

Sexual harassment is in the news every week. And on June 26, the topic made news again, as the United States Supreme Court issued rulings on the final two cases in a trio of sexual harassment lawsuits this year-the first of which was ruled on March 4—having important implications for employers and HR managers.

In one case ruling, for the first time since Title VII of the Civil Rights Act of 1964 became law, employer liability for sexual harassment between members of the same gender was clearly defined. In another case ruling, sexual harassment by supervisors has been outlawed, and in the third case ruling, an employee can now sue an employer for harassment, even if the employee suffered no tangible job loss because of the misconduct.

Take a deep breath, folks, because these three cases mean big changes. Some of these changes are favorable for employers, but some aren't. The implications of the Supreme Court's decisions are clear: Sexual discrimination and harassment won't be tolerated in America's workplaces. The legal arena is making sure of it. Here's what was decided and what it means for your organization:

**CASE I:** Oncale vs. Sundowner Offshore Services Inc. (No. 96-568)
  **Decision date:** March 4, 1998
  **Key question:** Is it sexual harassment when misconduct is between members of the same gender?
  **Facts of the case:** Joseph Oncale was hired as a roustabout (a deckhand or waterfront laborer) through Sundowner Offshore Services' (SOS) Houma, Lou-

isiana, office. He was assigned to work with an eight-man crew on a Chevron USA oil platform in the Gulf of Mexico.

In 1991, three of the crew members, including two

supervisors, forcibly subjected Oncale on numerous occasions to humiliating, sex-related actions, some in front of the rest of the crew.

The two supervisors, John Lyons, a crane operator, and Danny Pippen, a driller, physically assaulted Oncale in a

---

*Jennifer Laabs is the associate managing editor at WORK-FORCE. E-mail laabsj@workforcemag.com to comment.*

AP/WIDE WORLD PHOTOS

*Supreme Court Justice Antonin Scalia (opposite page) agreed sexual harassment is actionable based on conduct. Joseph Oncale (above, center) and Beth Ann Faragher (below) were plaintiffs in two of the harassment cases.*

sexual manner, and one of the supervisors even threatened Oncale with rape. A third co-worker, Brandon Johnson, also participated in the harassment.

Oncale complained of the blatant sexual misconduct to his supervisor, the company's safety compliance clerk. But instead of doing anything about the problem, the clerk replied that he, too, had been picked on by two supervisors who had called him a name suggesting that he was homosexual.

Oncale also reported the misconduct to the highest-ranking supervisor on the rig, who neither investigated nor intervened. Oncale ultimately quit because of the verbal abuse and harassment. He testified in his deposition that he thought if he didn't leave his job, he'd be raped or forced to have sex. SOS later explained the supervisors' behavior as mere horseplay.

**U.S. Supreme Court ruling:** Unanimous (9–0)

The Supreme Court unanimously declared that sexual harassment is actionable, even when the people involved are of the same sex. In Justice Antonin Scalia's opinion, what matters is the conduct at issue, *not* the sex of the people involved and not the presence or absence of sexual desire, whether heterosexual or homosexual. The Supreme Court noted that the law equally protects men and women against workplace discrimination.

**CASE II:** Burlington Industries, Inc. vs. Ellerth (No. 97-569)

**Decision date:** June 26, 1998

**Key question:** Is it sexual harassment when there's no tangible job detriment?

**Facts of the case:** Kimberly Ellerth, a former marketing assistant at Burlington Industries' mattress-fabric division in Chicago, claimed her boss, Theodore Slowik, a divisional vice president for sales and marketing, had made repeated "passes" at her in 1993 and 1994 during her employment. She claims he made inappropriate comments to her, such as "You know, Kim, I could make your life very hard or very easy at Burlington," and "Are you wearing shorter skirts, yet, Kim, because it would make your job a whole lot easier."

Despite rebuffing his advances, Ellerth never suffered any tangible job detriment because of the harassment. And although Ellerth was familiar with the company's anti-sexual harassment policy, she never informed management about her supervisor's misconduct. Ellerth even received a promotion before quitting. Fifteen months after resigning, she sued Burlington.

**U.S. Supreme Court ruling:** Majority vote (7–2)

An employer can be liable for sexual harassment and can be sued regardless of whether a supervisor's threats against an employee—for example, no promotion without sexual favors (quid pro quo,)—are carried out. However, the Supreme Court says employers can assert an "affirmative defense"—meaning that an employer may be relieved of liability in the absence of tangible job detriment if it can show that it exercised reasonable care to prohibit and remedy sexual harassment, and if it can show that the employee unreasonably failed to take advantage of the corrective opportunities offered by the employer.

**CASE III:** Faragher vs. City of Boca Raton, Florida (No. 97282)

**Decision date:** June 26, 1998

**Key question:** Is an organization liable for sexual harassment when the organization is unaware of a supervisor's misconduct?

**Facts of the case:** Once an ocean lifeguard for the city of Boca Raton, Florida, Beth Faragher claimed she endured repeated sexual harassment from two male supervisors during the five years she worked on the city's beaches.

Now a lawyer, Faragher says she and seven other female lifeguards worked for two men, Bill Terry and David Silverman, who would request sexual favors, grab them by the breasts and buttocks, try to break into their showers and referred to them regularly by vulgar epithets. Faragher says she didn't report the problem to higher-ups because she feared retaliation. However, Faragher did speak to one police lieutenant about the behavior, but he didn't think it was his place to act upon workplace complaints.

Attorneys for the city of Boca Raton argued that the city shouldn't be held liable because it had a clear policy against sexual harassment since 1986, and because the male supervisors were acting on their own—not as representatives of the city. The city, however, had failed to disseminate the policy to its lifeguard employees or supervisors. Therefore, neither Faragher nor her supervisors had any knowledge of the policy.

**U.S. Supreme Court ruling:** Majority vote (7–2)

The Supreme Court said that an employer is liable for a pervasive, hostile atmosphere of harassment, and an employer is potentially liable for its supervisors' misconduct, whether the company was aware of the harassment or not.

**Sexual harassment: Unlawful between people of the same gender.**

Of the three sexual-harassment cases decided this year, Oncale vs. Sundowner was the only unanimous decision handed down, which means a clear message for employers: Harassment between two or more men, or between two or more women, is still harassment. However, while on its way to the High Court, the Oncale case was perhaps the most misunderstood of the three harassment cases.

The confusion probably stems from the fact that whenever the word "sex" is involved in a discussion about sexual harassment, people get confused about what the term means. Does "sex" refer to the gender of the harasser or the victim? Or does it refer to the type of behavior? Or all three? That's exactly the confusion that plagued lower courts with this case, and it was the issue that the nine Supreme Court justices agreed to answer.

Here's what they had to work with: Title VII of the Civil Rights Act provides, in part, that "it shall be an unlawful employment practice for an employer . . . to discriminate against any individual with respect to his compensation, terms, conditions or privileges of employment because of such individual's race, color, religion, sex or national origin." It's the "because of . . . sex" phrase that has created all the controversy and confusion over the years.

Until now, Title VII was unclear whether it covered sexual harassment between members of the same gender because of its original intent to prohibit employers from discriminating against women in jobs traditionally held by men. Because of the law's origins, some lower courts ruled that in cases like Oncale, same-sex sexual harassment lawsuits could be brought to court only if the harasser was gay, but dismissed lawsuits when the harasser was heterosexual. Other courts suggested that in cases in which the victim was gay or lesbian, he or she wasn't protected because the harassment was considered sexual-orientation discrimination, which Title VII has been held *not* to prohibit.

In an amicus brief sent to the Supreme Court to consider while deciding this case, Lambda Legal Defense and Education Fund—a legal organization based in New York City that defends the civil rights of lesbians, gay men and people with HIV and AIDS—urged the Supreme Court to recognize that Title VII should be applied without regard to the sex or sexual orientation of the harasser or victim.

"Lambda, with the ACLU, NOW, Women's Legal Defense Fund and many other civil rights groups, urges the Supreme Court to recognize that sexual harassment is about subjecting employees to unfair working conditions by taking advantage of them at a very vulnerable, sexual level," said Ruth E. Harlow, Lambda managing attorney, who assisted in writing the brief, and who was quoted in an article compiled by Badpuppy's *GayToday,* a daily news publication for the global gay and lesbian community. "Every instance of severe sexual harassment plays upon the sex of the targeted employee and is unlawful under Title VII, regardless of the gender or sexual orientation of the perpetrators," she said.

Interestingly enough, Oncale identifies himself as a heterosexual, and didn't realize that he would become an icon for gay-rights advocates. "He started out living a very closed existence, not having much contact with gay people," his lawyer told *The Advocate,* a gay issues publication, last year. "But during this process, he has learned what gay people face in terms of discrimination. If his case can help them out, he's happy about that."

In the end, sexual orientation wasn't the issue. Disparate impact "because of sex" was the issue. In its final decision, the Supreme Court held that Title VII showed "a congressional intent to strike at the entire spectrum of disparate treatment of men and women in employment." So even though sexual harassment isn't expressly prohibited in federal employment discrimination statutes, the Supreme Court has said it is actionable as a form of sex discrimination under Title VII.

In making the decision, the Supreme Court looked to the law of racial discrimination, which makes it clear that it's possible for an employer to discriminate against members of its own race, not just members of another race. The Supreme Court bolstered its opinion with a sports metaphor to connote that context is everything: "A professional football player's working environment is not severely or pervasively abusive, for example, if the coach smacks him on the buttocks as he heads onto the field, even if the same behavior would reasonably be experienced as abusive by the coach's secretary (male or female) back at the office."

"I think for most major employers, [the Oncale case decision] is just a blip on their radar screen because their policies already prohibit harassment of any form—not only sex, but also racial, religious, ethnic and any type of harassment based on any protected characteristic," comments Paul Salvatore, a New York City-based labor and employment law partner and an expert on sexual harassment issues at Proskauer Rose LLP. "It came as no great surprise, I think, to most employers of any size with any sophisticated human resource function that this was the way the Supreme Court was going to go on this case." Salvatore emphasizes that this case isn't a big deal for most big employers that already have had policies against same-sex harassment in place for a while.

That's exactly how Bob Hamilton, human resources diversity consultant for E.I. du Pont de Nemours and Co. (DuPont), based in Wilmington, Delaware, sees it. "We've always treated sexual harassment among the same gender as inappropriate," says Hamilton, "but up until the Su-

preme Court rulings, it depended on the various district courts as to whether it was actionable [under the law] or not. So the Supreme Court finally made clarity around this issue."

DuPont's HR team, which won the 1997 WORKFORCE Optimas Award for its laudable approach to diversity issues, identified same-sex harassment as a "no-no" years ago. Since 1988, before most companies had even acknowledged the term "sexual harassment," DuPont had its training program, "A Matter of Respect," up and running.

The training, which involves a series of video vignettes that emphasize nondiscriminatory behavior in the work environment, clearly shows workers how to treat each other on the job—and serves as a model program for other employers to emulate. "From our nondiscrimination policy and from our policies about treating people with respect, we try to let people know that whether it's [happening between members of] the same sex or not, [discriminatory] behavior is inappropriate."

Although it's been a no-brainer to treat same-sex harassment the same as opposite-sex harassment for big-name firms like DuPont, the majority of most larger, mid-sized and smaller organizations aren't quite so enlightened. Most experts say there's going to be quite a bit of tweaking of policies, practices and training going on over the next few years to comply with the new law because of the Oncale case. Says one attorney who wished not to be identified: "We all know same-sex harassment is now covered. But it's a little unclear under what circumstances." The lower courts are bound to have to address that question over the next several years.

**There doesn't have to be a tangible job detriment for harassment to be actionable.**

The key question raised by the Ellerth vs. Burlington Industries case was if nothing happened to an employee in terms of a tangible job threat or detriment, such as a salary reduction, a less-desirable job assignment or denial of a promotion, could he or she claim sexual harassment? The Supreme Court affirmed that when harassment has a tangible consequence, like a poor work assignment, employer liability is absolute.

But what's more interesting is that the court took the law a step further by saying that even when there's no tangible job detriment to an employee because of sexual harassment, an employer may still be responsible. The Supreme Court is saying, in effect, that harassment is defined by the ugly behavior of the perpetrator, not by what happens to the worker subsequently.

And the Supreme Court clearly outlined employer liability when this concrete tangibility isn't present. Employers can be held for liability or damages unless: 1) They have a clear policy against harassment, including how to report such behavior, and 2) Such a policy exists, but the employee bringing suit "unreasonably" failed to take advantage of it. These two conditions of liability are called, in legalese, an *affirmative defense.*

"The million dollar question now is what impact will the affirmative defense have? Will it be a complete defense to liability? Or will it simply be a defense that lessens the amount of damages for which the company is responsible?" asks Gerald L. Maatman, Jr., a partner in the law firm of Baker & McKenzie in Chicago, specializing in sexual harassment issues. The Supreme Court has made it unclear because it used the word "or"—liability *or* damages. There's no way of predicting exactly how lower courts may interpret this in future court decisions.

The good news for employers is that the second prong of the affirmative defense implies employees have a bigger role to play than they previously had to. Under the old rules, workers needed to tell *someone* if they were experiencing sexual harassment. Under the new rules, workers now need to tell *someone with decision-making power* if they're experiencing sexual harassment. Both the Ellerth and Faragher cases make it clear that a worker who's being harassed must report it. The employee has "a corresponding obligation of reasonable care to avoid harm." The Supreme Court made it more of a two-way street.

Says Salvatore: "Before, we were kind of reading the tea leaves and reading between the lines. Now we have a definitive statement from the Supreme Court."

**Employers are now liable for supervisor misconduct.**

Up until now, most sexual harassment cases have been known as "hostile work environment"—when someone is the victim of a pervasive pattern of unwanted advances, touching and other misbehavior in a given workplace.

Many employers have had no trouble getting such cases thrown out of court. That's been mostly because employee plaintiffs had to prove negligence—that a company knew,

or should have known, about the offensive behavior. Under the old rules, a manager who didn't know about sexual harassment among his or her employees usually wasn't responsible for the behavior. That has changed—dramatically.

"There's been a definite change in the standard of liability when the harassment is done by a supervisor in the hostile work environment context, changing from a basically negligent standard—the 'knew or should have known' standard—to vicarious liability with an affirmative defense," explains Ellen McLaughlin, a partner in the law firm of Seyfarth, Shaw, Fairweather & Geraldson in Chicago. McLaughlin specializes in sexual harassment liability issues. Now, the manager will be held strictly liable for a harasser's actions, unless a company has a strong system of dealing with such problems, as outlined in the previous section.

That means plaintiffs now have an easier path to sue because a company will be held liable for its supervisors' misconduct. Supervisors need to be advised of their responsibility and know how to handle such problems.

"For once, being in Connecticut is an advantage," quips Jim Carabetta, director of HR for Fosdick Corp. in Wallingford, Connecticut. He explains: "Connecticut has its own, more stringent harassment laws, which require every employee with the authority to hire, fire, promote, discipline, direct, review or effectively recommend any of the above within six months of hire or promotion into the mandated group, and have two hours of approved sensitivity/harassment prevention training in a course that meets the state's criterion for content." Carabetta says his firm sticks by these guidelines, and trains its managers accord-

# Steps to Protect Your Company Against Sexual Harassment

The three new rulings by the U.S. Supreme Court imply that an employer may have to take the fall for sexual harassment, even if it's got all the right policies and practices in place. That's the bad news. However, if you do all the right things that the best minds in sexual harassment law and training suggest, you'll have a fighting chance. Here's what the experts suggest every organization do to protect itself from sexual harassment problems:

• Have a state-of-the-art policy that clearly says your organization won't tolerate harassment, including harassment between members of the same gender.

• Widely disseminate the policy at regular intervals (annually or more often is ideal), post the policy on your intranet, keep records of when the policy was disseminated and keep signatures on file that employees received the policy.

• Make at least two reporting venues available to employees—one *must* be someone other than employees' supervisors (HR, an ombudsperson, supervisors, managers, 800 number, open-door policy, internal review procedure or others).

• Conduct training for employees, supervisors and managers on anti-discrimination and anti-sexual harassment policies and practices. Ideally, have the firm's leader introduce the sessions to nail down the point that senior management is serious about non-discrimination. Make sure everyone understands what constitutes discriminatory behavior and why it won't be tolerated.

• Investigate all reports of sexual harassment promptly (including harassment between members of the same gender) and ensure that employees who report such misconduct aren't retaliated against.

• Take swift and appropriate action against employees who are found to have violated company policies on sexual harassment and anti-discrimination.

• Hold supervisors, managers and executives accountable for communicating anti-discrimination and anti-sexual harassment policies and practices to their work groups, and dealing appropriately with any misconduct.

*—JL*

ingly. Because he's already been up to speed with the supervisor training, the new rulings by the Supreme Court won't have much effect on how he proceeds with sexual harassment training.

**So where are we on the sexual harassment spectrum?**

Employers are collectively standing at the crossroads on the issue of sexual harassment. These three cases make it clear that employers, and HR in particular, can't afford to ignore the topic. This is happening with good reason: Everyone's predicting more lawsuits. The courts are already flooded with such cases, especially since 1991, the year that the Anita Hill-Clarence Thomas hearings made headline news and plaintiffs were first eligible for punitive damages.

Maatman explains: "The bottom line is simple—employers should be prepared to be named in more lawsuits, and to incur a much greater risk of liability." He says the net result of the rulings is that it's easier for a plaintiff to state a case so that more people who go visit a lawyer will be told they have enough evidence to file a case. Whereas before, it might not be worth the time and effort to even file a lawsuit. "Also, it will be easier for a plaintiff to recover [damages], at least in a case of a company sued for what its supervisor does," adds Maatman.

These three high-court decisions are forcing a lot of employers to take stock. "Employers are quickly revisiting their policies and modifying them," says Seyfarth, Shaw, Fairweather & Geraldson's McLaughlin, who recently gave a seminar on these Supreme Court decisions to a group of 260 people, mostly HR pros.

And she adds that companies are scrambling to get training programs together. "At many companies, especially if they're having a bad financial year, training may be one of those things that goes. But I've heard some HR pros say, 'I'm going back to my boss and tell him or her we really need to put training about sexual harassment back in the budget, given what's occurred with these Supreme Court decisions.' " Those who've already been vigilant on this issue remain convinced they need to stand firm in their actions. "Essentially, the rulings have no immediate effect on us because we've had a long-standing policy in place," says DuPont's Hamilton.

And Los Angeles-based Atlantic Richfield Co. (ARCO) is taking the same strong stance it has always had on the issue, as well. "For California employers, the Supreme Court cases, while interesting, aren't that big a deal," says Lloyd Loomis, the firm's senior corporate counsel, employee relations. Of course, ARCO has also been a pioneer in taking zero tolerance to sexual harassment for years. Despite being in a male-dominated industry, the firm has created a system of awareness about such issues, including a 15-page section on sexual harassment on the firm's intranet called "You Just Can't Do That!" that's available to all 20,000 employees. Even with such extraordinary measures, the company found itself firing an oil-tanker captain several years ago for sexually harassing co-workers. Clearly, even firms with the best of policies find themselves continually dealing with the issue.

"If you're trying to get ahead of the curve, be practical and want to do the right thing, you simply have to do what the Supreme Court is telling you a responsible employer should do," says Maatman. "Then if you still get sued, at least you have all the potential arguments available to you that [suggest] the case ought to be kicked out of the system in the first 30 days. If the court says no, it simply goes to damages, and you will be in the best and strongest position possible, should you have to face the jury and argue the case."

**The issue of sexual harassment isn't primarily a legal one.**

Employers should remember that sexual harassment is a behavioral and cultural problem in Corporate America, and it should be dealt with on both the individual and cultural level. Indeed, when 1,700 employees at medium- to large-sized U.S. companies were asked by Walker Information, a global research firm based in Indianapolis, to complete a national business integrity survey, employees said the top ethical problem in their organizations is sexual harassment.

Says Jennifer Blalock, a Cincinnati-based trainer who specializes in conflict resolution and preventing workplace harassment: "The issue of sexual harassment forces us to examine human behavior and ask, 'Why does it require an elaborate set of laws to get people to respect each other? Where would we be if there were no laws holding us accountable for our behavior?'"

Blalock has a good point. She says companies should focus on the average individual. People need to learn how to communicate with each other. "A policy is useless unless people use it. Most research indicates that a small fraction of employees ever say or do anything about harassing behavior. It's best to intervene and provide solutions before they escalate into full-blown, formal complaints," Blalock adds. Which brings us back to the Supreme Court decisions.

"I don't think that anyone is running for the hills or throwing up their hands and saying, 'The sky is falling' as a result of these three rulings," says Maatman. "Instead, they're redoubling their efforts at training, circulation and dissemination of policy statements."

What employers should keep in mind is this: If you didn't pay much attention to the issue of sexual harassment before, the Supreme Court just gave you at least three compelling reasons to do so. It has raised the bar, so to speak. If you already had a pretty good handle on the issue, make sure you tweak your policy and procedures so that they fall in line with the new rulings. As the experts say, this issue still isn't going away—so make sure you're doing what's appropriate to deal with it.

# Unit 2

## Unit Selections

## Key Points to Consider

❖ Job requirements and working conditions have changed over the past several years. What changes do you foresee in the workplace in the next 10 years? How do you see the use of disabled employees in the workforce developing?

❖ The first step in the process of working is getting hired; the last step is termination, whether for cause, leaving for a new job, retirement, or a "reduction in force." What trends do you see in the workforce concerning individuals and their careers?

❖ The current economy is causing labor shortages in a variety of organizations. What are some of the new sources and avenues when looking for new employees?

❖ How do you see computerization being applied to human resources, and how will this change human resources?

 **Links**    **www.dushkin.com/online/**

13. **America's Job Bank**
*http://www.ajb.dni.us*
14. **AmericanRecruitment**
*http://www.americanrecruitment.com*
15. **Labor Consultants of America**
*http://www.laborconsultants.com/index.htm*
16. **National Center for the Workplace**
*http://socs.berkeley.edu/~iir/ncw/execsum.html*

These sites are annotated on pages 4 and 5.

Organizations, whether profit or nonprofit, are more than collections of buildings, desks, and telephones. Organizations are made of people—people with their particular traits, habits, and idiosyncrasies that make them unique. Each individual has different needs and wants, and the employer and the worker must seek a reasonable compromise so that at least an adequate match may be found for both.

The importance of human resource planning is greater than ever and will probably be even more important in the future. As Thomas Peters and Robert Waterman have pointed out:

> Quality and service, then, were invariable hallmarks of excellent firms. To get them, of course, everyone's cooperation is required, not just the mighty labors of the top 200. The excellent companies require and demand extraordinary performance from the average man. (Dana's former chairman, Rene McPherson, says that neither the few destructive laggards nor the handful of brilliant performers are the key. Instead, he urges attention to the care, feeding and unshackling of the average man.) We labeled it "productivity through people." All companies pay it lip service. Few deliver.
> —Thomas Peters and Robert Waterman, *In Search of Excellence*, New York, Warner Books, 1987

In the future, organizations are going to have to pay more than just lip service to "productivity through people" if they want to survive and prosper. They will have to practice it by demonstrating an understanding not only of their clients' and customers' needs but also of their employees' needs. The only way that they will be able to deliver the goods and services and achieve success is through those same employees. Companies are faced with the difficult task of finding the right people for the right jobs—a task that must be accomplished if the organization is going to have a future.

Organizations are trying to meet the needs of their employees by developing new and different approaches to worker's jobs. This means taking into account how society, the labor force, the family, and the nature of the jobs themselves have changed. Training and development will be key in meeting future human resource requirements. Employers will have to change the way they design their positions if they are to attract and keep good employees; they must consider how society has changed and how those changes have affected the labor force; they will have to consider how the labor force has changed and will change in the future, with fewer young people and more middle-aged employees as well as dual-career couples struggling to raise children; and they will have to consider how the very nature of jobs has changed in society, especially from predominantly blue-collar to white-collar jobs. There would seem to be little in the way of a

future for the traditional workplace. True, it will continue to exist, but working at home and telecommuting will play a larger role in the future.

Human resource planning, selection, and recruitment are going to be even more critical in the future. Companies will have to go to extraordinary lengths to attract and keep new employees. There is no mystery about the reasons for this situation. America is aging, and there are fewer people in their late teens and early twenties to take the entry-level jobs that will be available in the future. Women, who for the past 20 years have been the major source of new employees, now represent almost half the workforce. As a result, new groups must be found, whether they are retirees, high school students, workers moonlighting on a second job, minority group members, people with disabilities, or immigrants. One thing is certain: The workforce is changing and organizations will need to unlock the potential of all their employees.

Another aspect of human resource planning involves both the selection process and the termination process. The days of working for only one company and then retiring with a gold watch and a pension are over. People are going to change jobs, if not companies, more frequently in the future, and many of the tasks they will be doing in the next 10, 15, or 20 years do not even exist today because of technological change. Midlife and midcareer changes are going to be far more common than they have been in the past, requiring people to change and adapt. Potential employees will be looking for a number of things from their employers that they did not look for in the past, including training and preparation for their next job or assignment as well as respect.

Human resources information systems offer important tools in managing human resources. The ability of computers to handle large amounts of data is now being applied to human resource management with very interesting results. These practices apply to hiring and internal information management and mean greater automation of human resources in the future. The Web offers many interesting potential innovations in the human resources area, not the least of which is the ability to attract workers and to find information.

Meeting the human resource needs of any organization in the future is a difficult task. Assuming that the economy continues to grow at an acceptable rate, the need for workers will continue to increase, but many of the traditional sources of supply for new workers will be either exhausted or in decline. Management must plan for this shortage and consider alternative sources of potential employees. In turn, the individual employee must be ready to adapt quickly and efficiently to a changing environment. Job security is a thing of the past, and workers must remain flexible in order to cope with increased uncertainty.

# Meeting Human Resource Requirements

# There Is No Future
## For the Workplace

**John Challenger**

**How will tomorrow's managers and supervisors lead self-directed teams whose members are spread out over multiple states? Is it even possible to lead such a group? Employers will need to prepare for this new kind of management now.**

If you want a snapshot of tomorrow's workplace, bring your camera to Fremd High School in Palatine, Illinois. There you will see Motorola engineers working closely with students to solve real engineering problems. You might also take a picture of the billboards in central Florida, where Walt Disney World advertises for help.

Teens working on real-world engineering projects and billboards advertising jobs give an accurate picture of today's labor shortage. Companies like Motorola are working with high schools to attract more students to the engineering profession and to their companies, while Disney and many other firms are creatively advertising their need for help.

The impact of this shortage on tomorrow's workplace is not clear. If it continues, how will it affect the way we work in the future?

I think two key factors—population and technology—will determine the landscape of tomorrow's workplace. As I discuss how these factors can affect the next generation of workers, I exclude the impact of economic policies, which can alter the trends in these areas.

## A Continuing Shortage of Workers

I see a future economy with continued worker shortages created by consumer demand, coupled with an employment population too small to meet that demand. The next generation of workers will continue to be a scarce commodity for employers.

Traditional want ads will be replaced with "situation wanted" ads: workers will place these ads on the Internet or other media and wait for companies to call them. They will have good reason to expect a call back. The U.S. Bureau of Labor Statistics projects 151 million jobs existing by 2006 and 141 million people employed. As often happens today, many of these workers will be working two jobs.

To attract new workers, companies will need to offer different kinds of perks and benefits. Money alone is not going to be the deciding factor. Businesses will need to add benefits to address the specific needs of workers.

For example, a worker who needs daycare for two young children may be attracted to an employer willing to make that service part of the compensation and benefits package. Another employee, who may need substantial help with retirement financing, may get special payroll deductions that can be directly deposited into a personal mutual fund or investment portfolio. Companies will provide free financial counseling.

Companies will no longer view benefits as companywide provisions. Instead, they may want to allocate a budget for benefits and authorize hiring managers to provide funds to employees within the limits of that budgeted amount. Such a change could affect many companies that currently provide benefit services, including major medical care.

Reprinted with permission from the February 1999 issue of *Public Management* magazine, pp. 20-23. Published by the International City/County Management Association, Washington, DC.

The employer of tomorrow may wish to find alternate ways to help employees fund medical insurance. Because of the nature of this kind of expenditure, I see major medical insurance becoming an expense shared by employer, employee, and private or publicly funded assistance.

The need to tailor benefits will become more crucial as the demographics of the workforce change. I expect these changes to come from two diverse groups: teens and people over 50.

The teen population is on the rise. The U.S. Education Department reports that high school enrollment will jump 13 percent over the next 10 years, adding another 1.9 million students by 2007.

Another important trend is that many older workers are retiring later in life. The U.S. Bureau of Labor Statistics reports that the number of workers aged 65 and older increased by 31 percent (3.8 million people) between 1985 and 1995. As the over-50 population rises, I suspect there will be even more workers in their 60s and even 70s.

The so-called Generation X'ers will probably become the minority age group in the workplace of tomorrow, sandwiched between the teens and the over-50 workers. Employers could face two potential scenarios: the two groups could form a strong connection, or they could become polarized. Employers will need to avoid the polarization between teens and the over-50 workers, and to develop policies that will bring them together.

I like to use the grandparent/grandchild model. Take a close look at families with strong relationships: if the grandparents are still around, you are likely to see an intimate bond between them and the teenaged grandchildren. That bond usually develops when the grandchild is young and continues through the child's adult years.

Employers will need to find ways to bring that relationship to the workplace. One way is to let the over-50 workers know they are expected to mentor the younger employees. Pairing teens and over-50 workers on specific assignments will help build these connections. Remember, most people in these two age groups will have grandparents or grandchildren at home and should easily relate to this relationship model.

Of course, employers should not forget the problems of the generation in between. Generation X has the potential to see itself as a separate tribe needing defense against the other two groups. For this reason, companies will rely more and more on the maturity and levelheadedness of the over-50 worker to maintain a good balance among all employees.

## The Impacts of Technology

The other major trend changing tomorrow's workplace will be technology, which has al-

**Traditional want ads will be replaced with "situation wanted" ads: workers will place these ads on the Internet or other media and wait for companies to call them. They will have good reason to expect a call back.**

ready made it possible for American business to become more productive. Computers and robots are now doing the work of two or three people, helping to keep total wages in check and to hold down inflation. These are the most obvious results of technology.

Less noticeable and more interesting is the impact that technology will have on the nature of leadership.

The Bureau of Labor Statistics reports that 27 percent of the civilian labor force worked flexible schedules last year. This is an increase of almost 83 percent over 1991, when only 15 percent of workers had flexible hours. These figures show that exactly when people do their jobs is becoming a less important factor than they meet deadlines.

Add to this trend the increasing number of telecommuters who work at home or in their cars, and it becomes obvious that employees need not always be at predetermined locations to get their jobs done. As long as the brain is working, the employee is working, or at least potentially.

That word "potentially" is a critical one. How will companies direct and manage a workforce that can be almost anywhere?

Before the infusion of technology into our lives, people reported to work at a specific time of day and went home at a set time, too. There was a supervisor or manager who assigned work and directed employee activity. It was understood that from 8 a.m. to 5 p.m., the employee was dedicated to the job.

In our high-tech society, the worker might be taking a shower, watching "Oprah" or having lunch with his or her daughter between 8 a.m. and 5 p.m. While the supervisor is watching the evening news, the employee might be putting the finishing touches on a report needed for a presentation tomorrow morning.

Technology has shown employers that it does not matter how the employee spends

his or her time as long as the job gets done to everyone's satisfaction. This makes for a significant change in the way we function. Even workers on the assembly line are experiencing a change in workplace organization. The structure we identify as a workplace is disappearing.

Most management layers have been downsized out of American corporations during the 1990s. Today, there are fewer managers to report to and fewer decisions that require their input. The concept of empowering workers has left an indelible mark, not only on the workforce but on the marketplace as well. Consumers are expecting and getting better service from companies, and businesses are doing more to improve the service they give.

As technology helps companies deliver greater satisfaction to their customers, it also changes the workforce. Workers of tomorrow can no longer rely on brawn to get them a job. The days of unskilled, manual labor are fading into the past.

Today's factories are becoming laboratories of technology. There are technical jobs in manufacturing that did not exist 10 years ago. Computers have even made an impact on the repair and maintenance field: your auto mechanic, for instance, is just as likely to hook your car up to a computer terminal as he or she is to remove your carburetor.

The result of such technological development is that new opportunities have been created for women in fields that have traditionally been dominated by men. The most recent figures compiled by the Bureau of Labor Statistics show that in 1996 almost 61 percent of U.S. technicians, engineers, sales engineers, and technical sales support staff were women. This trend is likely to continue as demand for engineering and technical jobs exceeds the supply.

**The U.S. Bureau of Labor Statistics projects 151 million jobs existing by 2006 and 141 million people employed.**

Although industry leaders are attempting to attract young talent into technical areas—like Motorola, maintaining its partnership with Fremd High School—fewer students are graduating with the appropriate college degrees. U.S. Education Department figures for 1995 show a drop in the number of students completing college-level programs in computer and electrical engineering since 1990. Yet the Commerce Department estimates that the demand for information technology workers alone will reach a million by 2005.

Factories may be hit the hardest by the lack of competent workers: in a National Association of Manufacturers survey, 88 percent of respondents reported a shortage of skilled help in at least one job category. More than half of respondents reported employee shortcomings in basic math, writing, and comprehension skills.

Training will become the next boom industry as employers are forced to take on the responsibility of educating unskilled workers. The new economy will not allow American industry to wait for the politicians to fund public education. Employers will need to become the public schools of the next generation.

These results point to what we can expect over the next 25 years. Workers will be more independent and self-directed, and companies will need to form partnerships with educators to prepare young people for the high-technology workplace.

## Turning Managers into Leaders

So, what about leadership? How will tomorrow's managers and supervisors lead self-directed teams whose members are spread out over multiple states? Is it even possible to lead such a group? Employers will need to prepare for this new kind of management now.

Today's job descriptions are outdated the moment they are written. Most people would probably admit that their job descriptions are not accurate. So why do we keep them?

An alternative to composing the traditional job description might be to write job goals. Goals focus on accomplishments, which the company leadership can track; job descriptions focus on tasks, which are untraceable and often unimportant.

I use the term "company leaders" instead of "managers" for a reason: supervision of tomorrow's workers will not require managers. Managers want to control tasks in the hope of predicting outcomes. Leaders want to plant seeds in the hope of harvesting unprecedented crops. Leaders operate in the mercurial world of the poet: they are the dreamers of corporations.

The only job a leader has is to inspire greatness, then get out of the way. To do that today requires some personal contact. I do not believe, for example, that we can fully appreciate someone's leadership qualities simply by reading his or her words. We gain so much more by seeing and hearing that person utter the words. A leader's communication style and sincerity make a greater impression on us, perhaps a lasting one.

But in the high-tech world of tomorrow, leaders will have fewer opportunities to talk to people in person. They will need to rely on electronic devices to express their ideas. Perhaps the CEO will make a multimedia CD that employees can explore at their leisure. Will that kind of communication be a good substitute for personal contact?

A shop superintendent can quickly communicate with the president of the firm simply by sending an e-mail message. A decision can be made quickly and implemented in one-third of the time it used to take. But what if the president wants to convey how crucial this particular decision is to the success of the company? Can the executive do it through e-mail?

## Exactly when people do their jobs is becoming a less important factor than whether they meet deadlines.

These are the demands that will be placed on tomorrow's business leaders. Their ability to convey ideas to teams composed of people working in different parts of the country will be a major challenge.

One problem the new leader already faces is the isolation of self-directed workers. With so many people working from their homes and cars at all hours, it is difficult to maintain a sense of belonging. People can lose touch with their organizations and begin to miss the normal camaraderie of the traditional workplace.

It is critical that business leaders provide opportunities for the next generation of workers to get together periodically. This will allow employees to see each other and make direct connections. It will also give the leaders of the company an opportunity to communicate one-on-one.

I believe this sense of isolation will be serious enough to create a new job category: the director of socialization, who will be responsible for helping workers connect with each other while giving them a chance to express themselves to someone other than the boss.

The need for people to feel a part of a human organization is crucial to achievement. People want to connect with other individuals, not just electronic message pads or laptop computers. This will be just as true in 2020 as it is today.

## Working for the Customer

My world exists on the edge of job creation and job destruction. My firm works with companies struggling to find the right balance between workers and need. This is no easy task, and many companies fail to do it correctly. However, the workers they shed are quickly absorbed by other firms eager to satisfy their need for growth. The result is a "just-in-time" employment system that will continue well into the next millennium. This system will force the American worker and employer to rethink ideas of loyalty and commitment. Few employers will guarantee jobs to everyone, and few workers will be able to afford to rely on employers to develop their skills and careers.

The workplace will become an environment dedicated to fulfilling customer demand. The needs of employers and employees will be subordinate to the need to satisfy customers.

Perhaps the New Economy is really nothing more than a consumer economy. Economic growth may rely less on government and more on companies, large and small, successfully satisfying an unrelenting consumer who wants more products and services, faster and at a better price.

Our worker populations will need to be better prepared for this kind of demand. Only those workers who are adequately educated will be able to handle the ever-changing technology designed to help us compete effectively in this market of world consumers.

The current trends in population and technology challenge us to rethink our goals for education and work. We cannot hope to sustain our economic health over the next 25 years unless we ensure that every able-bodied person can effectively participate in that growth.

Like most projections for the future, mine ends with a warning: Invest in education, or suffer the consequences.

We need to commit more than money, however. We need to set education standards that will prepare the next generation to build a future. As business and professional people, we need to invest ourselves and participate in the development of these standards. We need to make them relevant to the marketplace. Only then will our investment in education bring solid returns for everyone: employers, workers, and consumers.

---

*John Challenger is executive vice president of Challenger, Gray & Christmas, Inc., Chicago, Illinois. This article is based on his presentation at the World Future Society 1998 Annual Meeting in Chicago. It is reprinted with permission from the October 1998 issue of* The Futurist *magazine, Bethesda, Maryland.*

**Affirmative action is bad. Banning it is worse.**

# IN DEFENSE OF PREFERENCE

## By Nathan Glazer

The battle over affirmative action today is a contest between a clear principle on the one hand and a clear reality on the other. The principle is that ability, qualifications, and merit, independen of race, national origin, or sex should prevail when one applies for a job or promotion, or for entry into selective institutions for higher education, or when one bids for contracts. The reality is that strict adherence to this principle would result in few African Americans getting jobs, admissions, and contracts. What makes the debate so confused is that the facts that make a compelling case for affirmative action are often obscured by the defenders of affirmative action themselves. They have resisted acknowledging how serious the gaps are between African Americans and others, how deep the preferences reach, how systematic they have become. Considerably more than a mild bent in the direction of diversity now exists, but it exists because painful facts make it necessary if blacks are to participate in more than token numbers in some key institutions of our society. The opponents of affirmative action can also be faulted: they have not fully confronted the consequences that must follow from the implementation of the principle that measured ability, qualification, merit, applied without regard to color, should be our only guide.

I argued for that principle in a 1975 book titled, provocatively, *Affirmative Discrimination*. It seemed obvious that that was what all of us, black and white, were aiming to achieve through the revolutionary civil rights legislation of the 1960s. That book dealt with affirmative action in employment, and with two other kinds of governmentally or judicially imposed "affirmative action," the equalization of the racial proportions in public schools and the integration of residential neighborhoods. I continued to argue and write regularly against governmentally required affirmative action, that is, racial preference, for the next two decades or more: it was against the spirit of the Constitution, the clear language of the civil rights acts, and the interests of all of us in the United States in achieving an integrated and just society.

It is not the unpopularity of this position in the world in which I live, liberal academia, that has led me to change my mind but, rather, developments that were unforeseen and unexpected in the wake of the successful civil rights movement. What was unforeseen and unexpected was that the gap between the educational performance of blacks and whites would persist and, in some respects, deepen despite the civil rights revolution and hugely expanded social and educational programs, that inner-city schools would continue to decline, and that the black family would unravel to a remarkable degree, contributing to social conditions for large numbers of black children far worse than those in the 1960s. In the presence of those conditions, an insistence on color-blindness means the effective exclusion today of African Americans from positions of influence, wealth, and power. It is not a prospect that any of us can contemplate with equanimity. We have to rethink affirmative action.

In a sense, it is a surprise that a fierce national debate over affirmative action has not only persisted but intensified during the Clinton years. After twelve years under two Republican presidents, Ronald Reagan and George Bush, who said they opposed affirmative action but did nothing to scale it back, the programs seemed secure. After all, affirmative action rests primarily on a presidential executive order dating back to the presidencies of Lyndon Johnson and Richard Nixon which requires "affirmative action" in employment practices from federal contractors—who include almost every large employer, university, and hospital. The legal basis for most of affirmative action could thus have been swept away, as so many noted at the time, with a "stroke of the pen" by the president. Yet two presidents who claimed to oppose affirmative action never wielded the pen.

Despite the popular majority that grumbles against affirmative action, there was (and is) no major elite constituency strongly opposed to it: neither business nor organized labor, religious leaders nor university presidents, local officials nor serious presidential candidates are to be found in opposition. Big business used to fear that affirmative action would undermine the principle of employment and promotion on the basis of qualifications. It has since become a supporter. Along with mayors and other local officials (and of course the civil rights movement), it played a key role in stopping the Reagan administration from moving against affirmative action. Most city administrations have also made their peace with affirmative action.

Two developments outside the arena of presidential politics galvanized both opponents and defenders of affirmative action. The Supreme Court changed glacially after successive Republican appointments—each of which, however, had been vetted by a Democratic Senate—and a number of circuit courts began to chip away at the edifice of affirmative action. But playing the largest role was the politically unsophisticated effort of two California professors to place on the California ballot a proposition that would insert in the California Constitution the simple and clear words, taken from the Civil Rights Act of 1964, which ban discrimination on the basis of race, national origin, or sex. The decision to launch a state constitutional proposition, Proposition 209, suddenly gave opponents the political instrument they needed to tap the majority sentiment that has always existed against preferences.

While supporters of affirmative action do not have public opinion on their side, they do have the still-powerful civil rights movement, the major elites in education, religion, philanthropy, government, and the mass media. And their position is bolstered by a key fact: how far behind African Americans are when judged by the tests and measures that have become the common coin of American meritocracy.

The reality of this enormous gap is clearest where the tests in use are the most objective, the most reliable, and the best validated, as in the case of the various tests used for admission to selective institutions of higher education, for entry into elite occupations such as law and medicine, or for civil service jobs. These tests have been developed over many years specifically for the purpose of eliminating biases in admissions and appointments. As defenders of affirmative action often point out, paper-and-pencil tests of information, reading comprehension, vocabulary, reasoning, and the like are not perfect indicators of individual ability. But they are the best measures we have for success in college and professional schools, which, after all, require just the skills the tests measure. And the test can clearly differentiate the literate teacher from the illiterate one or the policeman who can make out a coherent arrest report from one who cannot.

To concentrate on the most hotly contested area of affirmative action—admission to selective institutions of higher education—and on the group in the center of the storm—African Americans: If the Scholastic Assessment Test were used for selection in a color-blind fashion, African Americans, who today make up about six percent of the student bodies in selective colleges and universities, would drop to less than two percent, according to

a 1994 study by the editor of the *Journal of Blacks in Higher Education.*

Why is this so? According to studies summarized in Stephan and Abigail Thernstrom's book, *America in Black and White,* the average combined SAT score for entering freshmen in the nation's top 25 institutions is about 1300. White applicants generally need to score a minimum of 600 on the verbal portion of the test—a score obtained by eight percent of the test-takers in 1995—and at least 650 on the mathematics section—a score obtained by seven percent of the test-takers in 1995. In contrast, only 1.7 percent of black students scored over 600 on the verbal section in 1995, and only two percent scored over 650 on the math. This represents considerable progress over the last 15 years, but black students still lag distressingly far behind their white counterparts.

There is no way of getting around this reality. Perhaps the tests are irrelevant to success in college? That cannot be sustained. They have been improved and revised over decades and predict achievement in college better than any alternative. Some of the revisions have been carried out in a near-desperate effort to exclude items which would discriminate against blacks. Some institutions have decided they will not use the tests, not because they are invalid per se, but because they pose a barrier to the increased admission of black students. Nor would emphasizing other admissions criteria, such as high school grades, make a radical difference. In any case, there is considerable value to a uniform national standard, given the enormous differences among high schools.

Do qualifications at the time of admission matter? Isn't the important thing what the institutions manage to do with those they admit? If they graduate, are they not qualified? Yes, but many do not graduate. Two or three times as many African American students as white students drop out before graduation. And the tests for admission to graduate schools show the same radical disparities between blacks and others. Are there not also preferences for athletes, children of alumni, students gifted in some particular respect? Yes, but except for athletes, the disparities in academic aptitude that result from such preferences are not nearly as substantial as those which must be elided in order to reach target figures for black students. Can we not substitute for the tests other factors—such as the poverty and other hardships students have overcome to reach the point of applying to college? This might keep up the number of African Americans, but not by much, if the studies are to be believed. A good number of white and Asian applicants would also benefit from such "class-based" affirmative action.

(I have focused on the effect of affirmative action—and its possible abolition—on African Americans. But, of course, there are other beneficiaries. Through bureaucratic mindlessness, Asian Americans and Hispanics were also given affirmative action. But Asian Americans scarcely need it. Major groups—not all—of Hispanic Americans trail behind whites but mostly for reasons we understand: problems with the English language and the effect on immigrant children of the poor educational and economic status of their parents. We expect these to improve in time as they always have with immigrants to the United States. And, when it comes to women, there is simply no issue today when it comes to qualifying in equal numbers for selective institutions of higher and professional education.)

How, then, should we respond to this undeniable reality? The opponents of affirmative action say, "Let standards prevail whatever the result." So what if black students are reduced to two percent of our selective and elite student bodies? Those who gain entry will know that they are properly qualified for entry, that they have been selected without discrimination, and their classmates will know it too. The result will actually be improved race relations and a continuance of the improvements we have seen in black performance in recent decades. Fifteen years from now, perhaps three or four percent of students in the top schools will be black. Until then, blacks can go to less competitive institutions of higher education, perhaps gaining greater advantage from their education in so doing. And, meanwhile, let us improve elementary and high school education—as we have been trying to do for the last 15 years or more.

Yet we cannot be quite so cavalier about the impact on public opinion—black and white—of a radical reduction in the number of black students at the Harvards, the Berkeleys, and the Amhersts. These institutions have become, for better or worse, the gateways to prominence, privilege, wealth, and power in American society. To admit blacks under affirmative action no doubt undermines the American meritocracy, but to exclude blacks from them by abolishing affirmative action would undermine the legitimacy of American democracy.

My argument is rooted in history. African Americans—and the struggle for their full and fair inclusion in U.S. society—have been a part of American history from the beginning. Our Constitution took special—but grossly unfair—account of their status, our greatest war was fought over their status, and our most important constitutional amendments were adopted because of the need to right past wrongs done to them. And, amid the civil rights revolution of the 1960s, affirmative action was instituted to compensate for the damage done to black achievement and life chances by almost 400 years of slavery, followed by state-sanctioned discrimination and massive prejudice.

Yet, today, a vast gulf of difference persists between the educational and occupational status of blacks and whites, a gulf that encompasses statistical measures of wealth, residential segregation, and social relationships with other Americans. Thirty years ago, with the passage of the great civil rights laws, one could have reasonably

expected—as I did—that all would be set right by now. But today, even after taking account of substantial progress and change, it is borne upon us how continuous, rooted, and substantial the differences between African Americans and other Americans remain.

The judgment of the elites who support affirmative action—the college presidents and trustees, the religious leaders, the corporate executives—and the judgment even of many of those who oppose it but hesitate to act against it—the Republican leaders in Congress, for example—is that the banning of preference would be bad for the country. I agree. Not that everyone's motives are entirely admirable; many conservative congressmen, for example, are simply afraid of being portrayed as racists even if their opposition to affirmative action is based on a sincere desire to support meritocratic principle. The college presidents who support affirmative action, under the fashionable mantra of diversity, also undoubtedly fear the student demonstrations that would occur if they were to speak out against preferences.

But there are also good-faith motives in this stand, and there is something behind the argument for diversity. What kind of institutions of higher education would we have if blacks suddenly dropped from six or seven percent of enrollment to one or two percent? The presence of blacks, in classes in social studies and the humanities, immediately introduces another tone, another range of questions (often to the discomfort of black students who do not want this representational burden placed upon them). The tone may be one of embarrassment and hesitation and self-censorship among whites (students and faculty). But must we not all learn how to face these questions together with our fellow citizens? We should not be able to escape from this embarrassment by the reduction of black students to minuscule numbers.

The weakness in the "diversity" defense is that college presidents are not much worried about the diversity that white working-class kids, or students of Italian or Slavic background, have to offer. Still, there is a reputable reason for that apparent discrepancy. It is that the varied ethnic and racial groups in the United States do not, to the same extent as African Americans, pose a test of the fairness of American institutions. These other groups have not been subjected to the same degree of persecution or exclusion. Their status is not, as the social status of African Americans is, the most enduring reproach to the egalitarian ideals of American society. And these other groups have made progress historically, and make progress today, at a rate that incorporates them into American society quickly compared to blacks.

This is the principal flaw in the critique of affirmative action. The critics are defending a vitally important principle, indeed, the one that should be the governing principle of institutions of higher education: academic competence as the sole test for distinguishing among applicants and students. This principle, which was fought for so energetically during the 1940s and 1950s through laws banning discrimination in admission on the basis of race, national origin, or religion, should not be put aside lightly. But, at present, it would mean the near exclusion from our best educational institutions of a group that makes up twelve percent of the population. In time, I am convinced, this preference will not be needed. Our laws and customs and our primary and secondary educational systems will fully incorporate black Americans into American society, as other disadvantaged groups have been incorporated. The positive trends of recent decades will continue. But we are still, though less than in the past, "two nations," and one of the nations cannot be excluded so thoroughly from institutions that confer access to the positions of greatest prestige and power.

On what basis can we justify violating the principle that measured criteria of merit should govern admission to selective institutions of higher education today? It is

## Testing Texas

The University of Texas Law School is ground zero of the post-affirmative action world. In a 1996 case, *Hopwood* v. *Texas*, the Fifth Circuit Court of Appeals struck down the law school's affirmative action policy. To ensure that each entering class of 500 or so included about 75 black and Hispanic students, the law school had been operating, in effect, a "dual" admissions system under which minority and non-minority students were being admitted by separate criteria—a method that the Supreme Court had struck down in the 1978 *Bakke* case. This fall, at the beginning of the first semester since *Hopwood*, 26 Mexican-American students, and four blacks, enrolled in Texas's first-year class—only a few more than the law school had had during the late '60s. Back then, the lack of minority representation hadn't been a big issue at the law school. Now, it is seen as a political and marketing disaster. Qualified minority students, whom schools fight over like star quarterbacks, are proving reluctant to apply to Texas. And so are the kind of progressively minded, out-of-state white students who help make the law school a national, rather than local, institution. "There have been times at recruitment events when majority and minority students approach the table together and say 'What does the entering class look like?' " Shelli Soto, the law school's assistant dean of admissions, told me.

Since *Hopwood* the law school has labored mightily to thread the eye of a legal needle—to admit large numbers of minority students without applying explicitly racial or ethnic criteria. The law school's application now includes an optional "Statement on Economic, Social or Personal Disadvantage"—an effort to tease more minority applicants out of the pool. " 'Qualified' really means a combination of your accomplishments and your experiences," Soto

explains. But this effort to side-step such statistical criteria as LSAT results doesn't really work. Black students do not have more extracurricular activities than whites and do not have better grade-point averages relative to their LSAT scores. And, because so few black students from truly disadvantaged backgrounds do well enough academically to qualify even under affirmative action criteria, "call-based" affirmative action doesn't help either. It seems the only way to admit large numbers of blacks is to admit them *because* they are black.

When I posed this problem to William Cunningham, the chancellor of the U.T. system, he said that the University of Texas Medical School had already adjusted its admissions criteria. "They want to look at people's motivation," the chancellor said, "the human traits that have to do with their wanting to be doctors." Was this being done in the hope that it would have a "race-positive effect?" I asked. Cunningham paused for a long, careful moment. "I don't want to say 'race-positive,' " he said. It wasn't clear what he *could* say without violating *Hopwood*. "We want to have a diverse student body," he said, "and we want to look at broader criteria than we have in the past to insure that we have a diverse student body." I told Cunningham that some law school faculty members were concerned about diluting admissions standards. The chancellor said very carefully, "I do think this is a time for us to be thoughtful and flexible." Was it possible to be "flexible" without either violating the terms of *Hopwood* or lowering standards? "It is," Cunningham sighed, "a difficult problem."

U.T.'s administrators are also looking over their shoulders at the Texas state legislature. A quarter of a century ago, it was virtually all white; now it has significant, and growing, black and His-

panic representation. As Russell Weintraub, a professor of contracts at the law school who was uneasy about affirmative action, says: "If the majority of people in this state are going to be Mexican-American and African American, and they are going to assume many of the leadership roles in the state, then it's going to be big trouble if the law school doesn't admit many minority students—it's going to be a bomb ready to explode."

Indeed, a few small bombs have detonated already. Soon after the *Hopwood* decision the state legislature passed a law that would require the University of Texas undergraduate college to accept the top ten percent of graduates from every high school in the state. This law, which would increase minority enrollment by automatically admitting the best students from heavily minority high schools, effectively reinstated a rule the college had abandoned three years ago in order to strengthen its standards.

The legislature then passed another law that requires public universities to apply the minimum grade-point average demanded of entering students to everyone—including athletes admitted on scholarship. The law, whose interpretation is now a matter of debate, would destroy the Texas Longhorn football team. Its sponsor, Ron Wilson, is a black State Assemblyman from Houston who attended both U.T. and U.T. Law. Wilson freely admits that the bill was designed to punish the university, which he saw as complicit in the *Hopwood* ruling. "If you're just a regular African American student with a two-point-five grade-point average, you can't get into the University of Texas," he told me. "But, if you can play the court jester out there on the football field and earn the university a million dollars, you can get in. As far as I'm of some significance to begin with that we in the United States have always been looser in this respect than more examination-bound systems of higher education in, say, Western Europe: we have always left room for a large degree of freedom for institutions of higher education, public as well as private, to admit students based on non-academic criteria. But I believe the main reasons we have to continue racial preferences for blacks are, first, because this country has a special obligation to blacks that has not been fully discharged, and second, because strict application of the principle of qualification would send a message of despair to many blacks, a message that the nation is indifferent to their difficulties and problems.

Many, including leading black advocates of eliminating preference, say no: the message would be, "Work harder and you can do it." Well, now that affirmative action is becoming a thing of the past in the public colleges and universities of California and Texas, we will have a chance to find out. Yet I wonder whether the mes-

---

concerned, that's hypocrisy. My bill says you can't have it both ways."

Wilson's real goal, of course, is not to exclude the athletes but to force the university to take everyone else. One solution, Wilson said, was "open admission." I asked if that wouldn't lead to a lowering of standards. Wilson said: "I don't look at academic standards as the Bible for academic excellence. There hasn't been enough input into those standards from African Americans and Hispanics to make them relevant to their community." And he added one more threat: if the university couldn't counteract the effect of *Hopwood*, he said, "We're going to move the money to follow the students to historically black colleges, if necessary."

The revenge of the legislature implies that the costs of doing away with affirmative action may turn out to be higher than the costs of keeping it. One of the most intriguing documents of the post-affirmative action era is an amicus brief which three professors at U.T. Law submitted to the Supreme Court in an affirmative action case last year. The three made the usual case in favor of affirmative action—but added a more novel, purely pragmatic argument: "A large public institution that serves the whole state cannot maintain its legitimacy if it is perceived to exclude minority students." The authors described the two bills that had passed the Texas legislature and noted that the University of California system is considering waiving its SAT requirement. If *Hopwood* becomes law for the country as a whole, the authors declared apocalyptically, "there will eventually be no great public universities—not for the nation and not for the white plaintiffs either."

In other words, affirmative action represents not a threat to academic standards but the surest means of pre- serving them. This argument sounds so perverse that it's hard to take seriously, but it's not without foundation. Douglas Laycock, one of the authors of the brief, said: "We're in the middle of a full-blown attack on every means we have to measure merit and on the very idea of merit, and it's mostly driven by the issue of race." What Laycock was suggesting is that, in a straightforward battle between the old meritocratic principle on which conservatives make their stand and the new ideals of diversity and inclusion, meritocracy is likely to lose. And, several weeks later, *The New York Times* inadvertently confirmed his point in a front-page story headlined, "COLLEGES LOOK FOR ANSWERS TO RACIAL GAPS IN TESTING". Donald M. Stewart, president of the College Board, lamented the "social cost" of relying on standardized tests on which minority students fare poorly. "America can't stand that," Stewart said.

Should we regret the political and marketplace dynamics that essentially force institutions like the University of Texas Law School to practice affirmative action? The original rationale for affirmative action was that it helped disadvantaged students overcome the effects of discrimination, both current and historical. No one questions that U.T. Law is guilty of past discrimination. The school was off-limits to black students as a matter of state law until a celebrated 1950 Supreme Court decision, *Sweatt* v. *Painter*. But most of the black students who attend the law school now come from other states, and they are scarcely more likely than the white students to come from a disadvantaged background.

What about "diversity"? The diversity argument has rapidly eclipsed the past-discrimination argument, because it is so much rosier and more consensual. It's hard to dispute the notion that institutions benefit from "diverse" points of view. But is that a large enough good to justify disadvantaging whites? And there's something arbitrary about the math. Randall Kennedy, a professor at Harvard Law School and another uneasy supporter of affirmative action, says: "I have my problems with the idea that we've got to have diversity because in the year 2000 the census says this and this about a jurisdiction. Does that mean that, if you're in Maine, you don't have to have more than one black student?"

The simple and painful truth is that affirmative action rests on a bedrock of failure. The reason why the University of Texas Law School needed affirmative action in the first place is that, according to a university deposition in *Hopwood*, only 88 black students in the entire country had a combination of grades and law boards in 1992 that reached the mean of admitted white students; only one of those black students came from Texas. One lesson of post-*Hopwood* Texas is that eliminating affirmative action would virtually wipe out the black presence in top schools. For conservatives, that's just the way the meritocratic cookie crumbles, but for most Americans, justly proud of the extent to which our leading institutions have been integrated over the last quarter century, that's likely to be an unacceptable outcome.

Affirmative action is, at bottom, a dodge. It allows us to put off the far harder work: ending the isolation of young black people and closing the academic gap that separates black students—even middle-class black students—from whites. When we commit ourselves to that, we can do without affirmative action, but not before.

JAMES TRAUB

JAMES TRAUB is a staff writer for *The New Yorker*.

sage of affirmative action to black students today really ever has been, "Don't work hard; it doesn't matter for you because you're black; you will make it into college anyway." Colleges are indeed looking for black students, but they are also looking for some minimal degree of academic effort and accomplishment, and it is a rare ambitious African American student seeking college entry who relaxes because he believes his grades won't matter *at all.*

One of the chief arguments against racial preference in college and professional school admissions is that more blacks will drop out, the quality of blacks who complete the courses of instruction will be inferior, and they will make poorer lawyers, doctors, or businessmen. Dropping out is common in American higher education and does not necessarily mean that one's attendance was a total loss. Still, the average lower degree of academic performance has, and will continue to have, effects even for the successful: fewer graduating black doctors will go into research; more will go into practice and administration. More blacks in business corporations will be in personnel. Fewer graduating black lawyers will go into corporate law firms; more will work for government.

And more will become judges, because of another and less disputed form of affirmative action, politics. Few protest at the high number of black magistrates in cities with large black populations—we do not appoint judges by examination. Nor do we find it odd or objectionable that Democratic presidents will appoint more black lawyers as judges, or that even a Republican president will be sure to appoint one black Supreme Court justice. What is at work here is the principle of participation. It is a more legitimate principle in politics and government than it is for admission to selective institutions of higher education. But these are also gateways to power, and the principle of participation cannot be flatly ruled out for them.

Whatever the case one may make in general for affirmative action, many difficult issues remain: What kind, to what extent, how long, imposed by whom, by what decision-making process? It is important to bear in mind that affirmative action in higher education admissions is, for the most part, a policy that has been chosen (albeit sometimes under political pressure) by the institutions themselves. There are racial goals and targets for employment and promotion for all government contractors, including colleges and universities, set by government fiat, but targets on student admissions are not imposed by government, except for a few traditionally black or white institutions in the South.

Let us preserve this institutional autonomy. Just as I would resist governmentally imposed requirements that these institutions meet quotas of black admissions, so would I also oppose a judicial or legislative *ban* on the use of race in making decisions on admission. Ballot

measures like Proposition 209 are more understandable given the abuses so common in systems of racial preference. But it is revealing that so many other states appear to have had second thoughts and that the California vote is therefore not likely to be repeated. (A recent report in *The Chronicle of Higher Education* was headlined "LEGISLATURES SHOW LITTLE ENTHUSIASM FOR MEASURES TO END RACIAL PREFERENCES"; in this respect, the states are not unlike Congress.)

We should retain the freedom of institutions of higher and professional education to make these determinations for themselves. As we know, they would almost all make room for a larger percentage of black students than would otherwise qualify. This is what these institutions do today. They defend what they do with the argument that diversity is a good thing. I think what they really mean is that a large segment of the American population, significantly not only demographically but historically and politically and morally, cannot be so thoroughly excluded. I agree with them.

I have discussed affirmative action only in the context of academic admissions policy. Other areas raise other questions, other problems. And, even in this one area of college and university admissions, affirmative action is not a simple and clear and uncomplicated solution. It can be implemented wisely or foolishly, and it is often done foolishly, as when college presidents make promises to protesting students that they cannot fulfill, or when institutions reach too far below their minimal standards with deleterious results for the academic success of the students they admit, for their grading practices, and for the legitimacy of the degrees they offer. No matter how affirmative action in admissions is dealt with, other issues remain or will emerge. More black students, for example, mean demands for more black faculty and administrators and for more black-oriented courses. Preference is no final answer (just as the elimination of preference is no final answer). It is rather what is necessary to respond to the reality that, for some years to come, yes, we are still two nations, and both nations must participate in the society to some reasonable degree.

Fortunately, those two nations, by and large, want to become more united. The United States is not Canada or Bosnia, Lebanon or Malaysia. But, for the foreseeable future, the strict use of certain generally reasonable tests as a benchmark criterion for admissions would mean the de facto exclusion of one of the two nations from a key institutional system of the society, higher education. Higher education's governing principle is qualification—merit. Should it make room for another and quite different principle, equal participation? The latter should never become dominant. Racial proportional representation would be a disaster. But basically the answer is yes—the principle of equal participation can and should be given some role. This decision has costs. But the alternative is too grim to contemplate.

# is *anybody* out there?

## TODAY'S BARREN LABOR LANDSCAPE IS FORCING DESPERATE CORPORATIONS TO RETHINK THEIR HIRING STRATEGIES AND PUMP UP THE PERKS.

### BY ALEX MARKELS

i t's tough enough to fill the hundreds of vacancies for computer programmers at Microsoft Corp. But try searching for qualified candidates when you can't even find enough workers to do the hiring.

That's the predicament in which recruiting director David Pritchard finds himself. Although his staff has swelled to more than 80 (from only 60 two years ago), he's still struggling to fill five positions—two of which have remained open for more than a year. The result: longer searches and skyrocketing hiring costs. Not just for technology developers but for the numerous jobs that support them. "We need salespeople, financial analysts—you name it," says Pritchard. Indeed, in Microsoft's 18,000-strong U.S. work force, approximately 2,000 positions are currently open.

Pritchard is going to unprecedented lengths to fill them. In the past year, his office has doubled the number of colleges it recruits from and drastically increased its advertising budget and hiring presence on the Internet. "Even then," he says, "we had to quadruple the number of headhunters on contract."

MICROSOFT'S PREDICAMENT IS HARDLY UNIQUE. WITH THE UNEMployment rate at a 20-year low, the growing labor crunch is affecting companies from high-tech firms to gift wrap makers.

For the first time in at least a decade, the tables have turned on companies, which have long held the upper hand in hiring. Sign-on bonuses for college graduates have become de rigueur. So has the need to start new employees with the same vacation benefits they'd accrued in their former jobs instead of the typical two weeks. Desperate to fill critical slots, employers that never paid relocation expenses now also foot the bill for placing spouses in new jobs and children in day care or private school. Meanwhile, both new and veteran employees demand,

and are likely to receive, greater leeway to work from home or rearrange their schedule to accommodate outside commitments.

Some employers are looking to fill vacancies with downsized workers—until recently considered by many recruiters as castoffs not desirable enough for their original employer to keep. "We've started talking to outplacement firms, which we never used to do," says Matthew Weinberg, chief executive of the Weinberg Group, a scientific and management consulting firm based in Washington, D.C. A key managing consultant position there has remained open for 14 months.

At the entry-level end of the hiring spectrum, some managers say they have been forced to lower standards—taking on workers unable to speak fluent English or those without the employment history or references previously required to land a job. Absenteeism, once a cause for dismissal, is tolerated. "We're definitely more lenient on disciplinary action," says Mike Davies, president of Flagship Converters, a fast-growing manufacturer of gift wrap and ribbons in Danbury, Connecticut. "We just can't afford to let a lot of these people go."

Edward L. Gubman, a management consultant and the author of *The Talent Solution: Aligning Strategy and People to Achieve Extraordinary Results*, assesses the situation bluntly: "Employers are starting to scrape the bottom of the barrel. And when you do that, you're more likely to bring on people with drug and alcohol problems and criminal records."

Yet many employers have avoided doing one thing that could fill jobs: increasing wages. Although salaries for computer programmers have risen by as much as 8.8 percent in the last year, government statistics show that hourly earnings for the average American worker increased by a meager 2.1

# "Employers are starting to scrape the bottom of the barrel because all of the qualified people are gone."

percent. And despite reports of hiring bonuses and a recruiting feeding frenzy on college campuses, recent graduates still earn about 9 percent less (in real terms, adjusted for inflation) than they did a decade ago, according to a study by the Economic Policy Institute, a Washington research organization.

"On the whole, employers still aren't willing to increase real wages for workers," says John Schmitt, a labor economist who worked on the study. And while bulging want-ad sections

and worker shortages suggest increasing upward pressure on pay, he says, "the overall result of the so-called labor shortage appears to be a more balanced, flexible work life."

THEREIN LIES THE reason some experts refer to the current hiring predicament as the "so-called labor shortage." In their view, qualified workers exist to fill the numerous vacancies, but they are either unwilling to change jobs without a pay increase or choosing a more flexible career path.

That's why companies are starting to accommodate employees' lifestyles. Take, for example, Coopers & Lybrand, where some jobs require long hours and constant travel. "We don't disqualify candidates now because they say, 'I'm terrific, and I'd like to work four days a week,'" says Iris Goldfein, vice chairman of human resources at the Chicago office of the accounting and consulting giant. "There was a time when we would not have hired that person. But that's not an option anymore."

Anxious to hold on to valued employees

as well as fill vacancies, many companies have introduced telecommuting programs. At Servus Financial Corp. in Herndon, Virginia, a loan processor complained that she would have to quit after buying a home far from work. CEO Douglas Dolton instituted a program to allow processors to work from home three days a week. "We've got to be progressive, or we're going to lose people," he says.

Many employers have been forced to offer more flexible arrangements throughout their ranks in response to the demands of today's graduates for greater control over their schedules and working conditions. For many managers who entered the job market in the 1970s (when high unemployment and stagnant economic growth compelled them to put their best foot forward), courting these young, often cagey applicants is downright uncomfortable.

"It's the Gen X problem," says Michael R. Gaulke, the 52-year-old CEO and president of Exponent, a 650-employee engineering and scientific consulting firm in Menlo Park, California. "Candidates are turning the tables and asking, 'Why should I work for you?' Gone are the days when candidates carefully selected which bond of paper to put their résumés on," he says. "There's a real lack of formality in the application process now, which makes it a lot harder to assess communications skills and level of interest."

Indeed, today's young workers start their careers with demographics on their side. *Workforce 2020*, a book published by

## PLAYING YOUR CARDS RIGHT

### COURT THEM, KEEP THEM

There's a skilled customer service rep in the waitress who served your Caesar salad at lunch. Just ask Provident Bank of Maryland. Eager to find top-notch customer service employees, the bank has turned a simple card into a career come-on.

Provident gives employees referral cards to dole out to talented service providers in any industry. The cards compliment people on their customer service skills and advertise that the bank is actively seeking such employees. Staffers who refer new hires receive $150 to $350, depending on the positions filled. It's a simple, inexpensive way to attract new talent, and it has given the bank's employer appeal a tremendous boost.

Human resources director Jeanne Uphouse says that since introducing the program last year, Provident has hired more than half the applicants attracted by a card come-on. In addition, employees on the lookout for recruits have become mindful of what constitutes good service, and, she says, recipients "get a huge charge out of the cards," which brings the bank welcome recognition.

—**Geanne Rosenberg**

## EXERCISING CAREER CONTROL

### COURT THEM, KEEP THEM

Forget lunchtime aerobics: Since last November, Unisys Corp. has focused on keeping its workers' careers fit. And the only exertion on the employee's part is the click of a mouse. Anyone on the Unisys payroll—anywhere in the world—has only to log on to the company's interactive intranet-based Career Fitness Centre to access a listing of potential mentors, direct links to skills-training Web sites, career advice, and job postings.

After years of downsizing, the Blue Bell, Pennsylvania-based technology giant switched into hiring mode. The best way to build career-long relationships with its new employees was to reach out to them via the Web. Just as important, says David Aker, senior vice president of human resources, the program helps Unisys "re-recruit" existing employees, reducing the likelihood that they will seek opportunities elsewhere.

Knowledge is power, and Unisys hopes that by sharing forecasts of the company's direction and job growth, it will empower employees to map out long-term career paths within its global ranks.

—**G.R.**

# "Candidates are turning the tables, asking, 'Why should I work for you?' There's a real lack of formality now."

the Hudson Institute in Indianapolis, reports that fewer Americans were born between 1966 and 1985 than during the previous two decades—an 11 percent drop. The result: "There just aren't enough 21- to 28-year-olds entering the work force," says Gubman. "And until the baby boomlet starts to work in 2004, there's going to be a continuing shortage of young talent."

Even worse, colleges aren't churning out enough graduates with the skills most in demand. "We're moving from a mass labor force to an elite one," says Jeremy Rifkin, president of the Foundation on Economic Trends in Washington and the author of *The End of Work: The Decline of the Global Labor Force and the Dawn of the Post-Market Era*. Elite workers—experts in esoteric disciplines such as bioinformatics, genetics, and computer forensics—represent a small but growing segment of the work force. "They're the ones who really stand to benefit from the labor shortage," Rifkin says.

For example, computer science jobs are expected to nearly double, to more than 2.5 million, within the next decade, while the number of people earning computer science degrees remains essentially the same as it was a decade ago.

Armed with this knowledge, younger workers in many industries, who are more tech-savvy than their predecessors, are job hopping like never before. "You sense that younger folks don't have any sense of loyalty," says Flagship's Davies. He's had some success hiring and training young graduates, "but after six months, they want to leave. There's the feeling that anybody can get work if they want it. So you can afford to give up your job for a while because you can go elsewhere."

Even workers still in college have the same attitude. "They get their paycheck, and they bolt," says Dolton. To combat the problem, his firm offers lucrative compensation to sales specialists—with a hitch. "We sit down with them and ask, 'What is your commitment to us?' If, say, they agree to stay for at

least six months, we tell them we'll pay them $11 per hour, but that they don't get the eleventh dollar until they reach the six months."

IRONICALLY, BURNT-OUT BABY boomers may be learning a few things about work-life balance from the younger generation. Weary after years of restructuring at their companies, many who survived the downsizing era are beginning to reap the rewards of a rising stock market. As they become financially secure, they're eager to lead more balanced lives, opting to step off the career ladder to start their own businesses, consult part-time, travel, or even move up their retirement dates.

Economists expect the situation to snowball as the majority of boomers begin retiring en masse around 2010. Until then, "employers are going to have an increasingly difficult time with their manpower planning," says Carol D'Amico, co-author of *Workforce 2020*. "They're going to have aging employees requiring a different set of benefits and working arrangements."

The immediate impact of the graying labor pool is a dearth of experienced mid- and upper-level managers. "I've got some great high-level positions available," says Charles W. Sweet, president of A. T. Kearney Executive Search in Chicago. "But when I approach people, they say, 'Look, I'm thinking of making [career] changes, but it's going to be a whole lot different from what I'm doing now.' They're thinking of volunteering for a nonprofit or just dropping out and

# PROMOTING PETS

## COURT THEM, KEEP THEM

You can bring Fido to work, get your pearly whites fixed aboard a mobile dental van, and ease away tension with a massage in the conference room. These are just a few of the perks offered at the Mountain View, California, campus of Netscape Communications Corp.

To Margie Mader, Netscape's human resources director (her business card reads *bringing in the cool people*), such appealing programs are "a tremendous recruiting tool." The perks are particularly helpful in Netscape's romancing of graduating college students. Says Mader, "They go a long way toward describing the culture here."

Netscape's on-site offerings also serve a more practical end: as "productivity tools, because a lot of the little things are being taken care of." Employees can spend more time at work without neglecting the errands normally performed after hours.

Thanks to Netscape's pets-allowed policy, dogs and rabbits come to the office, but there are limits. Some employees are allergic to cats.

—G.R.

seeing if life with no formal work is attractive. And if it's not, they know the labor market is so tight they can always go back. It's a very prevalent theme."

If this reluctance to stay on the fast track presents challenges for recruiters like Sweet, it nonetheless feeds demand for their services from companies frantically seeking management talent. "We've gone from paying nothing to hire new managers to forking over 20 to 30 percent of the individual's first-year salary," says Matthew Weinberg.

Last year, the executive search industry had revenues of some $6.5 billion, an 18 percent increase over 1996. "And this should be another boom year," says Stephen H. Collins, editor of *Executive Recruiter News,* which tracks the industry. His firm predicts that by 2000, industry revenues will hit $10 billion. It's a trend that makes the search for recruiters at Microsoft all the more exasperating to David Pritchard. "A lot of recruiters want to go into business for themselves," he says. "Instead of working as our employees, they can come to us with a few candidates, maybe get one or two hired, and earn a big placement fee."

Like many corporations, Microsoft once shied away from using headhunters. But market conditions in the last two years have forced it to increase the number of search firms now on contract to more than 100, from only 25 in 1996. "We're at the point where it doesn't matter where candidates are coming from," Pritchard says. "If they're qualified, we want to talk to them."

---

ALEX MARKELS *is a former staff reporter at* The Wall Street Journal *and is currently writing a book. He can be reached at alexm@email.com.*

# Job-hunting Professionals
## Are Looking for Respect

It's a job-searcher's market, and professional-level employees are more than happy
to leave the companies they feel "done them wrong." Here's why they're leaving,
what they're looking for and how to keep the ones you've got.

### By Gillian Flynn

David Mitchell, a middle manager at an East Coast telecommunications firm, talks the spit-mad talk of a scorned lover when he speaks of his company. With machine-gun frequency, out shoot words like "betrayed," "used" and "disrespected."

Lucky man. Just when Mitchell felt like he couldn't take anymore, like he had to get out of this failed relationship, along came a honey of a job market—4.3 percent unemployment at press time. After 12 years, he's looking to get out, and it's going to be very easy.

And very satisfying. Revenge is sweet, you know.

That's right, all you downsizers and 'reengineer-ers,' all you executives who talked about the pain of laying off workers on the way to the golf course. All you employers who stretched and stretched the workweeks, who put careers on the back-burner, and brushed families to the side. All you companies who treated employees poorly—just because you knew they had nowhere else to go. You had it good for most of the '90s. No more. It's payback time—and you know what they say about paybacks.

Even if your company really did its best, you're in for a tough time. The anti-employer sentiment runs deep. It's a job hunter's market, and employees are looking (even the ones you think aren't). Smart HR people will take the time to find out just why they're leaving (because they CAN), what they're looking for (R-E-S-P-E-C-T) and how to hold on to the ones you've got.

WORKFORCE talked to job-hunters (whose names have been changed within this article), and along with E-span, an online job-posting service, conducted a survey of professional and managerial employees to give HR people the information they need for hiring—and retaining—this much-coveted group. (For more information on the survey and its results, see "Money Isn't Everything and Other Revelations of the WORKFORCE/E-span survey.")

**Wake-up call: Do you know where your managers are?** For the past five years, Mitchell would begin the workweek in a sweat and get worse from there. The firings came on Fridays, so as the 14-hour workdays ticked down, the stress built up. Once Friday was over and his job was still intact, he'd take a deep breath, then start the cycle again. He considered himself fortunate—he was a rare bird, a middle manager with a job. But with the market as it is now, he's had time to lick his wounds—and build his resentment.

"This upswing in the economy is a blessing," he says. "I'm getting out."

Adam Kind, a supervisor at a Midwest manufacturer, also speaks of Friday firings and the loss of co-workers, of years "waiting for the ax to fall." Like Mitchell, he sees his imminent resignation as just desserts for a company that "did a really poor job of [reengineering]. There was no communication. The executives didn't share their grand plan with anyone below the director level . . . I feel like, hey it's my turn to make you guys sweat it. I'm holding the cards, and it feels really good."

In Kansas City, Missouri, Barry Jackson, workforce planning and staffing director for Hallmark Cards Inc., says he hears this refrain repeatedly from managerial employees proffering their resumes. They're coming to Hallmark, he says, because the card company offers a balm for employees who feel they've been burned by their employers.

"They're looking for an organization that will be committed to them, and Hallmark has that image," he says. "We're seeing more people looking at us because they're tired of the vagaries of what Wall Street does to the public sector, or what their public company has done to them in the way of downsizing. Our private ownership allows us to be more long-term focused; we're not driven by the stock market or by quarterly earnings reports."

But it's not just employees hit (or missed) by a downsizing who are bitter. Many others feel they've been poorly treated, whether by career stagnation, lackluster management or a generally unhealthy corporate culture.

And the very scary part is, you probably won't be able to pick out the ones harboring resentments. Most of the job searchers WORKFORCE spoke with said they'd kept dissatisfactions to themselves because they felt their superiors or HR didn't really care—and didn't need to care—with the job market as tight as it was for most of the '90s.

They complained that the only time their superiors asked them if they had problems or concerns was during the shaky ground of a performance review, when, conventional wisdom goes, the smart employee nods and smiles and waits to hear whether there's going to be a raise.

That is, if they got a performance review—another chief complaint. What to executives is a six-month delay to an employee is a half-year insult. Anne Flaherty, a sales director for a Minnesota computer products company, is looking for a job that will give her more customer contact. Asked if she had ever told her supervisors this, Flaherty replied, "They've never asked. They give performance reviews when they feel like it. They don't care enough to do it on time. And it's not just about the money. It's the one time a year when you have one hour of your boss's complete attention. I waited eight months for my last one. It's not just bad business, it's rude and thoughtless. I don't care if you're busy—to me it signals you don't give a damn."

It's not that employees are expecting a corporate Nirvana to come floating their way—few wear those kind of rose-colored glasses anymore—but many think they can do better.

In fact in the WORKFORCE/E-span survey, of 114 professional-level employees who planned to change jobs in the next 12 months, 85 percent said the culture and values of the organization would influence their decision.

As Mitchell, who's willing to move and take a pay cut for the right position, explains: "Right now I just want control over my life. Sane hours and a company that respects me."

**The most important of your company's offerings may be simple respect.** It's not a better paycheck most job searchers want (OK, it's not JUST a better paycheck—89 percent of 115 job-hunters surveyed said salary would play a role in their search).

But just as important, employees want to believe their company really cares about them. That can take form in a number of ways, but it generally boils down to career development, adult treatment and appreciation for a job well done.

Tracy Bumpus, a job-search coach for First Impressions in Murfreesboro, Tennessee, says most of her clients—and she has many these days—are already employed but seriously looking. "People who've been working jobs for paychecks are now seeing an opportunity to work for a company they love."

Kevin Daniels, a marketing manager in Memphis, is looking for a company that will give him room to grow—unlike his current employer. Despite five years of gushing reviews and satisfactory raises, he feels like he's been stagnating. The problem: The company's outdated seniority system. Promotions aren't based on merit, Daniels says, but on the number of years an employee has punched in. He worries that he could languish another decade in the same job, with the same skills before someone leaves and opens a position.

"I'm looking for a company that takes its people seriously," he says. "I'm interviewing with a company right now for a position at my current level and same pay. But this company has its own corporate school, and they pay for university work. They really seem to want their employees to do well. Which, of course, makes sense."

Indeed, of the surveyed job-hunters who plan to jump ship in the next year, 94 percent said job responsibilities would be "very" to "extremely" influential in their decision.

In that line, corporate training is one thing Gary Beu, partner in charge of HR for the Chicago office of Arthur Andersen LLP, has long emphasized to candidates. He says that most recruits mention Andersen's reputation for commitment to continuing education, opportunities to advance and its wide range of client services that helps employees develop new skills. "Those are the qualities that have always attracted top people to us," he says.

Bumpus agrees that job searchers want an organization where they can grow. "Lots of my clients have been stuck at companies not offering any employee development. That's the difference between leaving and staying for most of them."

Erni Bridges, technical recruiter at Data Systems Analyst Inc. in Fairfax, Virginia, says she also hears job hunters talk of the desire for a place to stay and grow—and, in the white-hot market of information technology, she needs as many as she can get. So she sells the entrepreneurial spirit of DSA, and the length of service, which averages twelve and one-half years.

And she gives them a healthy dose of the R word. "People want to associate themselves with companies that are really doing it, not just lip synching it: respecting individuals." She starts "doing it" right from the get-go. When she meets a promising professional at one of the 12-plus job fairs she attends a year, she immediately faxes his or her resume to managers back at base—and lines up interviews right on the spot. A quick response shows DSA is serious—and respects the job hunter's time.

For other professionals, respect falls more into the quality-of-life category. Surprisingly, this seems to have less to do with work-family goodies like daycare and more to do with basic work-life respect, such as flexible scheduling. (In fact, only 9% of those surveyed said child-care considerations would affect their decision to stay or leave their companies.)

Alice Dawson, a Dallas business consultant, is looking for an organization that will give her exactly what her former company refused her four years ago: some control over her time. When Dawson had twins in 1994, she realized full-time work and full-time mommying weren't feasible, so she asked to cut back her hours. "If they'd shown even the slightest interest in my situation—even letting me [use flextime] or take one day a week off, I'd have stayed, because we really needed that second paycheck."

Instead, Dawson started her own consulting business to bring in extra money. But with the twins ready to start school this year, she wants to get back in a company fold. "But I won't go to a company that doesn't have a really amazing work-family structure, that realizes employees are living people with lives outside work."

That's a quality Jan Bremner, deputy director of HR at Illinois State University in Normal, can brag on. Being an educational institution, Bremner says, ISU puts a lot of emphasis on flexibility and family. In fact, the school has done so well in attracting people, it's never had to really sell itself. "We've always had good work-life benefits, but we never really called them that," she laughs. "But people in the community hear about them and know this is a good place to work: flexible schedules, and the whole environment is pretty laid back."

That's not something Ed Simon would ever say about his Boston employer. Simon, an account manager, says he's tired of being treated like a college kid, with his superiors marking the time he comes in, the time he leaves, even how long his lunches are.

"The culture is ridiculous. It's like all the employees are pitted against each other. You feel like if you take a long lunch you have to explain to everyone that you'll stay an hour later—when it's really nobody's business as long as you're doing your job. I'm sick of coming into work already defensive . . . I want to work with grown-ups."

**How do you hold on to the employees you've got?** You know why they're leaving, you know what they're looking for . . . can you keep them? The answer is . . . maybe. You're in for a bumpy ride if you're in the technology business (but you probably already know that). With salaries expanding exponentially, companies may just have to do what Janet Leavey, an East Coast computer engineer suggests: "Show me the money! Whatever company gives me the best bid, that's where I'm going." Leavey says there's a realization among tekkies that these are the last of the good old days—in just a few years, college grads will flood the market with the very skills now in such short supply. "I figure I'd better lock in while the going's good," she says.

Of course, money is an issue with most professionals. But that doesn't mean you have to keep upping the paychecks. It goes back to respect—employees want to feel fairly treated.

At Inland Star Distribution Centers in Fresno, California, an ESOP does just that. Eighty-two percent of the company is owned by employees. Kerry Haverty, director of human resources, says that's just the key to getting people to stick with the transportation firm: She doesn't know of any other companies in Inland's particular industry that offer ownership. The other catch, of course, is that employees aren't fully vested until they've been there six years. "I think that helps keep people here," she says.

Seventy-five percent of job-hunters surveyed agreed—they said long-term rewards such as stock ownership would influence their decision to stay at a current job.

But in the end, keeping employees often means giving them what they came to the company for in the first place. At Andersen, that's development, development, development. Of course, a company can't be all things to all people. Beu knows, through exit interviews, that some people grow weary of the stress, long hours and frequent travel Andersen's career path requires.

And occasionally, that careful training and development makes employees so desirable they get raided by other companies—or even Andersen's own clients. But Beu and the other executives accept this as an inevitability. "We often soothe our frustrations over losing people by recognizing it as a tribute to our ability to attract outstanding talent and shape it further. We're the victims of our own success in that regard," Beu laughs.

Hallmark is another promise-keeper. It promises a family atmosphere and a concerned management team, and it delivers, Jackson says.

Employees really are part of the fold—owning one-fourth of the company has that effect. And, through flexible hours and the like, they really do have more time for themselves.

Of course, the other side to that coin, Jackson admits, is that Hallmark doesn't have the highest compensation package in the market—but the high payers, he points out, are also more demanding of time. "We don't ask for your soul when you show up at this place," he says. "That's not what we're about."

Finally, the company really does take an interest in development: Approximately 90 percent of management positions are filled internally. It all pays off. The average employee tenure is just over 14 years. Even employees who quit may not be gone for long: 16 percent of those who left in '96 came back. The reason they cited for their return? They missed Hallmark's people and culture (a culture that won the company the 1996 Quality of Life Optimas Award from WORKPLACE).

Maybe the current job-switching trend all boils down to a favorite saying of Jackson's: "Most companies today say employees are their greatest assets. My question then is, why do they treat them like they're liabilities?"

If they do, they'd better stop. Right now. Just like any relationship you want to thrive, HR professionals need to take good care of their workforces. Limit downsizings, or at least make them respectful. Ensure career growth, or at least show interest. Work with employees to give them the schedules they want, or at least the schedules they need. Treat employees right. Of all the tricky, complicated tasks HR professionals must perform, this should be one of the easiest—and most pleasurable.

---

*Gillian Flynn is the editor-at-large for Workforce. E-mail gflynn2@aol.com to comment.*

# Money Isn't Everything and Other Revelations of the WORKFORCE/E-span Survey

**B**ecause it's just the perfect weather for job-hopping right now, WORKFORCE decided to join E-Span, an on-line job-posting service, to conduct a survey that would give HR professionals the information they needed for hiring managerial- and professional-level employees.

We sent 2,000 surveys to *Businessweek* subscribers with managerial or professional titles, and received 471 responses. Of those, 115 said they were very to somewhat likely to change jobs in the next 12 months. Below are some of the more enlightening interests, traits and characteristics of those job-hunters.

## WHAT PROFESSIONALS WANT

Percent who said these were "extremely" to "very" influential in their decision to stay or leave their company:

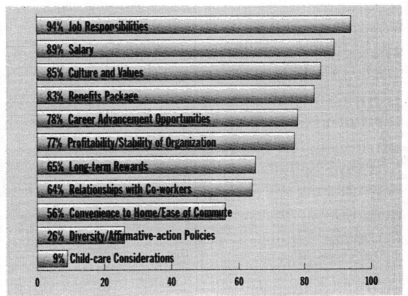

## HOW THEY GET IT

Importance of the following resources when looking for a new job. Percent who said these were "extremely" to "very" important:

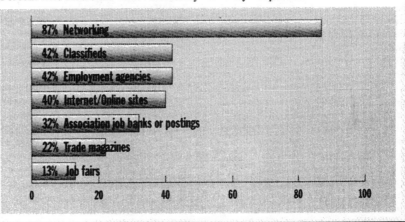

BY MIKE FROST

# Essential Bookmarks:
# Start Your Web Research with These 10 Sites.

Pretend, for a moment, that you are a busy HR executive. There are already too few hours in the day to accomplish all that needs to be done as part of your job. So, when the time comes to venture onto the World Wide Web—to research a policy, to track down a government regulation, to recruit a potential employee—you don't have a lot of time to waste scouring the thousands of web sites with HR-related services and information.

Maybe that scenario doesn't require a very long stretch of imagination.

Yet, many HR professionals end up wasting a lot of time scouring search engines and clicking through web sites that may—or may not—contain accurate and up-to-date information. Despite the array of HR-related World Wide Web sites, we find that there are certain sites we come back to again and again, for current, reliable information, presented in a logical manner.

Here is a list of 10 of these essential HR sites. You can make your use of the Internet more efficient by using these as starting points when conducting research on the World Wide Web.

Our criteria for inclusion on this list: In addition to containing valuable and accurate information, the bulk of the site has to be available for free use by anyone on the internet. Also, sites must be refreshed on a regular basis, to include timely information.

• **SHRM Online** (http://wwwshrm.org/). Forgive the immodesty, but the Society's web site does rate as one of the best sources for free HR information on the Internet. Daily news updates in the *HR News* section (http://www.shrm.org/hrnews) ensure that the site reflects the latest HR information. Other online publications—including *HRMagazine* (http://www.shrm.org/hrmagazine), *Workplace Visions* (http://www.shrm.org/issues/visions), *Mosaics* (http://www.shrm.org/diversity/) and *Washington Insider*

(http://www.shrm.org/government)—contain up-to-date analysis of the current and future trends. HR-related job openings from around the world are posted thrice weekly (http://www.shrm.org/jobs/). Member exclusives include an extensive library of research papers (http://www.shrm.org/whitepapers) and a bulletin board area (http://www.shrm.org/hrtalk).

• **Department of Labor** (http://www.dol.gov). Next time someone challenges you to name a government program that works, respond by saying "the Internet." Not only is the Internet as we know it a result of initiatives launched by the federal government, but some of the most informative sites on the Internet are operated by government offices.

## WHAT'S NEW

Keeping track of state-related employment laws has become easier. CCH, Inc., now provides SHRM members with monthly updates of statutes enacted around the country. To view the page, visit http://www.shrm.org/cch/. SHRM membership log-in is required.

• Two years' worth of *HRMagazine* book reviews are now available in the SHRMStore (http://shrmstore.shrm.org). The reviews include links that allow users to order the books online. Members receive special discounts. First-time users must register before they can order books online. See the SHRMStore for more details.

Put the Department of Labor web site at the top of that list. The DOL home page includes legal guidance, statistics and management advice. Offices within the Labor Department also offer useful web sites, including the Bureau of Labor Statistics (http://stats.bls.gov) and the Occupational Safety and Health Administration (http://www.osha.gov).

Social Security Administration (http://www.ssa.gov). Another excellent web site provided by the federal government, the SSA page includes resources for employers, such as wage reporting guidelines. Information on employees' Social Security benefits makes this site a valuable link for your HR intranet.

# From the E-mailbag

Have you run across a web site that provides assistance in recruiting in Europe, specifically United Kingdom countries?" Since we have no practical experience when it comes to recruiting on the other side of the pond, we posed this question on the Institute for International HR bulletin board (http://www.shrm.org/international), and to contacts in the U.K. The consensus: While the United States is ahead of the rest of the world when it comes to online recruiting, there are a number of fine sites that specialize in recruiting in the U.K.

Domestic users will welcome the familiar look and feel of CareerMosaic UK (http://careermosiac-uk.co.uk) and The Monster Board UK (http://www.monster.co.uk), which strongly resemble their American cousins. TheJob (http://thejob.com) draws applicants and employers not only from England, but from thoughout Europe. The Appointments (http://www.taps.com) and Work-Web (http://www.workweb.co.uk) are recruiting mega-sites, complete with virtual recruiting centers for employer, resume databases, and useful information for both employers and potential employees.

Useful indices of British recruiting sites can be found on the Riley Guide (http://www.dbm.com/jobguide) and Yahoo U.K. (http://www.yahoo.co.uk/Regional/Countries/United_Kingdom/Business_and_Economy/Employment/Jobs/).

---

- **Cornell University's School of Industrial and Labor Relations** (http://www.ilr.cornell.edu). The online Catherwood Library provides an electronic bookshelf of labor-related government documents. It also offers Work.Index, a directory of Internet sites relevant to the field of industrial and labor relations.

- **InsideHR** (http://www.insideHR.com). The most valuable features of this newcomer, presented by the Research Institute of America, include news updates, a best practices library and bulletin boards. Registration is required, but the site is free. InsideHR's fee-based companion service, HR Wire, is also useful.

- **Law Journal Extra's Employment and Labor Law** (http://www.ljextra.com/practice/laboremployment/labcol.html). Updated virtually every day, this web site contains analysis of major court decisions involving personnel and labor law. It's particularly strong in reporting cases in the New York/NewJersey area.

- **HR Live** (http://www.hrlive.com). The cornerstone of JWTWorks' HR Live is the weekly Layoff Updates, which reports on layoff actions around the country. Unfortunately, while the information contained in sections such as "Vital Stats" and "Reports" is useful, it's also in need of an update.

- **The Riley Guide** (http://www.dbm.com/jobguide). With thousands of sites featuring some form of recruitment advertising, how do you know where to turn when you want to hire via the Net? Start with the Riley Guide, which catalogs recruitment web sites and news groups by geographic location and industry. Special sections feature web sites dedicated to international recruiting and resources for women and minority group members.

- **JobSmart's Salary Surveys** (http://jobsmart.org/tools/salary/). More than anything else, people write to us asking where they can find salary information on the Internet. The Bay Area Library in Oakland has managed to find hundreds of salary studies online and provides links to them from its site. While you are unlikely to find the entire contents of a salary survey online (such studies are expensive to produce, so publishers are loath to give the results away), you will be able to see executive summaries and sample tables that may provide you with the information you need.

- **The Salary Calculator** (http://www.homefair.com/homefair/cmr/salcalc.html). The original "cool" HR-related site, the Salary Calculator is powered by statistics provided and updated quarterly by the Center for Mobility Resources. Users can compare cost-of-living expenses for hundreds of cities across the country.

## BOOKMARK THESE SITES THE EASY WAY

You can easily add these URLs to your bookmark list by downloading a file containing links to all of the sites contained on this list.

How do you do that? Point your web browser to http://www.shrm.org/cyberspace/hrmarks.htm, and save the file on your computer by going to your "File" pulldown menu and select the "Save as" option. Be sure to note the file name and directory you assign to the files, then follow these instructions to import the bookmark list.

*For Netscape users:* Go to the "Bookmarks" pulldown menu and choose "Go to Bookmarks." From the Bookmark screen, select the "File" pulldown menu, and select the "Import" option. Click the file you just saved (hrmarks.htm). The bookmark file will then be added to your existing bookmarks, under the heading "Essential HR Bookmarks."

*For Internet Explorer users (including America Online subscribers):* Go to the "File" pulldown menu and open the file you just saved (hrmarks.htm). Then, go to the "Favorites" icon and select "Add to Favorites." Select the file to link to the web sites.

*You can submit questions to this column by writing Mike Frost at frost@shrm.org. Or, you can fill in a form available on the HR Cyberspace home page (http://www.shrm.org/cyberspace).*

---

*Mike Frost is director of online services for SHRM.*

## JUST BROWSING

**Go Figure** That's what you can say to employees with questions about retirement planning. The Scudder University Web (http://scudder-u.working4u.com) offers workers a variety of calculators to estimate paycheck savings from pre-tax retirement plan contributions, see how investing money can add up for retirement and model a loan from an employer's retirement plan account. The site also includes a news section with market news and personal finance updates, a primer on employer retirement plan investing and FAQs.

## Unit Selections

## Key Points to Consider

❖ Getting people to accept ideas and adopt them as their own is one of the most difficult tasks facing management. What are some things you might do to motivate employees, especially in a downsizing environment?

❖ Do you think financial incentives work or are there other kinds of incentives that might motivate the workforce in addition to money?

❖ What strategies could you employ to communicate more effectively with your peers or your instructor? What things can destroy effective communication? What role does empowerment play in organizational communication? How does the organization communicate its values?

 **Links**  | **www.dushkin.com/online/**

These sites are annotated on pages 4 and 5.

Whenever anything is being accomplished, it is being done, I have learned, by a monomaniac with a mission.

—Peter Drucker

For years, management theorists have indicated that the basic functions of management are to plan, direct, organize, control, and staff organizations. Unfortunately, those five words only tell what the manager is to do. They do not tell the manager how to do it. Being a truly effective manager involves more than just those five tasks. It involves knowing what goals to set for the organization, pursuing those goals with more desire and determination than anyone else in the organization, communicating the goals once they have been established, and having other members of the organization adopt those goals as their own.

Motivation is one of the easiest concepts to understand, yet one of the most difficult to implement. Often the difference between successful and mediocre organizations is that people in successful organizations are motivated. They are enthusiastic about the company, about what they do for the company, and about the company's products or services. Effective organizations build upon past successes, recognizing the truth of the old saying, "Nothing succeeds like success." If people feel good about themselves and good about their organization, then they are probably going to do a good job. Whether it is called morale, motivation, or enthusiasm, it still amounts to the same fragile concept—simple to understand, difficult to create and build, and very easy to destroy.

In order to maintain a motivated workforce for any task, it is necessary to establish an effective reward system. A truly motivated worker will respond much more effectively to a carrot than to a stick. "Turned-on" workers are having their needs met and are responding to the goals and objectives of the organization. They do an outstanding job because they want to, which results in an outstanding company.

Perhaps the single most important skill for any manager, or for that matter, any human being, is the ability to communicate. People work on this skill throughout their education in courses such as English and speech. They attempt to improve communication through an array of methods and media, which range from the printed word, e-mail, and television, to rumors and simple conversation. Yet managers often do not do a very good job of communicating with their employees or their customers. This is very unfortunate, because ineffective communication can often negate all of the other successes that a firm has enjoyed. Managers and the firms they represent must honestly communicate their goals, as well as their instructions, to their employees. If the manager does not do so, the employees will be confused and even distrustful, because they will not understand the rationale behind their instructions. If the manager is successful in honestly communicating the company's goals and ideals to the employees and is able to build the motivation and enthusiasm that are necessary to accomplish those goals successfully, then he or she has become not just a manager but a leader, and that is indeed rare.

Creating a positive work environment is not easy. Communicating with and motivating people, whether employees, volunteers, citizens, or Boy Scouts, is difficult to do. However, managers are faced with the task of doing exactly that. Creating a positive work environment is a key to the success of any organization. Organizations that lack that kind of environment are doomed to spend their time in destructive internal politics and fighting within the organization.

# Memory bankers

Buzzwords and bandwagons come and go, but knowledge management is a vehicle that personnel professionals should jump aboard if they are serious about adding value to their businesses, according to **Andrew Mayo.** In the opening article of a new series, he highlights a small number of companies that are already making the most of their intellectual capital

The best news in decades for personnel professionals is the recent upsurge in interest in intellectual capital. Forever fretting over whether "serious" business people see the function as adding value, HR now has no excuse for failing to make a major contribution.

The new argument is simple: organisations must increase value for stakeholders or shareholders (depending on your persuasion). The value is what someone would be prepared to pay for the business.

The most commonly understood components of this value are tangible: fixed assets and other money-related items that appear on the balance sheet. But in almost all organisations, these tangible assets represent less than half, and sometimes as little as 5 per cent, of the true valuation. Even heavily capital-intensive companies find that two-thirds of their value lies in intangible assets—intangible in that they are hard to measure and sometimes difficult to hang on to.

But the key to increasing value lies in understanding and managing these intangible assets. So what are they? Recent books on the subject have defined them in different ways, but the most widely accepted divisions are:
• externally related or customer assets, including brands, customer relationships and reputation;
• internal or structural assets, such as systems, patents, processes, culture, documented experience and knowledge;

• human assets—the people available to the organisation, their brains, skills and experience—and how they are led and motivated.

All of these elements need attention to ensure that they are being maintained and enhanced. The first two categories contrast with the third in that they are owned by the organisation. They are what is left when the people have gone home.

Tom Watson Jr, former president of IBM, went so far as to say: "All the value of this company is in its people. If you burnt down all of our plants and we just kept our people and information files, we would soon be as strong as ever. Take away our people and we might never recover."

One key to managing these assets is to transfer as much as possible of what is in the third category to the second. Skills and attitudes are essentially personal, but knowledge, wisdom and experience should be captured for the benefit of all employees.

This interest in intellectual assets is one of three driving forces behind the development of the term "knowledge management". The second factor is the recent focus on the learning organisation. In trying to establish what this is in practice, companies have found that

---

*Andrew Mayo, a writer and conference speaker, is director of MLI, a consultancy specialising in developing human capital. He can be contacted on 01727 843424*

From *People Management*, January 22, 1998, pp. 34–38. © 1998 by Andrew Mayo. Reprinted by permission.

their greatest need is to capture and use the knowledge available to them.

Bob Garratt, author of *The Learning Organisation*, offered an early description of such an enterprise as one that possessed "systems for capturing knowledge and moving it to where it is wanted". But restructuring in the 1990s has broken up teams and relationships, removing staff who used to co-ordinate corporate synergy of knowledge and resources.

When reducing staffing levels is the main priority, the value of people as assets often takes second place. In the past, devolved organisational structures have led to unconnected "islands" in which information-sharing loses priority.

All of this has an effect on the bottom line. Many of the resulting costs remain hidden, but wasted effort and repeated mistakes that arise from a failure to manage knowledge and experience across an organisation are a continual drain on resources. So a crucial element of a true learning organisation is a system and a culture for sharing learning.

The third development that has heightened interest in knowledge management is information technology. The most significant recent advance to affect both the lives of people and organisations is probably the growth of electronic communication—in particular, the Internet. The pace of change in this area is phenomenal. Many terms familiar today were unheard of three years ago. Although too few IT departments have given priority to such systems (I am amazed at the number of large companies that still do not use e-mail), the potential for such systems to enhance organisational learning is rapidly being realised.

There is still a great deal of mystery about what the term "knowledge management" means, but my definition would be: the man-agement of the information, knowledge and experience available to an organisation—its creation, capture, storage, availability and utilisation—in order that organisational activities build on what is already known and extend it further.

Of course, many companies have been doing this for decades. Hewlett-Packard and 3M have served as role models in innovation and sharing ideas. Thirty years ago, I worked for Procter & Gamble, where it was normal to receive bulletins about experiences and innovations from plants around the world. While they were expected to be innovative, managers also had to observe simple routines of accessing and reporting library information. But it is surprising how few companies, whether global or national, use these disciplines on a regular basis.

A knowledge management system will include the following processes:
• managing the generation of new knowledge through learning;
• capturing knowledge and experience;
• sharing, collaborating and communicating;
• organising information for easy access;
• using and building on what is known.

It is easy to assume that all an organisation needs to do in order to achieve effective knowledge management is to ask its IT specialists to create a network that will allow access and retrieval of information, and then to train people to use it. Indeed, many IT departments see it as exactly that.

Unfortunately, the problem is more complex. There are human and organisational factors that can defeat even the most well-designed system (see diagram, below). First, people must begin by making intelligent decisions about what kind of data and experience is valuable enough to retain and pub-

## Knowledge management - a socio-technical system

Knowledge architecture

| Motivation for input | input user interface | System for managing, storing and distributing knowledge | output user interface | Motivation for access |
|---|---|---|---|---|

# Fountain of knowledge

Anglian Water Services is a rare example of a UK company that has embraced knowledge management as part of its transformation into a learning organisation.

Among other initiatives, it is currently developing an "encyclopedia of water"—a data base of information about all aspects of water, such as treatment technology and services management.

The database contains much of the knowledge currently held in books, articles, plant manuals and process descriptions and is contained on its intranet system, Hawk (Harnessing Anglian's Water Knowledge), along with annual reports and other business information.

The company is also tapping the "tacit" knowledge of its experts by challenging them to run master classes before they leave the company. These are then recorded and entered into the encyclopedia. The first to take up the challenge was a retiring senior executive, Brian Croll, who ran the pilot class as one of his final assignments.

The project complements the company's experience in developing its Aqua Universitas. This is a "company university", consisting of open-learning centres and other resources. It aims to create work environments that promote learning, encourage knowledge creation and enable collaboration with external partners, especially higher education.

The open-learning centres provide a focal point for obtaining advice and sharing ideas, which is particularly important because employees are scattered around several counties. The company has deliberately stimulated informal networks on disciplines, such as treatment technology or environmental planning, to exchange ideas and develop knowledge. It is particularly keen to develop a network of former employees, known as "associates".

The networks include groups that have been involved in a novel company action learning programme, known as the Transformation Journey, in which teams of ordinary employees embark on the kind of projects most companies reserve for senior executives. One team, for instance, created a well in an Ivory Coast village to improve the drinking water. This extended learning lasts for up to two years.

The drive for the transformation came from the former managing director, Alan Smith, now retired and replaced by Chris Mellor. But Anglian's senior management team was also instrumental in leading the change.

Peter Matthews, who claims to be one of the first directors of innovation appointed in a British company, stresses the connections between total quality management, customer service, continuous improvement, the learning organisation and knowledge management. "The learning organisation is a logical progression towards the knowledge-creating company and our university provides the opportunities for this process to take place."

**Jane Pickard**

---

lish in the central system (the knowledge architecture). The data has to be useful, relevant and not there simply for its own sake.

Typically, the information is stored in a combination of databases and an "intranet", using hypertext mark-up language (HTML), that allows people to cross-reference and link documents easily. One of the most advanced intranets shown at the Knowledge Management 97 conference last month was one used by AT&T. The company aims to provide a "dynamic environment where the enterprise can easily and securely communicate, collaborate and transact with employees, business partners, suppliers and customers anytime, anywhere."

Input of, and access to, information must be easy. Many readers will empathise with the frustrations of Internet search engines, complicated layers of menus and so on. Information overload is a real problem, so people have to be able to "navigate" effectively. The good news is that developments are occurring at an amazing speed and the often-used excuse that people "don't know how to use the system" will soon by removed for even the most technically illiterate individuals.

But an organisation must still persuade people to use its system. The greatest enemies of knowledge-sharing are the time that is required to input and access information and the lack of motivation among potential users. The latter results from some common human characteristics, such as the need to feel secure by retaining personal knowledge. People may also be overconfident of their own abilities, they may lack respect for others or they may be impatient with the communication process.

A favourite excuse given by organisations that withhold information is one of "commercial sensitivity", which reflects an unwillingness to trust employees with information.

Salary surveys are a good example of this. In how many organisations is such data freely available to all interested employees?

## Suspicious minds

But why are we often so afraid of facts being in the hands of people who might misinterpret them? The problem is often rooted in a regrettable lack of respect for others and what they have done—the "not-invented-here" syndrome, in which people are reluctant to accept colleagues' ideas, no matter how positive they may be.

Jorma Ollila, chief executive of Nokia Telecommunications, offered a strong response to these emotional blocks. Introducing a new cultural direction in his 1994 annual report, he wrote: "Knowledge in Nokia is only power when it is shared."

People like to publicise their achievements and specialist areas of know-how. But it requires a trusting and blame-free culture for them to feel comfortable about logging their mistakes into the corporate memory, even though such experiences could be the critical contributor to learning. Lack of time and discipline can also mean that people fail to input data that they are happy, in principle, to share.

Personnel specialists have an important role to play in resolving these issues. But at Knowledge Management 97 only about 15 per cent of participants were from human resources. Slightly more had an IT background, but, overall, interest came from a range of departments. This is an issue that transcends internal functions and is undoubtedly the new battleground of competitive advantage.

The potential contribution that personnel practitioners can make to the creation of knowledge-sharing organisations is currently being undervalued within the profession. Speakers at the conference repeatedly stressed that success was dependent on people. It is the cultural foundation of norms, disciplines and values that gives some companies a leading edge over others. And so an intranet should be viewed as nothing more than a slice of the knowledge management "cake". Personnel should be helping to define, articulate, encourage and facilitate the necessary learning culture.

The personnel function needs to focus on top management to encourage processes that will enable cross-boundary learning and sharing. This includes helping to set up and, possibly, fund networks, as well as defining and developing the skills of learning from other people.

Hewlett-Packard and Procter & Gamble are companies in which collaboration and sharing have always been the norm. In Hewlett-Packard, for example, any employee who feels they have made an important development publishes details and invites colleagues to a seminar to discuss them. Such an enterprise is considered money well spent.

Nokia is one of many companies dedicated to creating the right culture. It has established a team of "knowledge champions" to determine what this culture should be and to put it into practice. The team describes the key elements as: "Shared mindsets, visions and strategies; new values and attitudes; networking and teamworking; recognition and reward of knowledge sharing; and trust."

The HR function at Nokia has a catalytic role in defining and managing these changes. It also devises initiatives aimed at enhancing learning and increasing the capability of teams and individuals. General Motors has addressed the perennial problem of how to encourage people to share learning with colleagues after they have undergone training.

Wendy Coles, GM's director of knowledge network development, has developed competency descriptions that include a positive attitude to sharing and collaborating, skills in managing learning processes and the ability to use knowledge effectively. The overall aim of the system is to capture "learning in action"—the wisdom and experience that is used in the daily task of making decisions.

The ability to share knowledge and collaborate are all too often missing in our organisations. Recruiters should look for these capabilities in new employees, as well as assessing what new knowledge they can bring to an organisation. Part of the induction process for recruits should involve "capturing" their knowledge and experience. Most new employees bring useful specialist experience with them that few people ever get to access.

But induction should also be about passing on the experience of predecessors to new employees. When people leave, the HR department asks for their company car keys and so on. Why not conduct a recruitment interview in reverse to retrieve information? Of course, by that time it may be too late—there may be no motivation for the employee to help the company he or she is about to leave.

### Wrongful dismissals

Reward systems must support the culture of sharing knowledge. Do people receive signals to encourage such behaviour? What criteria is used for promoting staff? Are instances in which the business has benefited from sharing learning publicly celebrated? Are mistakes made that could have been avoided if it had been known that similar errors had happened in the past? People tend to shrug off these occurrences as an occupational hazard, but it is HR's role to design reward and recognition systems that support strategic initiatives.

Personnel normally plays a key role in designing and restructuring organisations. It should consider the effect such processes have on knowledge-sharing, particularly when teams and customer relationships are broken up, or when the changes create a risk that valuable people will be lost.

During mergers and acquisitions, HR professionals have a much greater role to play than merely assessing contracts, union arrangements and conflicts of procedure. They should ask key questions such as where does the organisation's knowledge lie? Has this been captured into a central system? What are the procedures in knowledge management? Who are the people who hold the core of the organisation's experience? What are the capability profiles of these people and of specific teams?

The HR function can also act as a role model for networking, benchmarking and sharing good practice. It can build "sharing routines" into its work and ensure that any blame culture is outlawed.

Lastly, the measurement of intellectual and human assets provides a real opportunity for HR to be firmly linked with stakeholder/shareholder values. Skandia Assurance is a pioneer in this area and other companies, such as Dow Chemical, are making significant progress. But only a handful of HR directors appear to have taken any interest in this.

Knowledge management directors and functions are appearing everywhere. Consultancies have led the way, both in internal management and in providing services to clients. For instance, Ernst & Young has its own knowledge management centre.

These new posts are usually set apart from other functions, in order that they may take the broadest view. But too few knowledge management leaders are coming from within personnel (one notable exception is ICL's Elizabeth Lank, who will feature in a forthcoming article).

Our understanding of knowledge-sharing is growing rapidly. It is about making the most of the added value that our human assets can provide. If that is not a central concern for HR professionals, then I do not know what is.

**The WORKFORCE Magazine Optimas Award for *Competitive Advantage* is given to a department that has developed a program or policy that has recognized competitive issues for the organization and has helped it maintain or develop a competitive advantage.**

# Remedy Cures Work Doldrums

**Working fun yields retention and savings.**

## By Gillian Flynn

**W**ork is fun. It's a statement that gives one pause at the very least. But Remedy Corp. has a case. Here's a company whose managers have been known to don hula skirts and sumo-wrestling suits. Their version of a serious job fair is a romp at a mini race-car track. And they actually encourage employees to goof around during the workday, sponsoring pinball games and foam-ball shootouts.

And yet, as much as executives here kid around, their humor has serious payback. The software company, based in Mountain View, California, has doubled its size, revenue and customer base for five consecutive years. Its product line—internal help desks that identify glitches on computer networks and maintain databases to record the problems—earned the young company revenue of $37.1 million in the third quarter of 1997.

Remedy's success, impressive even in the exploding, voracious Silicon Valley, is tied inextricably to its ability to attract and retain the best employees in the exploding, voracious Silicon Valley. Remedy executives do this better and cheaper than the average industry employer, and they have fun doing it.

**Remedy plays the recruiting game—literally.**   When Remedy's three founders, Larry Garlick, Dave Mahler and Doug Mueller, started the company in 1990 in a tiny backyard cottage, they were adamant that their business should be fun as well as profitable. The challenge became, then, growing as rapidly as they needed to while still keeping the spirit they started out with. So when they realized their kind of growth meant doubling the employee base every year, they launched a seriously amusing strategy. The theory: Show candidates that work doesn't have to be all stress and straight faces, and employees will come running.

"Recruiting in Silicon Valley is probably one of the toughest things any company in this area can face," says Cara Jane Finn, vice president of employee services. "But our

Retention of core employees is key to success in the ultracompetitive Silicon Valley. Remedy takes this notion seriously—albeit in a fun way. One recent tactic the company employed was having managers show their appreciation to their workers by washing all of their cars. The company has gotten mileage from the event by communicating it in recruitment efforts.

recruitment practices haven't changed since we began. It's not like we started doing a lot of flashy things because the hiring is so difficult. We do what we do because it's part and parcel of our culture."

What the HR staff does is launch continual job fairs designed to present a relaxed atmosphere in which candidates can really get a feel for the company. They often rent out a local mini race-car track, conducting interviews at the track and then inviting applicants to take a few spins. They also have invited applicants to flights on a virtual-reality simulator, with interviews following.

All candidates at these special events already have been through one round of screening, and the second round serves as a means to see how well the candidate and the company fit. "The intention is to be more informal and relaxed, but you also see how people act in unusual circumstances," Finn says. "You see how they respond to our rapid culture as well as whether or not they respond to a spirit of enjoyment about work."

To keep the applicant pool brimming, Remedy also sponsors a fairly lucrative employee-referral program. Employees whose referrals are hired receive between $2,000 and $5,000 once the new hire has worked 60 days.

Money keeps employees interested, while theme-based referral campaigns keep them amused. For one recent theme—"Starship Remedy, the search for intelligent life"—HR performed a Star Trek/Star Wars spoof at an employee meeting and gave out "biogarments designed just for you to shield the upper part of your life form." For employees whose referrals were hired, Remedy also named a star after them or a friend and filed the names with the U.S. Copyright Office.

Another recent campaign—"It's a Jungle in Here"—combined recruiting with Remedy's philanthropic effort. The kickoff meeting featured all the Remedy executives, including the CEO and the CFO, in full animal costumes. Employees whose referrals were hired received a referral fee, and Remedy made a $25 dollar donation to the World Wildlife Fund in their names.

**Remedy executives get down to business.** Finn says as good as Remedy is at generating interest from potential employees, it's even better about getting them to join the team. "The first attempt to reach us must be met with enthusiasm and speed. A lot of new hires said our managers are so responsive that they'd been hired before other companies had even called them back." Finn says the average hire takes only three weeks. Martin Doettling, a recently hired director of product marketing, says it was his interviewing experience at Remedy that convinced him to leave a company he'd been with almost eight years. First he met informally over breakfast with the vice president of marketing. That was just the start. Doettling ended up interviewing with 17 people during three rounds. What impressed him most was their thoroughness. They had done as much homework on him as he had on Remedy.

"I met with the engineering people here. The co-founders probed me in terms of how well I can push back, how well I argue my points and whether I could speak the engineering language," he said. "That, as a candidate, makes me feel very confident about this company and my future here."

Remedy's combination of light-hearted and serious recruiting pays off. An average of 45 percent of the company's annual hires

come through the referral program—140 of the company's current 530 employees are referrals. During the first half of 1997, 43 percent of Remedy's hires, 66 people, came through the program with HR paying out $200,000 to employees for their tips. Even with this cost, the program has kept Remedy's cost-per-hire at $6,100, thousands below the industry average of $8,450.

John Wentworth, president and CEO of the Wentworth Company Inc., a recruiting firm in San Pedro, California, says such success is beyond impressive in Silicon Valley. "Companies are trying everything, leaving no stone unturned," he says. "The demand [for technology workers] has simply outstripped the supply. A firm that can get actual good employees instead of warm bodies has a serious advantage."

**Keeping employees in the game.** If hiring is difficult in Silicon Valley, retention is even trickier. So Remedy's HR professionals pay special attention to keeping the work atmosphere enjoyable—particularly in the wake of the company's 1995 initial public offering. "When Remedy was pre-public, a lot of people stayed to see if they could grab that golden ring," Finn said. "But once they had the golden ring, the question became, 'What are you going to do to keep people here now, Cara?' So our energy [in HR] is spent on making this place a good place to work, not just fun, but a place with camaraderie, where you can make a difference, get recognition and feedback."

Little things like refusing to have employees wear name badges—unusual in high-tech companies—forge a closeness, Finn says. It forces people to get to know each other.

On the first day of work, each employee also receives a Take a Chance card. The *Take a Chance* program encourages employee risk taking—it's basically a license to take action without fear. The card entitles its bearer to push the envelope in making decisions or creating projects. Like Monopoly® Get Out of Jail Free cards, the Take a Chance cards can be cashed in when employees' risk taking doesn't pay off. "All employees get one; managers get more because they're expected to take more risks," says Finn. "I have my own supply. When you give it to a manager, it obligates that manager to take your decision in a broader context." One engineer stapled a card to his resignation letter—he wrote that Remedy had been so nurturing about his risk taking, he felt there was nothing he couldn't do, so he was striking out to start his own firm. Finn has turned in several in her quest to focus the company on a four-year plan for the future, which she says, "Takes a lot of guts when everything's going so well now as it is."

The main reason things are going so well is Remedy's executives. They maintain a healthy workforce because they have such a strong sense of enjoyment. They look for reasons to play—it helps offset the long days most employees put in. "With people working harder and harder these days, we sometimes forget to do the smaller things," explains Leslie Yerkes, co-author of "301 Ways to Have Fun at Work" (Berrett-Koehler Publishers Inc. 1997). "One of the first things we forget to do is have fun, but fun is the best antidote to stress. Good leaders facilitate joy and fun. Top-performing companies tend to have the more fun workplaces. That's especially true for Silicon Valley."

## AT A GLANCE

**ORGANIZATION**

Remedy Corp.

**INDUSTRY**

Client/server applications

**EMPLOYEES**

530

**HR EMPLOYEES**

7

**CHALLENGE**

Remedy competes for hi-tech talent in the exploding Silicon Valley.

**SOLUTION**

Nurture its "fun" culture.

**RESULTS**

Attrition is just over 8 percent annually in an industry that hovers between 10 percent and 12 percent; retention averages 42 months while the industry's average is 20 months; cost-per-hire is $6,100 compared with an industry average of $8,450.

It's a notion exemplified by Remedy. Last year, new hires padded up and got to sumo wrestle their managers. At a picnic, they got chances to dunk the Remedy executives into cold-water tanks. Other workers have become human foos-ball players, linked to each other by lengths of pole as they played soccer in the Remedy parking lot. An employee-appreciation day could have managers out washing every employee's car.

A department head may also decide to take the whole team to a movie or to Disneyland. "We try hard to keep a balance of seriousness and enjoyment," Finn says. "You get a different sense of your executives when you see them riding a tricycle in a race, and then see them in the hall. You know they're real human beings." This type of camaraderie has given Remedy's charm remarkable staying power: Attrition is just over 8 percent annually in an industry that hovers between 10 percent and 12 percent. Remedy's retention averages 42 months; the industry's average is 20 months. The company has become an employer of choice in the valley, with some employees driving 90 miles one way from as far north as Berkeley and as far south as Santa Cruz.

This loyalty, of course, helps the bottom line: Remedy's market share now exceeds that of the company's top three competitors combined.

Good times combined with good business results—sounds like good HR.

---

*Gillian Flynn is editor-at-large for* WORK-FORCE. *E-mail anfusod@workforcemag.com to comment.*

# Practical Lessons for Designing an Economic Value Incentive Plan

by Don Delves

Seeking ways to make their incentive plans ever more effective, savvy compensation professionals today are considering financial performance measures like Economic Value (EV).

An EV incentive can be a powerful tool or just fancy pay. It all depends on how the plan is designed and whether EV is right for your company. Economic Value measures more and can tell management more than other performance measures. It is a valuable financial measurement tool that has tremendous potential power to drive performance—if properly used in the right situations. (See sidebar, "How Economic Value Works.")

The way in which a company incorporates EV into an incentive plan and the degree to which it takes the characteristics of its people—both senior management and lower level workers—into account is critical. It can make the difference between a program that improves workers' business understanding and drives performance and one that creates misunderstanding and confusion. That is why the human resources (HR) role is so important in companies that are considering implementing an EV-oriented incentive plan. More often than not, the EV initiative originates in a company's finance department or with the CEO; the HR department is often playing catchup, trying to learn what EV is and how it works. In the process, HR (and specifically the compensation professional) can lose track of what its job is in designing and implementing the incentive.

What works and what doesn't in EV incentive design? Using examples based on practical, ground-level experience with numerous companies, this article will describe how to harness the power of EV. Let's begin with the three basic steps to designing an EV incentive:

1. Define the plan's purpose and objectives.
2. Determine whether EV is right for your company.
3. Develop the scope and mechanics of the plan.

## Define the Plan's Purpose and Objectives

The desire to implement EV can take on a life of its own. Part of the compensation professional's role is to step back and ask "why"—to help management clarify what it is trying to achieve.

Clear objectives for an incentive plan are synonymous with a strong plan. Too many companies are limited and narrow, or just perfunctory with their incentive plan objectives. They think simplistically about attracting and keeping people rather than getting the most out of them. If keeping people is the extent of your company's vision for its incentive plan, then don't bother with a sophisticated performance measure like EV. However, if the goal is to maximize performance, productivity and efficiency, then careful selection of the right performance measure(s) is critical, and EV should be among those considered.

Often management confuses EV objectives with incentive plan objectives in general. It is important to distinguish the objectives that can be achieved with incentives from the objectives the company is specifically trying to achieve with EV.

For example, a major equipment manufacturer we worked with had a burning desire to implement EV. EV was its solution for a problem it had not adequately defined. With our help, the company defined the problem more clearly as low accountability in its existing incentive plan. The existing plan's mechanism for determining individual incentive awards involved a "black box" calculation that smoothed out performance differences between divisions. The process was mostly a mystery to the individuals concerned and resulted in little differentiation in bonus awards. This nullified its effectiveness as an incentive to drive results. The major change the company made was to eliminate the black box and open up the process of how it calculated awards and how it divvied up awards between divisions and managers. While the company did introduce an EV component into its incentive plan, this played only a minor role in improving the company's performance.

Any incentive design process should start with defining the purpose and objectives of the plan. Here's what the compensation professional needs to determine when considering an EV plan:

1. *What are the purpose and objectives the company is trying to achieve with its incentive plans?* Make sure the company's incentive plans support its purpose, objectives, and strategy.

**2.** *How well are current plans meeting the purpose and objectives?* Review existing plans to see where they meet and don't meet the purpose and objectives.

**3.** *What is the company trying to accomplish with EV?* Look at the specific goals the company is trying to achieve with EV and assess what changes the company will have to make to meet those goals.

**4.** *What kind of change is required?* Be aware that it's usually a lot easier and often more effective to modify an existing plan than to design a totally new one.

Before embarking on an EV incentive design project, engage your company in developing thorough answers to these four questions. Once you have used these questions to set a context for what your company is trying to do with EV, you can assess whether it is right for your company.

## Is EV Right for Your Company?

Economic Value is not right for every company in every situation. The criteria for determining whether EV is appropriate for your company fall into three categories: *industry factors, business factors, and people factors.* (See Exhibits 1 and 2.)

*Industry Factors.* Because EV measures how effectively a company uses assets, it is most effective for companies that use a fair amount of physical assets (buildings, factories, equipment, or inventory). These include companies that manufacture, distribute, or extract a product, or that use a lot of equipment and other assets in providing a service. It is not a particularly good measure for professional services firms or other organizations in which human capital is the primary asset.

EV also is not very effective for super high-growth companies. Typically, these companies are generating huge economic losses but are still creating value. EV does not capture the less tangible and more speculative things that the market values in these companies.

Economic Value can be measured for financial services firms (banks, insurance companies and investment firms), but it is a more complex calculation, requiring a relative risk measure; thus, it will not be discussed in this article.

*Business Factors.* EV basically measures the cash that a business generates and the effective use of assets. While these are theoretically the main drivers of value, they may not be the most important *strategic factors.* For example, an automotive supply company we work with is very financially astute and fully grasps the EV concept. However, gaining market share is much more critical for this company's success over the next few years. Therefore, it includes a market share measure along with two other specific financial measures in its incentive plans.

*Management style* is another important variable in the EV decision. Many companies use EV as the sole measure and determinant of incentive awards. Most also use it as a common measure across all divisions. This reliance on one measure may not match the way senior management runs your company. If your CEO likes to communicate specific goals using MBOs and tailored financial measures for each business unit, then EV is not likely to support his or her management style.

*People Factors.* In order for EV to work, employees have to understand it and management has to like it. EV is a different and sometimes difficult concept, so it requires some selling and some educating. The CEO and his or her direct reports should understand the concept and be in favor of it. The heads of each business unit and their controllers should understand the concept well enough to tell you several things they would do to increase EV. The company must also make a significant commitment to education and training when it rolls out the EV incentive.

If the company is not ready to meet these conditions, slow down and consider some interim steps. For example, the CEO and the strategic planning people at a large food processing company thought EV was a good idea for the company. Strategically it was; but the level of buy-in and understanding was minimal. Most of the finance department was even unfamiliar with the concept. Management realized that an EV incentive would be too much too soon, so they took two interim steps. The company embarked on a yearlong EV training program, starting with senior management, finance, and HR. At the same time, it added a "return on capital" measure to its incentive plan to underline the importance of managing assets. Even with these initiatives, it was two years before the company was ready to introduce EV into an incentive plan.

*Accountability* is another key variable to consider in determining whether EV is right for your company. Because EV measures more, including it in an incentive implies holding people accountable for more. In fact, most successful EV initiatives are at least in part an attempt to increase the accountability in a company. This is a critical point. If improved accountability is not a major objective of implementing an EV incentive, then it can easily end up being no more than a fancy pay delivery mechanism.

We recently got a call from a large public company that has had fancy EV incentives in place for a number of years but whose internal accountability is low. The head of HR complained that "we used to manage budgets, now we manage payouts." In other words, people have always gamed the system. With EV only the game changed. The company's primary motivation in implementing EV was to impress the stock market and to hope that EV would somehow magically make people do the right things. The plan is technically good, but it has so

**EXHIBIT 1**
**EV Readiness Test**

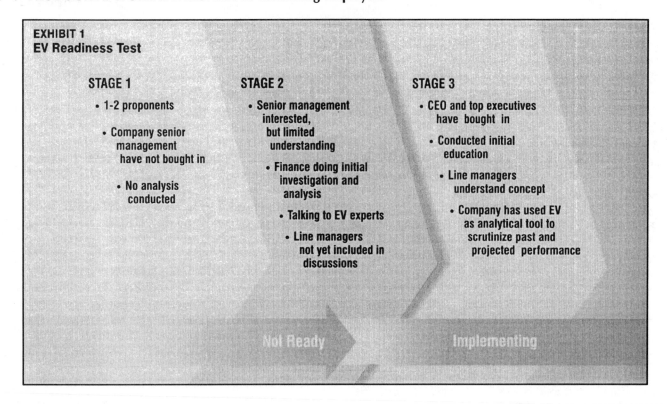

STAGE 1

- 1-2 proponents

- Company senior management have not bought in

- No analysis conducted

STAGE 2

- Senior management interested, but limited understanding

- Finance doing initial investigation and analysis

- Talking to EV experts

- Line managers not yet included in discussions

STAGE 3

- CEO and top executives have bought in

- Conducted initial education

- Line managers understand concept

- Company has used EV as analytical tool to scrutinize past and projected performance

Not Ready

Implementing

many administrative loopholes that special exceptions and adjustments have become the rule. As a result the plan has paid out handsomely in almost every year since its inception, but the company's stock has been virtually flat. The company's board is unhappy with the plan and is putting pressure on management to get rid of it.

If, after considering all these factors, you still think that EV is right for your company, then it's time to start designing the scope and mechanics of the incentive plan.

### Develop the Scope and Mechanics

There are a variety of issues that must be addressed in designing any incentive plan. We will concentrate here on seven issues that are particularly pertinent to an EV incentive.

1. *Annual vs. Long-Term.* While a great deal has been written about how important it is to incorporate EV into all incentives, most companies choose to incorporate the measure into either the annual or the long-term incentive, but rarely both. They continue to use one or more other incentives to achieve other purposes. This is illustrated by the following two companies.

• The first company, a privately held distribution business, focused on its long-term incentive. The CEO was very happy with the control and direction he was able to exert and the results he was able to produce—or at least influence—through the annual incentive plan. However, as principal owner of the company, he had a strong desire to focus his management team on building the value of the company over a 10–20 year period. He

wanted a stable and loyal management team that had a personal, vested interest in seeing the long-term value grow. Building EV into a new long-term incentive was a natural solution.

• At the second company, the situation was quite different. A large, publicly traded manufacturer of transportation equipment, the company had a long-term incentive tied to a variant of EV. It also had stock options on a stock whose performance was flat. The problem, everyone suspected, was a very lucrative (and inclusive) annual incentive that drove short-term earnings to the exclusion of all else, including investment management, inventory control, receivables management, and maintaining margins. Fixing what was measured and rewarded annually was critical to the redirection and success of the company. By changing the performance measure in the annual plan from earnings to a version of EV, managers began almost immediately to focus on reducing inventories and improving productivity in their plants.

2. *Who will participate?* EV is an excellent measure of corporate, division, and plant performance. So, executives and man[a]gers that play a direct role in managing any business entity down to the plant level should be included in the plan. However, below this level of direct influence, the plan should no longer include people in an incentive that measures Economic Value directly. Instead, it should measure and reward them for improving the drivers of value over which they have direct influence.

Rewarding lower level employees for improving value drivers may or may not require revisions or redesign of their existing incentives. The company may al-

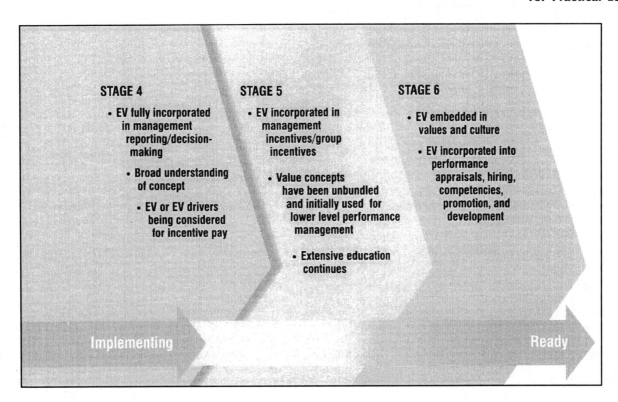

STAGE 4
- EV fully incorporated in management reporting/decision-making
- Broad understanding of concept
- EV or EV drivers being considered for incentive pay

STAGE 5
- EV incorporated in management incentives/group incentives
- Value concepts have been unbundled and initially used for lower level performance management
- Extensive education continues

STAGE 6
- EV embedded in values and culture
- EV incorporated into performance appraisals, hiring, competencies, promotion, and development

Implementing → Ready

ready be rewarding the right things. However, some analysis is required to identify what the key drivers are. A number of companies have done this successfully using the "value tree" process of analysis to help identify the drivers of economic value. To be effective, incentives at lower levels in the company should be based on these drivers, which are the components of EV (See Exhibit 3.)

Salespeople also should be excluded from the EV incentive. They do not have enough influence over the various factors that drive EV. Their focus should be on selling. Any attempt we have seen to include salespeople directly in the EV plan has been an unproductive distraction to the selling effort. However, it may be appropriate for sales management to be included in the EV plan.

That said, some companies have successfully trained their salespeople in the discipline of EV so they can better understand and add value to their customers' organizations.

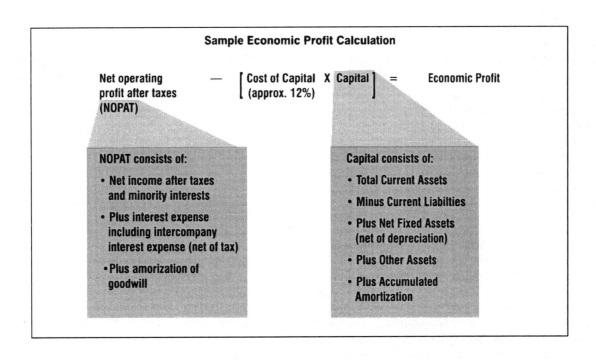

**Sample Economic Profit Calculation**

Net operating profit after taxes (NOPAT) — [ Cost of Capital (approx. 12%) X Capital ] = Economic Profit

NOPAT consists of:
- Net income after taxes and minority interests
- Plus interest expense including intercompany interest expense (net of tax)
- Plus amorization of goodwill

Capital consists of:
- Total Current Assets
- Minus Current Liabilties
- Plus Net Fixed Assets (net of depreciation)
- Plus Other Assets
- Plus Accumulated Amortization

---

# How "Economic Value" Works

Economic Value can help a company maximize both its return on investment and the amount of cash it generates. This combination creates value. The compensation professional who understands this principle can be a more effective business partner and contributor to the company's success.

Economic Value is a new way to measure profits. EV does two things that traditional "accounting profits" (profits calculated by traditional accounting methods) don't do.

First, EV measures the amount of net cash that a company generates. This cash figure is similar to the amount of earnings, or profits the company makes—but it's not identical. Because of how accounting rules work, the company usually has to make some adjustments to earnings to determine the net cash generated.

Second, EV measures how well the company is using its assets. To measure this, the company subtracts an "asset charge" (or "capital charge") of 10%–15% of its assets from the amount of cash generated. That asset charge can be likened to the assets' "owners" charging the company rent for the use of the assets. It is the amount that the company's owners (the landlords) need to get paid for the assets they invested in the company. If the company can't make this minimum "return" on its assets, then it really isn't making a true—that is, an "economic"—profit. It's like business owners forgetting to pay themselves. If they pay everyone else but haven't paid themselves for their time and for the assets they put into the business, then they're really losing money. They could have invested their time and their money somewhere else and made more.

Many companies show accounting profits in their annual reports, but they are not actually making an economic profit. One manufacturing company we worked with knew it was having problems, but it hadn't been overly concerned because it was still increasing its accounting profits. Then we ran the EV numbers and management saw big negatives—large economic losses. In its efforts to increase accounting profits, the company had pumped more and more money into the business. However, every additional dollar it invested was generating less and less profit. The company was increasing its absolute profit, but its return on each new dollar invested was decreasing. It would have been better to put all that additional money into a money market account. From an Economic Value point of view, this company was destroying value.

Of course, the point is to create, not destroy value. So, the goal of an EV incentive plan is to reward growth in economic profits as well as reduction of economic losses. The chart below shows a sample economic profit calculation.

---

**3. _Carry-Over Features._** The folks at Stern Stewart & Co., who deserve most of the credit for popularizing EV, have also popularized an incentive concept called "banking." With banking, the company defers part of the annual incentive into an account that builds up over time. Each year, if performance is good (i.e., EV grows), the account grows. However, if performance is poor (i.e., EV decreases), the account decreases.

Our experience indicates that banking is an interesting idea, but one that has some fairly major drawbacks and that few companies have adopted. Its major drawbacks are its complexity, and the fact that banking a portion of the payout reduces current year awards. Nevertheless, the concept has merit. It adds a long-term element to an annual incentive and creates a real potential downside for poor performance. Let's look at two examples of companies that have overcome the drawbacks and implemented carry-over, or "banking," features.

• The privately held distribution company mentioned earlier has a long-term incentive with four-year performance cycles. Each year, the company adds an amount to each individual's incentive account based on the EV performance of the company and/or that individual's division. Poor performance reduces the balance in the account, but not below zero. At the end of the four-year period, the company pays the individual a percentage of the amount in the account. The percentage paid is based on the individual's years of service with the company.

For example, an employee with 5 years of service would get 40%, while an employee with 10 years would get 90%. The company carries the rest over until the end of the next four-year period, at which point it pays a larger percentage (because of longer service). The employee who had 5 years of service will now have 9, so this individual's payout percentage will increase to 80%. However, a portion (at least 10%) of the account is always carried over and builds up until retirement. A growing portion of the account balance is vested and payable if the employee leaves the company. The long-term balance accrues interest at a rate that is tied to company performance.

• Another concept recently adopted by a large automotive supplier is to set EV goals in advance for the next three years and pay incentives annually based on whether performance is at, above, or below the three-year EV goal trend line. If the company does not achieve the first year's goal, the goal for the second year does not change. The three-year trend line remains fixed. However, if the company recovers and hits the second year goal after missing the first, half of the missed bonus from the first year is carried over and paid out in the second year—on top of the second year bonus. Amounts can be carried over for up to two years.

**4. _Corporate, division and plant level measurement._** Far too often, companies only measure and reward EV at the corporate level. They limit themselves to an EV

| Decision Factors | | **EXHIBIT 2** **Is EV Right for Your Company?** | |
| --- | --- | --- | --- |
| | | Yes | No |
| **Industry Factors** | *Capital Intensity* | Manufacturing, distribution, extraction companies using buildings, plant, machinery, equipment, and inventories to make money | Professional services and other businesses using little physical capital |
| | *Growth Rate* | Low, Medium, High | Super High |
| **Business Factors** | *Management Style* | Prefers 1-2 measures in incentive plans; same measures across all operations | Prefers MBOs and/or specific financial measures for each business unit |
| | *Strategic Importance* | EV incorporates most important strategic drivers of business | Other drivers or strategic initiatives are more critical |
| **People Factors** | *Accountability* | Management desires to improve accountability with EV incentive | Incentive plan accountability is low; improving it is not an objective |
| | *Buy-in* | CEO, management and other managers are proponents | Few proponents, many skeptics |
| | *Understanding* | Widespread, especially in operating units | Limited to finance |

plan that measures only corporate EV and may include only the most senior executives. This misses the true power and potential of the measure, which is an excellent tool for assessing division and plant performance and for highlighting and helping to explain differences in performance. As an incentive measure, EV is effective because it is responsive to and is easily influenced by the actions and decisions of division and plant managers. Most of the division and plant level managers we have worked with have readily grasped the EV concept and have used it to better understand their operations. They have also been able to quickly identify the steps they would take to improve their EV performance.

On the other side of the coin, an important caveat is to avoid getting so focused on measuring and rewarding business unit performance that you forget about corporate performance. Senior management must be accountable for the EV performance of the entire organization. This may seem obvious, but there is a temptation to assume that if all business units are managing their EV, corporate EV will take care of itself. Not so! There are many critical drivers of EV that can be measured and controlled only at the corporate level, such as corporate overhead, taxes, excess cash and other investments, and the company's capital structure.

In a recent project, we measured EV for a large manufacturing company and its three divisions over the last five years. All three divisions showed consistently positive EV numbers, yet the company's EV as a whole was negative. What was wrong with this picture? Part of the problem was corporate overhead, but the real culprit was a huge balance of uninvested cash that the company was sitting on. In order for the company to generate a positive EV, it would have to find some productive uses for that cash.

5. *EV as a single performance measure or combined with others.* Choosing EV as the sole measure of performance in an incentive plan is a risky move. The CEO and senior management should give it careful consideration. Annual and long-term incentives are primary means of controlling and directing people and the company. The measures used in these plans are literally the drivers of company performance. Consequently many CEOs are reluctant to place all control in a single performance measure, and rightfully so.

The private distribution company mentioned earlier used EV as the sole performance measure in its long-term incentive, but maintained flexibility in its annual incentive plan. The annual plan allowed the CEO to set specific goals and objectives tailored to each business unit, and to each of his senior man[a]gers, all under the umbrella of a long-term objective of increasing the value of the company.

A major manufacturing firm had historically used only one measure of performance in its annual plan: quarterly operating earnings. This had caused managers to make questionable investment decisions and virtually ignore inventory and receivables levels. There was no accountability in the incentive system for managing assets and investments wisely. On the other hand, senior management saw the power that the single measure incentive had to direct people's performance. People in this company worked hard, and they were very motivated

**EXHIBIT 3**
**Economic Value "Tree"—Identifying the Drivers of EV**

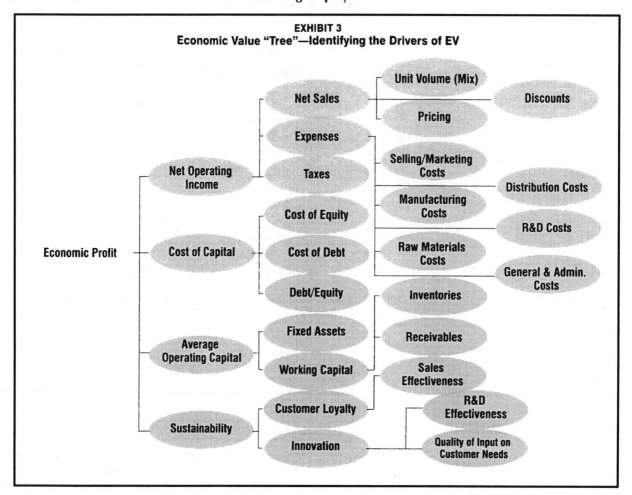

by their lucrative annual incentive, even though it encouraged them to do some shortsighted things.

Consequently the company's management sought in EV a single measure that would encourage and reward people both for generating short term operating earnings and for managing assets. Exhibit 4 compares the objectives of the long-term plan implemented by the diversified company with the objectives of the annual incentive plan implemented by the major manufacturing company

**6. Measuring EV amount generated or change in EV.** Economic profit generally must go up from one year to the next in order for the business to create additional value. Consequently, we generally want to reward only those divisions that are generating increases in EV. However, this would also include divisions that are generating an economic loss, but which reduce the loss from one year to the next.

This practice works in theory, but many companies have divisions that consistently generate large amounts of economic profit but are unlikely to increase it much. These "EV cows" are engines that help drive and fund the rest of the company. Often, they are very well run divisions that have invested and managed their assets wisely but are in mature businesses. The large amounts

of cash they throw off are better invested elsewhere in the company. These divisions should be rewarded for the *amount* of EV they produce, even if it isn't growing.

The private distribution company deals with this issue in a creative way. The EV incentive account for each individual is funded by a percentage of the *amount* of economic profit generated as well as by a separate percentage of the *change* in economic profit generated by that individual's business unit. The company adjusts the two percentages from one business unit to the next to reflect the relative importance of *amount* versus *change* in EV. Newer, growth businesses are rewarded primarily for increases in EV (or dinged for decreases), while more mature slower growth businesses are rewarded primarily for the amount of EV produced. Most of the company's businesses, however, are rewarded for a *combination* of increases in EV and amount of EV.

**7. Treatment of new capital expenditures.** One of the most often raised concerns about EV plans is that the asset charge could discourage managers from making significant investments that, while good for the company in the long term, would reduce EV in the short run. This is a legitimate concern and companies should deal with it explicitly in the EV incentive plan design. There are three basic ways to deal with major new capital expen-

---

**EXHIBIT 4**
**Comparison of Objectives for Two EV-Based Incentive Plans**

**DIVERSIFIED COMPANY**

**Long-Term Incentive Plan**

- Define and communicate a common and consistent framework for value creation.

- Reward value creation at both corporate and business unit levels.

- Provide a sense of ownership to the company's key executives to encourage a long-term business partnership.

- Create a long-term wealth accumulation opportunity.

- Create "golden handcuffs" to retain key executives.

**MAJOR MANUFACTURER**

**Annual Incentive Plan**

- Maintain the highly motivational features of the existing plan.

- Focus the entire management of the company on more effectively managing assets and investments.

- Create greater accountability for business unit results.

- Implement change gradually over 3-4 years.

- Make changes understandable—use known terminology wherever possible.

---

ditures for acquisitions, new plants, major expansions, etc.:

• *Make no adjustment.* New investments have to start generating an economic profit ASAP, and managers will suffer until they do. Some very aggressive companies have such policies, but they work best in long-term plans.

• *Phase in the investment* over 18 months to three years, depending on how quickly the company expects managers to generate an economic profit from the new investment. The company gradually adds the amount of the new investment to the asset charge calculation (e.g., 30% the first year, 70% the second year, and 100% the third year).

• *Make adjustments to the EV goals* based on the projections the company used to justify the investment. Most companies require detailed projections and net present value calculations in order to justify and authorize any major capital expenditure. These calculations can easily be converted into EV projections and used to adjust EV goals. This effectively holds managers accountable for producing the results they promised from a new investment.

Most companies we know of have been using the *phase-in* method. One company phases in new investments over eighteen months to two years. Most of its new investments are either new plants or plant expansions, and senior management feels strongly that any new facility should be economically profitable within this 18–24 month period. Another company makes most of its new investments in new business ventures and acquisitions. Since each of these investments is unique, the company prefers more discretion and flexibility in determining the phase-in period. Consequently the CEO and

CFO determine how long the phase-in period will be for each new investment.

A growing number of companies *adjust the EV goals,* primarily because this makes division managers accountable for producing the results they promise when they request funding for new investments.

## Summary

Better, more accurate performance measures and well-designed incentives are important tools for compensation professionals to make meaningful contributions to the success of their companies. The intent of this article was to provide these professionals with the perspective and knowledge required to play a pivotal role in determining whether EV is the right measure for their companies, and if so, how they should incorporate it into an incentive plan. The key steps in the process are to:

**1.** Establish the purpose and objectives of the incentive plan and make sure they are achieved.

**2.** Assess whether EV is right for the company—given industry, business, and people factors.

**3.** Design the incentive plan so it is workable, understandable, and motivational.

Implicit in all three steps is the fact that no performance measure is perfect and that the unique human factors in your company will be most important in determining what will work and what won't.

---

*Don Delves, CPA, is a senior consultant with Sibson and Company based in Chicago. Since completing his MBA in finance at the University of Chicago, Delves has spent almost 20 years working with executives and boards of directors to improve organizational accountability, communication, and performance. His areas of expertise include performance measurement, communication, and incentive design.*

# True Tales *AND* Tall Tales

## The Power of Organizational Storytelling

Storytelling is a vivid, memorable way to pass on an organization's history, values, and vision. Everyone has a story to share and the capacity to become a great storyteller.

### By Beverly Kaye and Betsy Jacobson

A question: How did you first come to know about camels? At what point did you begin not only to see them as beasts of burden, but also to understand them as animals with eccentric personalities and stubborn demeanors? You might have glimpsed a photo of these ships of the desert in an encyclopedia, but you probably didn't get a feel for their distinct characters. That more likely happened when you were read a story or two about a specific camel and its behavior–such as the lazy camel in Rudyard Kipling's "How the Camel Got His Hump" or the affectionate Camel With the Wrinkled Knees who accompanied Raggedy Ann and Andy on their adventures.

Because many of us share that camel lore, we also share a collective conception about camels. Thus, we nod knowingly when we hear that "a camel is a horse designed by a committee." We have a common understanding of that metaphor.

Here is the typical sequence in storytelling:

☐ The story. Someone tells it; someone (or some people) listens.

☐ The understanding. The people who hear the story, and the teller, start to understand something that was known to them only superficially before.

☐ The shared meaning. Groups use their shared understanding of one thing as a metaphor and a kind of shorthand that facilitates a wider understanding of other things.

In that simple, three-part sequence lies the key to the power of storytelling–whether the stories are true tales or tall tales. Because stories can be vivid and memorable, they help us understand in ways that are meaningful and relevant. Because storytelling is a collective act, it encourages us to share meanings and establish a cohesion that might otherwise be beyond our reach.

### Beyond the watercooler

When organizational stories are communicated in ways that enhance people's understanding, the stories create and disseminate valuable shared meaning. A leader can tell stories that help people understand the organization's heritage. Savvy strategists can relate stories that explain how behind-the-scenes machinations guide the outcome of complex negotiations. Mentors and coaches can provide personal narratives that illuminate options for handling difficult situations. A CEO can paint his or her vision through a saga and symbols.

Stories about past organizational events are vivid, memorable vehicles for learning from past experience— our own and that of others. They're also an effective way to forge and understand an organization's culture and build organizational identity. A good story taps into the intellect and emotions of the audience; it leaves listeners enriched in their learning and feelings. In truth, only a story can accomplish that. Lectures, question-and-answer sessions, seminars, and coaching dialogues are not as likely to be as powerful.

The idea of storytelling as a positive organizational force isn't new. Managers have told "war stories" for decades, perhaps centuries. Speakers typically open with a story. But only recently are stories being recognized as an especially effective means of communication for leaders. In his book *Leading Minds,* Howard Gardner writes: "The true impact of a leader depends on the story that he or she relates or embodies, and the reception to that story by the organizational audience." Gardner distinguishes between "innovative leaders," who use stories to revive neglected or existing themes that need to be communicated, and "visionary leaders," who create new stories to inspire transformation. Gardner says that both kinds of leaders use words and symbols "to convince others of a particular view and that the story is the best way to convey their point."

Communicating vision and influencing people to act on the message aren't the only products of stories. A recent study of a 300-member, not-for-profit organization found that storytelling—in the form of relating past events—created shared meaning and purpose among the employees. In that way, stories can be vehicles for

> ## When my father was a college student, he was returning by car one Sunday from singing in a gospel quartet in the Appalachian Mountains. He and his friend stopped to fix a flat tire in front of a small, rural soap-making factory. Somehow, they got to talking with the factory owner and the next thing they knew, they were soap salesmen. They loaded up the car with so much soap that the back bumper was only inches from the ground. Hood ornament pointed skyward, they headed down the road.
>
> My father and his friend learned quickly that war-rationed America was eager for soap. They sold all that they had in just a few days. It was too easy to believe. They started making plans—talking about national territories, color-coded maps, projections, extrapolations. They wondered whether they even needed to finish college. They discussed which college mates they'd hire and which they wouldn't.
>
> In their determination to do things right, they decided to solicit testimonials. So, they went back to one of their first customers, the godly wife of the college's most prominent Bible professor. Surely, her recommendation would go a long way with the other women of the town. But instead of praising the soap, she asked "Is this normal?" holding out her bright, red hands. My father looked at his friend and knew that owning the soap-selling rights in California didn't mean as much as it had the day before.
>
> *Adapted from Daniel Taylor's* The Healing Power of Stories.

capturing people's experiences and communicating them in ways that relate an organization's traditions, values, beliefs, and priorities. Stories can also create and maintain a sense of community among diverse people in an organization, and stories can foster widespread understanding of the subtle cultural and political realities of an organization's life.

Storytelling can also help leaders build leadership. Veteran leaders conserve and communicate their learning through telling stories about how they viewed a certain issue, how they dealt with a problem, and so forth. Sharing such experiences as stories with the next generation of leaders is an example of "wisdom stored forward."

Part of the warp and weave of organizational yarns are the personal stories told by individuals. As each of us strives to fulfill the promise of a satisfying life, we can find patterns and themes that create our own narratives. In *The Healing Power of Stories,* Daniel Taylor writes that the ability to see our lives as stories rather than unrelated, random events increases the possibility for significant and purposeful action. If we view our lives as a movie rather than a slide show, we can see connections among our actions and see significance in our experiences. Simply, we get to know

ourselves, our motivations, and our effect on the people around us.

Storytelling can

☐ communicate a leader's vision of the future and invoke others' commitment

☐ create a collective sense of shared purpose and meaning that can enhance cohesion around an organization's culture

☐ build leadership through "wisdom stored forward," by capturing and disseminating learning to the next generation of leaders

☐ enable people to find patterns in their lives, enhancing self-knowledge and a productive interpretation of experiences

☐ inspire alignment in support of a change initiative.

## Once upon a time

Stories also entertain, influence, teach, inform, and uplift. All organizations can benefit from sharing stories, and everyone is potentially an excellent source or teller of stories, with some coaching (and perhaps coaxing). Some people are natural yarn spinners, but almost anyone can acquire the ability to put across an expressive, meaningful story. Storytelling is a form of communication that can be learned.

Peter Drucker tells a memorable story that occurred many years ago when he went to the opera, *Falstaff,* and was so impressed that he decided to look into the life of its composer, Giuseppe Verdi. Drucker, a young man at the time, learned that Verdi was 80 years old when he wrote *Falstaff,* after a lifetime of fame and accomplishments. When Verdi had been asked why he wanted to take on the demands of writing another opera, he replied, "All of my life as a musician, I have striven for perfection. It has always eluded me. I surely had an obligation to make one more try."

Drucker resolved then and there that he too would always strive for perfection, even if it eluded him. He learned from Verdi's story, and that learning has guided his life. Drucker has also passed the learning on in written and oral form as a story that might continue to guide others.

*Adapted from* My Life as a Knowledge Worker, *by Peter Drucker.*

Coaching, role modeling, planning, and practice can help.

The most valuable stories told in organizations–those that teach, inspire, motivate, and add meaning–are created from personal experience in the past, from ideas and questions concerning the present, and from a personal vision about the future.

## Identify your imperfections. Mistakes, failures, and even derailments make wonderful stories—probably the best.

Here are some tips for creating a repertoire of stories.

**Look for patterns.** Examine the plots and themes of your life–your values, priorities, concerns, interests, and experiences together create patterns. Some may relate to advice for dealing with adversity, obtaining scarce resources, or overcoming challenges. When we see the multiple incidents of our lives as essential parts of a pattern, we find value in the stories that created the pattern. Taylor says that stories turn chronology into purposeful plot and thereby into

meaning. If we discern some purposeful action to our lives, we're more likely to take our lives and ourselves seriously.

**Look for consequences.** Determine the cause and effect of your choices. If we look back on our lives chronologically, we see that one thing happened and then another thing happened. The events might not be interesting–not worth a story. But if we search for the consequences of our choices as leading to the next event or action, the narrative of our lives becomes more interesting and sometimes highly instructional. We can make meaning from our experiences instead of just reciting incidents: One choice resulted in another, and that result made it possible to take action in another area.

**Look for lessons.** When we think back on events or our actions as they unfolded, we can find stories in the answers to these questions: What did I learn from that? What did I discover about myself and others that has changed me in some way? If we have an *aha!* as we observe or participate in contract negotiations, strategy sessions, financial manipulations, or supervisory practices, it's likely that the *aha!* has value for others if passed on in a story. But, first, we need to reflect on our work to cull the learning and interpret how and why the learning took place. Stories that impart lessons are often the best way to advise others, especially staff or colleagues. The usual advice about patience, persistence, timing, interpersonal interaction, and other realities of organizational life can be di-

dactic and prescriptive. But when the same advice is given in the form of a recalled experience that demonstrates a personal lesson, it's generally easier for the other person to embrace.

**Look for utility.** Recall your successes. They are fertile ground for organizational narratives. When we reflect on the kinds of successes that might make good stories, we need to dig for hidden principles. They're what make a story transferable to other situations and, possibly, applicable to someone else's successes. Finding the utility in a situation and emphasizing it in a narrative involves examining in detail exactly how the events unfolded towards success. How essential were the timing, people, financial resources? Of what importance were vision, strategy, leadership? Those elements, not the success itself, lend utility to the experience and make it a story worth telling.

**Look for vulnerability.** Identify your imperfections. Mistakes, failures, and even derailments make wonderful stories–probably the best. Such narratives have powerful qualities: They invoke people's intellect by motivating them to probe for causes and better approaches to problems, and they invoke people's emotions by giving them a feel for the pain and frustration of negative results. Such stories are usually the most interesting and memorable (consider how "bad news" dominates the media). In reality, many stories don't have happy endings and the people in them don't live happily ever after. When an organization's leaders tell such stories, they show their vulnerability and increase their credibility. An always successful person can be harder to learn from than someone who has made mistakes and bounced back from failure.

**Look for the future experience.** Be creative. Organizational researcher and consultant James March says in his book *Organizational Scenes* that much of valuable development comes from learning from one example. By that, he means that we learn well from one-time experiences and that we learn well from experiences we haven't yet had, by imagining how we might behave. Observing what's happening around us–how a project is being managed, how a negotiation is being handled, how a presentation is being prepared–can help us create our own scripts for how we would handle similar situations. We learn from imagination as well as from an actual experience. When we turn the scripts into creative stories, other people can also learn. When a script is enlarged into a vision, it becomes a scenario for success.

**Look for recollections.** Go over the meanings and memories of your past. Let the stories of literature guide you–for example, the surprise endings in O. Henry's short stories. You might be reminded that a personal experience had a surprise ending and, thus, would make an interesting story. Similarly, you could become aware of a potential story by recalling the messages in *Alice in Wonderland,* in *Catcher in the Rye,* or from stories told by your grandparents.

A story that is worth sharing is already within you, and another one is in the making. But, for now, it may exist only as an untapped experience, idea, or value until you reflect and imagine the possibilities.

## Wait till you hear this

The term *story communication* may sound as if it means only "telling a story," but it's more than that. Though an oral narrative to a receptive audience might be the most obvious, and sometimes most effective, way to get a message across, it's not the only way. Another, subtler way is to communicate by what Gardner calls "embodying the story." He means that leaders convey their stories by the kinds of lives they lead and by what they seek to inspire in other people. The identity of the storyteller and his or her relationship to the audience are crucial. For example, a story that verifies and amplifies the message "the customer is always

| A Stories Framework | | | |
|---|---|---|---|
| **STORY TYPES** | **STORIES WE TELL OURSELVES** | **STORIES WE TELL OTHERS** | **STORIES WE EMBODY** |
| Personal Histories | Memoirs capturing self | Autobiographies communicating self | Journals relating self |
| Events, Experiences | Tales reflecting meaning | Guides to building wisdom | Lessons showing possibilities |
| The Future | Fantasy, daydreams | Sharing a vision for the future | Adventures embracing opportunities |

right" is best told by someone who has substantial customer contact and who is viewed as embodying the value of customer relations.

As stories are passed on, they're heard differently by different organizational members, depending on their own experience and their relationship to the person telling the story. Each receiver of a story makes his or her own meaning. Sometimes, the storyteller can communicate the message in a way that everyone takes

> **Good stories that build leadership and enhance corporate culture can happen in hallways, meeting rooms, offices, parking lots, or training rooms.**

the same meaning.

Storytellers are also their own audiences. In many cases, they're their first audiences. The stories we tell ourselves shape our responses to our environments and our perception of our capacities. Through such stories, often in the form of daydreams or fantasies, we set personal goals, develop a vision of our future, determine how to relate to others, and plan

our daily moves. Stories we tell ourselves are the first step towards embodying stories in an outward, evident way–such as through a metaphor or an attitude. Before a leader can use stories as vehicles for passing on learning or a vision, they must tell themselves the stories (self-definition), and then move on to disseminate the learning.

Stories can be communicated verbally, through embodying, or by revealing something to ourselves through reflection and imagination. You can apply those approaches to numerous topics that amount to what the story is about. Storytelling as effective learning in organizations and among leaders generally falls into these areas:

☐ Personal histories. These stories tell about the storyteller's origins, journey, feelings, and coping strategies.

☐ Events and circumstances. These stories relate the details of occurrences and occasions to show the inner workings of success or failure in ways that create learning.

☐ Future possibilities. These stories communicate potentialities and plans in ways that inspire and motivate people to share the same vision.

That short list can be integrated with the ways stories are told to form a framework of the possibilities for communicating them. When we examine the framework, we see that different types of stories told in different ways have different meanings and uses. Some are personal building blocks for people–such as personal histories that are stories we tell ourselves. Others are the events and experiences that contribute to organizational learning by creating collective meaning.

## Story time

Learning through stories can happen at almost any time, in any place. Good stories that build leadership and enhance corporate culture can happen in hallways, meeting rooms, offices, parking lots, or training rooms. Stories don't have to be highly amusing or entertaining to be lasting and meaningful, and they don't have to be delivered with a perfectly timed punch line or clever moral. The best corporate storytelling builds on people's experiences and observations to pass on the legacy of leaders who care deeply about sustaining leadership into the future. That is the essence of wisdom stored forward.

Fortunately, everyone has the capacity to tell a good story–to relate experiences, observations, or stories they've heard.

Many opportunities for storytelling exist in organizations and can also be developed. These opportunities or channels by which storytelling happens in organizations are

☐ spontaneous–casual, opportunistic occasions for storytelling

☐ existing–regular, ongoing occurrences during which storytelling can happen

☐ deliberate–planned opportunities for exchanging and sharing stories with the goal of organizational learning.

**Spontaneous channels.** Managers can find many opportunities for storytelling in their everyday world. Staff meetings, project kickoffs, sales debriefings, performance appraisal discussions, weekly status reports, team meetings, and spontaneous discussions in the hall are rich playing fields for sharing stories, not just for tending to tasks.

For example, a sales team might report quota figures in a monthly meeting. A manager could ask them to also recount their best and worst experiences of that reporting period through a story. Such stories could provide the team with memorable vignettes and valuable lessons that

could make the static numbers reports more meaningful.

One-on-one interactions such as performance appraisals and development discussions create superb arenas for relaying a story. Though appraisals are usually a time for managers to talk about behaviors they've observed and changes they'd like to see, such meetings can be an opportunity to emphasize certain points. A manager can share his or her own experience–handling a project or overcoming a failure. During a development discussion, a manager might talk about goals and needs, but he or she can also ask an employee to talk about aspirations–in other words, tell a story. The manager can tell a story about paths people have taken to remind the employee that others have traveled the same road and there's no one correct route.

**Existing channels.** Other channels for storytelling are part of the ongoing work of the organization and can be directed towards the story platform. Probably the best example is orientation programs. Recently, many organizations are revamping them because they've found that they lose talented new employees in the first year or two. Orientation sessions are superb opportunities for senior members to share their perspective on the organization and to personalize their viewpoints through a story. This type of orientation fosters an esprit de corps and welcomes new members rather than seeming to indoctrinate them.

Exit interviews are another excellent opportunity for stories. They can reveal the reasons for employees

wanting to leave, but this valuable information has to be reported to the organization in a timely, useable way.

**Deliberate channels.** Deliberate channels are opportunities created specifically for enhancing organizational learning through storytelling. You can create a forum for shared learning by designing events with significant, specific pathways to open the field for storytelling. Such learning forums are how people exchange stories about organizational life, which often doesn't happen in the pressure of everyday problems. A learning forum is more like a campfire gathering than a seminar. It needs few props. We've found that slides, overheads, and computer presentations detract from the chance for human interaction and connection. Learning forums centered around storytelling build community.

Another deliberate channel we've used is the learning group. You can develop such groups as part of other organizational interventions, including high-potential programs, new-recruit programs, and action learning efforts. Diverse groups that share some common experience and commit to meeting for at least a year will find that the storytelling experience becomes more meaningful. Any member, the leader, or an invited visitor can instigate a story in these groups.

## The rest of the story

All of the channels typically require the following type of planning and support.

---

**Arnold Pitcher, a top executive** with DuPont many years ago, loved to relate the story of a young man who appeared in his office one day touting his development of a new and bold chemical wizardry. He needed a big company's support to implement and market his idea, and he was certain that the big company would benefit greatly. "How about DuPont?" the young man asked.

DuPont executives were accustomed to a full-court press from small inventors with labs in their garages, but after Pitcher and the others took a quick look at the young man's idea, they were skeptical. They sent Edwin H. Land on his way—to the enormous success of the Polaroid Land Camera.

The story, in its telling and retelling, has become a classic in the annals of "the fish that got away" and is also a fine example of a leader sharing his vulnerability.

**Storyteller coaching.** Coaching for leaders who tell stories should emphasize the importance of their insider's view, including their own family issues, thoughts, struggles, concerns, role models, and so forth. What makes learning forums and other such groups memorable is sharing what's important to organizational life but often doesn't get shared. The key to this type of coaching is to emphasize openness and even suggest story topics. The coaching can also advise how long a story should be and not to use slides and overheads.

**Topic assistance.** In learning groups and forums, topics don't always come naturally. "I don't know what to tell a story about" is a common comment. People often need prompts such as, "How about a story from your experience that relates when a vision moved the organization in a new direction?" or "Why not tell a story about a risky career move you or someone else made that worked out well?" Using another kind of prompt, sentence stems, you can also help someone pick a topic. At a meeting of a learning forum, a sentence stem to prompt a story might be, "I came into the office and found that my desk had been moved...." The storyteller then needs to take it from there. Another possible stem: "It made no sense that we're having a meeting to plan the marketing of a new product...." Sentence stems may be all a person needs to jog a recent event that could turn him or her into a storyteller.

**Audience consideration.** When telling stories, consider the audience carefully. The topic and the storyteller are only two important ingredients; the third is the audience. The listeners need to understand why they're there, and they should want to be there. Uncomfortable differences, deeply held opinions, and other relationship issues can make or break a good story and the storyteller. A story's appropriateness for the audience and its ability to create the right ambience are big determinants for the story taking hold.

**Debriefing.** Some stories have to be digested over time by the listeners for them to get the full meaning and learning. A facilitator working with them can help their understanding by asking these questions:
☐ What did you think when you heard about the decision to scrap the first phase of the project?
☐ How does the way the sales division got started tell you about control and influence?
☐ What seemed to be the most important considerations for our storyteller when she decided not to accept the assignment?

The interaction between the story and the listeners as they think about and discuss what they've heard and what the story means is a powerful collaboration in the learning process.

There are a lot of good reasons for the rising interest in storytelling; many have to do with the power of a story to propel informed change. If experience is a great teacher, then stories based on experience—the storyteller's or others'—may be the next best thing to actual experience. Stories tap into our emotions and intellect in ways that get us to remember and to use the information and wisdom of the past to help us make informed choices in the future.

Storytellers also learn something when they retell their stories, by adding new interpretations and meanings. In constant change, stories provide continuity—a link to the past. What a great story that makes!

---

**Beverly L. Kaye** *is a consultant with Beverly Kaye & Associates, 3545 Alana Drive, Sherman Oaks, CA 91403; 818. 995.6454; BevKaye746@aol.com.*

**Betsy Jacobson** *is a consultant with Betsy Jacobson & Associates, 363 Patty Lane, Encinitas, CA 92024; 760.943.1677;X1628@aol.com.*

# Show Them Where You're Headed

## *The more you can communicate your company's vision, the more committed employees will be.*

By Jennifer Laabs

Change is an accepted given by today's employees. Having survived the layoff era of the mid-'90s, what employees are looking for now is how well their companies are led, where those companies are heading and how well organizations can handle change. Workers also want to know whether they can be involved in planning the change and to feel that their ideas are welcome. Employees who find these qualities in an employer are much more committed and likely to stay. They're asking—and demanding answers to—the tough questions about a company's culture before making any commitments.

According to Linda Lewis, vice president, transition, for Oakland, California-based Kaiser Permanente—a health care organization that underwent a cultural change process a few years ago—company culture is important because it acts as the glue that holds the organization together. It also provides a sense of meaning and identity for both the group and the individual, and it establishes communication patterns.

Each of these are important issues in the new dance between employers and employees—it has become more of a give-and-take in which both sides give more, and both sides take more.

## Communicate both the big picture and the little picture.

What are employees looking for from their companies? According to the "1997 Workplace Index" study by Boston-based Towers Perrin, an international management consulting firm, a big part of what they're looking for centers on management effectiveness. In the past, the average employee wasn't expected to know much about the big picture in terms of company strategy, profitability, the competitive market and so on. Now companies are sharing business and financial information to help connect employees to the business and give them more concrete direction about what they should do and how they should do it.

In fact, according to Towers Perrin's study, three-quarters of the employees who were surveyed say they understand the big picture, how that picture relates to their

---

■ **Now employees want a solid commitment from management to give them the information they need to get their jobs done. They want to know what their role is. If that isn't clear to each person, the relationship falls apart.** ■

---

day-to-day activities (their roles and responsibilities), and how they can have an impact on company success. Interestingly, the more employees understand, the more they feel a sense of personal accomplishment and contribution.

Among employees who say they understand what makes the business successful, 84 percent also say they're motivated to help create that success. In contrast, among employees who don't feel they understand the business'

---

*Jennifer Laabs is the associate managing editor at WORK-FORCE. E-mail laabsj@workforcemag.com to comment.*

success factors, just 46 percent say they're motivated. Among employees who say they do understand how they can help achieve company goals and who believe their own activities influence success, 91 percent say they're motivated to help create success. But among those who don't understand their piece of the puzzle and believe they have little personal impact on results, only 23 percent say they're motivated.

So the critical questions that affect employee commitment are: Do employees understand company goals? Can they have a direct impact on company success? And are their roles and responsibilities distinctly communicated? "Clearly, people today understand these things," says Stephen M. Bookbinder, a principal with Towers Perrin and author of both his firm's employee commitment studies. "But where it gets much more negative is whether they understand about the things that affect them within the organization."

According to Towers Perrin's 1997 Workplace Index, people feel they're working hard, but they don't always see others working hard. More than half of the study's respondents now feel that employees at their companies "pass the buck." With the growing workload and the pressure employees feel to keep up their skills and performance, they have little tolerance for co-workers who aren't fully engaged in their work and for managers who allow this behavior. "In a sense, the individuality of things is rising to the surface," comments Bookbinder.

"In the future, managers increasingly will become business leaders and their role will be to inspire employees, then get out of the way," says John A. Challenger, executive vice president of the international outplacement firm Challenger, Gray & Christmas, Inc., based in Chicago. Employees want managers who inspire and coach them, and above all, communicate well and often.

Seven out of 10 respondents (69 percent) of 612 employed persons who responded to a nationwide survey conducted in September by In Touch®, a Minneapolis-based employee opinion and management consulting firm, said it was "very important" to "somewhat important" for top management to do a better job of listening to employee ideas and concerns. After all, employees heard the empowerment message of the early '90s loud and clear. Now they want a more solid commitment from management to give them the information they need to get their jobs done. They want to know what their role is—the "little picture," if you will. If that isn't clear to each and every person, the whole relationship falls apart. And that isn't good for commitment—either way.

## Frequent communication supports the organization's goals.

"Employees are the heart and soul of this organization," said Sharon Faltemier, vice president, people and communications, for Rocketdyne Propulsion & Power in Canoga Park, California (a division of The Boeing Company, based

in Seattle), at The Conference Board's 1998 West Coast HR conference in January. At the conference, Faltemier discussed the firm's vision for 2016 to "be the best provider of rocket propulsion, space power and high energy laser systems in the world." To reach this vision, the firm's two measures of success will be the growth and increase of shareholder value and having involved, committed employees.

Rocketdyne's plan is to gain employee commitment through the following five steps: enable people to work together, provide meaningful assignments, practice highest ethical standards, increase personal growth and employability through training and development, and recognize personal and team contributions. Faltemeier explained that each work group throughout the company must take ownership for its success through a vision support plan that's

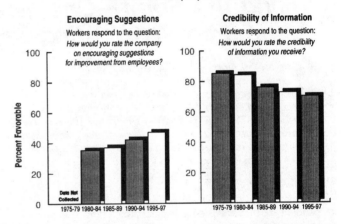

**Workers Rate Company Communications**

Although ratings on how well firms encourage sugestions from employees have consistently gone up (left), the credibility of information employers give workers has decreased (right).

Source: The 1998-'99 Hay Employee Attitudes Study, Hay Group, Inc., Philadelphia

reviewed quarterly. The company formulates a leadership-expectations plan each year. In 1998, the firm's leadership activities have centered on leadership, quality culture, continuous learning and metrics-based management.

Bentley College in Waltham, Massachusetts, also has initiated a goal system that defines the overall goals of the college and then develops division, department and individual goals. By ensuring that individual goals are tied to the overall goals of the college, each employee is able to identify his or her personal contribution to the company goals.

Bentley also has recently strengthened merit-raise programs so exceptional performers receive more than average performers. The president holds regular "town meetings" to let employees know what's happening and to ensure that everyone knows where the college is headed. All of this helps fulfill the strong need for communication and recognition that our sampling of employees said was important to them.

And at Parker Aerospace Corp. in Irvine, California, several initiatives contribute to the organization's effort to enhance loyalty, including frequent communication, opportunities for strong peer interaction, and reward and recognition programs. Linda Walker, vice president of HR, says the company maintains communication through newsletters, one-on-one meetings and other ways with the more than 5,600 employees in her division to keep workers in the loop.

An interesting part of the new employee-commitment rules is that workers' relationships with their managers and managers' relationships with their teams also have become much more important. Workers have been known to stay with a team and not accept job offers at other places because they have a great relationship with their bosses

and they're afraid they may not find that elsewhere. It's true, the grass isn't always greener on the other side.

So the more a company can encourage the communication channels between employees and their supervisors, the stronger the employee's commitment to the entire company will become. After all, people go to work every day and usually interact with their team, not with a big conglomerate. The more a company does to enhance and leverage those close relationships, the stronger the performance bond will be.

### Employees are more committed to winners.

Employees want to be part of a winning team. And winning companies are being identified through various

## *Killing the Spirit—One Worker Goes From Committed, To Wanting To Be Committed*

There are 30 months that Carrie Pierce would really rather forget. Unfortunately, she can't. Pierce was the victim of an employment relationship that went terribly wrong—turning from commitment into condemnation. Although she can now joke that she may need therapy to help her put the whole experience into perspective, it's no laughing matter. While it's hard to believe that such loyalty lapses are happening in today's workplace, Pierce's story provides insight into how employee commitment can quickly sour when the wrong ingredients are poured into the workforce mix.

Pierce had worked in the film industry for years as an independent aesthetician doing makeup, including special-effects makeup. She had owned her own business for several years and consulted with many firms when she was recruited by a cutting-edge, start-up skin-care company (which shall remain nameless at Pierce's request) that was based in Japan, but had a couple of U.S. divisions. The firm had several thousand employees between its overseas and American locations.

Pierce was first hired as a consultant, bringing all her experience as a makeup artist to bear in letting the firm in on the pulse of the skin-care and makeup industry. Initially, she helped the company design packaging, ran test formulations and consulted on price points. From there, she became the company's director of education, teaching the growing company's internal and field employees about the company's products, customer service techniques and basic company philosophy, and also wrote training manuals.

Later, she was promoted to vice president of sales and marketing, but also handled all the employee-relations issues—even though she had no formal HR title. It was expected that she keep all her old duties, even though she was given executive responsibilities, as well. "When I first started, and even to the point I was promoted to vice president, I was very pleased [with the company]," says Pierce. "At the beginning, they seemed to understand what I was bringing to the company and I saw a great deal of potential. But as I went on, it became clear to me that many people were very unhappy. I've never met so many discontented people in my whole life." One of the biggest reasons, she says, is that the

president of her division was a conniving, crooked, underhanded man. "When I finally left, several other people also left and a whole division of the company just collapsed because of this one man's mismanagement," she says. Pierce explains that the president, and most of those directly below him, had questionable, often unethical, ways of doing business.

Outwardly, it seemed like the perks and benefits were good. She admits she got a big salary and great benefits. But as time went on, she discovered that another executive in the same position at the firm's sister company was earning $60,000 more a year than she did—and was doing less than she was. Pierce describes how she brought in several national accounts and designed a marketing plan that went gangbusters—none of which her counterpart did. "I think the attitude was so bad in the company because most people assumed she was sleeping with the boss," says Pierce. "And everyone talked about it. It's kind of like a Clinton thing."

On a management level, the president was completely disorganized and was loyal to whoever was in front of him at any given time, then he'd turn on them behind their backs. He'd keep "dead wood" around because he was afraid to fire people, even though everyone knew who the non-performers were, and resented them.

All the while, Pierce couldn't believe she found herself in the middle of such a predicament. "It knocked the wind out of my sails for many, many months afterward," says Pierce. "I don't know that I'll ever approach work the same way. It was such a foul, negative environment."

Pierce now writes industry-related articles in the beauty business and also writes children's books. "I guess I went from a high-falutin' power structure to wanting to just sit and draw pictures," she adds. "I want something cuddly and fluffy in my life."

*The moral of the story is: There's no substitute for ethical, visionary leadership. Like attracts like. Companies that don't shape up will see employees shipping out.*

—JL

> ■ **Winning vision usually translates into greater employee commitment. But employees want to be invited to ride the train, rather than stand on the sidelines watching it go by.** ■

forms—the media, employee surveys, benchmarking, national and local awards, and so on.

"One of the things we find is that when workers believe in the direction their company is headed, they have stronger commitment. That's because they think their company will be one of the winners in the global marketplace," says David L. Stum, president of The Loyalty Institute™, an Aon Consulting Worldwide division based in Ann Arbor, Michigan.

Leaders at Sun Microsystems Inc. based in Mountain View, California, know what a winner looks like. They're already sixth on *Fortune* magazine's 1997 list of the world's most admired companies in the computers and office equipment category. But the firm isn't stopping there. Leaders there have a vision of what they want their firm to look like by the turn of the century: One million Solaris licenses. Two million systems. A $1 billion SPARC company.

"Sun's course is set," said Lora Colflesh, vice president of human resources operations, in a presentation at The Conference Board's West Coast HR Conference in January. In presentation materials, she talked of a committed workforce that's "engaged with the SMI vision, customer-focused, highly productive, teamwork-oriented and dedicated to continuous improvement. Employees are open to paradigm shifts, and willing to initiate difficult changes needed to meet business objectives. Throughout Sun, employees will be empowered to take initiative, and will be accountable for results."

Winning vision usually translates into greater employee commitment. But employees want to be invited to ride the train, rather than stand on the sidelines watching it go by. All the experts and studies say that the more you can involve employees in the direction the company is moving, the faster it will get to its destination—and everyone can share the rewards.

## Provide context and support for change.

For most employees, cultural changes such as reorganizations or mergers can feel like the company has pressed the "fast forward" button and let the tape spiral out of control. It's utter turmoil for people, unless they have an understanding of what's really going on. If they're not in on the secret of corporate change, they'll often resist. "The truth is most resistance is tough to diagnose—and even tougher to overcome," says Ken Hultman in *Making Change Irresistible* (Davies-Black Publishing, 1998).

The good news is, according to Aon's study, a large portion of employees (79 percent) feel their organizations are ready to make the changes needed to stay competitive. However, they have slightly greater confidence in the ability of their own work groups (74 percent) to make changes quicker than the company's overall ability (69 percent) to move quickly when changes are needed. Fewer employees (66 percent) feel encouraged to participate in change efforts, perhaps because workers feel their organizations don't want them to "make waves." These are critical areas for HR professionals to understand as they're immersed in change management projects and organizational change efforts.

Aon's experts suggest that to make any change effort more successful, you need to investigate the expectations of your workforce, create opportunities for employee input, support and reward employee initiatives for improvement, and improve communication—especially during organizational turbulence. There's that communication theme again. The more you have an open-door policy and mean it, the more your people will stick with you during the good times and the difficult ones. Change may never be easy in the business world, but if employees are engaged in the change, it could be easier. Who knows? It might even be fun.

## Involve employees in decisions regarding leadership, culture and change.

The big theme in leadership is: Give them better communication—of the big picture all the way down to their role. It's more important than ever for companies to lead with a clear vision, communicate that vision and involve workers in implementing it.

Human resources professionals, who often are embroiled in their firms' change management and cultural-change processes, have a front-seat opportunity to involve employees in their organizations' strategy. Employees want to be in on the company's projects, and to be in on the action, they want improved communication from co-workers, managers and the company in general. As one employee anonymously puts it: "I get frustrated when upper management manipulates news just to get a particular spin and invoke a certain mood with employees. We're intelligent folks—we can separate spin from facts."

Perhaps HR pros would do well to remember the saying: "We have met the enemy and they are ours" (Oliver Perry, 1813). Employees are clearly saying: "We're not the enemy. We're on your team. Treat us that way."

# Unit 4

## Key Points to Consider

❖ Organizations spend a great deal of money on training and development. Why do many organizations feel it is necessary to provide courses in-house? Why do other organizations spend money on outside programs? Why might the training programs of some firms be inadequate, even though a great deal of money is spent on them? What are some of the questions that organizations should be asking of their training and development operations? What are some strategies that can be used to train "Generation X"?

❖ What are your career plans, and how do you plan to implement them? How do you see the role of women changing in organizations? How do you plan to make the change from school to work?

 **Links** **www.dushkin.com/online/**

These sites are annotated on pages 4 and 5.

Every organization needs to develop its employees. This is accomplished through a number of activities, including formal corporate training, career development, and performance appraisal. Just as society and the economy will continue to change, so will the human resource needs of organizations. Individuals and their employers must work together to achieve the effective use of human resources. They must plan together to make the maximum use of their abilities in order to meet the challenge of the changing environment in which they live.

American industry spends approximately the same amount of money each year on training and developing employees as is spent by all colleges and universities combined. It also trains roughly the same number of people as there are students in traditional postsecondary education. Corporate programs are often very elaborate and can involve months or even years of training. In fact, corporate training and development programs have been recognized by academia for their quality and excellence. The American Council for Education has a program designed to evaluate and make recommendations concerning corporate and government training programs for college credit. Corporations themselves have entered into the business of granting degrees that are recognized by regional accrediting agencies. For example, McDonald's grants an associate's degree from "Hamburger U." General Motors Institute offers the oldest formalized corporate degree-granting program in the United States, awarding a bachelor's in industrial management; Ernst and Young offers a master's in accountancy; and a Ph.D. program in policy analysis is available from the Rand Corporation. American industry is in the business of educating and training employees, not only as a simple introduction and orientation to the corporation, but as a continual and constant enterprise of lifelong learning so that both the firms and the employees can meet the challenges of an increasingly competitive world. Meeting these challenges depends on knowledge, not on sweat, and relies on the ability to adapt to and adopt technological, social, and economic changes faster than competitors.

The key to corporate training and development for it to be effective is that it needs to be in line with the objectives of the firm. That is really the difference between corporate training and education and the more traditional forms of education and training. Companies must spend their dollars on training and education that will directly benefit them and their employees.

There is an important difference between jobs and careers. Everyone who works, whether self-employed or employed by someone else, does a job. Although a career is made up of a series of jobs and positions over an individual's working life, it is more than that. It is a sense of direction, a purpose, and a knowledge of where one is going in one's professional life. Careers are shaped by individuals through the decisions they make concerning their own lives, not by organizations. It is the individual who must ultimately take the responsibility for what happens in his or her career. Organizations offer opportunities for advancement, and they fund training and development based on their own self-interest, not solely on workers' interest. Accordingly, the employee must understand that the responsibility for career development ultimately rests with him- or herself.

To ignore the development of the potential of the employees of any organization is to court disaster—not only for the organization, but for the employee. People who have stopped developing themselves are cheating themselves and their employers. Both will be vulnerable to changes brought on by increased competition, but the workers will be the ones who join the ranks of the unemployed.

Developing Effective Human Resources

# Sharpening the Leading Edge

**The State of the Industry Report reveals the steps companies must take to ascend to the top of the training field.**

By Laurie J. Bassi and Mark E. Van Buren

**D**ata from more than 750 organizations that participated in ASTD's 1998 Benchmarking Service (reporting figures from 1997) is in. And the evidence shows that employer-provided training in the United States is clearly on the rise. Both the amount of money invested in training and the percentage of people trained increased substantially in 1997. However, the survey also shows that the gap between the leaders in company-provided training and the average organization is growing in many respects through the foreseeable future. The average organization has improved its training investments and practices, but at a slower rate than the leading edge.

In the ASTD State of the Industry Report covering 1996, we revealed the drama unfolding between leading-edge firms and the state of the employer-provided training industry. Based on 1996 numbers, we designated 32 companies (out of 500) as leading-edge firms. The leading-edge firms represent the pinnacle of training practice in the United States in terms of the amount of training and the types of human performance practices they provide. We also reported that leading-edge firms distinguished themselves in their use of learning technologies and their levels of outsourcing, as well as their performance. (See the box, The Cast, for more information on the leading edge.)

Using the same methods, this year we identified 55 organizations, or 7.2 percent of the Benchmarking Service participants as leading-edge firms. This small group at the apex of the training industry again led their counterparts in the amount of training they provided, the resources they invested in employee development, the practices in which they engaged, and the means by which they delivered their training.

Perhaps your organization looks more like a typical company than a leading-edge firm. You may be wondering what it would take for your organization to transform itself into a firm at the forefront of training in the United States. Our Key Ratios for the training industry show the gap that you'd have to cover to catapult your company into this elite group. The Ratios reveal that, along most dimensions, this divide is expected to widen in the coming years. The slope to the top is becoming steeper. So, if your organization aspires to be on the leading edge, the sooner you start the better. The evidence suggests that your bottom line will thank you.

## Your leading-edge makeover

Before describing what transforming your organization into a leading-edge firm would entail, you may be wondering whether it can be

From *Training and Development Journal,* January 1999, pp. 23-33. © 1999 by the American Society for Training and Development. All rights reserved. Reprinted by permission.

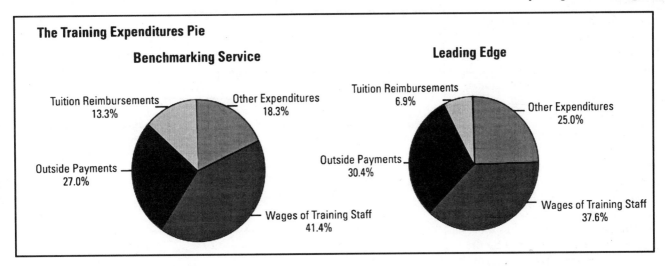

**The Training Expenditures Pie**

**Benchmarking Service**

Tuition Reimbursements 13.3%
Other Expenditures 18.3%
Outside Payments 27.0%
Wages of Training Staff 41.4%

**Leading Edge**

Tuition Reimbursements 6.9%
Other Expenditures 25.0%
Outside Payments 30.4%
Wages of Training Staff 37.6%

accomplished at all. The answer is yes. Of the participants in the last two years of the Benchmarking Service,

85 organizations reported data for both 1996 and 1997. Six of those organizations are leading-edge firms,

based on their 1997 numbers. Four of the six were also among our leading edge for 1996. The other two, however, are examples of firms that moved from the ranks of average organizations into the leading edge in just one year. One firm nearly doubled the percentage of employees trained and its spending on training per employee. The other complemented an already high volume of training with a number of leading-edge human performance and training practices. The data reveals that you can emulate leading-edge firms by focusing your change efforts in these areas:

☐ human performance practices
☐ number of employees trained
☐ training expenditures
☐ outsourcing
☐ course topics
☐ delivery methods
☐ review and evaluation.

**Start with the system.** A good starting place for your leading-edge makeover isn't how much you spend on training, but rather the things you do to improve workplace learning and performance in general. As was true last year, a coherent system of human performance practices is a critical feature of a leading-edge firm. Such firms align their training with a number of innovative practices that can be categorized into these groups:

☐ High performance work practices (such as self-directed teams, access to business information)

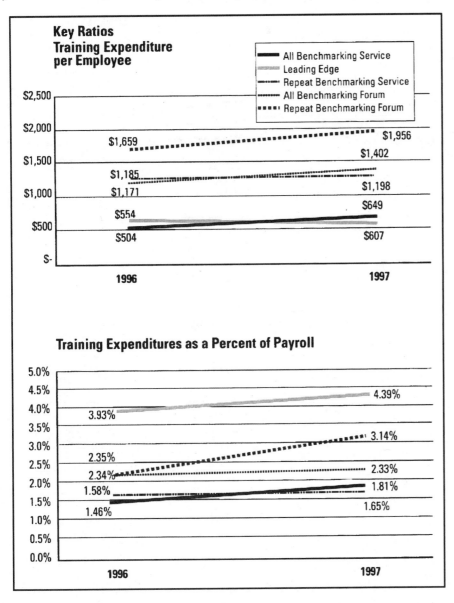

**Key Ratios Training Expenditure per Employee**

All Benchmarking Service
Leading Edge
Repeat Benchmarking Service
All Benchmarking Forum
Repeat Benchmarking Forum

$1,659 → $1,956
$1,402
$1,185 / $1,171 → $1,198
$554 → $649
$504 → $607

1996 / 1997

**Training Expenditures as a Percent of Payroll**

3.93% → 4.39%
2.35% → 3.14%
2.34% → 2.33%
1.58% → 1.81%
1.46% → 1.65%

1996 / 1997

◻ Innovative compensation practices (such as profit sharing, group-based pay)

Innovative training practices (such as mentoring or coaching programs, training information systems).

(For a complete list of the practices in each group, please see the full State of the Industry Report that accompanies [the January 1999] issue of *Training & Development*.)

To join the leading edge, you will need to use an average of 13 of the 17 practices we placed in those groups, rather than the 11 used by the typical organization. Your company will also have to reach at least 50 percent of your employees with six of the practices. In most organizations, only 4.5 of the practices reach more than 50 percent of employees.

**Training for everyone.** Once you have the whole system of leading-edge human performance practices in place to support your training efforts, your next task may be to increase the amount of training you provide. Fortunately, here we have some good news: This is the one area in which the slope to the top may not be as steep. Many organizations gained ground on leading-edge firms from 1996 to 1997 in the percentage of employees trained. And we expect to see that the gap has narrowed even further when 1998 data is reported. This is partly because, for leading-edge firms, there are few employees who aren't already being trained. If your company is like most organizations, you train about 74 percent of your employees. This figure would have to be increased to more than 86 percent. For the typical organization in our Benchmarking Service, with slightly more than 5,000 employees, that would mean training an additional 600 employees.

**It doesn't come cheap.** Although you may not want to start with the issue of money, training more people and surrounding your training with leading-edge training practices will require a greater financial investment. The leading edge is rapidly raising the bar of excellence in training expenditures.

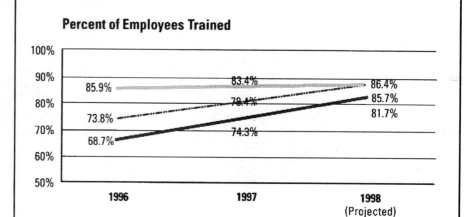

**Percent of Employees Trained**

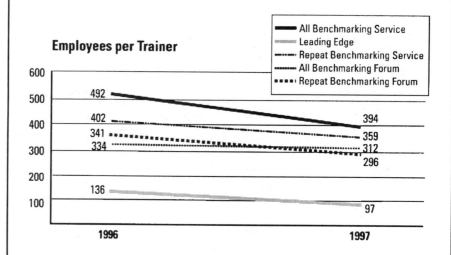

**Employees per Trainer**

All Benchmarking Service
Leading Edge
Repeat Benchmarking Service
All Benchmarking Forum
Repeat Benchmarking Forum

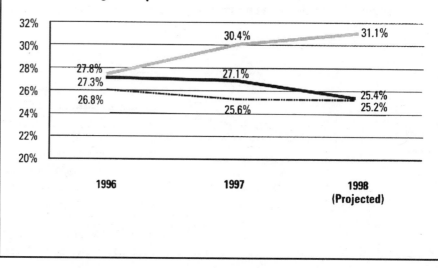

**Percentage of Expenditures to Outside Firms**

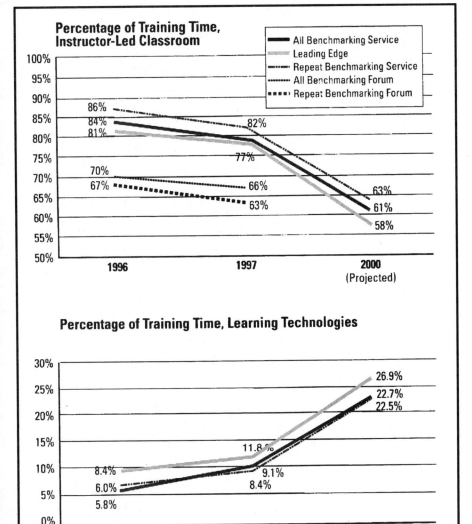

**Percentage of Training Time, Instructor-Led Classroom**

Legend:
- All Benchmarking Service
- Leading Edge
- Repeat Benchmarking Service
- All Benchmarking Forum
- Repeat Benchmarking Forum

86%, 84%, 81%, 82%, 70%, 77%, 67%, 66%, 63%, 63%, 61%, 58%

1996, 1997, 2000 (Projected)

**Percentage of Training Time, Learning Technologies**

26.9%, 22.7%, 22.5%, 11.8%, 9.1%, 8.4%, 8.4%, 6.0%, 5.8%

1996, 1997, 2000 (Projected)

Key Ratios: training expenditures per employee and total expenditures on training as a percent of payroll. Viewed from that vantage point, the spending gap appears even more difficult to close. The average leading-edge firm has fewer than half the number of employees of the typical company and an appreciably smaller payroll. As a result, you would have had to triple your 1997 training expenditures per employee just to match the leading edge's 1997 figures. While the sample average grew by about $150 per employee, the leading-edge average rose by about $300 per employee.

Total training expenditures as a percentage of payroll paint a similar picture. Both the industry as a whole and the leading edge raised this Key Ratio between 1996 and 1997. However, the gap also grew during the same period. To pull even with the leading edge on this measure in 1997, your organization would have had to double its spending level. Using those two measures of spending, our Key Ratios chart also reveals that Benchmarking Forum organizations, though world-class in many respects, fall somewhere between the leading-edge firm and the average organization.

**Spreading it around.** OK. So now you know that you have a high hurdle to jump on your way to the top when it comes to spending. It might be helpful to know where the top firms put their money.

One way to look at expenditure allocations is to examine the pieces that make up our total training expenditure pies:

☐ wages and salaries of trainers
☐ payments to outside training firms
☐ tuition reimbursements
☐ other internal expenditures (for example, facilities, materials, administration, and trainer travel expenses).

A first glance reveals that spending priorities between the leading edge and general practice are similar. Both groups spend the largest percentage of their money on trainers' wages and salaries, followed by payments to external firms, other expenditures, and

On the bright side, most organizations reported significant increases in their total amount of spending on training between 1996 and 1997. Topping the charts, of course, were our mostly large Benchmarking Forum organizations, whose average total expenditures rose from $29.8 million in 1996 to $32.7 million in 1997. In fact, average total expenditures for the BMF firms that reported for both years grew by $8 million during that period.

The average total expenditures for the sample as a whole are much more modest, but reveal the same upward trend. The typical firm spent about $2 million on training in 1997, up from $1.4 million in 1996. Projected total expenditures for 1998 were expected

to be up slightly as well ($2.1 million). Leading-edge firms, meanwhile, increased their spending even more. Total expenditures for the typical leading-edge firm grew from $3.4 to $4.1 million between 1996 and 1997. In 1998, average total training expenditures are projected to be $4.7 million per firm. This rate of growth means that the gap between the leading edge and general practice is likely to grow from $2 million to $2.6 million in two short years.

Total training expenditures, however, do not provide a good basis for comparison across organizations because training expenditures are heavily influenced by the size of the organization. More accurate comparisons can be made using two of our tuition reimbursements. Closer examination, however, shows that your leading-edge makeover would entail reducing wages and salaries by about four percentage points and increasing outside payments by the same amount. Similarly, you would spend about 6.5 percentage points less on tuition reimbursements and about the same amount more on other expenses. Because leading-edge firms spend more on training to begin with, that means that while you shift the allocation of your spending across categories, you'll also have to increase your spending in all categories.

The percent of payments to outside firms deserves a special look, because this figure serves as our Key Ratio on outsourcing. Outsourcing is the only area in which our data suggests divergent trends between the training industry as a whole and the leading edge. The percentage of expenditures to outside firms is going up for leading-edge firms, but headed downward for the training industry in general. Although the percentage was about the same for both groups in 1996, leading-edge expenditures to outside training providers were three percentage points higher in 1997. Benchmarking Forum companies, which track external expenditures differently, also reported a decrease in outside spending from 1996 to 1997.

Another measure of outsourcing is the percentage of organizations using outside training and consulting firms. The percentage of leading-edge firms using outside providers in 1997 remained constant at 91 percent, but for the sample as a whole, the figure increased from 73 percent to 76 percent. Taken with the percentage of outside spending for training, these numbers suggest that the typical organization has become more likely to use outside providers, but spending on services has not risen at the same rate as it has among the leading edge. By either measure, your transformation into a leading-edge firm will require allocating more funds for outside training than in 1996.

**Slices by the course.** Another way to slice expenditures on training

is by topic or course type. We tracked training time in 1996 and training expenditures in 1997, making comparisons between the two years difficult to draw. In 1996, more than a quarter (26 percent) of all training time went to technical training, either computer applications training or job-specific technical skills training. In 1997, technical training courses accounted for more than 29 percent of expenditures in the typical company. The figure for leading-edge firms was only slightly higher (31 percent). Those expenditures were most often spent on sales and dealer training, executive development, and professional skills training. Leading-edge firms opt less frequently for customer service training, management and supervisory training, and safety and compliance training. None of the differences would amount to more than two or three percentage points.

**Getting it there.** Your journey to the top would not be complete without some changes in the way you deliver training to employees. First of all, no matter which organizations you consider, you'll see that our Key Ratio on delivery methods—instructor-led classroom training as a percent of training time—is declining. In 1997, most organizations delivered about 4 percent less of their training by instructors in a classroom setting. Projections to the year 2000 hint that figure may drop by another 20 percentage points. For the typical organization, that indicates traditional training will drop from more than 80 percent to just over 60 percent. Large corporations, such as many of those in the Benchmarking Forum, reported figures at or below 70 percent for 1997.

Based on the numbers reported in both years of the Benchmarking Service, the difference between leading-edge firms and the overall sample in instructor-led, classroom-based training is expected to hold constant at about five percentage points through the year 2000. That means your organization has less than two years to close the gap and take another step toward becoming a leading-edge firm.

## BUSINESS SECTOR OVERVIEW

### Agriculture/Mining/Construction (2%)

Comprises agriculture producers; mining, oil, exploration, and extraction companies; construction companies; fisheries; and forestry. These companies have one of the highest percentages of employees receiving training yet invest the least money as measured by their low training expenditures. This industry lags in its implementation of learning technologies and in its provision of computer literacy and applications and job-specific technical skills training. These companies have fewer internal trainers per employee and use a large percentage of independent training consultants and firms.

### Information Technology (15.3%)

Comprises computer, electronics, and communications equipment manufacturers; software designers; telecommunications services; and information technology services and consulting firms. These companies show a solid commitment to training investments, with the highest training expenditures as a percentage of payroll and one of the highest expenditures per employee. They lead in their use of all presentation and delivery technologies, and they predict a continued shift in favor of those technologies. Although reporting one of the highest levels of internal trainers per employee, these companies also use a large percentage of outside trainers and independent consultants, educational institutions, and product suppliers.

### Nondurable Manufacturing (9.3%)

Comprises manufacturers of nondurable goods such as food and beverages, apparel, textiles, plastics and chemicals, paper and pulp, rubber, petroleum products, and leather. Includes printers, publishers, and refineries. With a low number of internal trainers per employee, this industry relies on outside and independent consultants and trainers, including product suppliers and educational institutions. With both total and outside expenditures on the low end of the spectrum, these companies have shown minimal improvement in their overall performance. Although their use of delivery technologies is limited, they predict declines in classroom training and increases in the use of learning technologies. Light CBT users, they opt for interactive TV, multimedia, CD-ROMS, voicemail, and LANs. The focus of their training lies in quality, competition, and business-practices training along with job-specific technical skills. Little emphasis is placed on computer literacy and applications training.

### Durable Manufacturing (9.6%)

Comprises manufacturers of durable goods such as wood products, stone and glass, fabricated metal products, machines and electrical equipment and transportation equipment. This industry has maintained stable training expenditures, with little improvement in overall performance. However, a significant increase in outside training expenditures means that these companies rely heavily on external trainers, including product suppliers and educational institutions. A large percentage of employees receive training; content is focused on quality, competition, and business-practices training along with basic skills training. Predicting a significant increase in their use of learning technologies, these companies plan to reduce their commitment to classroom-based methods. A heavier user of CBT, teleconferencing, and interactive TV than other industries, this industry also forecasts a slight increase in its use of EPSS.

### Transportation and Public Utilities (8.2%)

Comprises power, water, and gas utilities; trucking and warehousing companies; airlines and railroads; water transportation companies; and parcel services. These companies spend a large amount on training, with the leading percentage of total expenditures per employee and one of the highest total training expenditures. Strong multimedia, EPSS, and virtual-reality users, members of this industry predict an increase in the use of CBT.

They are more likely to use learning technologies as their delivery mechanism than other industries, favoring intranets, LANs, and simulators. They teach primarily basic skills, executive development, and job-specific technical skills.

### Trade (5.3%)

Comprises retail and food stores; home furnishings and equipment stores and food and beverage facilities; apparel and accessory stores; building materials, hardware, garden supply, and mobile home dealers; and wholesale trade or distributors. A combination of a high percentage of employees receiving training and the lowest training expenditures results in low expenditures per employee. This industry is more likely to rely on independent consultants and trainers than other industries, and it has a low number of internal trainers per employee. These companies project significant increases in the use of CBT, multimedia, and groupware for training. Training content focuses on customer service; sales; and dealer, management, and job-specific technical skills training, while underemphasizing computer literacy, computer applications, and professional skills training.

### Finance, Insurance, and Real Estate (14.6%)

Comprises banks and other financial institutions, insurance companies, securities brokers, and real estate companies. These companies tend to invest more in training than other industries and they report improvements in their overall performance. This industry focuses more on computer literacy and applications than job-specific technical and basic skills training. It has a high number of internal trainers per employee in comparison to other industries, yet uses a significant percentage of outside trainers, consultants, and product suppliers. The leading user of EPSS, this industry predicts a decline in classroom training and a general increase in learning-technology delivery methods.

### Services (18.4%)

Comprises hotels; business and personal services; automotive repair com-

panies; professional services; educational, legal, social, and other consumer services. These companies spend a larger percentage on training than companies in most other industries. They also tend to use more internal trainers per employee, and they project notable increases in the use of learning technologies. These companies are heavy users of CBT, teleconferencing, and EPSS methods, and they predict increases in interactive TV and groupware training. Training content focuses on professional skills training and new-employee orientation.

### Health Care (10.4%)

Comprises hospitals, clinics, doctors' offices, and home care companies. These companies have the highest percentage of employees receiving training, yet the lowest training expenditures per employee and as a percentage of payroll. These companies have a higher level of new-employee orientation training and computer literacy application training. Light users of CBT and EPSS compared to other industries, this industry prefers groupware, teleconferencing, and interactive TV over other technologies. These companies predict a significant decline in their commitment to classroom training.

### Government (6.9%)

Comprises federal, state, and local government organizations or agencies. Although government organizations have a high level of spending on training, their expenditures as a percentage of payroll rank near the bottom. This industry uses outside training consultants and companies more heavily than other industries. Governments place a particular emphasis on computer literacy and applications, job-specific technical skills, and basic skills versus professional skills training. Preferring classroom-based training, this industry predicts minimal increases in its use of learning technologies. Although government agencies use CBT and multimedia less than most companies, they tend to be heavier users of interactive TV and groupware. Government organizations did not report substantial improvements in their overall performance.

## Benchmarking Forum Members

Aetna Incorporated
Allstate Insurance Company
American Express
Ameritech Services
Andersen Worldwide
AT&T
Banc One
Bank of Ireland
Bank of Scotland
Bell Atlantic
Boeing
Caterpillar
Chase Manhattan Bank, N.A.
Chevron
Citibank, N.A.
Colgate-Palmolive
COMPAQ
Corning, Inc.
Cummins Engine Company
Delco Electronics Corporation
Dow Chemical Company
Duke Energy
DuPont
Eastman Chemical
Eli Lilly and Company
ISVOR Fiat S.p.A.
Florida Power & Light
Ford
Freddie Mac
General Motors
GTE
Hallmark Cards
Hoffmann-La Roche
Iams Company
IBM

Intel Corporation
Johnson & Johnson
KPMG Peat Marwick LLP
Larsen & Toubro Limited
Levi Strauss & Company
Lockhead Martin
MCI
Moore Corporation Ltd.
Motorola
Polaroid Corporation
PricewaterhouseCoopers
Procter & Gamble
Qualcomm
SBC Communications
Scandinavian Airlines System
South African Breweries
Southern California Gas Co.
SPRINT
Tennessee Valley Authority
UNISYS
United Parcel Service
USAA
US Department of Energy
US Department of Health and
  Human Services
US Department of Transportation
US Office of Personnel
  Management
US Postal Service
Xerox

See the Research section of the ASTD Website at *www.astd.org* for the most current roster of Benchmarking Forum Members.

A large part of the tremendous change in the delivery of training is driven by learning technologies such as CD-ROMs, intranets, local area networks, and the Internet. Our Benchmarking Service estimates reveal that learning technologies account for a relatively small, but growing, percentage of training time. Leading-edge firms delivered 11.8 percent of their training in 1997 using learning technologies, compared to the training-industry average of 9.1 percent. Those figures are up from 8.4 percent and 5.8 percent respectively in 1996.

The divide between the leading edge and general practice is projected to widen even further by the year 2000. By then, you'll have to deliver more than a quarter (27 percent) of your training using learning technologies to be on the leading edge. The overall average will also rise, but only to 22.5 percent. Either way, the shift away from traditional instructor-led, classroom-based training portends a major change in both the ways training is delivered and the ways people learn.

Several technologies in particular are leading the way. In 1997, about half of all organizations in the sample delivered training via CD-ROMs, and roughly a third delivered training via electronic mail and local area networks. By the year 2000, 80 percent expect to be using CD-ROMs; intranets (70 percent) and the Internet (58 percent) ranked second and third. In fact, both forms of Web-based training are projected to triple in use between 1997 and 2000. As you would expect, to join the ranks of the leading edge by the year 2000, you would be even more likely to use CDROMs (93 percent), intranets (85 percent), and the Internet (62 percent).

More indicative of the degree to which those technologies are being used for training is the actual percent of courses for which they are the primary delivery method. Organizations that use CD-ROMs, for instance, used them only for slightly more than 9 percent of their courses in 1997. By 2000, that figure is expected to double. Electronic mail and LANs, by contrast, were used for 18 and 19 percent of courses respectively in 1997, with little increase expected over the next three years. The leading learning technology by the year 2000 is expected to be the company intranet. The typical organization expects to use its intranet to deliver more than 22 percent of its courses by that time.

Another piece of good news is that the percentages of courses leading-edge firms deliver via learning technologies are not any higher than in the typical organization. In fact, for some technologies, such as CD-ROMs and the Internet, the leading-edge percentages are lower. In other words, to join the leading edge, your organization won't have to use the technologies you currently have for more courses. Rather, you'll have to use a greater variety of learning technologies to deliver your training than you currently do.

**Come full circle.** Before completing your journey to the leading edge, there are a few other important issues to consider. One is how you manage the performance of your employees to ensure that they're making the most of your leading-edge training.

## The Cast

### The Benchmarking Service

Established in 1997, ASTD's Benchmarking Service is a free service open to all organizations around the world that desire to assess the strengths and weaknesses of their employer-provided training efforts. Participants receive a customized report showing how their training investments, practices, and outcomes stack up against those of other organizations in their industry and overall benchmarks. To participate in the Benchmarking Service, look for the *ASTD Measurement Kit* packaged with the March 1999 issue of *Training & Development*, or request a free copy from the Benchmarking Service; 703.838.5841; bench-service@astd.org.

### All Benchmarking Service Organizations

Of the 801 participants in the 1998 Benchmarking Service from the United States, 754 organizations provided a sufficient amount of valid and comparable information on their 1997 training investments and practices to be included in our overall averages. (More than 400 organizations from outside the United States were excluded for the purposes of this report. Look for a full report on these participants in an upcoming issue of *Training & Development*.)

More than half of the organizations (56 percent) reported data for the entire organization while the rest reported for a specific unit or division. The average organization employed 5,147 employees in 1997, with an annual payroll of $139.8 million. Nearly 40 percent had fewer than 500 employees, and 64 percent were for-profit companies.

### Repeat Benchmarking Service Organizations

Of the 754 eligible 1998 Benchmarking Service organizations, 85 reported data for the same unit in the 1997 Benchmarking Service. These organizations were similar to the other participants in 1998, except that a lower proportion were located in the service sector and a higher proportion were from the finance, insurance, and real estate sector. Data from these organizations was used to determine whether changes between 1996 and 1997 estimates were due to changes in the composition of participants in the Benchmarking Service in each year.

### Leading-Edge Firms

Using a statistical technique known as cluster analysis, 55 participants in the 1998 Benchmarking Service were identified as firms on the leading edge of training. These firms scored high on all of the following criteria:

☐ percentage of employees trained

☐ training expenditures per employee

☐ use of innovative training practices

☐ use of high performance work practices

☐ use of innovative compensation practices.

The typical leading-edge firm employed fewer than 2,250 employees in 1997, at an annual payroll of $113.7 million. Leading-edge firms were more likely to be for-profit companies (78 percent) and located in the information technology sector. None of the leading-edge firms were located in the health care sector.

### The Benchmarking Forum

Since 1991, ASTD's Benchmarking Forum has provided a venue for world-class organizations to benchmark their training, learning, and performance improvement processes, practices, and services. Members benefit from a broad array of services and products, including comparative data analysis and benchmarking, member-to-member surveys, excellence-in-practice search and dissemination, trends research, working groups, detailed member profiles, and semi-annual meetings. Membership, determined by an application and peer-review process, comprises both private- and public-sector organizations that exhibit world-class training, learning, or performance improvement, and are committed to raising the quality and effectiveness of their workforce development efforts. For more information about the Benchmarking Forum or to apply for membership, please contact Scott Cheney, director, 703.683.9206; scheney@astd.org.

### All Benchmarking Forum Organizations

In 1998, 92 organizations reported data to the ASTD Benchmarking Forum. Of these, 71 eligible organizations provided data for the entire organization or a specific business unit. The typical Benchmarking Forum company employed more than 26,700 people, with an annual payroll of $1.4 billion. The Benchmarking Forum organizations represent all major industry groups with high concentrations from the information technology and manufacturing sectors and a low concentration from the service sector.

### Repeat Benchmarking Forum Organizations

Of the 71 eligible 1998 Benchmarking Forum organizations, 45 reported data in 1997. These organizations were not appreciably different from the other 36 reporting companies. The repeat Benchmarking Forum organizations serve the same purpose as the repeat benchmarking service organizations: to sort out changes in estimates due to changes in composition.

## Thank You

We would like to thank the following organizations for their support and sponsorship of the ASTD State of the Industry Report

- AchieveGlobal
- Disney Institute
- The Forum Corporation
- Franklin Covey
- New Horizons Computer Learning Center
- PACE Group
- PricewaterhouseCoopers
- Provant
- U.S. Department of Labor/America's Learning eXchange

As in last year's report, our leading-edge firms exhibited a much heavier reliance on performance management practices that give high-quality individualized feedback, including 360 feedback and peer review, individual development plans, and annual performance reviews. Almost all leading-edge firms conducted annual performance reviews for most of their employees in 1997, versus only 85 percent of the total sample. Three-quarters provided individual development plans and one-third provided 360 feedback for most of their employees. The comparable figures for the sample as a whole were 50 percent and 10 percent respectively.

Another way organizations ensure the quality of their training is to evaluate their training outcomes using methodologies such as Kirkpatrick's four levels of evaluation. The estimates for 1997 reveal that between 4 and 8 percent more leading-edge firms evaluate their training for reactions (Level 1), learning (Level 2), and behaviors (Level 3) than the sample as a whole. Those percentages were expected to rise at roughly the same rate for both groups by the year 2000. Although about a quarter of both groups performed Level 4 (business results) evaluations in 1997, a higher percentage of leading-edge firms expect to be doing those evaluations by the year 2000 (58 versus 53 percent). The difficulty of evaluating training for its impact on business results should not be overlooked, however. Even leading-edge firms anticipate evaluating only 25 percent of the courses they provide for business results in the year 2000.

You've now seen that moving up into the ranks of the leading edge involves a complete transformation of your training efforts as well as numerous other practices and systems that support your training. The transformation requires increasing your use of leading-edge human performance practices, the percentage of employees you train, training expenditures, your adoption of new learning technologies, and your use of performance-management and training-evaluation practices. It will

also involve a somewhat different mix in your reliance on external versus internal trainers and the types of courses you provide.

Put all of those pieces together into a coherent aligned system of practices and you have the makings of a leading-edge firm. But start your transformation sooner rather than later. Most indications are that the lead held by the leading edge in the level and quality of training investments and practices is likely to grow in the coming years.

## Training investments provide results

Perhaps you're asking, "Why would I want my organization to be on the leading edge? What will being a leading-edge firm mean for us? Where's the payoff for all of the effort it will take to make this transformation?" The payoff is in the bottom line.

Last year, we demonstrated how the investments of leading-edge firms resulted not only in aligned systems of practices, but also in higher performance. We found that leading-edge firms reported better levels of performance on such measures as sales, overall profitability, and the quality of products and services. Increases in expenditures between 1995 and 1996, among leading-edge firms in particular, were associated with improved overall performance during the same period. And those with higher Key Ratios (spending per employee and spending as a percentage of payroll) than other leading-edge firms reported better overall performance than their peers.

Evidence from Benchmarking Service organizations that reported data for two straight years bolsters even more the relationship between investments in training and performance. Our data reveals that those firms designated as leading-edge in 1996 reported significantly higher overall performance in 1997, compared to other organizations. Several of the defining characteristics of leading-edge firms appear to account for this relationship. For instance, among our repeat Benchmarking Service or-

ganizations, we find that their level of 1996 expenditures per employee has a stronger relationship with their 1997 performance compared to other organizations than it does with their 1996 performance. Likewise, our analyses of this group show that companies that increased their training expenditures per employee and as a percentage of payroll, and the percentage of employees they trained from 1996 to 1997, also improved their performance over the same period. The percentage of employees trained and spending per employee, however, are only two of the defining characteristics of leading-edge firms. Data from the same firms also showed that a greater use of innovative training practices in 1996 was associated with better performance versus other organizations in 1997.

These findings of a time lag between training investments and practices and performance suggest that the biggest benefits from investments in training are not immediate but may occur down the line. This is good news for organizations that have begun to enhance the quality and level of their training efforts but have yet to see the fruits of their labors. However, a word of caution: Our data suggests a direct causative relationship between training and performance but doesn't prove it. As the Benchmarking Service grows, the data will establish more precisely if and when you can look for these payoffs to occur.

The drama that unfolded last year between the leading edge and the industry as a whole has intensified. The tremendous gap between the leading edge and average organizations is projected to grow. There are significant benefits to being on that leading edge. It's neither impossible nor too late for your organization to position itself at the forefront of the training industry.

**Laurie J. Bassi** *is vice president for research at the American Society for Training & Development.* **Mark E. Van Buren** *is a senior research officer at ASTD.*

# Aligning Training With Business Objectives

While working on learning transfer and ROI with the training director and training professionals of a large manufacturing company, I asked the group, "What are the five major initiatives or corporate objectives your organization is attempting for next year?" No response. The silence was telling. Not a single person could provide the initiatives. After some talking, they were able to come up with a couple, but management's initiatives were clearly not part of their HRD planning process. Is it any wonder that management views many of HRD's efforts as ineffective? To correct this perception, HRD must start aligning with the organization's business objectives and become more internal customer-oriented.

Do you ever wonder how outside vendors are able to access senior management and sell multi-million dollar programs to your organization? Why do managers bypass you and buy programs from outside sources and then expect you to support the roll-out? Like it or not, many senior managers perceive that outside sources have a better understanding of their business issues and see vendor programs as providing a partial solution. Why? Because vendor account managers learn about your company and your business issues. They then position themselves and their programs as a solution to an identified need. Again, to correct this situation, you must start aligning with your organization's business objectives.

Organizations have mission statements, goals and objectives, and strategies. A mission statement answers the question, what business are we in? The strategies are the methods to fulfill the mission. The goals and objectives set the targets, and actions or tactics are the means for meeting the goals and objec-

tives. These terms are put into operation through strategic plans and operational plans, the latter being a shorter-term focus, usually one or two years. All of these plans, objectives and strategies should be in the context of the marketplace in which an organization finds itself competing.

## LEARNING TO LINK

The problem arises when HRD efforts are not linked to the business objectives of the organization or business unit. To alleviate the problem the HRD organization needs to look at each business unit as its internal customer and senior management as its clients. HRD must understand both the goals/objectives and strategies of its internal customers and clients. It must then respond with learning initiatives that address those business issues.

**1 CREATE MISSION STATEMENT.** The mission statement communicates what business the clients are in to internal and external parties. In smaller organizations, there is one mission statement. In larger organizations each business unit will have its own mission statement which aligns with the overall direction of the corporations. More than just a philosophical stance, mission statements spell out what the firm or business unit does. Therefore, to understand the business unit and client, begin with the mission statement.

**2 IDENTIFY CLIENT'S STRATEGIES.** Identify the client's strategies that support the mission and set the direction for the organization. These may include reengineering and process initiatives to improve the business, focusing on core competencies resulting in outsourcing, entering new markets, and/or forming

alliances to achieve business results. In many cases they have specific strategies related to developing their workforce.

**3 TRANSLATE INTO GOALS AND OBJECTIVES.** Clients translate their mission and strategies into operational goals and objectives. Identifying these goals and objectives is essential to understanding how management expects to make its strategy work and how the company or business unit believes it can turn in a financial performance that will please its shareholders. Some examples include increasing market share, increasing productivity, improving customer satisfaction, reducing costs, reducing time to market, increasing sales.

**4 CONDUCT BUSINESS ANALYSIS.** Each operational goal can be categorized by functions as operations, engineering, marketing, etc. At this level, the operational goals become more measurable and function specific. Individuals are held accountable for the attainment of these operational goals and welcome any help needed to achieve them. Your task is to understand these operational goals and determine where you can add value. Each function has demands that have HRD implications that can be met by securing HRD programs and services. For example, if a marketing and sales function wants to increase its market presence and market share by taking its existing products into new markets, what are some possible HRD implications? HRD implications could include training about the new vertical markets and decision processes within those markets, product benefits to the new customers, and/or knowledge of the new competitors and competitive strategies. If an organization wants to improve profits, the idea is to increase revenue and cut costs. To increase revenue may mean to increase sales and/or margin on sales. This could have implications for sales training. Cutting costs could affect the operations/manufacturing organization through reduced scrap, overtime and/or inventory. For business units, reduction in costs may mean a reduction in turnover. It is your job to determine the HRD implications embedded within your clients' operational goals and objectives. From a design/development perspective, in this step you are conducting a business analysis.

5 TAKE ACTION. The focus of your efforts become your actions, which support the partnering and help clients to reach their operational goals and objectives. You are now aligning HRD actions and capabilities with clients' priorities and accountabilities. The actual response to Step 4 through the design/development and implementation of courseware or other HRD interventions that directly relate to the HRD implications identified are some actions for HRD. You may need to provide management coaching to help reduce turnover or training on interviewing techniques to get a better person/job fit, or provide training in workforce management/

scheduling to reduce overtime, or training in inventory management techniques to reduce inventory. From a design/development perspective, you are now conducting the needs analysis and then providing the appropriate interventions.

By following these five steps, the result is a repositioning away from HRD products, courses and services toward the needs of the client.

## GETTING THE INFORMATION

You ask, "Where do I get this information?" It is readily available. Some sources include your organization's annual report and operating plan, the organization's goals and objectives by business unit, and business unit planning sessions and staff meetings. Also look at interviews with key individuals, the performance objectives of managers and professionals, annual reviews and internal publications such as newsletters and monthly reports. Valuable information is available in internal and external executive presentations and in industry reports on your company.

An HRD professional with a customer orientation believes that the achievement of department goals de-

pends on understanding the needs and wants of clients/customers and delivering high-quality, customized programs and services more effectively and efficiently than a competitor. In this case, the HRD function tries to "pull" its programs and services, thus creating demand, through understanding and meeting client and customer needs.

The customer-oriented operating principle is to provide programs and services that directly address the identified needs of the client/customer. This results in customized programs and services that provided added value to the client/customer. The box on this page indicates the difference between a more traditional approach and a customer-oriented approach.

Currently, your HRD organization may not be positioned for alignment and a customer-oriented approach to doing business. To solve the problem, you may need to add or change some roles to allow for continued access into the business units. While the more popular role is "performance consultant," this role is really that of an "internal account manager." The role is to work with business units (much like an account representative works with outside customers) to understand their needs and then orchestrate a response from the HR and HRD organizations. Some responsibilities include:

➤Conducting ongoing research and study to understand the current and future operations of an assigned business unit, including strategies, goal and objectives, customers, products, etc.

➤Working with the business units to identify business needs and business performance issues.

➤Collaborating with business units to identify the HRD implication of their needs and performance issues.

➤Securing support for agreed-upon initiatives.

➤Orchestrating a comprehensive response to those identified needs.

➤Providing on-going communication and feedback to your clients.

➤Educating management of its role/responsibility for the support of joint initiatives.

➤Measuring your contribution to the bottom line.

➤Identifying key players and continuing to build relationships with the business units.

➤Positioning HRD as a key partner for their success.

## A COMPARISON: TRADITIONAL VS CUSTOMER/CLIENT-ORIENTATION

| CHARACTERISTIC | TRADITIONAL APPROACH | CUSTOMER/CLIENT-ORIENTATION |
|---|---|---|
| Starting Point | HRD Function | Client/Customer understanding |
| Focus | Existing programs/services | Customer business issues |
| HRD Means | "Selling"—or "You take what we offer" | Customer-oriented practices; customized programs and services |
| HRD Ends | Number of participants enrolled; number of courses; budget variance | Client/customer satisfaction; bottom-line impact |
| Organizational Ends | Skill development | Customer's goal attainment and impact |
| Revenue | Central budget (through number of courses and/or participant days) | Client provides revenue based on alignment with needs and satisfaction with deliverables |
| Planning Horizon | Short term | Long term—position for the future |
| Operating | Getting employees and management to take what is offered | Understanding customer business needs and meeting those needs |

## HOW TO BECOME MORE CUSTOMER-ORIENTED

1. Identify customers within each function.

2. Demonstrate an understanding of each customer's business and of industry trends.

3. Use needs assessment to discover your customer's specific needs.

4. Partner with these customers for planning.

5. Set objectives that are meaningful to the customer and evaluate these objectives for organizational impact.

6. Have account managers or performance consultants for each business function.

7. Focus communication and promotional efforts on client benefits, not on programs and services offered. Develop separate communication for each customer.

8. Set client satisfaction objectives, monitor satisfaction and respond to input and evaluation data.

9. Develop programs and services for the specifically identified customer needs. Deliver these programs and services according to your customers' schedule and deliver the learning experiences by a methodology agreed to by your customers.

The concepts discussed here are not revolutionary. Find out what keeps your clients/customers up at night, and provide a solution to their insomnia. In most cases, HRD offers part of the solution. While it sounds relatively simple, HR has a difficult time doing it. Some barriers you may face in developing the relationship include not knowing:

➤The business of your clients or your internal operations.

➤The marketplace and industry.

➤The business acumen.

➤Business and marketing concepts.

➤How to approach your client and develop the relationship that can become a partnership.

➤How to work the internal politics to gain access to the client on a continuing basis.

➤The importance your clients put on HRD for their business unit.

➤How to position HRD to be value-added.

## WHERE DO YOU GO FROM HERE?

How do you overcome these barriers? First, start studying your organization and the marketplace. Second, begin a reading program or taking classes in marketing, distribution, operations management and finance. Third, seek out coaching. Your organization's account managers can provide insights into how to establish and develop relationships with clients. Fourth, set an appointment and begin the process. Fifth, continue in your efforts. While your clients will welcome your initiative and help, they may at first question your direct link to their business needs. This is where you can put on your consulting hat and help build the bridge.

Your business units and senior managers are very open to collaborating with you in helping them achieve their objectives. You bring critical expertise to their team. You can and must be a part of their team in providing success stories for the organization.

---

*DONALD V. McCAIN is founder and principal of Performance Advantage Group in Brentwood, Tenn., which provides design/development, evaluation and certification consultation for companies.*

# Use the Web to check out those job applicants

**by Phillip M. Perry**

**P**re-employment background checks can save your business from the costly error of hiring a bad apple. Got a hot prospect for a supervisory position? You'll want to check out the authenticity of that college degree he claims to have. How about the bright applicant for the bookkeeping job? Make sure she wasn't fired for raiding the till on her last go-round. As for the fellow who wants to drive the car emblazoned with your business logo: If he already has a desk drawer stuffed with traffic violations, you'll want to know about it.

You face even greater risks because of the growing menace of workplace violence. Fail to check the background of a new employee who ends up attacking fellow workers or customers, and you'll end up on the losing side of a costly negligent hiring lawsuit.

"Negligent hiring is an attractive theory for attorneys looking to make money from your business," cautions Daniel Cohen, a labor and employment law attorney with the firm of

---

## Web-based employee screening services.

Here are some active web-based employee screening services. Prior to using these services, check with your attorney for guidance on complying with state law as well as with the federal Fair Credit Reporting Act.

- www.informus.com. Information includes credit, criminal records, driving reports, workers compensation, employment history, address verification, professional licenses, education, personal references. Prices vary from $10 to $30. Speed varies from immediately up to 3 days. Offers an "IntroScan" which includes key data for high turnover positions, for a fee of $12.50.

- www.knowx.com. This company, which advertises itself as a "courthouse on the web," gets its information from publicly available legal records. Information includes liens, lawsuits, judgments, bankruptcies, assets, DBA's, residential addresses. Records are from $5 to $25. Offers an "ultimate people finder time saver search," combining many of the most commonly requested items, for a flat fee of five dollars.

- www.data-trac.com. This online service claims to provide access to "billions" of records. Address histories, motor vehicle records, real property searches, others. Prospective users must register and provide professional credentials of status as corporate human resource departments. Search fees may be as low as $10 with extra charges for more detailed reports.

- www.advsearch.com. This is more of a special order service, in which you fill out a form and are billed for work accomplished. Criminal convictions, civil lawsuits, address histories, bankruptcies, workers compensation records, credit reports, and others. Same-day service is available for an extra fee. You can also find similar businesses by searching for "employee screening" in the web search services such as Yahoo and Alta Vista.

A reference list of other employee screening services is maintained at http://www.hitekinfo.com/snoop/employee_screening.html. Many of these services will do the search for you. They require that you place an order by mail or fax.

---

 From *New England Printer and Publisher,* February 1999, pp. 34-36.

Charfoos, Reiter, Peterson, Holmquist, and Pilchak, in Farmington Hills, Mich. "You can be sued if there was something in a new hire's background which created a risk to your workplace, and you did not bother to try to find out that information."

All this raises a practical question.

Some of these services are listed in the accompanying sidebar, "Web-based employee screening services." Used correctly, they can save you from hiring individuals with bogus resumes or dangerous backgrounds. The fact that you engaged in this background checking can be a good de-

employment law arsenal, without getting bruised by a courtroom recoil.

## Don't violate the Fair Credit Reporting Act

When gathering information about a prospective employee, the number one risk is falling afoul of the Fair Credit Reporting Act (FCRA) which was amended in September 1997 to require disclosure of all background checks to individuals applying for work.

"The FCRA is a major issue that a lot of employers don't know about," says Kevin Prendergast, vice president and general counsel at Research Associates, Inc. (RAI), a pre-employment background checking firm in Cleveland. "If you run a background check you must comply with this law."

---

## Consider higher end investigative services.

Web-based services have their limitations. They may provide access to publicly-available records, but they cannot provide the insights into character or work habits that can be all-important in a new hire. Neither can they reveal the incidence of previous employment problems that were swept under the rug when the individual was let go.

Higher end investigative service agencies will conduct personal interviews with former employers and with references. The charge can range upwards of $350 per report.

"There is a lot of stuff you won't find in public records," says Kevin Prendergast, vice president and general counsel to Research Associates, Inc. (RAI), a private investigative firm in Cleveland.

"Many times, employees with workplace problems are handled quietly and the person is allowed to resign with no record. Suppose the individual was quietly let go for threatening other employees, and for bringing a gun to work. This is something you will want to know."

---

Just how do you get this valuable background information, anyhow? If you've placed many calls to check references, you know that former employers are all too often reluctant to disclose anything beyond dates of employment.

That's because they fear their departed employees will sue them for making damaging, inaccurate statements, under a legal theory called "negligent referral."

Well, the World Wide Web rides to the rescue, with a growing number of online employee screening services. These services offer background checks that include credit reports, criminal conviction records, workmen's compensation claims, court judgments, lawsuits, personal address histories, and many other reports. Depending on what you are looking for, the expense may range from $10 to $200.

That's cheap insurance against the cost of hiring the wrong person.

fense against charges of negligent hiring.

But watch out: Used improperly, employee screening services can lead to costly lawsuits for violation of federal law, employment discrimination, or invasion of privacy.

"Generally speaking, one has the right to access and rely on information obtained in background checks," says Michael G. Cleveland, an employment law attorney with Chicago-based Vedder Price Kaufman & Kammholz. "But there are risks that lurk out there for the uninitiated. Some information is protected by law, and in some cases use of information can result in unlawful discriminatory decision making."

Okay. The secret to walking the fine line between prudent investigation and illegal intrusion is to know what the law requires. In this article, Cleveland and other attorneys show how to fire this new weapon in the

## Here are key points from the law:

- Prior to obtaining any pre-employment report, you must notify the individual in writing, in a document consisting solely of this notification. Also get the person's written authorization before you retrieve the report.
- If you rely only partly on the report for an adverse job action you must give the individual a "pre adverse action disclosure" that includes a copy of the report, along with a copy of *A Summary of Your Rights Under the Fair Credit Reporting Act,* which you can get from the Federal Trade Commission. The person must be given time to respond.
- After you have taken the adverse action you must give the person an "adverse action notice."

These FCRA notification requirements kick in whenever you obtain information about a job candidate from third parties. These include the web-based employee screening services. And the FCRA stipulations must be met even with seemingly minor background checks, such as scanning public records for driving violations or past residential addresses. Failure to produce the proper documents subjects you to costly penalties, as well as possible lawsuits by the affected employees.

For more guidance on how to stay out of hot water, refer to the excellent document, *"What Employers Need to Know,"* posted by the Federal Trade Commission (FTC) at tp://www.ftc.gov/bcp/conline/pubs/buspubs/credempl.htm.

Once you understand what the CRA requires, fulfilling its mandate is straightforward. "The FCRA requirements are not much of a problem in the application process," says Cohen. "After all, the prospect that refuses to authorize the report can apply elsewhere."

Things get dicey, though, when you find you must run a background check on a current employee. Suppose an employee starts to exhibit violent behavior on the job. This violates your company behavior guidelines, so you are obligated to initiate an investigation. And if you want to run a background check as part of that investigation, under the rules of the FCRA you have to ask the employee to sign a form authorizing the check. "Now you have to provide notice to someone who might be a dangerous person that you are accessing this information," says Cohen. "That might upset the person, and if he has a mental disability it might make him more dangerous."

You can't get around the problem, by the way, by asking all employees to sign blanket forms authorizing such investigations when they join your business. According to FCRA requirements, every time you launch a new investigation you must draw up a new set of forms.

This places you in a difficult position. Cohen suggests one solution: the FCRA does not apply if you access the information directly. "The FCRA is triggered when you retain a third party to perform the investigation," he says. "If you go to the courthouse

## New protections against negligent referral

So you call your job applicant's former employer to request a reference. What happens? You get nothing but name, rank and dates of employment from a business that fears a lawsuit for negligent referral if they go any further.

That's a common scenario in today's workplace—but times are changing. "Over two dozen state legislatures have enacted immunity laws designed to protect the provision of job references by former employers," says Kevin Prendergast, vice president and general counsel to Research Associates, Inc. (RAI), a private investigative firm in Cleveland. "The employer who gives a reference in good faith, and has back-up documentation in the personnel files, is immune for suit."

That's good news, and you should find out if your state has enacted such laws. But even if it has not, you can take some steps to loosen the lips of former employers.

"I recommend that you have all job applicants sign forms authorizing your business to get employment history, and releasing the former employers from liability as a result of your inquiries," says Daniel Cohen, a labor and employment attorney with the law firm of Charfoos, Reiter, Peterson, Holmquist, and Pilchak, in Farmington Hills, Mich. "If you fax that form to the former employer, and invite them to show it to their labor counsel—they will be much more comfortable sharing information with you." Cohen adds a further point: Include in the release form a clause allowing you to provide a good faith reference to the next employer down the line, should that employee come aboard your business.

yourself, you do not have to disclose the investigation." This means you need to get some training in researching court records.

## Beware employment discrimination.

It all sounds so easy. You run background checks on your computer, discover which of your job applicants lack clean slates, and toss their employment applications in the wastebasket.

Not so fast. You've already seen how you can easily violate the FCRA. But there's another way you can find yourself on the losing end of a crippling lawsuit or government action. Many states have laws that prohibit use of specific records in making employment decisions. New York State, for example, limits an employer's ability to make decisions on incarceration records. And in Michigan, you may not access or rely on criminal arrests which did not result in convictions. (Notice the first part of that statement: even *looking* at

arrest records is considered discriminatory.)

"You need to understand that the law varies by state," says Cohen. "You have to find out what your state allows prior to reviewing records." Indeed, one of the drawbacks of the Web-based employee screening services is their national scope. Some of their information may be legally accessed in some states but not in others.

Because members of certain minority groups are subject to more arrests and convictions than other people, some court judgments have said that basing employment decisions on such records is discriminatory.

It's less risky to rely on actual conviction records than arrest records. But even then, says Cleveland, using such records carries peril. "Some opinions from the Equal Employment Opportunity Commission state that since some minority groups have been convicted more often of crimes, having a policy of disqualifying people with criminal backgrounds is racially discriminatory." The courts don't always rule that way, says

Cleveland, but you are taking a chance if you go too far.

The solution, says Cleveland, is to tie your hiring criteria to the requirements of the job. "If you say, 'I won't hire anyone with a criminal conviction, no matter what its nature,' you are being too aggressive," says Cleveland. "I think it's wiser to ask this question: 'What does the criminal conviction have to do with the particular job that is involved?' "

Suppose you are hiring someone for a position involving money handling. If the individual was convicted of theft, that criminal record would be relevant. "On the other hand, would conviction for driving under the influence be a pertinent consideration?," poses Cleveland. "Maybe not. To successfully defend against a discrimination charge, go beyond compli-

ance with the letter of the law. Make sure you are able to defend your decision on a rational basis."

## Avoid lawsuits for invasion of privacy.

Once you obtain the information you need, keep it under lock and key. If details are shared with the wrong people, and the workplace gossip mill starts grinding, the investigated individual can sue for invasion of privacy. "Don't disclose why you did not hire someone to people who do not have a need to know," says Cleveland. "You run the risk of defamation."

It's prudent to lock up the information in files devoted to that purpose. "You need to maintain confidentiality of information in an appropriate way,

for people you hire and don't hire," cautions Cleveland.

Despite the risks involved, conducting background checks is essential. Today's business climate is characterized by a fluid movement of workers from one employer to another. "One bad apple can poison a company," warns attorney Prendergast. "You can't afford not to check the backgrounds of people you hire."

**About the author:**
*Phillip M. Perry is the author of syndicated articles. He has 20 years experience on both sides of the editorial desk. A member of the New York Business Press Editors, he has published over 3,000 articles and two books.*

# RECRUITING SECRETS

## of the smartest companies around

**How far will you have to go to find the best people?
No matter what your business is, the answer is the
same: further than you've ever imagined**

### BY CHRISTOPHER CAGGIANO

$C$*AMBRIDGE MASS.—Totally Apocryphal Technologies
(TAT), a fast-rising player in the rapidly expanding field
of genetic engineering, recently announced that it would
proceed with a controversial program to take tissue samples from top-performing members of its engineering,
sales, and management staff. Rather than using the samples to screen for illegal drug use or preexisting medical
conditions, TAT hopes to use its recently developed hu-
man-cloning technology to address a critical lack of available talent. In a recent statement, TAT CEO Hugh R.
Keating described the project as "a logical application of
our core technology in what continues to be an extremely
tight labor market."*

Sorry, but the story above is fictitious. And even if clon-
ing should become an option for today's employee-starved
companies, it will be too late for Mark Roesner. Only a
year ago, with sales at his filtration-and-fluid-handling-
products company doubling every year, Roesner de-

# WANT ADS

**How can you make your help-wanted ads stand out? It helps to have a sense of humor—and a photogenic CEO, like Roger Mody of Signal Corp.**

cided to take a drastic step in response to the job glut: he sold his company. "One key reason was the current job market," he says. "I decided it was impossible to grow and maintain our profitability level."

Roesner's solution may seem extreme, but his predicament is all too familiar. Thomas Kenyon, president of Pettit Fine Furniture, in Sarasota, Fla., grew so frustrated with the dearth of good people that he recently declared a 90-day growth freeze for the $1-million furniture-manufacturing company. "We told our sales reps to put a moratorium on finding new dealers," he says. "It was frustrating, but I knew it was the right thing to do." Kenyon says he still has to limit his growth (for instance, by not expanding into the Washington, D.C., area, where there's some demand for his furniture) because of the difficulty in finding qualified woodworkers.

Right now lots of folks are infuriatingly stalled, tantalized by the opportunity for record revenue growth but limited by their inability to locate qualified personnel. Frazzled CEOs are also lamenting increased employee workloads and the concomitant decreased customer satisfaction. It's becoming clear that for fin de siècle entrepreneurial companies, successful recruiting will make the difference between growth and stagnation—maybe even between life and death.

And the human drought shows no signs of letting up. According to Bill Styring, senior fellow at the Hudson Institute, "It's going to get a lot worse," He points to the ratio of probable workers (ages 25–64) to probable retirees (ages 65 and over), which currently stands at four to one, as it has for the past three decades. However, in 2011 the first baby boomer will reach 65 and will be looking to retire, with 76 million fellow boomers right behind. That's when the ratio will start dropping, down to three to one in 2020, and to nearly two to one in 2030. "That's a demographic fact that business needs to deal with," he says. "The population of available workers is going to implode like you wouldn't believe."

As the need for employees becomes acute, CEOs are finding that their stand-by staffing methods aren't enough anymore. Two years ago, Lou Hoffman, president of a $5-million public-relations firm in Silicon Valley, was in the enviable position of being able to grow without necessarily adding new business, mostly because his high-tech clients were growing so quickly. If only he could find the staff to meet the demand.

Hoffman figured he needed to at least double the Hoffman Agency's staff of 25. He hired a recruiting consultant to generate leads. "Once we have the names, our close rate is pretty good," says Hoffman. "The problem was, our funnel was empty." Hoffman says his slot for group account manager—the chief liaison between the company and all its customers—went unfilled for 10 months, and his inability to meet client demand was starting to affect client satisfaction. Hoffman and other high-ranking officials took turns filling the void, but he says it was "only so long before clients started to feel there was no one giving them full-time attention."

That's when Hoffman realized his recruiting practices needed to be a lot more systematic. Previously the company hired on an as-needed basis, with Hoffman himself taking the hiring helm. Now, although his company wasn't always hiring, it needed to be always recruiting. Hoffman likens it to painting the Golden Gate Bridge: by the time the painting crew is done, it has to start over. By the time Hoffman's recruiting process has found a good candidate, he'll probably have a job for that person.

But for that to work, Hoffman's recruiting efforts needed to expand. So he replaced his 20-hours-a-week human-resources person with a full-time staffer hired primarily for her crack recruiting skills. "I know that sounds obvious," he explains, "but we were trying to limit 'unnecessary' functions, positions that didn't generate revenue. But it was foolish not to invest in full-time human resources." Hoffman also hired a 28-hours-a-week consultant to head up the company's on-line recruiting efforts, which include searching through Web databases, placing banner ads on third-party recruiting sites, and attending on-line career chats.

In addition to bringing in the specialists, Hoffman insisted that everyone join in the recruiting effort. Members of the management team are required to engage in two "profile-raising" activities a year, and also to make two recruiting-related phone calls a week. Hoffman also monitors the time it takes to fill a position and recruiting quality, which partly determine the size of employees' annual raises. At the account-executive level, Hoffman measures team-hiring input and recruiting-idea generation to "put recruiting on everyone's radar."

# BUT WAIT— THERE'S MORE

For more information on recruiting and the tight labor market, see these articles from recent issues of *Inc.* (To view an article on-line, go to www.inc.com/incmagazine/archieves /[insert archive number here].html.)
**HANDS ON:** "Beyond Campus Recruiting," April 1998, page 115, archive number 04981151
**OWNER'S MANUAL:** "The People Chase," May 1998, page 125, archive number 05981251
**FURTHER READING:** "Zero-Defect Hiring," March 1998, page 74, archive number 03980741
**FEATURE STORY:** Motherhood, Apple Pie, and Stock Options," February 1998, page 84, archive number 02980841
**FEATURE STORY:** "How're You Gonna Keep 'Em Down On the Firm?," January 1998, page 70, archive number 01980701
**FEATURE STORY:** "The Right Fit," *Inc.* 500, 1997, page 104, archive number 14971041
**WHAT'S HOT:** "On-Line Recruiting," August 1998, page 108, archive number 08981081
**BUSINESS 101:** "Think All Noncompetes Stink?" October 1997, page 114, archive number 10971141

Hoffman has transformed his business so that it is now a recruiting firm as much as a PR company—which is what most growth companies will have to be to stay competitive. As Hoffman did, CEOs can start by rethinking what they've done in the past and trying one new idea at a time. The first group of ideas that follows consists of refreshing variations on familiar-but-stale standard tactics, whereas some of the other ideas that follow may seem downright outlandish. But in whatever direction you decide to go to expand your recruiting repertoire, sooner or later you're sure to come to this realization: what you're doing right now isn't nearly enough.

Editor's note: See the following pages for Parts 1, 2, and 3 of "How to Hire."

*Additional reporting for this story was provided by Ilan Mochari.*

... CEOs can start by rethinking what they've done in the past and trying one new idea at a time

# HOW TO HIRE PART ONE
## sharpening the old tools

**Classified Ads: New Looks, New Locations** When Hoffman did a reverse audit of his hiring practices in 1996, he found that no one he had hired in the previous two years had come to him through newspaper ads, on which he was spending upwards of $20,000. Like Hoffman, many company builders are finding newspaper ads increasingly ineffective: too much clutter and not enough quality response.

Those that still find newspaper ads useful have found that they need to make their ads stand out. Roger Mody of Signal Corp., an information-technology-services provider in Fairfax, Va., uses humor. One recent ad in the *Washington Post* featured a messy-faced Mody shortly after taking part in a company pie-eating contest, with the tag line "And you should see us on *casual* day." Other ads have featured stock photos of Wally Cleaver ("Gee whiz, Wally, Signal sure has some swell job opportunities!")

Increasingly, CEOs are widening their advertising efforts to include such nontraditional recruiting media as radio and TV. Recently, Michael Pehl of i-Cube, an IT-consulting-services company in Cambridge, Mass., began running a series of large billboards in the Boston area, including one targeting drivers exiting from Logan Airport that immodestly touts i-Cube as "An Incredible Place to Work." Even at a cost of $10,000 to $15,000 a month (including design fees), the billboards represent quite a bargain in Pehl's view. "We'd pay the same thing to run a tiny one-day ad in the *Boston Sunday Globe*," he says, "but the billboard sits there for 30 days."

**Referral Bonuses: Bribe Strangers, If You Have To.** Another long-standing practice that's getting refined in today's labor market is the venerable referral bonus. Paying employees to do your recruiting for you has always been a smart tactic—with the employee acting as a cost-effective quality check—but lately the bounties have been getting larger and more creative. To make sure employees are thinking about the long term when they refer prospects, Brett Brewster of Mitec Controls, a $5.5-million fire- and life-safety company in Norcross, Ga., spreads the bonus payments out: the employee gets half at the referral's 90-day mark and the rest when the referral

has been working for six months. As an added dose of accountability, Brewster requires employees to spend time orienting the people they refer, which Brewster says improves the chances of retaining new recruits.

Linda Blaser, a contract recruiter for Exchange Applications, an IT company in Boston, has set up a referral program that gives employees more money for more valuable referrals: $3,000 for most positions and $5,000 for "hot jobs" that Blaser needs to fill with particular urgency. Recently, for every successful referral they made, employees were entered into a drawing for a Caribbean trip. Blaser periodically provides employees with a list of available positions and a fun reminder of the trip, such as a bag of fish-shaped candies. And it's not just Exchange Applications employees who can cash in. The company offers a $2,500 bounty to people outside the company, be they vendors, customers, strangers, even journalists. (You know whom to contact if you're interested.)

## REFERRAL BONUSES
are getting increasingly creative—from TVs to housecleaning services. But Brett Brewster prefers the old standby—cash.

If you're growing particularly fast, you may want your referral program to inspire repeat participation. Michael Pehl of i-Cube has developed a program that rewards employees in ongoing quarterly and annual campaigns with progressive and changing incentives. For example, in addition to a $2,000 bonus, anyone making a successful referral for the third quarter of 1998 received a 32-inch TV. And if the candidate started in August, Pehl tacked on a VCR. Annually, anyone making three referrals receives a choice of either two mountain bikes or a year's worth of laundry and housecleaning services. For five hires the choice is between a spa trip and an adventure vacation. And anyone making eight successful referrals for the 1998 calendar year will receive a new Jeep Wrangler. "The most important thing about a recruiting system isn't what you do," says Pehl, "but that you have a framework in place to get people thinking about finding people."

**Networking: Passively Schmooze, and You'll Lose.** Travel time needn't be just a chance to catch up on reading the latest books. Whenever Kathi Jones, human-resources and recruiting manager at Aventail Corp., in Seattle, is flying out on business, she arrives at the airport an hour early, and not because of increased security measures. She reads other people's luggage for company tags featuring the names of such big-time competitors as Cisco Systems and Raptor Systems, and takes the opportunity to chat up the owners of the luggage. She also keeps an eye out for folks wearing competitors' T-shirts and baseball caps and engages the sporty travelers in employment-related conversation.

When Barry Brodersen, cofounder and vice-president of Domino Equipment Co., in Clinton, Okla., hears about a particularly good service or construction specialist, he tries to get as much information about that person as he can and looks for opportunities to become acquainted. Once Brodersen pursued a hot service specialist (armed only with the fellow's name, a vague physical description, and the name of his employer), tailgating him for 30 miles. When they stopped, Brodersen introduced himself and said, "Why don't you come work for me?" Now the man is a service manager for Brodersen, whose company installs and services petroleum equipment.

While some people look for opportunities to reach out to others in their industries, others prefer to manufacture those opportunities. Dave Clark, president of Mindsource, a technical staffing company in Silicon Valley, has created a monthly industry-networking session called "Birds of a Feather" (BOF) at which he and his employees hobnob with other Internet protocol folk in the Silicon Valley area. Word has gotten around about the monthly fete—mostly through E-mail and various newsgroups—to the point where Clark says the gathering has become a "centerpiece for our particular niche." It has also, he admits, become a source for the occasional hire.

**Campus Recruiting: Beyond the Old College Try.** One of the classic recruiting spots is the college campus, especially for companies seeking newly minted M.B.A.'s. Doug Evans, president of Doug Evans + Partners, an Internet, electronic-commerce, and technology consulting company in New York City, found that he needed a bit

of chutzpah to get attention from the M.B.A.'s, whose eyes tend to fix on *Fortune* 500 names. Evans began planning in May 1996 for presentations he'd make starting that November. When he first approached Columbia Business School, he says the administration wouldn't even talk to him. When it finally responded, all it gave him was a tiny room from which to recruit. To achieve a larger on-campus presence, Evans called a client who was a Columbia grad, who helped him get the pricey-but-prime suite where IBM and Arthur Andersen made their presentations. Evans also networked with on-campus organizations, and he inundated candidates with E-mails, direct mail, and telephone calls to maximize attendance at his presentation. As a result of the Columbia presentation, he netted three new employees.

**Résumés: Making a Paper Trail.** For some people the practice of ferreting out prospects borders on obsession. Cathy Lanier, president and owner of Technology Solutions Inc., a $3.3-million technology-staffing firm in Columbia, S.C., never throws a résumé away. She rarely seeks entry-level personnel, but nevertheless she enters every résumé she gets into a database. Then, every two years, Lanier peruses the database and sends out an E-mail questionnaire to see what prospects have added to their résumés, including a checklist of computer systems and languages in which she asks candidates to rate their proficiency. She also asks for their current location, salary range, and references. Most important, she says, is asking for a contact person who will always know the prospect's whereabouts in case she somehow loses touch. "It takes a detective mentality," she says, "getting enough information to track them down later if you need to."

When Herb Sizemore was CEO of Kansas Communications, in Lenexa, Kans. (he recently sold the company), he kept a file of all the "People on the Move" columns in his local paper and called people a year after they'd taken a new job to see if they were happy with their situation. Louise Wannier of Enfish Technology Inc. keeps a "people book" of everyone she meets and scans through it periodically, keeping in touch with key prospects.

## ALWAYS RECRUITING

When traveling, Kathi Jones keeps an eye peeled for competitors' luggage tags and then makes her pitch.

. . . for fin de siècle entreprenurial companies, successful recruiting will make the difference between growth and stagnation —maybe even between life and death

# HOW TO HIRE PART TWO
## picking up the new tools

**New Sources: Casting the Widest Net.** In 1991, Jeff Moler, CEO of Protek Electronics Inc., a $9-million electronics designer and manufacturer in Sarasota, Fla., received a call from the local Easter Seals office offering physically and mentally challenged individuals for Moler's assembly line. Moler accepted, and he reports that with a little extra training, those recruits have become a tremendous asset. "But lately even they haven't been available," he laments. Apparently, other local companies have caught on, creating much local demand for handicapped workers. So Moler went offshore—1,500 miles, in fact—to set up a second manufacturing plant in Costa Rica. "It was the only answer," he says. "We couldn't find people fast enough." Costa Rica offered a large number of available educated workers, many with technical-school or college backgrounds.

Of course, one relatively quick way to staff up is to buy another company. When Shiv Krishnan, CEO of Indus Corp., a systems-integration company in Vienna, Va., acquired the Washington, D.C., and North Carolina assets of Vigyan Inc., in 1996, one of his primary motivations was the 30 staff members he would be adding to his staff of 25. But Krishnan warns that there are perils to recruiting by acquisition, especially since sale-price expectations in the IT field are so high. "The culture fit has to be right," he says. "If not, they'll leave and you'll have to sit on these huge acquisition costs while 75% of your assets have walked out." He says he was able to avoid that by ensuring that his soon-to-be acquired personnel were open to an acquisition. The Vigyan staff were working with fairly old technology and relished the chance to move into new areas.

**Internet Recruiting: Finding the Right Connections.** Recently, Dan Maude, president of Beacon Application Services Corp., a systems-integration company in Framingham, Mass., made the switch to recruiting exclusively from the Internet, primarily because it's effective and comparatively cheap. "A year's worth of Web recruiting for us costs less than one agency fee," he explains. It's also faster: rather than wait for candidates to see and respond to the Sunday help-wanted ads, he can post jobs and get responses in the same day.

Maude says he's found certain third-party-recruiting Web sites to be very effective, particularly Career Mosaic (www.careermosaic.com), the Monster Board (www.monster.com), and Yahoo (www.yahoo.com/Business_and_Economy/Employment). Maude's

listings include a link back to Beacon's Web site (www.beaconservices.com) and a special E-mail address to which candidates can send their résumés (resumes@beacon.com). Since Beacon Application Services is one of 61 exclusive PeopleSoft partners, candidates can also find out about job opportunities through a link from the vendor's master site back to the company site. Aside from links, there are other ways of attracting potential employees to your site. Tony Petrucciani of Single Source Systems, a systems-integration business in Fishers, Ind., offers Web surfers a free chance at such prizes as a Palm-Pilot personal organizer just for visiting the company's Web site.

## FRESH OUT

**College recruiting involves much more than setting up a table on the campus green. Because your competition is doing the same thing.**

Now you might be thinking, Sure, it makes sense for technology-based companies to recruit on the Web, but what about my business? Well, you can find more than just the tech types in cyberspace. Currently there are job-related Web sites catering to restaurant workers (www.starchefs.com), truck drivers (www.truckers.com), and funeral directors (www.funeralnet.com), to name a few.

**Web-Spinning: Working the Virtual Room.** Beyond databases and Web sites, there are other corners of the Web that many companies are only beginning to discover. For example, there's Usenet, a Web-based network of topic-specific newsgroups or bulletin boards. Kathi Jones, at Aventail, starts at Deja News (www.dejanews.com), where she can search for newsgroups that are of interest to her typical recruit and read through the postings to find the smartest posters. She also quietly lurks through Web-based forums or chats, where attendees share ideas and advice on technical questions.

Don't be discouraged if you can't find a Web forum to suit your needs. Toni Marie Finn of Creative Financial Staffing decided to create her own career-specific Web chat at www.wbs.net, a Web-based "community." She advertised the occasional forum on

CFS's company Web site, as well as on other message boards and chat sites. Finn claims she got hundreds of attendants, from which she generated 24 quality leads and 12 interviews, which ultimately resulted in two hires. It cut her advertising costs by two-thirds, she says. "And," adds Finn, "I could interview over the Net, in real time."

**Long-Term Prospecting: Cultivating Your People Pipeline.** Finn became very active in the local Chamber of Commerce partly to help create new training programs and internships to groom high school students for potential accounting careers. Finn also teaches a local Junior Achievement class on "Life after High School: How to Prepare for Work," which has actually already netted three temps for her to place.

Joe Martinez takes the outreach process a step further. The CEO of Productive Data Systems, an IT staffing and services company in Englewood, Colo., Martinez wonders why everyone seems to be screaming at Congress to increase the number of visas for high-tech workers from abroad. "There are a ton of people right here we can train to take these new, information-age jobs," he says. "Give the local people a chance, instead of importing these guys from India or Israel." Martinez has formed a nonprofit called Technology Transfer Solutions, which works with various Colorado organizations to help high school-equivalency students get entry-level IT jobs. Martinez concedes that the effort does not directly benefit his businesses—at least not yet. "We don't hire entry-level people, so it's not feeding right into our workforce," he says.

Andrew Levi took the spin-off strategy in a different direction: The president and CEO of Aztec Systems Inc., a systems-integration company in Dallas, started a separate recruiting company. Levi had grown increasingly frustrated with most of the more than 10 headhunters he had engaged. "They were charging these huge fees and delivering substandard people," he says. One particular recruiter had succeeded in bringing in a stream of decent candidates, so Levi approached her about starting up on her own under Aztec's aegis. Now that she's up and running, "our recruiting problem has totally disintegrated," says Levi. His current recruiting clients include companies that he otherwise competes against. Does that bother him? "Other people will place those people anyway," he says. "We might as well get the fees. And even if we don't place them with us, we build a relationship for down the road."

# HOW TO HIRE PART THREE
## your new 'marketing' mind-set

Ultimately, getting your company geared up to become the recruiting machine it needs to be involves more than sharpening old hiring tools and acquiring new ones. More important is the mind-set you apply to the task. Think of the energy and discipline you bring to courting prospective customers, and you'll get some idea of the intensity you need to bring to the recruiting table.

In the first six months of 1998, Dan Maude took his employee base from 40 to 70, with a goal of having 100 staffers by year-end 1998. Recognizing that the process was more a marketing job than a classic "personnel" function, Maude put his vice-president of marketing at the helm of the recruiting effort. "Sales is not the problem," Maude notes. "Getting customers is the easy part."

Often the biggest selling point a growing company has, and the most difficult to copy, is its culture. Which is why Bill Ziercher, CEO of Sterling Direct Inc., a direct-marketing and communications company in Earth City, Mo., goes out of his way to make sure his company is a fun place to work. The company has ongoing "contests" such as "Pat the Pig," in which a porcine Beanie Baby sits on the sloppiest desk of week, with this week's winner awarding the pig to the next week's recipient. And then there's the "Smiley Face Game," in which, if a fellow employee goes out of his way to be nice to you, you can enter his name into a weekly drawing for a T-shirt, a free limo ride, even tickets to a Cardinals game. The company also holds regular events, such as a recent beach party, during which the lunchroom was equipped with a karaoke machine and Super Soaker water guns. Those who refused to sing got soaked. "But that wasn't a worry," says Ziercher. "Once you get acclimated to the culture here, you just jump on in." Fun events get employees talking. "Happy associates tell their friends," says Ziercher. "That helps you communicate to the outside world that this is a fun place to be."

To attract the best salespeople, Chris Taylor, cofounder of $18.5-million International Postal Consultants Inc. (IPC), which sells international-mailing services, uses a system whereby salespeople earn "royalties" on their accounts: in addition to a commission, salespeople receive a percentage of the profit an account brings in for the life of the account. "We wanted to make it open-ended," says Taylor, "so there wasn't any reason for them to leave and try it on their own." Doesn't Taylor consider the system overly generous? "We hope all our reps make huge six-figure incomes," he says. "A lot of people have said we're giving the shop away, but we've never lost a rep in six years." Plus, word gets around on the street that IPC has this lucrative commission plan, "and that makes recruiting a lot easier."

Brett Brewster of Mitec Controls has gone so far as to change the entire structure of his company to make it more attractive to potential recruits. "We had to find a new way to compete," he says. "We kept losing people to the high-tech industry." Brewster divided his company into five limited-liability corporations, surrounding each of five account managers with one to three testing teams each. Whereas those testing jobs used to start at $14 an hour, now the teams are paid based on the profitability of the account. For example, on a $2,000 contract, about $1,200 would go directly to the people on the team, after they paid for company costs, overhead, and their own materials. "So they work to be productive instead of just being on the clock," says Brewster. "Their overall income goes up greatly." So when Brewster is recruiting, he can point to people on his staff making upwards of $40,000, and to the fact that they have some direct control over how much they make.

As important as it is to get the word out about your company through as many channels as possible, it's also important to ask for and collect feedback. Beverly Kelly, human-resources manager at Robert Charles

Lesser & Co., a real-estate consulting firm in Los Angeles, asks candidates about other companies they're interviewing with, and what makes a particular company attractive. She also queries current employees about what they liked and disliked about the hiring process. And she sends an E-mail inquiry to people who have declined an employment offer, asking why. Kelly says she's made numerous changes based on all that feedback, particularly on the company's Web site (www. rclco.com), which now features more "eye-grabbing" graphics, plus explications of the company's interview process, training schedule, and samples of client work.

Kelly has by no means finished tinkering; she thinks of her recruiting efforts as a self-correcting process. As does Lou Hoffman, who is optimistic about the changes he's making in his ever-evolving recruiting process. "We've seen some improvement, but we still need to get better," he says. "We started making changes two years ago, and it's really only kicked in the past six months." Next, Hoffman plans to focus more on marketing to get the message out about his company. He's already created a corporate annual report for direct-mail recruiting efforts. He also hands them out at first interviews. "We thought it was the right vehicle to tell our story," he says. The report highlights the company's perks, which include an outside-training allowance, a paid-sabbatical program, profit sharing, and flextime. It also includes sample client-project case studies and even company revenues and gross revenue per employee. Thanks to his contacts in the business, the report costs him only $35,000 a year to produce, and Hoffman says that when he asks recent hires, as well as people who have declined recent offers, "What gave you a favorable impression about us?" the annual report nearly always comes up. "It gives people a sense of what we're about," he says. "None of our competitors has anything like that."

# Unit 5

## Key Points to Consider

❖ Companies are involved in worldwide competition, often with foreign organizations with much lower wage rates. What should management do to meet this competition? What do workers need to do to meet this competition?

❖ How would you implement a merit/incentive program in a staff department such as research and development or data processing? In a line department such as sales or production?

❖ Explain why you believe some senior executives are overpaid. Do you feel some are underpaid? Cite examples and reasons for your conclusions.

❖ One of the problems facing American industry is an increase in violence. What can be done about it? What would you do about substance abuse?

❖ The increase in the cost of benefits—especially health insurance—is a major concern for most organizations. What are some things that could be done about this?

 **Links**   www.dushkin.com/online/

25. **BenefitsLink: The National Employee Benefits Web Site**
    *http://www.benefitslink.com/index.shtml*
26. **Executive Pay Watch**
    *http://www.paywatch.org/paywatch/index.htm*
27. **Social Security Administration**
    *http://www.ssa.gov*
28. **WorkPlace Injury and Illness Statistics**
    *http://www.osha.gov/oshstats/bls/index1.html*

These sites are annotated on pages 4 and 5.

Money makes the world go around . . . the world go around!
—From "Money" in the musical *Cabaret*

Individuals are usually paid what others perceive their work to be worth. This situation is not necessarily morally correct. In fact, it does not even have to be logical, but it is reality. Police officers and college instructors are often underpaid. They have difficult jobs, requiring highly specialized training, but these jobs do not pay well. Other professions pay better, and many illegal activities pay better than law enforcement or college teaching.

When a company is trying to determine the salary of individuals, two markets must be considered. The first is the internal structure of the firm, including the wages that the company pays for comparable jobs. If the organization brings a new employee on board, it must be careful not to set a pay rate for that individual that is inconsistent with those of other employees who are doing the same or similar jobs. The second market is the external market for employees. Salary information is available from many sources, including professional associations and the federal government. Of course, both current and prospective employees, as well as organizations, can easily gain access to this information. To ignore this information and justify pay rates only in terms of internal structure is to tempt fate. The company's top producers are the ones in whom the competition is the most interested, and no organization can afford a mass exodus of its top talent.

One recent development in the area of compensation is a return to the concept of "pay for performance." Many firms are looking for ways to directly reward their top performers. As a result, the idea of merit pay has gained wide acceptance in both industry and government. Pay for performance has been used in industry for a long time, most commonly in the sales and marketing area, where employees have historically worked on commission plans based on their sales productivity. Theoretically, merit pay and other types of pay for performance are effective, but they can easily be abused, and they are often difficult to administer because measuring performance accurately is difficult. Sales and production have numbers that are easily obtained, but research and development is a different situation. How does a firm measure the effectiveness of research and development for a particular year when such projects can often take several years for results to be achieved?

One issue that has evolved over the past several years is the question of pay for top executives. During times of economic recession, most workers are asked to make sacrifices in the form of reduced raises, pay cuts, cuts in benefits, other compensation

reductions, or layoffs. Many of these sacrifices have not been applied to top management. Indeed, the compensation for top management has increased substantially during the past several years. When former president George Bush traveled to Japan with a number of top auto industry executives, this situation was highlighted. The auto industry in the United States had been doing very poorly, while the auto industry in Japan had been very successful—especially when compared to its U.S. counterpart. A comparison of the salaries of American auto executives with those of their Japanese rivals revealed that the Japanese executives received only a fraction of the compensation of the Americans. This might lead one to question who is worth more—senior management of a successful Japanese firm or of a less successful American firm? Are chief executives overpaid, and if so, how did they get that way, and who should set their pay? There has been some new thinking in recent years on how to determine executive compensation and to address this questionably disproportionate situation.

Health and safety are also major concerns of employers and employees. The workplace has become more violent as workers act out against their employers for unfairness—whether real or imagined. The history of industrialization in the United States is filled with examples of industry's abuse of the safety and health of workers. To prevent this, there is now OSHA (the Occupational Safety and Health Administration) and there are child labor laws. Today, issues concerning safety and health in the workplace include AIDS, burnout, and substance abuse. These issues reflect not only changing social conditions but also a greater awareness of the threats presented by unsafe working conditions. Violence in the workplace has become a major issue for employers with death on the job being one of the major causes for death among young women. The problem of an employee's dark side is likely to be a continuing issue for organizations and one which must be faced.

Benefits represent one of the major means of compensating employees. Health care is a significant portion of the benefit package that most employees have, and, of course, this has been a major area of concern as the health care bill continues to increase. Finding ways of addressing this need on the part of the worker while at the same time minimizing the cost is one of the important issues facing industry.

All in all, salaries, wages, and benefits represent a major expense and a time-consuming management task for most firms, and health and safety requirements are a potential area of significant loss, in terms of both dollars and lost production.

# Implementing Compensation, Benefits, and Workplace Safety

# Pros & Cons of Pay for Performance

**Are pay-for-performance programs good for the company or bad for morale?**

## By Scott Hays

Somewhere in Corporate America, a human resources manager is tweaking her company's employee-incentive program. Maybe she's dumping last year's customized giveaways for this year's weekend getaway packages. Perhaps she's jettisoning the annual casino-awards party in favor of discreet distribution of personalized thank-you cards. What drives her is the theory that rewards and bonuses motivate employees to do their jobs better.

Still, it's only a theory—and one that a number of CEOs and human resources managers believe is no more valid than the notion that dispensing food to a rooster every time he pecks the piano guarantees he'll soon play Beethoven. In fact, no one out there really knows if incentive programs truly work, and a number of you are convinced they can cause significant harm.

### Pondering proffers.

Are incentive programs good for the company or bad for morale? It depends on whether the rewards help support corporate goals, such as increased profit and customer loyalty, or if they merely engender unhealthy competitiveness and back-stabbing among employees.

Seven years ago, CEO and president Rob Rodin eliminated all individual incentives for the 1,800 employees at Marshall Industries, an El Monte, California-based distributor of electronic components. To your average outsider, this may have seemed like a great way to cripple an entire workforce—take away the American Express certificates and Alaskan cruises and motivation drops faster than a helium balloon rises. After all, who wants to slog away at work if there's no food in the dispenser?

*Scott Hays is the department editor for* Workforce. *E-Mail hayss@workforcemag.com to comment.*

Rodin analyzed the five-year earning potential of each employee, concocted a formula, then went person-by-person and assigned salaries.

Profit-sharing potential was set at the same percentage figure for each employee, regardless of salary, based on the company's overall performance. "It wasn't as if we imposed communism," Rodin says, "but our company was divided by internal promotions and contests. We weren't working together with a common vision. Managers were fighting over the cost of a new computer because no one wanted to put it on his P&L, and departments were pushing costs from one quarter into the next to make budget. Fundamentally, we eliminated these distractions. Now we have collaboration and cooperation among sales people, and between divisions and departments."

And, he says, productivity per person has almost tripled.

Last year in Portland, Oregon, president and CEO Mary Roberts discontinued a bonus program for the 200 employees at Rejuvenation Inc., a company that manufacturers decorative brass lighting fixtures. The manufacturing managers, Roberts maintains, begged her to discontinue the program because craftsmen were stealing parts from other craftsmen to meet quotas, and workers were pacing the production of fixtures to gobble up overtime, then working like maniacs to achieve production bonuses.

"Incentive programs create competitiveness, and that's not necessarily best for a company like ours that's growing," says Roberts. "I don't think people are motivated by rewards and bonuses. I think they're motivated because they're excited about their jobs or because they're doing something that provides a service to the world."

Then why do so many companies claim otherwise—that incentive programs, administered effectively, improve company performance? "Personal recognition can be more motivational than money," asserts Bob Nelson, author of *1001 Ways to Reward Employees* (Workman Publishing,

1994). "You can obtain from your employees any type of performance or behavior you desire simply by making use of positive reinforcement."

At Dallas-based Texas Instruments (TI) Incorporated, rewards are used to foster loyalty. Recruiting and retaining employees is a nasty battle zone in the competitive semiconductor industry. Therefore, the company offers a unique and creative compensation package that includes bonuses as well as non-cash recognition ranging from personalized plaques to country ranch parties, movie tickets to golf lessons, team shirts and jackets to footballs and train kits. The number of TI employee recognitions between 1996 and 1997 jumped 400 percent from 21,907 to 84,260.

"Our managers wouldn't use a non-cash recognition program if it didn't bring value to the employees," says Kathy Charlton, TI's manager of workplace vitality. "We're part of an aggressive industry. Our people work hard and long hours. Rewards make a difference in their attitudes and performance. Hey, everyone has a need to be recognized, and not just once a year when there's a formal review process. And when recognition is tied to effort, you end up getting more bang for your buck."

## Do rewards undermine corporate goals?

It's wildly unrealistic to assume that *all* incentive programs work, or that by taking away individual rewards, productivity per person will triple. Maybe that's why commissions and bonuses and other rewards programs seem always half-assembled—no one has figured out yet how to devise the perfect system. Even though TI's Charlton emphatically defends her company's incentive programs, she has never been able to definitively link motivation and productivity to non-cash rewards. And although Marshall Industries' CEO Rodin loves to trumpet his company's new nonincentive system, some naysayers claim that, for example, salespeople will never perform without commissions.

According to a 1996 survey sponsored jointly by McLean, Virginia-based Wirthlin Worldwide and O.C. Tanner of Salt Lake City, 78 percent of CEOs and 58 percent of HR vice presidents say their companies feature rewards programs recognizing performance or productivity. Two-thirds of each group report their interest in service awards is constant, while about one-quarter claim their attraction to such programs is actually increasing.

"If you want to impact the bottom line, you must invest in people, and not just with money, but also with recognition rewards," says Steven Kimball, director of communications with O.C. Tanner (a provider, it should be noted, of corporate service/recognition award programs). "It's a matter of common sense and motivation theory that has been with us forever that says people work for more than just a paycheck. That should be proof enough."

However, John Parkington, practice director of organization effectiveness for the San Francisco office of Watson Wyatt, argues that in the past two decades, companies focused too much on measuring efficiency and production. In the process, he says, they weeded out anyone with entrepreneurial spirit. In other words, if you wanted to speed up the assembly of, say, brass lighting fixtures, and you weren't particular about quality, workers could be spurred to meet quotas by financial incentive. But that's not exactly want employers today want. These days, they want someone to design software that speeds up the assembly line.

The new economy demands that employees at every level be creative problem solvers, and this is where it gets sticky for managers to design strategies for creating high-performance organizations. "Now companies are asking themselves: 'What can we do to reward people for solving problems, for being innovative and for growing the top line,' " explains Parkington. "Managers have to be smart and inventive enough to figure out new ways to reward their employees for this sort of behavior."

But can you encourage this kind of thinking with team shirts and train kits? Parkington believes a company that wants people to take job-related risks must let employees know what's expected of them, offer them encouragement, provide the resources for innovation and proffer rewards with perceived value.

Certainly, money isn't the only incentive for people to stay with a company. In a 1998 "American Work" survey conducted by The Loyalty Institute of Aon Consulting in Chicago, 1,800 employees ranked pay only 11th as a reason for remaining with an employer, behind such factors as open communication with managers, ability to challenge the status quo, and opportunities for personal growth. Money is especially weak as an incentive when it comes to encouraging employees to think more creatively.

## Be careful not to punish employees with rewards.

Non-cash rewards don't engender increased quality, productivity or creativity, either, says Alfie Kohn, one of America's leading thinkers and writers on the subject of money as motivator, and author of *Punished by Rewards* (Houghton Mifflin, 1993). He believes rewards programs can't work because they're based on an inadequate understanding of human motivation. One of the most thoroughly replicated findings in social psychology, he points out, is that the more you reward people for doing something, the more they tend to lose interest in whatever they did to get the reward. And when interest declines, so does quality.

"You can get people to do more of something or faster for a little while if you provide them an appealing reward," says Kohn. "But no scientific study has ever found a long-term enhancement of the quality of work as a result of any reward system. Bribes and threats can get you a short-term effect, but that's it."

# *Should You or Shouldn't You?*

Before you implement or change an employee incentive program, ask yourself the following questions:

- How will the program help support our corporate goals, such as increased profit or customer loyalty?
- How will the program support customers' expectations of our products and services?
- How can I make sure the program criteria is objective?
- Which employees will be included?
- How much of a hardship, if any, will the program place on our organization?
- Am I committed to repeating the program or is it a one-shot deal?

Source: LaBov & Beyond, a marketing communicationscompany in Fort Wayne, Indiana.

Kohn says rewards may actually damage quality and productivity, and cause employees to lose interest in their jobs. Why?

•Rewards control behavior through seduction. They're a way for people in power to manipulate those with less power.

•Rewards ruin relationships. They emphasize the difference in power between the person handing out the reward and the person receiving it.

•Rewards create competitiveness among employees, undermining collaboration and teamwork.

•Rewards reduce risk taking, creativity and innovation. People will be less likely to pursue hunches, fearing such out-of-the-box thinking may jeopardize their chances for a reward.

•Rewards ignore reasons. A commission system, for example, may lead a manager to blame the salesmen when they don't meet quotas, when the real problem may be packaging or pricing.

"Managers typically use a rewards system because it's easy," adds Kohn. "It doesn't take effort, skill or courage to dangle a doggie biscuit in front of an employee and say, 'Jump through this hoop and this will be yours.' "

## The bottom line on growing the top line.

Cara Finn is vice president of employee services at Mountain View, California-based Remedy Corp., a software company that builds and distributes applications for business processes. To remain competitive in the hothouse of Silicon Valley, her company during the last four years has doled out to some 750 employees incentive rewards ranging from American Express gift certificates to spot bonuses and movie tickets. Only recently has Finn structured a "quality of life" program in which employees receive rewards after they've been with the company three, five or seven years.

"You can't separate longevity from performance," she says. "If an employee has been with our company for three years, he's performing." And because Remedy is a publicly-held company, with the attendant inevitable ups and downs, Finn believes rewards also help even things out. "We hold tightly to the philosophy that rewards are good, but they should neither be a deterrent nor a reason for someone leaving or coming to our company." Instead, the suggestion coming out of the Chicago-based National Association of Employee Recognition is to change your corporate culture using positive reinforcement on a daily basis to transcend those traditional programs that so often feel manipulative.

Barry LaBov, CEO of the Fort Wayne, Indiana-based LaBov & Beyond, a marketing communications company, suggests every good human resources professional find new ways to offer incentive rewards that help support specific corporate goals. "People are people and they want to be recognized," he says. "The programs that fail revolve around rewarding performance that doesn't support company goals. Improving sales performance, for example, is not enough. Today you need programs that support such issues as profitability, loyalty and customer satisfaction. And you have to do it without alienating other people within the organization."

If you're one of those people who still can't take it as gospel that the more you reward an employee the more he or she gets innovative and creative—because it's not just about the money in the first place—then maybe you need to listen to Kohn, who still firmly believes there's a solution to all the madness surrounding employee incentive and rewards programs. Sure you can motivate people with the proverbial carrot and stick, he says, but motivate them to do what? To work for the long-term interest of the company, or for some short-term personal goal? "Rewards are a matter of doing things *to* employees," he stresses. "The alternative is working *with* employees, and that requires a better understanding of motivation and a transformation in how one looks at management."

Kohn quotes from management theorist Frederick Herzberg, who said: " 'If you want people motivated to do a good job, give them a good job to do.' " In other words, create an organization in which people feel a sense of community, maximize the extent to which employees are brought in on decisions large and small, and "dump your company's rewards program," adds Kohn. "You need to pay your employees well, pay them fairly, and do everything possible to get their minds off money and on work."

Of course, the elimination of commissions and other rewards programs doesn't guarantee quality. In reality, it takes real talent and courage to create a workplace in which employees feel important, where their work matters to them, and where they care about each other—with or without an incentive program.

# New Thinking on How to Link EXECUTIVE PAY with PERFORMANCE

ARTWORK BY CURTIS PARKER

*Under current compensation schemes, senior managers are rewarded even when their companies underperform. But there's a way for boards to align executive pay with shareholder expectations.*

## by Alfred Rappaport

THE TOPIC OF EXECUTIVE COMPENSATION generates heated discussion. And, because stock options have become the fastest growing segment of executive pay, performance-related pay in particular attracts high-decibel debate. Stock options now account for more than half of total CEO compensation in the largest U.S. companies and about 30% of senior operating managers' pay. Options and stock grants also constitute almost half of directors' remuneration.

*Alfred Rappaport is the Leonard Spacek Professor Emeritus at Northwestern University's J.L. Kellogg Graduate School of Management in Evanston, Illinois. He directs shareholder value research for L.E.K. Consulting and is the author of* Creating Shareholder Value: A Guide for Managers and Investors *(Free Press, 1998). He can be reached at alrapp@pacbell.net.*

> The huge gains from options for below-average performers should give pause to even the most ardent defender of current corporate pay systems.

This trend is relatively new. The takeover movement of the 1980s provided a powerful incentive for companies to introduce compensation schemes tied directly to stock prices. Before that, executive pay was largely a matter of salaries and of bonuses that were paid out only if financial targets were met. It was widely thought that a company's stock price correlated with its ability to meet certain financial goals. A number of studies, however, cast doubt on the supposed relationship between bonuses, financial targets, and stock prices. For example, Michael C. Jensen and Kevin J. Murphy's often cited HBR article "CEO Incentives—It's Not How Much You Pay, But How" (May–June 1990) showed that there was virtually no link between how much CEOs were paid and how well their companies performed for shareholders.

In the early 1990s, corporate boards began to highlight shareholder value. They became convinced that the surest way to align the interests of managers with those of shareholders was to make stock options a large component of executive compensation. By the mid-1990s CEOs and other senior managers found themselves with significant stock and options holdings. As the stock market began its ascent, executive pay mounted. But the correlation between a CEO's pay and the stock market did not prove that a company was enjoying superior performance: when the market is rising, stock options reward both superior and subpar performance.

That's because *any* increase in a company's share price constitutes "positive performance" with conventional stock options. Any increase in share price will reward the holder of a stock option without distinguishing between good performance and bad. The almost 100% increase in major stock market indexes between 1995 and 1997 exposed this shortcoming. Executives with fixed-price options enjoyed a huge windfall from the long-running bull market that was fueled not only by corporate performance but also by factors beyond management control, such as declining inflation and lower interest rates,

How easy is it to earn a positive return when the stock market is rising? For the ten-year period ending in 1997, total return to shareholders—dividends plus increases in the share price—was positive for each of the 100 largest U.S. companies. The huge gains from options for below-average performers should give pause to even the most ardent defender of current corporate pay systems.

Fortunately, the gap between existing compensation practices and those needed to promote higher levels of achievement can be bridged. In doing so, all levels of the corporation, not just the top, must be considered. The ultimate goal of providing superior total returns to shareholders can be better accomplished by following three steps: first, by rewarding top managers only when they outperform the competition; second, by determining the real contribution of each business unit to the company's overall share price; and third, by involving frontline managers and workers in the quest for higher shareholder value. We'll examine how each of these steps can be carried out.

## Problems with Pay at the Top

For incentive compensation to work, corporate boards must choose both the right measures and the right levels of performance. In principle, stock options employ the right measure of performance for corporate executives who are responsible for the company as a whole. After all, the value of a stock option is driven by the share price, which is the largest component of shareholders' total return. Some managers protest that shareholders' expectations are unrealistically high, but the weight of evidence does not support that conclusion.

Surveys, for example—whether taken in rising or falling markets—consistently and overwhelmingly report that most CEOs believe their company's shares are undervalued. Companies are backing up this belief by repurchasing shares at record levels—and studies show that stock prices respond positively to announcements of repurchased shares. In addition, forecasted performance in a company's own long-term business plans is frequently well above the level needed to justify its current stock price. Finally, companies are increasingly using stock to finance acquisitions. Executives dedicated to increasing shareholder value would not do that if they believed that shares were undervalued. Most CEOs, in short, place a lot of stock in their company's share price.

If stock options set the right measure of executive performance, do they also set the right level? The answer is no. Shareholders expect boards to reward management for achieving superior returns—that is, for returns equal to or better than those earned by the company's peer group or by broader market indexes. That is how institutional investors distinguish performing from underperforming companies and also how the *Wall Street Journal* "Shareholder Scoreboard" compares performance in its annual rankings of the 1,000 largest U.S. companies. To help investors monitor executive pay, the Securities and Exchange Commission even requires companies in their annual executive compensation disclosure to report the total return to shareholders relative to their peers or to the market as a whole. But although many boards and CEOs publicly acknowledge the paramount importance of delivering superior returns to shareholders, current stock option schemes reward both mediocre and superior performance. In other words, boards are not setting the right level of performance.

The problem lies in the way conventional stock options are structured. The exercise price is established at the market price on the day the options are granted and stays fixed over the entire option period, usually ten years. If the share price rises above the exercise price, the option holder can cash in on the gains. Therefore, fixed-price options reward executives for any increase in share price—even if the increase is well below that realized by competitors or by the market as a whole.

Consider the following example. A CEO is granted options exercisable over the next ten years on 1 million shares at the current share price of $100. If the share price rises by 5% a year to $163 at the end of the period, the CEO will take home a gain of $63 million. But if the share prices of competitors grow at 15% a year during the same period, a convincing argument can be made that the CEO does not deserve to cash in the options. No reasonable board of directors would knowingly approve a plan that offers high rewards for such poor long-term performance.

Some stock option plans do target a higher level of performance than standard fixed-price options. Companies such as Colgate-Palmolive, Monsanto, and Transamerica, for example, have recently introduced premium-priced stock option plans. In those plans, exercise prices are fixed at a premium above the market price on the date the options are granted, and they remain at that level throughout the life of the options. The premium is usually 25%, 50% or even 100% of

> Fixed-price options reward executives for any increase in share price—even if the increase is well below that realized by competitors.

the market price. At those higher exercise prices, the share price for a ten-year option must rise about 2%, 4%, and 7% respectively each year if the option is to be exercised profitably when it expires. But those rates are still well below historical equity returns and investor expectations. More to the point, because the exercise prices remain fixed, premium-priced options hold no guarantee that the level of performance will be superior. During a period of rising markets, premium-priced options may still reward below-average performance. They also offer little or no reward to executives who outperform their competitors during times of modestly rising or declining markets.

## The Advantages of Indexing

Stock option plans don't have to be blunt instruments. By tying a plan's exercise price to a selected index, boards can increase the pay of superior performers while appropriately penalizing poor ones. Let's assume the exercise price of a CEO's options are reset each year to reflect changes in a benchmarked index. If the index increases by 15% during the first year, the exercise price of the option would also increase by that amount. The option would then be worth exercising only if the company's shares had gone up by more than 15%. The CEO, therefore, is rewarded only if his or her company outperforms the index.

In selecting an index, companies can choose either an index of their competitors or a broader market index such as the Standard & Poor's 500. The choice requires trade-offs. Stock options indexed to the market are easily measured and tracked. A market index, however, ignores the special factors that affect the company's industry. Although the S&P 500 index has risen spectacularly over the past few years, industries such as steel, heavy construction, pollution control, and paper products have done poorly in comparison. It is better to judge management's contribution using a peer group index. However, because many companies have diversified into a wide range of

# Misplaced Concerns About Indexed Options

The idea of indexed options is not new. Yet despite their appeal, very few companies have issued them. There are two possible reasons for that. First, current accounting treatment penalizes the use of indexed options; and second, investors may be concerned about the dilution of the value of their shares. Both concerns are largely misplaced.

**The Accounting Anomaly.** Under present accounting rules, companies must disclose the cost of fixed-price stock options in their financial statements. But they are not required to charge the cost against earnings. In the case of indexed options, however, the difference between the stock price and the exercise price must be reported each year as an expense. It defies economic logic that less costly indexed options must be expensed while more costly standard options are not. But this rule should not be a roadblock against the switch to indexed options. Executive stock options do not become more or less costly depending on whether the disclosure is made in a company's income statement or in its footnotes. Research shows that stock prices respond to disclosure of relevant information such as the cost of executive stock options. Investors are not fooled, and boards should not use the "investors won't understand the earnings hit" excuse to avoid implementing value-creating compensation arrangements.

Still, the requirement to expense indexed options does discourage companies from adopting indexed option plans. Companies do not voluntarily report lower earnings. The Financial Accounting Standards Board should take the lead by mandating a *consistent* treatment for all options. The critical choice for the FASB is not between footnote disclosure and expense recognition. What is important is that whatever the choice, it apply equally to all options. That would level the playing field. Bad accounting policy should not be allowed to dictate compensation.

**Fears of Dilution.** Shares reserved for outstanding and future grants under stock option and stock purchase programs have surged during the past few years. More than 13% of outstanding shares among the 200 largest public U.S.. corporations are reserved for such programs, and some investors believe that allocations have reached—if not exceeded—a reasonable upper limit. Because more indexed options than fixed-price options will have to be granted under the proposed conversion scheme, some shareholders might worry that their holdings will be further diluted.

That is unlikely, because there is a higher chance that indexed options will expire unexercised than is the case with fixed-price options. While indexed options have only about a 50% probability of being exercised (because only about half the companies in an index can enjoy superior performance), fixed-price options have had an exercise rate approaching 100% over the past ten years. Thus if two indexed options were granted in place of each fixed-price option, the increase in a company's outstanding shares would be about the same. Concerns over dilution should not focus on the number of options granted but rather on the number that can be exercised in the absence of superior performance. Because CEOs can be rewarded for weak performance under fixed-price plans, there is actually a greater risk of dilution with standard plans than with indexed plans.

---

products and markets, it is sometimes difficult to identify a group of peers.

Whatever index is selected, indexed options have clear advantages over fixed-price options. Indexed options do not reward underperforming executives simply because the market is rising. Nor do they penalize superior performers because the market is declining. They can keep executives motivated not only in the bull markets everyone has grown accustomed to but also in sustained bear markets. They link pay to superior performance in all markets.

Despite their merits, indexed options are likely to meet with opposition. Some objections are rooted in misplaced concerns; others are more fundamental. (See the insert "Misplaced Concerns About Indexed Options.") Underperforming executives are likely to balk at the more exacting performance standards of indexed options. Indeed, companies committed to providing superior returns to their shareholders will need to carefully consider how switching to indexed options will affect the moti-

vation of their senior managers. In addition, board members, who now receive almost half their compensation in stock grants and fixed-price options, must be persuaded to agree to the same standards for themselves if they are to credibly ask management to accept indexed options.

To persuade executives to accept indexed option packages, the packages should be structured so that exceptional performers can earn greater returns than they could with conventional options. Two incentives need to be incorporated into the packages. First, companies should increase the number of options they grant to executives; second, they should lower the exercise price. By taking those actions, boards can get senior managers to tie their pay to superior performance.

They would be able to do so because the managers would come out on top with such a plan. The evidence comes from a study conducted by L.E.K. Consulting, which examined the performance between 1988 and 1997 of 170 companies in 23 industries represented in the Dow Jones index. The study found that executives at two-thirds of superior-performing companies would have earned more with indexed options structured along the lines recommended here than they actually did.

**Increasing the Options.** To compensate executives for bearing higher risk, boards will need to offer them more options. To decide how many more, they first need to know how many indexed options would offer the same value as the conventional options that top managers currently possess. I call this number the "value ratio." Take a typical situation for a company whose share price is $100. As calculated by option-pricing models, the estimated value of a conventional stock option is $34.50, and the value of an indexed option is $21.60. The value ratio is then 34.50 divided by 21.60, or 1.6.

The value ratio is affected principally by changes in interest rates, stock price volatility, and the correlation between the chosen index and the stock price. Research conducted by the University of Toronto's John Hull has shown that although value ratios are sensitive to these factors, in most situations they can be expected to fall in a range of approximately 1.5 to 2.0. But in a competitive market for top management talent, many executives are unlikely to be convinced by such figures and will probably demand more options than the ratios would suggest. Thus in order to entice executives to convert, boards must start by offering them at least two indexed options for every fixed-price option in their current plan.

Although many CEOs may be reluctant to shift to a new compensation plan, high-performing ones will do better with indexed options than with conventional options if they convert at a two-for-one rate. Suppose, for example, that a company's stock price was $100 on the day the options were granted and that a peer index was established that had the same price. Over ten years, the index grows at an average of 10% per year and its price reaches $259. The company, meanwhile, grows by 20% annually so that its share price reaches $619. The profit on each indexed option would be $619 minus $259, or $360, while the gain for a fixed-priced option would be $619 minus $100 or $519. If two indexed options had been granted for each fixed-priced option, the gain from the indexed option package would be $720—that's 39% greater than the $519 from the fixed-priced option. (To gauge the impact of different scenarios, see the table "How Much Can Senior Managers Gain from Indexed Options?")

**Lowering the Exercise Price.** By offering two or more new options for each old one, companies will enable superior executives to earn even more. But only about 50% of executives can be above average. What about incentives for the others? One response is that they don't deserve incentive compensation. On the other hand, it's probably not in the best interest of shareholders to have a group of company executives who are less motivated than they could be because their indexed options are presently worthless.

One way to resolve the dilemma is to lower the exercise price for indexed options. There are several ways to do that. The most effective and easiest way is to grant what I call "discounted indexed options—options whose exercise prices are discounted by some specified rate. A discounted indexed option guarantees an index-generated exercise price while simultaneously allowing managers to profit at a performance level that is modestly below the company's peer group average. Discounted indexed options sweeten the package.

## How Much Can Senior Managers Gain from Indexed Options?

Superior managers will usually do better with indexed option packages than with conventional packages. And the better a company does relative to the index, the higher the gains. My research also shows that gains from indexed options relative to fixed-price options decrease if options are exercised early. Indexed options thereby encourage managers to stay for the long term.

| | | Annual growth of company's stock price minus the index's growth* | | |
|---|---|---|---|---|
| | | **5%** | **10%** | **15%** |
| Number of indexed options granted for each fixed-price option | **2.00** | -5 | 39 | 62 |
| | **2.50** | 19 | 73 | 102 |
| | **3.00** | 43 | 108 | 142 |

Percentage gains for senior managers on an indexed plan in comparison with a fixed-price plan

*The selected index is assumed to grow 10% annually, a rate that approximates the market's long-term price appreciation.

To see how such options would work, imagine a company whose board wants to issue them. The board could discount the selected index by a specified rate each year over the life of the option. For example, if in the first year the index rises from $100 to $120, a 1% discount would decrease the year end index from $120 to $118.80. Thus the exercise price of the stock would have risen by only 18.8% instead of 20%. This approach makes gains from indexed options accessible to more executives. Discounting options also provides further economic motivation for high-performing executives to remain with the company and to hold on to their options. By the end of the ten-year life of the typical option, the cumulative discount on the price of the index would be 10%.

Two additional questions must be answered before CEOs and other senior executives are likely to endorse an indexed option plan. First, how large does the spread have to be between the growth in a company's share price and the index price before the gains from indexed options exceed those from standard ones? In other words, by how much does a company have to outperform its peers? And second, how difficult is it for companies to reach and surpass the break-even spread?

## How Many Winners with Indexed Options?

Discounting options and increasing the value ratio makes it easier for companies to reach the break-even spread – the figure that allows holders of indexed option packages to equal the gains they would have obtained under fixed-price plans. The table shows the percentage of superior-performing companies from a total sample of 170 that would have surpassed the break-even spread for different types of indexed option packages.

| | | Annual discount from 1988 through 1997 | | |
| | | 5% | 10% | 15% |
|---|---|---|---|---|
| Number of indexed options granted for each fixed-price option | 2.00 | 29 | 43 | 64 |
| | 2.50 | 45 | 64 | 80 |
| | 3.00 | 55 | 75 | 88 |

Percentage of superior-performing companies whose senior managers would have gained more with indexed options than they would have with fixed-price options

Those questions can be answered by referring to the L.E.K. Consulting study mentioned above. The research shows that a company should outperform its selected index by about 5.4% for two indexed options to generate greater gains than one fixed-price option. That figure falls to about 3.9% if one introduces an annual 1% discount to the indexed options. How easy is it to achieve those spreads? Easier than might be expected. The table "How Many Winners with Indexed Options?" shows, for example, that executives at 64% of the superior-performing companies in the study would have gained if they had exchanged each conventional option for 2.5 indexed options discounted at 1%.

This research, of course, was conducted at a time when the stock market was rising very quickly. The average annual price growth of the S&P 500 index between 1988 and 1997 was 14.7%; the figure was 8.7% for the past 50 years. Would the percentages in the table be affected if price appreciation over the next ten years mirrored the longer-term average? The most reasonable guess is that the percentages would not change significantly. Although the size of break-even spreads is affected by the overall growth of the market or the selected index, the number of companies that reach or exceed that spread is not affected by the state of the market. In the 23 industries looked at in the study, increases in share price ranged on average from 4% to 24% per year over the ten-year period. I could find no relationship between those figures and the percentage of companies whose executives would have realized greater gains from indexed options than from fixed-price options. This suggests that discounted indexed options will provide a better deal for most managers regardless of stock market conditions.

## Judging the Value of Business Units

While CEO pay draws intense interest, the compensation of operating managers is far less scrutinized. It is, however, equally critical to the success of public companies. After all, the primary source of a company's value lies in its operating units. In decentralized companies that have a range of products and markets, operating executives make the important day-to-day decisions and investments. The way those executives are evaluated and paid affects their behavior and the business's results. In order to close the gaps between pay and performance at the operating unit level, performance targets and incentive pay must be aligned with the interests of shareholders.

Otherwise, CEOs will find it difficult to achieve gains from indexed options.

Corporate managers are well aware of the importance of motivating operating managers. Performance packages are now the dominant part of the compensation mix at the operating level. Pearl Meyer & Partners, a consulting firm that specializes in executive compensation, reported that for group heads managing businesses with annual

> **Granting stock options to business unit managers is even less a guarantee of performance than it is for CEOs.**

ight to be a good estimate of the value added he business, but these measures also suffer accounting problems. The most important lem, however, is that schemes using residual me measures typically set too low a level of mum performance. This conclusion may sure many managers. It is well established that agement creates value when the returns on orate investments are greater than the cost of tal. But that does not mean operating execu- should be rewarded for any value created. g the cost-of-capital standard as a threshold ncentive compensation ignores the level of d value already implied by a company's stock .

nagine a corporation whose cost of capital is . The price of its shares reflects investors' be- that the company will find opportunities to st and operate at an average expected rate of n on investment of 20%. If managers start to st in projects yielding less, say 15%, investors revise their expectations downward and the pany's shares will fall correspondingly. Few d argue that a manager should be rewarded such performance, even though he has ex- ed the cost of capital.

ow often does this gap occur between ex- d return on investment and the cost of capi- Although the differences vary widely from industry to another, the share prices of vir- y all publicly traded companies reflect the ex- tion that they will generate returns well e the cost of capital. According to a study by . Consulting, for example, the median base- line value for the 100 largest nonfinancial companies is approximately 30% of their stock price. In other words, if investors expected these companies to earn returns at the cost of capital, their shares would be priced at about 70% below current levels. (See the table "Expected Rates of Return Compared with Costs of Capital.")

**The Superior Shareholder-Value-Added Approach.** How is pay to be set using the right measure at the right level in a business unit? The best way is by valuing a unit as if it were a stand-alone business. The parent's share price, after all, largely

nancial measures include operating income, return on invested capital (ROIC), and return on equity (ROE). Earnings measures are not reliably linked to shareholder value because they do not incorporate the cost of capital and may be calculated using different accounting methods that can produce different numbers. ROIC and ROE have similar accounting shortcomings.

A growing number of companies have also embraced residual income measures, such as economic value added, which deduct a cost of capital charge from earnings. The resulting calculation is

## Expected Rates of Return Compared with Costs of Capital

Credit Suisse First Boston, using their own value-driver estimates, including the cost of capital, calculated the expected or minimum rates of return on investment needed to justify September 1998 share prices for the Dow Jones industrial companies. In every case, the expected returns were greater than the cost of capital.

The potential for undeserved payment is very high when cost of capital is the threshold. That is as true for business units as it is for corporations, and it applies whenever performance is based on accounting or residual income measures. That's because those measures rely on a company's historical investment rather than on the benchmark against which investors properly measure their returns—the company's current market value.

| | Expected Return | Cost of Capital | Difference |
|---|---|---|---|
| Coca-Cola | 24.8% | 8.8% | 16.0% |
| Merck | 22.8 | 8.9 | 13.9 |
| General Electric | 21.7 | 9.0 | 12.7 |
| Johnson & Johnson | 21.3 | 9.1 | 12.2 |
| AT&T | 19.3 | 8.4 | 10.9 |
| Caterpillar | 19.0 | 9.0 | 10.0 |
| J.P. Morgan | 18.6 | 9.0 | 9.6 |
| Wal-Mart | 18.1 | 8.5 | 9.6 |
| Philip Morris | 17.7 | 8.4 | 9.3 |
| DuPont | 16.8 | 8.1 | 8.7 |
| Boeing | 16.6 | 8.4 | 8.2 |
| Procter & Gamble | 16.5 | 8.9 | 7.6 |
| IBM | 16.4 | 7.7 | 8.7 |
| General Motors | 16.2 | 9.0 | 7.2 |
| Hewlett-Packard | 16.0 | 8.7 | 7.3 |
| Eastman Kodak | 15.5 | 8.2 | 7.3 |
| Disney | 13.9 | 8.2 | 5.7 |
| United Technologies | 13.9 | 8.9 | 5.0 |
| AlliedSignal | 13.5 | 8.0 | 5.5 |
| 3M | 13.3 | 8.6 | 4.7 |
| Travelers Group | 12.5 | 8.6 | 3.9 |
| McDonald's | 12.2 | 7.5 | 4.7 |
| Alcoa | 12.2 | 8.4 | 3.8 |
| Goodyear | 11.6 | 9.5 | 2.1 |
| International Paper | 11.0 | 6.7 | 4.3 |
| Sears | 10.7 | 7.5 | 3.2 |
| Union Carbide | 9.6 | 8.5 | 1.1 |
| American Express | 9.5 | 9.1 | 0.4 |
| Chevron | 8.9 | 7.8 | 1.1 |

lated by applying standard discounting techniques to forecasts of operating cash flows for a specific period and then subtracting the incremental future investments anticipated for that period. If a company is to deliver superior returns to its shareholders, its units must create superior SVA. Calculating superior SVA requires six steps:

• First, develop expectations for the standard drivers of value—sales growth, operating margins, and investments—by factoring in historical performance, the unit's business plan, and competitive benchmarking.

• Second, convert the expectations about value drivers into annual cash-flow estimates and discount them at the business unit's cost of capital in order to obtain the value of each operating unit.

• Third, aggregate the values of each operating unit to verify that the sum is approximately equal to the company's market value.

• Fourth, from the cash flows used to value the operating unit establish the annual expected SVA over the performance period—typically three years.

• Fifth, use year-end results to compute the actual SVA at the end of each year. The calculation will be the same as in the previous step, with actual numbers replacing the estimates.

• Sixth, calculate the difference between actual and expected SVA. When the difference is positive, you have superior SVA.

Value creation prospects can vary greatly from one business unit to another. An approach based on expectations establishes a level playing field by accounting for differences in business prospects. Managers who perform extraordinarily well in low-return businesses will be rewarded, while those who do poorly in high-return businesses will be penalized.

At what level of performance do you start rewarding business unit managers with pay for performance? The right answer would seem to be, "When they create superior SVA in their units." But just as they may with indexed options, boards may wish to set their SVA threshold targets at a discount. Setting a threshold that is modestly below expected SVA would be appropriate. Indeed, incentive plans for operating managers often set a threshold at 80% of a designated target. That makes sense, but the converse—imposing a cap—does not. Currently, many plans are capped once performance is greater than 120% of the target. Such a policy would send the wrong message to operating managers who otherwise would be motivated to maximize SVA.

When setting performance pay, it is important to note that value creation is a long-term phe-

reflects the aggregate expectations of its operating units. One way to evaluate business units is by considering "shareholder value added." SVA has one clear advantage over residual income measures: it is based entirely on cash flows and does not introduce accounting distortions. It can therefore serve as a sound basis for an incentive pay plan.

SVA puts a value on changes in the future cash flows of a company or business unit. It is calcu-

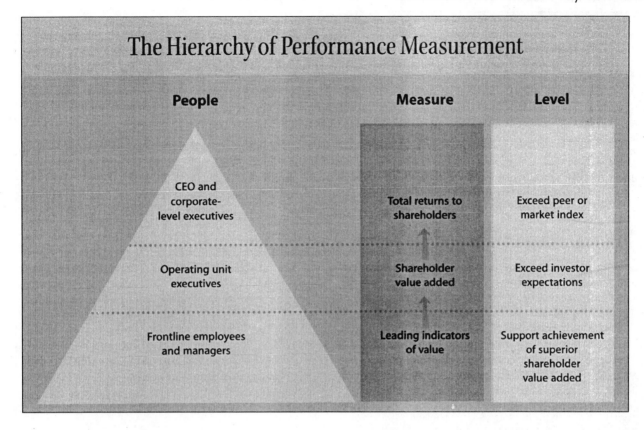

## The Hierarchy of Performance Measurement

| People | Measure | Level |
|---|---|---|
| CEO and corporate-level executives | Total returns to shareholders | Exceed peer or market index |
| Operating unit executives | Shareholder value added | Exceed investor expectations |
| Frontline employees and managers | Leading indicators of value | Support achievement of superior shareholder value added |

nomenon. Annual performance measures do not account for the longer-term consequences of operating and investment decisions made today. So looking at a single year reveals little about the long-term ability of a business to generate cash. To motivate managers to focus on opportunities to create superior SVA beyond the current period, the performance evaluation period should be extended to, say, a rolling three-year cycle. Companies can then retain a portion of incentive payouts to cover against future underperformance.

## The Front Line's Contribution

Using SVA performance to establish incentive pay is consistent with the responsibilities of the operating unit executive. But measures are needed at every level of an organization in order for it to realize superior total returns to shareholders. Indeed, finding measures that can guide hands-on decision making by frontline workers is the final piece of the puzzle. Although value drivers such as sales growth and operating margins are useful for identifying value-creating strategies and tracking SVA at operating units, they are not sufficiently focused to provide much day-to-day guidance. Middle managers and frontline employees need to know what specific actions they can take to ensure that expectations are met or exceeded. Even setting a three- or five-year perform-

ance period may not capture most of the SVA potential of high-growth businesses or of industries such as pharmaceuticals that have extended lags between their investments and their product sales. The solution to both problems lies in identifying what I call the "leading indicators of value." These indicators can be used both as a supplement to SVA analysis and as the basis for calculating incentives for frontline employees.

Leading indicators are current measures that are strongly correlated with the long-term value of a business. Examples include time to market for new products, employee turnover figures, customer retention rates, the number of new stores that are opened on time, and the average cycle time from order date to shipping date. These are all factors that frontline managers can directly influence. My research has shown that for most businesses, three to six leading indicators account for a high percentage of long-term SVA potential. Improving leading indicators is not a goal in itself; it is the basis for achieving superior SVA. The process of identifying leading indicators is challenging, revealing, and rewarding. It takes more than an impressive knowledge of customers, products, suppliers, and technology to understand a business's sources of value. Operating managers need to identify and focus on activities that maximize SVA and reduce costly investment in resources that contribute little to actual value.

# Home Depot's Leading Indicators of Value

## by Thomas H. Nodine

Home Depot ranks among the ten largest retailers in the United States. With an annual total return to shareholders of 44.8% over the past ten years, the company's performance easily exceeds the industry average of 21.6%. That extraordinary performance has raised the standards that management must meet in coming years. Over 70% of Home Depot's stock price is based on expected shareholder value added coming from future growth. It is essential that the company identify its leading indicators of value—the building blocks for its long-term SVA—in order to maintain its position.

The first step in finding leading indicators is to see which of the standard cash-flow drivers of value—sales growth, profit margins, and investments—are critical to a company's success. At Home Depot sales growth and profit margin are the critical drivers. Analyzing sales growth reveals two leading indicators of value—growth in new stores and revenue per store. A sensitivity analysis of those indicators reveals how significantly they are correlated with Home Depot's value. For each 1% shortfall in new store growth, the company's value falls by about 7%. Indeed, store growth is so important to Home Depot that a one-year delay in all currently scheduled new store openings would reduce the company's value by almost 16%.

The same process can be used to identify leading indicators of value associated with profit margins. These include average retail and wholesale prices, as well as freight, labor, and administrative costs as a percentage of revenues.

Understanding the relationship between leading indicators is essential for identifying value-creating strategies. For exam-

ple, although it is important that Home Depot maintain or exceed projected store growth, the company must not open new stores so quickly that they cannibalize sales at existing stores.

Leading indicators also provide management with a more sophisticated way to identify trends. For example, increases in Home Depot's average retail prices, together with falling average wholesale prices, signal greater future profitability. On the other hand, decreases in Home Depot's revenue per store as growth continues might indicate market saturation, showing managers that a period of lower growth lies ahead.

Home Depot is clearly focusing on leading indicators of value. To promote growth, it is aggressively adding stores in the United States while entering new markets in Canada and Latin America. The retailer is also monitoring store construction to ensure on-time openings, increasing store size to improve revenue per store, and introducing new store formats that promote higher average purchases. At the same time, Home Depot plans to increase margins by buying in bulk and optimizing its mix of products. By continuing to focus on these leading indicators of value, Home Depot's management can identify value-creating strategies and continue to exceed the high expectations of its shareholders.

---

*Thomas H. Nodine is vice president of L.E.K. Consulting in Chicago, Illinois.*

Identifying leading indicators helps management find strategies with the highest potential for increasing SVA. The insert "Home Depot's Leading Indicators of Value" shows how one company focuses on certain leading indicators to deliver superior value to shareholders.

Achieving superior returns is the ultimate goal for shareholders. It is, therefore, the only appropriate target for the CEO, the board, and corporate-level executives. Companies with superior performance standards in place at all levels send a powerful message to shareholders about their aspirations.

The focus on achieving superior returns is consistent with the broader duties of the CEO—the responsibility to be in the right businesses and to allocate the proper amount of capital to them. But the most significant source of superior total returns is the operating unit's level of SVA. And the

building blocks for SVA are the leading indicators that guide frontline managers. Without performance at those levels, shareholders will not be able to maximize their returns, and CEOs will be less likely to realize gains from their indexed options.

The concept of pay for performance is widely accepted, but the link between incentive pay and superior performance is still too weak. Boards of directors need to push through changes in executive compensation practices, including their own pay schemes. And reforms must be adopted at all levels of the organization. If indexed options are introduced for CEOs, then SVA-based measures should be introduced in business units. And on the front line, leading indicators should be followed. Shareholders will applaud changes in pay schemes that motivate companies to deliver more value.

# LET THE EVIDENCE SPEAK:

# Financial Incentives *Are* Effective!!

**Nina Gupta**
**Professor of Management**
*University of Arkansas*

**Jason D. Shaw**
**Assistant Professor of Management**
*Drexel University*

In an ideal world, everyone would be altruistic. In an ideal world, all jobs would be inherently interesting and challenging. But the fact of the matter is, we don't live in an ideal world; people are self-interested to a greater or lesser extent, and many jobs are dull and boring, or become so over time.

Methods for motivating people to do their best must be developed against this backdrop, not against idealistic fantasies. We must confront the inevitable fact that most of us are motivated by money—some more so than others. After all, even consultants who argue that money doesn't motivate charge huge amounts of it to dispense this advice, and authors of books arguing that money "punishes" keep the profits from book sales. This is why sports and movie stars are paid huge amounts: money matters—it matters to most of us. Why then should we not expect money to matter to line workers, to sales people, to food processors, and to the average working person?

Of course it matters. Economists through the centuries—St. Thomas Aquinas, Adam Smith—understood the importance of money. Isn't it time that management specialists did too?

We can make our work systems substantially more effective if we bite the bullet, accept this premise and proceed on it instead of daydreaming about the ideal world. That money matters and that money is an effective incentive are not simply matters of opinion. Rather, these premises are supported by logic and by decades of research and practice, all pointing in the same direction—money is a powerful incentive. When used prudently, it yields enormous benefits. When used foolishly, it can be quite dysfunctional.

## Why Does Money Motivate?

This philosophical issue has long been debated. Critical reasons for the motivational

*Much better than a raise, Fredericks, I've promoted you to V.P. You'll oversee our coffee distribution and trash removal teams.*

potential of money include its *instrumental* and *symbolic* meanings. The instrumental meaning of money concerns what we get for it. Money motivates because it can get us things—better houses, clothes, cars, and whatever. The symbolic meaning of money concerns how it is viewed by ourselves and by people in general. Money signals our status in and worth to society. Richer people are considered more successful than poorer people. By extension, then, if we have more money, we are more successful. These two aspects of money are intertwined throughout the fabric of society—terminology such as "put your money where your mouth is," "crime doesn't pay," "paying the piper," "hitting pay dirt," "you get what you pay for," and "there is no free lunch" underscores the centrality of money in all spheres of our lives. It is reasonable to assume that most people would rather have more money than less money. Having more money allows us to get more and better things; having more money increases our status, visibility, and respect.

### How Does Money Motivate?

Behaviors that are rewarded are repeated, behaviors that are punished are eliminated. When certain behaviors are followed by money, then, they are more likely to be repeated. This means that employees will do the things for which they are rewarded; it also means that they will ignore the things for which they are not rewarded. The term "rigid bureaucratic behavior"[1] captures this idea. It reflects the tendency for people to follow the

*The evidence consistently shows that financial incentives are associated with higher performance.*

reward system strictly, doing those and *only* those things that are rewarded. The classic example of rigid bureaucratic behavior is shown by sales "hawks" paid on commission basis— they try to get sales at all costs (another example of the pervasive use of monetary figures of speech) and ignore reshelving and other duties that the organization values but does not necessarily reward. For this reason

it is critical, when linking money to behaviors, to make sure that *all* relevant aspects of behavior are included in measurement. Incomplete measurement and rewards result in incomplete performance as well, i.e., employees doing only those things that are rewarded.

By "putting its money where its mouth is," management also shows employees what it values. People are cognitive processors—they understand and interpret management signals. They understand why the CEO is paid a lot more than is the janitor, for example. They also understand the difference between lip service and real commitment. Resources (the most visible resource being money) are devoted to things that management values. Media tycoon Ted Turner recently made a splash regarding the importance of the rich supporting various humanitarian causes—he donated a large amount of money to the United Nations while calling on other rich people to do the same. Would the splash have been as big if he had simply called for huge humanitarian efforts without the donation? Of course not.

In the same way, what management supports with money is given greater weight than what management supports simply with words. In short, money motivates by rewarding certain behaviors; it also motivates by showing people what is valued in the organization—it provides a cognitive map of the path people must take to succeed, i.e., to make more money.

### What Does the Research Say?

Research is tricky business. It does not always show what we want it to show. As rational beings, however, we must accept the evidence, whatever it may be. With respect to the motivating power of money, the evidence is consistent—financial incentives are associated with higher employee performance.

About a decade ago, Douglas Jenkins cumulated the evidence on financial incentives and performance. He concluded that financial incentives do indeed work, not just in laboratory settings but in real life as well.[2] But he used a nettlesome method, known as the "traditional voting method," of counting the number of studies showing positive, negative, and no effects, and then determining where the bulk of the studies fell. This method has problems. For example, it ignores the *strength* of the relationship between two variables; it treats studies with many subjects the same way as it does studies with only a few subjects.

More recently, we cumulated these studies, as well as those that had been done since 1986, statistically through a technique called meta-analysis.[3] Meta-analysis enables the identification of whether one factor (e.g., financial incentives) is related to another (e.g., performance), controlling for various statistical artifacts that may affect the results of any particular study. Meta-analysis also enables a determination of how *strongly* one factor affects another when the research evidence as a whole is considered. It considers *all* available research and thus prevents researchers from picking and choosing among studies for evidence supporting their arguments.

To conduct the meta-analysis, we searched for scientific studies examining the effects of financial incentives on performance. After considerable effort, we were able to identify only 39 such studies. Thus, the meta-analysis included 39 rigorously-designed studies of the effects of financial incentives on performance. We found a strong effect ($r = .34$) on performance *quantity* (i.e., financial incentives accounted for quite a bit of variation in performance quantity). This was true when the variations across studies were statistically controlled; this held true whether the study was conducted in the laboratory or in a real company; it remained true whether the job the person was doing was inherently interesting or not.

We wanted to examine the effects of financial incentives on performance *quality* also. Unfortunately, only six studies examined performance quality separately. Furthermore, it was unclear whether the incentive was contingent on performance quality, or whether performance quality was measured without a specific contingency being present. We did not find a consistent relationship between incentives and performance quality, in all likelihood because this issue is rarely investigated thoroughly. We can conclude from this that the jury is still out regarding the impact of financial incentives on performance quality. It is interesting to note that those who argue that money undermines performance quality *cannot* support this assertion with evidence; it is noteworthy that few rigorous studies even examined this issue.

The only studies included in the meta-analysis were carefully designed with good measurement instruments—they were much less susceptible to bias than anecdotes, case studies, and testimonials can be. With respect to performance quantity, then, the evidence is conclusive—financial incentives *improve* it. That on average only about one "good" study per year is conducted on the impact of financial incentives on performance is in and of itself telling. Despite a careful search, we found only 39 studies on this issue over 40 years that were well-designed and could really address the topic scientifically. The plethora of opinions on the positive *and* negative effects of money is counterbalanced by very few well-designed research endeavors. Clearly, more solid research is needed in this area. Still, over three dozen studies provide a good starting point.

## It doesn't matter what kind of work people do—financial incentives improve performance.

An issue sometimes raised is that financial incentives erode intrinsic motivation. Our meta-analysis explored whether the relationship between financial incentives and performance was stronger for *extrinsic* (i.e., dull and boring) tasks than for *intrinsic* (i.e., challenging and interesting) tasks. Presumably, if financial incentives erode intrinsic motivation, we would find them to be negatively related to performance for intrinsic tasks. The data show otherwise. It doesn't matter what kind of work people are doing—financial incentives improve performance.

Another meta-analysis performed by Cameron and Pierce addressed this issue more directly—it examined the effects of financial incentives on intrinsic motivation.[4,5] These authors argued (as we do) that the supposedly detrimental effects of rewards on intrinsic motivation have attained mythical, not to say apocryphal, proportions, despite considerable evidence to the contrary. It could be that some consultants are catering to the subconscious desire of certain managers—hopeful of keeping payroll costs down—by telling managers to ignore money; other consultants may be selling counter-intuitive anecdotes as scientific evidence. Nonetheless, what this meta-analysis found was that reinforcement and rewards led to worse performance *only* in rare cases—only when the reinforcement was used once, only when the reward was given regardless of how well the individual performed (or even whether the task was completed), and only when intrinsic motivation was measured in certain ways. That is, negative effects on performance occur only in extremely limited circumstances, circumstances unlikely to be prevalent in organizational settings.

Taken together, then, the hard data are unambiguous—financial incentives improve performance quantity; they *do not* erode intrinsic motivation.

In response to the argument that most motivational theories were developed from animal studies—and that people are not animals—we should note that while some behavioral studies were initially conducted among animals, our meta-analysis cumulated only *human* studies. Furthermore, it focused on real tasks and real money, not symbolic rewards. By contrast, studies which supposedly demonstrate the deleterious effects of money are typically conducted among children, using gold stars, candy, and other symbolic rewards. Surely there are problems extrapolating from children and candy to working adults and money.

When the appropriate populations are considered, i.e., working men and women in the real world, the data are consistent and clear. Money can be used as an effective motivator for performance improvement. Perhaps the repeated emergence of this finding will begin to dispel myths about money being a punishment.[6]

Of course, this does not mean that care shouldn't be exercised in tying financial incentives to performance. Quite the contrary. Theory, research, and practice provide several guidelines in this regard.

## The Dos and Don'ts of Financial Incentives

There are good ways and bad ways to use financial incentives. The following dos and don'ts are gleaned from a wealth of scientific and practical sources.

This information suggests that one should **DO** the following in designing financial incentive systems:

### The "DO" List

➤ **Do tie financial incentives to *valued* behaviors.** As noted above, people process signals cognitively. They will repeat behaviors that are rewarded. It is critical to ensure that rewarded behaviors are those that the company actively *wants* and *values*.

➤ **Do have good measurement systems.** Many merit pay plans are ineffective because performance is not measured accurately, perhaps because of exclusive or heavy reliance on subjective supervisory performance appraisals. An incentive system will be only as successful as the performance measurement system allows it to be.

➤ **Do have good communication systems.** People worry about money and talk to one another about money. People often assume the worst when information is not available. It is important to make sure that this information is accurate. Good communication systems ensure that (a) people know what they must do to make more money and (b) this information is *accurate*, not based on rumor and innuendo.

➤ **Do make the system *complete*.** As noted above, people repeat the behaviors that are rewarded and ignore those aspects of job performance which are not rewarded. For this reason, it is critical that incentive systems incorporate *complete* measures, meaning all relevant and valued aspects of performance.[7] Edward Lawler suggests that, instead of having one "big" incentive plan, a company may be better off with several smaller plans, each attached to a different aspect of performance. This approach of "riddling" the system with rewards may ensure completeness.

➤ **Do use financial incentives to *supplement* other rewards.** Financial incentives are excellent supplements to other reward systems. Of course, they are not substitutes for intrinsic, social, or other rewards that people also value. Using many rewards *simultaneously* is likely to yield good returns.

➤ **Do make *meaningful* differentiations.** Some of our other research shows that, to be effective, financial incentives must be "large enough."[8] In other words, if people get small "merit" raises or other financial incentives, their behaviors will not be substantially affected, and their attitudes may suffer as well. It is perhaps the use of insultingly small financial incentives that accounts for their mythical punishing qualities.[8]

➤ **Do set realistic goals.** A consistent finding in management research is that goals must be challenging but *achievable* for people to be motivated. If the goals are not realistic, people will not believe that they can reach them and will not try.

➤ **Do provide relevant skills and resources.** In a similar vein, people must have the ability to reach goals—training may be necessary to ensure this. They must also have the resources (information, materials, equipment) to do the job. There is nothing more frustrating than having to make decisions in the absence of relevant information.

➤ **Do emphasize long-term as well as short-term success.** Many incentive systems fail because they have a short-term focus. This means that employees will have a short-term focus also and will maximize short-term rewards *even if* this is dysfunctional in the long run. Long-term issues must be incorporated into successful incentive systems.

➤ **Do accept reality.** When people talk about incentives, they often talk idealistically—employees will appreciate "gold stars," students will study because of inherent love of studying, etc. But ask yourself this question: "How hard will *I* work for a gold star?" That's probably how hard the employees will work too. Reality dictates that we use the incentives that *do* work, not the incentives that *should* work.

➤ **Do be systemic.** Incentives work best when managers have incentives to reward supervisors for the "right" behaviors, supervisors have incentives to reward subordinates for the "right" behaviors, and so on. If there is nothing in it for supervisors to manage incentives well, why would they?

### The "DON'T" List

There are some factors that enhance the success potential of financial incentives. Coupled with these "dos," of course, are also a number of "DON'TS." According to theory, research, and practice, then,

➤ **Don't give in to hype and fad.** We all know that financial incentives make a significant difference in people's attitudes and behaviors. The best incentives are those that are carefully designed to suit the specifics of a situation. On the other hand, fads—skill-based pay, broad-banding, competency pay, etc.—come and go. Each of these pay systems is useful in some settings; none is useful in *all* settings. When a reward system is marketed, ask yourself whether it fits your company, your constraints, your organizational culture, and your strategic goals. Also ask yourself: "How would this system affect *my* behavior if I were under it?" In most instances, these are the best tests of how the system will work.

➤ **Don't be idealistic and unrealistic.** Good incentive systems are designed through a systematic and *realistic* assessment of the kinds of behaviors the company desires and the kinds of rewards people value. Local cultures and needs also vary—a system successful in one setting may well fail in another. Careful identification of both the valued behaviors and the valued rewards in each specific setting is critical to designing effective incentive systems.

➤ **Don't assume that working adults are identical to schoolchildren.** Many popular prescriptions about incentive systems are derived from work done among schoolchildren. But these two populations are fundamentally different. Effective incentive systems are derived from research and practice among working adults in organizational settings. Look for evidence among working adults.

➤ **Don't equate rewards and punishments.** Some consultants would have people believe that rewards and punishments are interchangeable. They aren't. Some people argue that lessons learned from the use of punishments can be applied *in toto* to rewards. They can't be. The psychological literature demonstrates conclusively that rewards affect people's attitudes and behaviors differently than do punishments. When assessing the value of rewards, look at the evidence with respect to *rewards*, not punishments.

➤ **Don't rely on invalid behavior measurement tools.** Many incentive systems fail to realize their potential, not because of inherent flaws in the design of the system, but because the behaviors on which the incentives are based are measured inadequately. Relying exclusively on supervisors for performance appraisals can be the Achilles' heel of incentive systems, unless the appraisals are carefully designed and used. Valid behavior measurement is central to effective incentive systems.

➤ **Don't keep things secret.** For incentive systems to work, people must have a clear and accurate picture of what they must do and what the consequences of their actions will be. It is important to make sure that people understand and accept the incentive system. Good communication is essential.

➤ **Don't violate employee expectations.** Often, incentive systems are introduced with much fanfare, but when difficulties arise, they are withdrawn. In the scheme of things, the company would have been better off never to have started the system in the first place than to have terminated it part way. Much damage can accrue from raising people's expectations and failing to meet them. This is why careful planning is necessary to design and implement effective incentive systems.

## Where Do We Go from Here?

There is a lot to be learned from what management evidence says, in theory and in practice, about the effective use of financial incentives. Unfortunately, there is also a lot of chaff out there, and it is up to rational readers and users to glean the wheat from the chaff. Nonetheless, the sum total of available scientific knowledge does provide some unambiguous answers—financial incentives improve performance, financial incentives *can be* and *have been* misused, and financial incentives, while useful, are not a panacea. The prudent manager should use financial incentives carefully, with systematic prior planning and with ongoing attention to ironing out the inevitable kinks, problems, and potential abuses inherent in these systems. When used wisely, financial incentives *can* and *do* provide many benefits for companies.

So let us accept the inevitable—money matters. It matters to us, it matters to you, it matters to employees, and it matters to managers and executives.

## Endnotes

1. Lawler, E. E., III and Rhode, J. G. 1976. *Information and control in organizations*. Pacific Palisades, CA: Goodyear.

2. Jenkins, G. D., Jr. 1986. Financial incentives. In E. A. Locke (Ed.), *Generalizing from laboratory to field settings*. Lexington, MA: Lexington Books.
3. Jenkins, G. D., Jr., Mitra, A., Gupta, N., and Shaw, J. D. 1997. *Financial incentives and performance: A meta-analytic review*. Presented at the Society of Industrial and Organizational Psychology meeting, St. Louis, MO.
4. Cameron, J., and Pierce, W. D. 1994. Reinforcement, reward and intrinsic motivation: A meta-analysis. *Review of Educational Research*, 64, 363–423.
5. Eisenberger, R., and Cameron, J. 1996. Detrimental effects of rewards: Reality or myth? *American Psychologist*, 51, 1153–1166.
6. Kohn, A. 1988. Incentives can be bad for business. *Inc.*, 10(1), 93–94; 1993. Why incentive plans cannot work. *Harvard Business Review*, 71(5), 54–63; 1993. *Punished by rewards: The trouble with gold stars, incentive plans, A's, praise, and other bribes*. New York: Houghton-Mifflin.
7. Gupta, N., and Jenkins, G. D., Jr. 1996. The politics of pay. *Compensation & Benefits Review*, 28(2), 23–20. See also Lawler and Rhode, 1976.
8. Mitra, A., Gupta, N., and Jenkins, G. D., Jr. 1995. The case of the invisible merit raise: How people see their pay raises. *Compensation & Benefits Review*, 27(3), 71–76.

*Dr. Nina Gupta (Ph.D., University of Michigan) is a professor of management at the University of Arkansas. She publishes and consults extensively in the area of compensation systems. She is a leading authority on skill-based pay systems, and on how people react to compensation strategies.*

*Dr. Jason D. Shaw (Ph.D., University of Arkansas) is an assistant professor of management at Drexel University. He studies strategic issues in the design and effectiveness of compensation systems, the effects of personality-environment congruence, and the value of family-friendly management policies.*

Editor's note: See next article, "Challenging Behaviorist Dogma: Myths about Money and Motivation," by Alfie Kohn.

RESPONSE

# Challenging Behaviorist Dogma: Myths About Money and Motivation

**Alfie Kohn**
*Author and speaker*

The idea that dangling money and other goodies in front of people will "motivate" them to work harder is the conventional wisdom in our society, and particularly among compensation specialists. Those of us who have challenged the Skinnerian orthodoxy that grounds this conviction have apparently caused its professional apologists to reassert in ever more emphatic and defensive language what most of their audience already takes on faith. (Hence the amusing spectacle of being admonished that it is "time that management specialists . . . understood the importance of money"—as though the field were guilty of attributing too little importance to it!)[1]

Lest there be any doubt, however, Gupta and Shaw [previous article, page 147] strain to frame the issue as a choice between anecdotes and hard science (the science unambiguously supporting their position, of course) or between utopian fantasy and the "real world." I propose that we try to examine a few of the many issues involved with a little more care and precision.

## 1. Does Money Matter?

The first response to this question by a reputable social scientist would be: "Well, what society are we talking about—and what historical period?" If indeed it turned out that a disproportionate number of contemporary Americans were preoccupied with money, that would hardly give us license to draw sweeping conclusions about "human nature" or to offer prescriptions premised on such conclusions.

As it happens, even in our own society maxims about the significance of money are offset by proverbial reminders about what can't buy happiness, what is the root of all evil, and so on. Then, too, we must be careful about attributing to everyone what is true of some. That the have-nots tend to think about having more tells us about deprivation rather than about the inherent centrality of money. Many of us pour our time and love into avocations—that is, activities for which we will never be compensated—nicely making the point that money for most of us is not the

From *Compensation and Benefits Review,* March/April 1998, pp. 27, 33–37. © 1998 by the American Management Association, New York. All rights reserved. Reprinted by permission.

point. (One thinks not only of the usual hobbies but also of raising children, an activity reasonably certain to produce a net loss.) Yes, there are affluent people whose lives nevertheless do seem to revolve around making money, but on some level we understand that this is a futile attempt to fill a psychological void, to make up for genuine needs that are not being met. New evidence suggests that the more people are driven by a desire to be wealthy, the poorer their psychological health on a range of measures.[2] Gupta and Shaw's article reminded me of an observation by the sociologist Philip Slater: "The idea that everybody wants money is propaganda circulated by wealth addicts to make themselves feel better about their addiction."[3]

Even if we confine our discussion to the workplace, numerous studies have shown that when people are asked what is most important to them about work, money ranks well behind such factors as interesting work or good people to work with. (Interestingly, when managers are asked what matters most to their employees, they tend to rank money at the top of the list—and then proceed to manage on the basis of that error.)[4] None of this is meant to imply that money doesn't matter to people, only to offer a nuanced alternative to declarations at the level of "most of us are motivated by money"—the first dubious link in a chain of assertions that is supposed to justify manipulating people with incentives.

## 2. Does Money Motivate?

The most important point to be made here is that this is a very different question from the first one. Even if money matters more—and to more people—than I think it does, that is by no means tantamount to showing that it *motivates* people. By one definition, nothing can meaningfully be said to "motivate" people. Various devices can be used to get people to do something, but that is a far cry from making people *want* to do something. Seminars and articles with titles like "How to Motivate Your Employees" should be avoided at all costs: not only is the basic premise psychologically misconceived, but the prescriptions are likely to involve attempts to control people and therefore to make things worse in the long run.

You could not ask for a crisper contrast with behaviorism, which assumes that all behavior is ultimately initiated by the external environment (in the words of one proponent). Intrinsic motivation is typically placed between quotation marks by Skinnerians as though to call its very existence into question. For the rest of us, who find it meaningful to distinguish between *intrinsic motivation* (where the task itself is experienced as appealing) and *extrinsic motivation* (where the task is seen as a means to an end, a prerequisite for receiving a reward or avoiding a punishment), the question then becomes not "How motivated are people at our organization?" but "*How* are our people motivated?" It is not the amount of motivation that matters, but the type. Hence we might agree (by a looser definition) that someone could be motivated by money, but then immediately add that this would probably signal a major problem, a motivational orientation that isn't associated with a high quality of work or quality of life.

## 3. What Does the Research Say?

On the questions that matter there are indeed very few relevant workplace studies. Probably this is because the conventional view that money "motivates" people, and hence that well-designed reward schemes are bound to be effective, is accepted as religious dogma—and there is no need for a scientific test of religious dogma.

Anyone can insist repeatedly, and in an ever more aggrieved tone, that what data do exist support one's own position "consistently," "clearly," "unambiguously," and so on, but that does not make it so. It's hard to comment on a meta-analysis that hasn't yet been published, but the earlier review of studies by Jenkins—presumably many of the same studies analyzed with a different statistical methodology—makes my case very powerfully. First, most of the research showing a positive effect of financial incentives looked only at short-term results. Second, the effect was most likely to be positive when subjects were given simple, indeed virtually mindless, tasks to do.

Third, as Gupta and Shaw acknowledge and then try desperately to "spin" away, incentives at best seem to be effective only in quantitative terms (e.g., getting people to do something faster). Jenkins was quite clear about the effect of incentives on quality: *they don't help*. While acknowledging that the five relevant studies he dug up didn't explicitly tie pay to quality, he wrote that "laboratory and field experiments alike appear to be u-nanimous: financial incentives do not improve performance quality."[5]

That finding needs to be understood in the context of at least two dozen studies in other settings demonstrating that rewards are not merely ineffective but actually counterproductive. Subjects offered an incentive for doing a task (or, in some of the studies, for doing it well) actually did lower quality work than subjects offered no reward at all. As University of Texas psychologist Janet Spence put it after discovering this surprising effect in an early study of her own, rewards "have effects that interfere with performance in ways that we are only beginning to understand."[6] One would never guess from their defiant assertions about how the research backs them up that the reality is very nearly the reverse of what Gupta and Shaw claim. The detrimental effect of rewards on performance has been demonstrated with children and adults, across cultures, with every kind of reward imaginable (including but not limited to money), and with a range of tasks—although the damaging effect is more pronounced as the tasks become more complicated and quality becomes more important.

I realize that the dispute to which Gupta and Shaw and I are treating you only seems to confirm the cynical, eye-rolling reaction that research can be cited to prove anything. But not all research is equally well designed, and not all studies are trying to show the same thing. I readily concede that studies often prove that "rewards work." But we should immediately ask: "Work to do what? And at what cost?" Like sticks, carrots can often elicit temporary compliance—or short-term blips in the quantity of performance at relatively simple tasks. To the best of my knowledge, though, *no controlled scientific study has ever found a long-term enhancement of the quality of work as a result of any reward system.* For five years, I have challenged defenders of incentive systems to provide an example to the contrary, and I have yet to hear of such a study.

The cost of rewards—and one of half a dozen compelling explanations for *why* performance isn't enhanced by their use—has to do with their effect on interest in the work itself. If you're willing to question the behaviorist penchant for collapsing intrinsic into extrinsic, and to look at *how* people are motivated, then it becomes disturbingly clear

## The research studies show that financial incentives may improve quantity of work but not quality.

that *the more you use rewards to "motivate" people, the more they tend to lose interest in whatever they had to do to get the rewards.* Extrinsic and intrinsic motivation not only are different, in other words—they generally are reciprocally related: as extrinsic goes up, intrinsic most often goes down. (There are qualifications to this, of course, but it's a reasonably accurate summary, as contrasted with the egregiously simplistic claim that rewards cause people to be "more motivated.")

At least 70 studies have found that rewards tend to undermine interest in the task (or behavior) itself; this is one of the most thoroughly replicated findings in the field of social psychology.[7] Gupta and Shaw essentially ignore that impressive body of research, relying instead on two claims. First, they say that because incentives can boost performance (that is, short-term quantitative performance) even on interesting tasks, it can be inferred that incentives don't reduce interest. I read that paragraph three times, trying without success to grasp the logic here. That people might temporarily work faster at a task in fact tells us absolutely nothing about how they feel about that task, or whether they'd want to do it again in the absence of rewards. Studies that *have* examined this question directly (unlike Gupta and Shaw's) have repeatedly shown that the more salient or reinforcing the reward is, the more it erodes intrinsic interest.

Second, they cite a meta-analysis by Cameron and Pierce whose methodology is, in my view and the view of research psychologists without a prior commitment to behaviorism, fatally flawed.[8] But even if one accepts its approach, these authors had to concede that the expectation of a tangible reward in connection with a task is indeed associated with less voluntary time spent on the task later as compared with a no-reward condition. This finding, whose significance Cameron and Pierce (like Gupta and Shaw) are at pains to minimize, stands as further confirmation of what most other reviews of the research have

## *The more you use a reward to motivate, the more people tend to lose interest in the task they had to do for it.*

found. (The Cameron and Pierce article, incidentally, was principally concerned with rewards in a classroom context and studies involving children. Apparently essays dealing with this population are acceptable to cite when they support one's position, whereas research demonstrating that rewards cause children to lose interest in what they're rewarded for doing can be dismissed as irrelevant to compensation issues.)

### 4. What Does It All Mean?

To those looking for reassurance that reward systems make sense, Gupta and Shaw's article will no doubt be well-received. For those interested in a dispassionate analysis of rewards, it will raise more questions than it answers. The idea that reward systems *don't* work very well is not particularly controversial—witness a cover article in *Incentive* magazine several years ago carrying the headline "Why No One Likes Your Incentive Program." And if you're not impressed by research, then just ask how long a typical reward program lasts before it's junked. Then ask: how many times does that have to happen before you finally realize that the problem isn't with the specifics of the program but with the psychological theory on which the whole *idea* of rewards is based. How many times do we earnestly attempt to carry out the advice of consultants, along the lines of the familiar suggestions offered at the end of Gupta and Shaw's article, before we realize that offering workers the equivalent of a doggie biscuit for doing what we demand is never going to be successful in any meaningful sense?

That rewards *can't* get us what we want is a heretical idea, but it emerges ineluctably from a critical analysis of motivation and work. What distinguishes behaviorists (and pop-behaviorists, who identify themselves not as Skinnerians but as "performance management" experts and suchlike) is not a pre-

dilection for using rewards so much as a tendency to focus on behavior—as though only that which can be seen and measured is real. The more reasonable view, I would argue, is that our behavior is just the outward manifestation of who we are: our thoughts and feelings, expectations and memories.

Once you start thinking about people rather than behaviors, you begin to ask questions like "What do people need—and what can we do to help meet those needs?" Psychologists tell us that people have a basic need for autonomy, so the challenge is to create a workplace that is democratic, where everyone has the opportunity to participate in making important decisions. Psychologists tell us that people have a basic need to feel related and to belong, so the challenge is to create a workplace that is collaborative and feels like a community. Psychologists tell us that people have a basic need to feel competent, so the challenge is not to induce people to do a fixed series of tasks but to re-examine the tasks themselves. (Frederick Herzberg put it best: "If you want people motivated to do a good job, give them a good job to do.")[9]

Now contrast such an organization, where the point of departure is asking what people need, with an organization whose fundamental question is, in effect, "How can we get the employees to do what we tell them?" The former sort of workplace is about *working with*; the latter sort is about *doing to*. Rewards, seen from this perspective, are just one more way of doing things *to* people. They are basically "control through seduction."[10]

To create a more democratic and collaborative workplace is not inconsistent with compensating people adequately for what they do. I am not arguing against money, which is necessary and even nice. I am arguing against (1) attributing more importance to money than it actually has, (2) pushing money into people's faces and making it more salient than it needs to be, and (3) confusing compensation with reward (the latter being unnecessary and counterproductive). The problem isn't with the dollars themselves, but with using dollars to get people to jump through hoops.

Thus, my formula for how to pay people distills the best theory, research, and practice with which I am familiar into three short sentences:

- *Pay people well.*
- *Pay people fairly.*
- *Then do everything possible to take money off people's minds.*

*The problem lies in using dollars to get people to jump through hoops.*

Notice that incentives, bonuses, pay-for-performance plans, and other reward systems violate the last principle by their very nature.

Another prescription, even less likely to be popular among comp experts, follows close on the heels of that one: Work with everyone in an organization to decide on an equitable basis for paying people—and then *move on!* Herzberg's career was devoted to proving the following revolutionary principle: just because paying people inadequately can be demotivating doesn't imply that paying people better (or more skillfully) will be motivating. The jazziest, most expensive and elaborate comp system ever devised can never do anything other than prevent some problems. It can take you only to the baseline, the zero point. And if you become preoccupied with the topic, it can distract you from attending to what *can* move an organization forward—projects such as meeting people's needs for autonomy, relatedness, and competence. The engineers who maintain the heating and cooling systems in an office building perform an analogous function: if they do their job poorly, then the air is too hot or cold or dry and people can't do their best work. But no matter how well they do their job, the best that can be expected is that people forget about the climate altogether and think about how to get better at—and really enjoy—what they do. No one hires a heating specialist to "motivate" the employees; it is equally ludicrous to expect that of a compensation specialist.

One of my favorite examples of a company that took this advice is Marshall Industries, a huge electronic components distributor based in southern California. Long locked into a pop-behaviorist sensibility, myopically concerning itself with the "dos and don'ts of financial incentives," they finally realized that none of this advice seemed to help and that the problem was with the premises on which the use of *any* financial incentive was based. It was the very existence of sales commissions and other rewards that was preventing the company from moving forward. Only when this light bulb clicked on did things begin to change. After a full year of listening, reflect-

ing, and "losing sleep," CEO Rob Rodin and his associates first got rid of all contests and other practices that set employees against each other, then eliminated management incentives, and finally replaced sales commissions and everything else smacking of pay-for-performance with a base salary.[11] The result: turnover (one of the many hidden costs of reward systems) was reduced by 80%; morale soared; salespeople began coordinating their efforts more effectively; and sales, along with profitability, grew dramatically. About five years ago, when Marshall began its deincentivizing process, its stock was about $8 and its annual sales were at $575 million; today, its stock trades in the $30–$40 range and annual sales have hit $1.3 billion.

We can all agree that this is an imperfect world. But the uncritical acceptance of traditional practices, particularly those based on an outdated and inaccurate view of human psychology, serves only to make our world that much more imperfect. The sociologist C. Wright Mills put it well: "Are not those who in the name of realism act like crackpots, are they not the utopians? Are we not now in a situation in which the only practical, realistic, down-to-earth thinking and acting is just what these crackpot realists call 'utopian'?"[12]

## Endnotes

1. Equally surprising is the news (revealed in the same paragraph) that St. Thomas Aquinas was an economist.
2. Tim Kasser and Richard M. Ryan, "A Dark Side of the American Dream; Correlates of Financial Success as a Central Life Aspiration," *Journal of Personality and Social Psychology*, vol. 65, no. 2, 1993, pp. 410–22; and "Further Examining the American Dream: Differential Correlates of Intrinsic and Extrinsic Goals," *Personality and Social Psychology Bulletin*, vol. 22, no. 3, 1996, pp. 280–87.
3. Philip Slater, *Wealth Addiction*. New York: Dutton, 1980, p. 25.
4. Some of the research is reviewed in Alfie Kohn, *Punished by Rewards*. Boston: Houghton Mifflin, 1993, pp. 130–31. Since that book's publication, another study replicated the finding: a randomly selected national sample of 3,400 men and women ranked "salary/wage" only sixteenth on a list of 20 reasons for taking a job, well behind such factors as open communication, stimulating work, control over work content, and opportunity to gain new skills. ("The National Study of the Changing Workforce," conducted by the Families and Work Institute, was described in the *New York Times*, 19 September 1993, p. F21.)
5. G. Douglas Jenkins, "Financial Incentives," in E.A. Locke, ed. *Generalizing from Laboratory to Field Settings*. Lexington, Mass.: Lexington Books, 1986, p. 172.
6. Janet Taylor Spence, "Do Material Rewards Enhance the Performance of Lower-Class Children?" *Child Development*, vol. 42, 1971, pp. 1461–70.

7. In *Punished by Rewards,* I reviewed the available research on the damaging effect that rewards have on the quality of performance (chap. 3) and on intrinsic motivation (chap. 5), as well as the application of this research to workplaces (chap. 7).
8. See the entire issue of *Review of Educational Research,* vol. 66, no. 1, 1996.
9. Frederick Herzberg, "Workers' Needs: The Same Around the World," *Industry Week,* 21 September 1987, p. 30.
10. This expression appears in a work by two of the leading students of motivational psychology: Edward L. Deci and Richard M. Ryan, *Intrinsic Motivation and Self-Determination in Human Behavior.* New York: Plenum, 1985, p. 70.
11. A quarterly profit-sharing distribution accounts for a small percentage of total compensation but—unlike gainsharing, which my friend Peter Scholtes defines as "MBO with a bribe attached"—it is not dangled conspicuously in front of employees as a means to "motivate" them.
12. C. Wright Mills, *Power, Politics, and People.* New York: Ballantine, n.d., p. 402.

*Alfie Kohn is the author of five books, including* Punished by Rewards *(Houghton Mifflin, 1993) and* No Contest: The Case Against Competition *(Houghton Mifflin, 1986). He has been described as the country's leading critic of competition, although he is quick to point out that there is not much competition for that title. His work has been discussed in* U.S. News and World Report, *the* Economist, *on the front page of the* Wall St. Journal, *and in a number of other business publications, while his own articles have appeared in the* Harvard Business Review, *the* New York Times, *the* Atlantic Monthly, *and most of the major education publications. Kohn lectures throughout North America and in Europe to researchers and educators, as well as managers at AT&T, NASA, Mattel, Pfizer, Dial, BMW, and many healthcare organizations. He has appeared on the "Today" show, "Oprah," and more than 200 other TV and radio programs. Kohn lives in Belmont, Mass. For reporting information, contact Alfie Kohn at 242 School Street, Belmont, MA 02178.*

Editor's note: See previous article, "Let the Evidence Speak: Financial Incentives *Are* Effective!!" by Nina Gupta and Jason D. Shaw.

*Many managers have bought into expensive fictions about compensation. Have you?*

# SIX DANGEROUS MYTHS ABOUT PAY

### BY JEFFREY PFEFFER

CONSIDER TWO GROUPS *of steel minimills. One group pays an average hourly wage of $18.07. The second pays an average of $21.52 an hour. Assuming that other direct-employment costs, such as benefits, are the same for the two groups, which group has the higher labor costs?*

• • • •

*An airline is seeking to compete in the low-cost, low-frills segment of the U.S. market where, for obvious reasons, labor productivity and efficiency are crucial for competitive success. The company pays virtually no one on the basis of individual merit or performance. Does it stand a chance of success?*

• • • •

*A company that operates in an intensely competitive segment of the software industry does not pay its sales force on commission. Nor does it pay individual bonuses or offer stock options or phantom stock, common incentives in an industry heavily dependent on attracting and retaining scarce programming talent. Would you invest in this company?*

• • • •

Every day, organizational leaders confront decisions about pay. Should they adjust the company's compensation system to encourage some set of behaviors? Should they retain consultants to help them implement a performance-based pay system? How large a raise should they authorize?

*Jeffrey Pfeffer is the Thomas D. Dee Professor of Organizational Behavior at the Stanford Graduate School of Business in Stanford, California. He is the author of* The Human Equation: Building Profits by Putting People First *(Harvard Business School Press, 1998).*

# Managers are bombarded with advice about pay. Unfortunately, much of that advice is wrong.

In general terms, these kinds of questions come down to four decisions about compensation:

- how much to pay employees;
- how much emphasis to place on financial compensation as a part of the total reward system;
- how much emphasis to place on attempting to hold down the rate of pay; and
- whether to implement a system of individual incentives to reward differences in performance and productivity and, if so, how much emphasis to place on these incentives.

For leaders, there can be no delegation of these matters. Everyone knows decisions about pay are important. For one thing, they help establish a company's culture by rewarding the business activities, behaviors, and values that senior managers hold dear. Senior management at Quantum, the disk drive manufacturer in Milpitas, California, for example, demonstrates its commitment to teamwork by placing all employees, from the CEO to hourly workers, on the same bonus plan, tracking everyone by the same measure—in this case, return on total capital.

Compensation is also a concept and practice very much in flux. Compensation is becoming more variable as companies base a greater proportion of it on stock options and bonuses and a smaller proportion on base salary, not only for executives but also for people further and further down the hierarchy. As managers make organization-defining decisions about pay systems, they do so in a shifting landscape while being bombarded with advice about the best routes to stable ground.

Unfortunately, much of that advice is wrong. Indeed, much of the conventional wisdom and public discussion about pay today is misleading, incorrect, or sometimes both at the same time. The result is that businesspeople end up adopting wrongheaded notions about how to pay people and why. They believe in six dangerous myths about pay—fictions about compensation that have somehow come to be seen as the truth.

Do you think you have managed to avoid these myths? Let's see how you answered the three questions that open this article. If you said the second set of steel minimills had higher labor costs, you fell into the common trap of confusing labor *rates* with labor *costs*. That is Myth #1: that labor rates and labor costs are the same thing. But how different they really are. The second set

of minimills paid its workers at a rate of $3.45 an hour more than the first. But according to data collected by Fairfield University Professor Jeffrey Arthur, its labor costs were much lower because the productivity of the mills was higher. The second set of mills actually required 34% fewer labor hours to produce a ton of steel than the first set and also generated 63% less scrap. The second set of mills could have raised workers' pay rate by 19% and still had lower labor costs.

Connected to the first myth are three more myths that draw on the same logic. When managers believe that labor costs and labor rates are the same thing, they also tend to believe that they can cut labor costs by cutting labor rates. That's Myth #2. Again, this leaves out the important matter of productivity. I may replace my $2,000-a-week engineers with ones that earn $500 a week, but my costs may skyrocket because the new, lower-paid employees are inexperienced, slow, and less capable. In that case, I would have increased my costs by cutting my rates.

Managers who mix up labor rates and labor costs also tend to accept Myth #3: that labor costs are a significant portion of total costs. Sometimes, that's true. It is, for example, at accounting and consulting firms. But the ratio of labor costs to total costs varies widely in different industries and companies. And even where it is true, it's not as important as many managers believe. Those who swallow Myth #4—that low labor costs are a potent competitive strategy—may neglect other, more effective ways of competing, such as through quality, service, delivery, and innovation. In reality, low labor costs are a slippery way to compete and perhaps the least sustainable competitive advantage there is.

Those of you who believed that the airline trying to compete in the low-cost, low-frills segment of the U.S. market would not succeed without using individual incentives succumbed to Myth #5: that the most effective way to motivate people to work productively is through individual incentive compensation. But Southwest Airlines has never used such a system, and it is the cost *and* productivity leader in its industry. Southwest is not alone, but still it takes smart, informed managers to buck the trend of offering individual rewards.

Would you have invested in the computer software company that didn't offer its people bonuses, stock options, or other financial incentives that could make them millionaires? You should have because it has succeeded mightily, growing over the past 21 years at a compound annual rate of more than 25%. The company is the SAS Institute of Cary, North Carolina. Today it is the largest privately held company in the software industry, with 1997 revenues of some $750 million.

Rather than emphasize pay, SAS has achieved an unbelievably low turnover rate below 4%—in an industry where the norm is closer to 20%—by offering intellectually engaging work; a family-friendly environment that features exceptional benefits; and the opportunity to work with fun, interesting people using state-of-the-art equipment.

In short, SAS has escaped Myth #6: that people work primarily for money. SAS, operating under the opposite assumption, demonstrates otherwise. In the last three years, the company has lost *none* of its 20 North American district sales managers. How many software companies do you know could make that statement, even about the last three months?

Every day, I see managers harming their organizations by believing in these myths about pay. What I want to do in these following pages is explore some factors that help account for why the myths are so pervasive, present some evidence to disprove their underlying assumptions, and suggest how leaders might think more productively and usefully about the important issue of pay practices in their organizations.

## Why the Myths Exist

On October 10, 1997, the *Wall Street Journal* published an article expressing surprise that a "contrarian Motorola" had chosen to build a plant in Germany to make cellular phones despite the notoriously high "cost" of German labor. The *Journal* is not alone in framing business decisions about pay in this way. The *Economist* has also written articles about high German labor "costs," citing as evidence labor rates (including fringe benefits) of more than $30 per hour.

The semantic confusion of labor rates with labor costs, endemic in business journalism and everyday discussion, leads managers to see the two as equivalent. And when the two seem equivalent, the associated myths about labor costs seem to make sense, too. But, of course, labor rates and labor costs simply aren't the same. A labor rate is total salary divided by time worked. But labor costs take productivity into account. That's how the second set of minimills managed to have lower labor costs than the mills with the lower wages. They made more steel, and they made it faster and better.

Another reason why the confusion over costs and rates persists is that labor rates are a convenient target for managers who want to make an impact. Labor rates are highly visible, and it's easy to compare the rates you pay with those paid by your competitors or with those paid in other parts of the world. In addition, labor rates often appear to be a company's most malleable financial variable. It seems a lot quicker and easier to cut wages than to control costs in other ways, like reconfiguring manufacturing processes, changing corporate culture, or altering product design. Because labor costs appear to be the lever closest at hand, managers mistakenly assume it is the one that has the most leverage.

For the myths that individual incentive pay drives creativity and productivity, and that people are primarily motivated by money, we have economic theory to blame. More specifically, we can blame the economic model of human behavior widely taught in business schools and held to be true in the popular press. This model presumes that behavior is rational—driven by the best information available at the time and designed to maximize the individual's self-interest. According to this model, people take jobs and decide how much effort to expend in those jobs based on their expected financial return. If pay is not contingent on performance, the theory goes, individuals will not devote sufficient attention and energy to their jobs.

Additional problems arise from such popular economic concepts as agency theory (which contends that there are differences in preference and perspective between owners and those who work for them) and transaction-cost economics (which tries to identify which transactions are best organized by markets and which by hierarchies). Embedded in both concepts is the idea that individuals not only pursue self-interest but do so on occasion with guile and opportunism. Thus agency theory suggests that employees have different objectives than their employers and, moreover, have opportunities to misrepresent information and divert resources to their personal use. Transaction-cost theory suggests that people will make false or empty threats and promises to get better deals from one another.

All of these economic models portray work as hard and aversive—implying that the only way people can be induced to work is through some combination of rewards and sanctions. As professor James N. Baron of Stanford Business School has written, "The image of workers in these models is somewhat akin to Newton's first law of mo-

# It's simpler for managers to tinker with compensation than to change the company's culture.

tion: employees remain in a state of rest unless compelled to change that state by a stronger force impressed upon them—namely, an optimal labor contract."

Similarly, the language of economics is filled with terms such as *shirking* and *free riding*. Language is powerful, and as Robert Frank, himself an economist, has noted, theories of human behavior become self-fulfilling. We act on the basis of these theories, and through our own actions produce in others the behavior we expect. If we believe people will work hard only if specifically rewarded for doing so, we will provide contingent rewards and thereby condition people to work only when they are rewarded. If we expect people to be untrustworthy, we will closely monitor and control them and by doing so will signal that they can't be trusted—an expectation that they will most likely confirm for us.

So self-reinforcing are these ideas that you almost have to avoid mainstream business to get away from them. Perhaps that's why several companies known to be strongly committed to managing through trust, mutual respect, and true decentralization—such as AES Corporation, Lincoln Electric, the Men's Wearhouse, the SAS Institute, ServiceMaster, Southwest Airlines, and Whole Foods Market—tend to avoid recruiting at conventional business schools.

There's one last factor that helps perpetuate all these myths: the compensation-consulting industry. Unfortunately, that industry has a number of perverse incentives to keep these myths alive.

First, although some of these consulting firms have recently broadened their practices, compensation remains their bread and butter. Suggesting that an organization's performance can be improved in some way other than by tinkering with the pay system may be empirically correct but is probably too selfless a behavior to expect from these firms.

Second, if it's simpler for managers to tinker with the compensation system than to change an organization's culture, the way work is organized, and the level of trust and respect the system displays, it's even easier for consultants. Thus both the compensation consultants and their clients are tempted by the apparent speed and ease with which reward-system solutions can be implemented.

Third, to the extent that changes in pay systems bring their own new predicaments, the consultants will continue to have work solving the problems that the tinkering has caused in the first place.

## From Myth to Reality: A Look at the Evidence

The media are filled with accounts of companies attempting to reduce their labor costs by laying off people, moving production to places where labor rates are lower, freezing wages, or some combination of the above. In the early 1990s, for instance, Ford decided not to award merit raises to its white-collar workers as part of a new cost-cutting program. And in 1997, General Motors endured a series of highly publicized strikes over the issue of outsourcing. GM wanted to move more of its work to nonunion, presumably lower-wage, suppliers to reduce its labor costs and become more profitable.

Ford's and GM's decisions were driven by the myths that labor rates and labor costs are the same thing, and that labor costs constitute a significant portion of total costs. Yet hard evidence to support those contentions is slim. New United Motor Manufacturing, the joint venture between Toyota and General Motors based in Fremont, California, paid the highest wage in the automobile industry when it began operations in the mid-1980s, and it also offered a guarantee of secure employment. With productivity some 50% higher than at comparable GM plants, the venture could afford to pay 10% more and still come out ahead.

Yet General Motors apparently did not learn the lesson that what matters is not pay rate but productivity. In May 1996, as GM was preparing to confront the union over the issue of outsourcing, the "Harbour Report," the automobile industry's bible of comparative efficiency, published some interesting data suggesting that General Motors' problems had little to do with labor rates. As reported in the *Wall Street Journal* at the time, the report showed that it took General Motors some 46 hours to assemble a car, while it took Ford just 37.92 hours, Toyota 29.44, and Nissan only 27.36. As a way of attacking cost problems, officials at General Motors should have asked why they needed 21% more hours than Ford to accomplish the same thing or why GM was some 68% less efficient than Nissan.

# TRUTH AND CONSEQUENCES: THE SIX DANGEROUS MYTHS ABOUT COMPENSATION

| Myth | Reality |
|---|---|
| 1. Labor rates and labor costs are the same thing. | 1. They are not, and confusing them leads to a host of managerial missteps. For the record, labor rates are straight wages divided by time—a Wal-Mart cashier earns $5.15 an hour, a Wall Street attorney $2,000 a day. Labor costs are a calculation of how much a company pays its people and how much they produce. Thus German factory workers may be paid at a rate of $30 an hour and Indonesians $3, but the workers' relative costs will reflect how many widgets are produced in the same period of time. |
| 2. You can lower your labor costs by cutting labor rates. | 2. When managers buy into the myth that labor rates and labor costs are the same thing, they usually fall for this myth as well. Once again, then, labor costs are a function of labor rates and productivity. To lower labor costs, you need to address *both*. Indeed, sometimes lowering labor rates increases labor costs. |
| 3. Labor costs constitute a significant proportion of total costs. | 3. This is true—but only sometimes. Labor costs as a proportion of total costs vary widely by industry and company. Yet many executives assume labor costs are the biggest expense on their income statement. In fact, labor costs are only the most immediately malleable expense. |
| 4. Low labor costs are a potent and sustainable competitive weapon. | 4. In fact, labor costs are perhaps the most slippery and least sustainable way to compete. Better to achieve competitive advantage through quality; through customer service; through product, process, or service innovation; or through technology leadership. It is much more difficult to imitate these sources of competitive advantage than to merely cut costs. |
| 5. Individual incentive pay improves performance. | 5. Individual incentive pay, in reality, undermines performance—of both the individual and the organization. Many studies strongly suggest that this form of reward undermines teamwork, encourages a short-term focus, and leads people to believe that pay is not related to performance at all but to having the "right" relationships and an ingratiating personality. |
| 6. People work for money. | 6. People do work for money—but they work even more for meaning in their lives. In fact, they work to have fun. Companies that ignore this fact are essentially bribing their employees and will pay the price in a lack of loyalty and commitment. |

For more evidence of how reality really looks, consider the machine tool industry. Many of its senior managers have been particularly concerned with low-cost foreign competition, believing that the cost advantage has come from the lower labor rates available offshore. But for machine tool companies that stop fixating on labor rates and focus instead on their overall management system and manufacturing processes, there are great potential returns. Cincinnati Milacron, a company that had virtually surrendered the market for low-end machine tools to Asian competitors by the mid-1980s, overhauled its assembly process, abolished its stockroom, and reduced job categories from seven to one. Without any capital investment, those changes in the production *process* reduced labor hours by 50%, and the company's productivity is now higher than its competitors' in Taiwan.

Even U.S. apparel manufacturers lend support to the argument that labor costs are not the be-all and end-all of profitability. Companies in this industry are generally obsessed with finding places where hourly wages are low. But the cost of direct labor needed to manufacture a pair of jeans is actually only about 15% of total costs, and even the direct labor involved in producing a man's suit is only about $12.50[1]

Compelling evidence also exists to dispute the myth that competing on labor costs will create any sustainable advantage. Let's start close to home. One day, I arrived at a large discount store with a shopping list. Having the good fortune to actually find a sales associate, I asked him where I could locate the first item on my list. "I don't know," he replied. He gave a similar reply when queried about the second item. A glance at the long list I was holding brought the confession that because of high employee turnover, the young man had been in the store only a few hours himself. What is that employee worth to the store? Not only can't he sell the merchandise, he can't even find it!

# Most merit-pay systems share two attributes: they absorb vast amounts of management time and make everybody unhappy.

Needless to say, I wasn't able to purchase everything on my list because I got tired of looking and gave up. And I haven't returned since. Companies that compete on cost alone eventually bump into consumers like me. It's no accident that Wal-Mart combines its low-price strategy with friendly staff members greeting people at the door and works assiduously to keep turnover low.

Another example of a company that understands the limits of competing solely on labor costs is the Men's Wearhouse, the enormously successful off-price retailer of tailored men's clothing. The company operates in a fiercely competitive industry in which growth is possible primarily by taking sales from competitors, and price wars are intense. Still, less than 15% of the company's staff is part-time, wages are higher than the industry average, and the company engages in extensive training. All these policies defy conventional wisdom for the retailing industry. But the issue isn't what the Men's Wearhouse's employees cost, it's what they can do: sell very effectively because of their product knowledge and sales skills. Moreover, by keeping inventory losses and employee turnover low, the company saves money on shrinkage and hiring. Companies that miss this point—that costs, particularly labor costs, aren't everything—often overlook ways of succeeding that competitors can't readily copy.

Evidence also exists that challenges the myth about the effectiveness of individual incentives. This evidence, however, has done little to stem the tide of individual merit pay. A survey of the pay practices of the *Fortune* 1,000 reported that between 1987 and 1993, the proportion of companies using individual incentives for at least 20% of their workforce increased from 38% to 50% while the proportion of companies using profit sharing—a more collective reward—decreased from 45% to 43%. Between 1981 and 1990, the proportion of retail salespeople that were paid solely on straight salary, with no commission, declined from 21% to 7%. And this trend toward individual incentive compensation is not confined to the United States. A study of pay practices at plants in the United Kingdom reported that the proportion using some form of merit pay had increased every year since 1986 such that by 1990 it had reached 50%.[2]

Despite the evident popularity of this practice, the problems with individual merit pay are numerous and well documented. It has been shown to undermine teamwork, encourage employees to focus on the short term, and lead people to link compensation to political skills and ingratiating personalties rather than to performance. Indeed, those are among the reasons why W. Edwards Deming and other quality experts have argued strongly against using such schemes.

Consider the results of several studies. One carefully designed study of a performance-contingent pay plan at 20 Social Security Administration offices found that merit pay had no effect on office performance. Even though the merit pay plan was contingent on a number of objective indicators, such as the time taken to settle claims and the accuracy of claims processing, employees exhibited no difference in performance after the merit pay plan was introduced as part of a reform of civil service pay practices. Contrast that study with another that examined the elimination of a piecework system and its replacement by a more group-oriented compensation system at a manufacturer of exhaust system components. There, grievances decreased, product quality increased almost tenfold, and perceptions of teamwork and concern for performance all improved.[3]

Surveys conducted by various consulting companies that specialize in management and compensation also reveal the problems and dissatisfaction with individual merit pay. For instance, a study by the consulting firm William M. Mercer reported that 73% of the responding companies had made major changes to their performance-management plans in the preceding two years, as they experimented with different ways to tie pay to individual performance. But 47% reported that their employees found the systems neither fair nor sensible, and 51% of the employees said that the performance-management system provided little value to the company. No wonder Mercer concluded that most individual merit or performance-based pay plans share two attributes: they absorb vast amounts of management time and resources, and they make everybody unhappy.

One concern about paying on a more group-oriented basis is the so-called free-rider problem, the worry that people will not work hard because they know that if rewards are based on collective performance and their colleagues make the effort,

# If you could reliably measure and reward individual contributions, organizations wouldn't be needed.

they will share in those rewards regardless of the level of their individual efforts. But there are two reasons why organizations should not be reluctant to design such collective pay systems.

First, much to the surprise of people who have spent too much time reading economics, empirical evidence from numerous studies indicates that the extent of free riding is quite modest. For instance, one comprehensive review reported that "under the conditions described by the theory as leading to free riding, people often cooperate instead."[4]

Second, individuals do not make decisions about how much effort to expend in a social vacuum; they are influenced by peer pressure and the social relations they have with their workmates. This social influence is potent, and although it may be somewhat stronger in smaller groups, it can be a force mitigating against free riding even in large organizations. As one might expect, then, there is evidence that organizations paying on a more collective basis, such as through profit sharing or gain sharing, outperform those that don't.

Sometimes, individual pay schemes go so far as to affect customers. Sears was forced to eliminate a commission system at its automobile repair stores in California when officials found widespread evidence of consumer fraud. Employees, anxious to meet quotas and earn commissions on repair sales, were selling unneeded services to unsuspecting customers. Similarly, in 1992, the *Wall Street Journal* reported that Highland Superstores, an electronics and appliance retailer, eliminated commissions because they had encouraged such aggressive behavior on the part of salespeople that customers were alienated.

Enchantment with individual merit pay reflects not only the belief that people won't work effectively if they are not rewarded for their individual efforts but also the related view that the road to solving organizational problems is largely paved with adjustments to pay and measurement practices. Consider again the data from the Mercer survey: nearly three-quarters of all the companies surveyed had made *major* changes to their pay plans in just the past two years. That's tinkering on a grand scale. Or take the case of Air Products and Chemicals of Allentown, Pennsylvania. When on October 23, 1996, the company reported mediocre sales and profits, the stock price declined from the low $60s to the high $50s. Eight days later, the company announced a new set of management-compensation and stock-ownership initiatives designed to reassure Wall Street that management cared about its shareholders and was demonstrating that concern by changing compensation arrangements. The results were dramatic. On the day of the announcement, the stock price went up 1-1/4 points, and the next day it rose an additional 4-3/4 points. By November 29, Air Products' stock had gone up more than 15%. According to Value Line, this rise was an enthusiastic reaction by investors to the new compensation system. No wonder managers are so tempted to tamper with pay practices!

But as Bill Strusz, director of corporate industrial relations at Xerox in Rochester, New York, has said, if managers seeking to improve performance or solve organizational problems use compensation as the only lever, they will get two results: nothing will happen, and they will spend a lot of money. That's because people want more out of their jobs than just money. Numerous surveys—even of second-year M.B.A. students, who frequently graduate with large amounts of debt—indicate that money is far from the most important factor in choosing a job or remaining in one.

Why has the SAS Institute had such low turnover in the software industry despite its tight labor market? When asked this question, employees said they were motivated by SAS's unique perks—plentiful opportunities to work with the latest and most up-to-date equipment and the ease with which they could move back and forth between being a manager and being an individual contributor. They also cited how much variety there was in the projects they worked on, how intelligent and nice the people they worked with were, and how much the organization cared for and appreciated them. Of course, SAS pays competitive salaries, but in an industry in which people have the opportunity to become millionaires through stock options by moving to a competitor, the key to retention is SAS's culture, not its monetary rewards.

People seek, in a phrase, an enjoyable work environment. That's what AES, the Men's Wearhouse, SAS, and Southwest have in common. One of the core values at each company is *fun*. When a colleague and I wrote a business school case on Southwest, we asked some of the employees, a number of whom had been offered much

# I would not necessarily say that external rewards backfire, but they do create their own problems.

more money to work elsewhere, why they stayed. The answer we heard repeatedly was that they knew what the other environments were like, and they would rather be at a place, as one employee put it, where *work* is not a four-letter word. This doesn't mean work has to be easy. As an AES employee noted, fun means working in a place where people can use their gifts and skills and can work with others in an atmosphere of mutual respect.

There is a great body of literature on the effect of large external rewards on individuals' intrinsic motivation. The literature argues that extrinsic rewards diminish intrinsic motivation and, moreover, that large extrinsic rewards can actually decrease performance in tasks that require creativity and innovation. I would not necessarily go so far as to say that external rewards backfire, but they certainly create their own problems. First, people receiving such rewards can reduce their own motivation through a trick of self-perception, figuring, "I must not like the job if I have to be paid so much to do it" or "I make so much, I must be doing it for the money." Second, they undermine their own loyalty or performance by reacting against a sense of being controlled, thinking something like, "I will show the company that I can't be controlled just through money."

But most important, to my mind, is the logic in the idea that any organization believing it can solve its attraction, retention, and motivation problems solely by its compensation system is probably not spending as much time and effort as it should on the work environment—on defining its jobs, on creating its culture, and on making work fun and meaningful. It is a question of time and attention, of scarce managerial resources. The time and attention spent managing the reward system are not available to devote to other aspects of the work environment that in the end may be much more critical to success.

## Some Advice About Pay

Since I have traipsed you through a discussion of what's wrong with the way most companies approach compensation, let me now offer some advice about how to get it right.

The first, and perhaps most obvious, suggestion is that managers would do well to keep the difference between labor rates and labor costs straight. In doing so, remember that only labor costs—and not labor rates—are the basis for competition, and that labor costs may not be a major component of total costs. In any event, managers should remember that the issue is not just what you pay people, but also what they produce.

To combat the myth about the effectiveness of individual performance pay, managers should see what happens when they include a large dose of collective rewards in their employees' compensation package. The more aggregated the unit used to measure performance, the more reliably performance can be assessed. One can tell pretty accurately how well an organization, or even a subunit, has done with respect to sales, profits, quality, productivity, and the like. Trying to parcel out who, specifically, was responsible for exactly how much of that productivity, quality, or sales is frequently much more difficult or even impossible. As Herbert Simon, the Nobel-prize-winning economist, has recognized, people in organizations are interdependent, and therefore organizational results are the consequence of collective behavior and performance. If you could reliably and easily measure and reward individual contributions, you probably would not need an organization at all as everyone would enter markets solely as individuals.

In the typical individual-based merit pay system, the boss works with a raise budget that's some percentage of the total salary budget for the unit. It's inherently a zero-sum process: the more I get in my raise, the less is left for my colleagues. So the worse my workmates perform, the happier I am because I know I will look better by comparison. A similar dynamic can occur across organizational units in which competition for a fixed bonus pool discourages people from sharing best practices and learning from employees in other parts of the organization. In November 1995, for example, *Fortune* magazine reported that at Lantech, a manufacturer of packaging machinery in Louisville, Kentucky, individual incentives caused such intense rivalry that the chairman of the company, Pat Lancaster, said, "I was spending 95% of my time on conflict resolution instead of on how to serve our customers."

Managers can fight the myth that people are primarily motivated by money by de-emphasizing pay and not portraying it as the main thing you get from working at a particular company. How? Consider the example of Tandem Computer

# Pay cannot substitute for a working environment high on trust, fun, and meaningful work.

which, in the years before it was acquired by Compaq, would not even tell you your salary before expecting you to accept a job. If you asked, you would be told that Tandem paid good, competitive salaries. The company had a simple philosophy—if you came for money, you would leave for money, and Tandem wanted employees who were there because they liked the work, the culture, and the people, not something—money—that every company could offer. Emphasizing pay as the primary reward encourages people to come and to stay for the wrong reasons. AES, a global independent power producer in Arlington, Virginia, has a relatively short vesting period for retirement-plan contributions and tries not to pay the highest salaries for jobs in its local labor market. By so doing, it seeks to ensure that people are not locked into working at a place where they don't want to be simply for the money.

Managers must also recognize that pay has substantive and symbolic components. In signaling what and who in the organization is valued, pay both reflects and helps determine the organization's culture. Therefore, managers must make sure that the messages sent by pay practices are intended. Talking about teamwork and cooperation and then not having a group-based component to the pay system matters because paying solely on an individual basis signals what the organization believes is actually important—individual behavior and performance. Talking about the importance of *all* people in the organization and then paying some disproportionately more than others belies that message. One need not go to the extreme of Whole Foods Market, which pays no one more than eight times the average company salary (the result being close to $1 billion in sales at a company where the CEO makes less than $200,000 a year). But paying large executive bonuses while laying off people and asking for wage freezes, as General Motors did in the 1980s, may not send the right message, either. When Southwest Airlines asked its pilots for a five-year wage freeze, CEO Herb Kelleher voluntarily asked the compensation committee to freeze his salary for at least four years as well. The message of shared, common fate is powerful in an organization truly seeking to build a culture of teamwork.

Making pay practices public also sends a powerful symbolic message. Some organizations reveal pay distributions by position or level. A few organizations, such as Whole Foods Market, actually make data on individual pay available to all members who are interested. Other organizations try to maintain a high level of secrecy about pay. What message do those organizations send? Keeping salaries secret suggests that the organization has something to hide or that it doesn't trust its people with the information. Moreover, keeping things secret just encourages people to uncover the secrets—if something is worth hiding, it must be important and interesting enough to expend effort discovering. Pay systems that are more open and transparent send a positive message about the equity of the system and the trust that the company places in its people.

Managers should also consider using other methods besides pay to signal company values and focus behavior. The head of North American sales and operations for the SAS Institute has a useful perspective on this issue. He didn't think he was smart enough to design an incentive system that couldn't be gamed. Instead of using the pay system to signal what was important, he and other SAS managers simply told people what was important for the company and why. That resulted in much more nuanced and rapid changes in behavior because the company didn't have to change the compensation system every time business priorities altered a little. What a novel idea—actually talking to people about what is important and why, rather than trying to send some subtle signals through the compensation system!

Perhaps most important, leaders must come to see pay for what it is: just one element in a set of management practices that can either build or reduce commitment, teamwork, and performance. Thus my final piece of advice about pay is to make sure that pay practices are congruent with other management practices and reinforce rather than oppose their effects.

## Breaking with Convention To Break the Myths

Many organizations devote enormous amounts of time and energy to their pay systems, but people, from senior managers to hourly workers, remain unhappy with them. Organizations are trapped in unproductive ways of approaching pay, which they find difficult to escape. The reason, I would suggest, is that people are afraid to challenge the myths about compensation. It's easier and less controversial to see what everyone else is doing and then to do the same. In fact, when I talk to executives at companies about installing pay systems that actually work, I usually hear, "But that's different from what most other companies are saying and doing."

It must certainly be the case that a company cannot earn "abnormal" returns by following the crowd. That's true about marketplace strategies, and it's true about compensation. Companies that are truly exceptional are not trapped by convention but instead see and pursue a better business model.

Companies that have successfully transcended the myths about pay know that pay cannot substitute for a working environment high on trust, fun, and meaningful work. They also know that it is more important to worry about what people do than what they cost, and that zero-sum pay plans can set off internal competition that makes learning from others, teamwork, and cross-functional cooperation a dream rather than the way the place works on an everyday basis.

There is an interesting paradox in achieving high organizational performance through innovative pay practices—if it were easy to do, it wouldn't provide as much competitive leverage as it actually does. So while I can review the logic and evidence and offer some alternative ways of thinking about pay, it is the job of leaders to ex-

ercise both the judgment and the courage necessary to break with common practice. Those who do will develop organizations in which pay practices actually contribute rather than detract from building high-performance management systems. Those who are stuck in the past are probably doomed to endless tinkering with pay; at the end of the day, they won't have accomplished much, but they will have expended a lot of time and money doing it.

---

1. John T. Dunlop and David Weil, "Diffusion and Performance of Modular Production in the U.S. Apparel Industry," *Industrial Relations,* July 1996, p. 337.

2. For the survey of the pay practices of *Fortune* 1,000 companies, see Gerald E. Ledford, Jr., Edward E. Lawler III, and Susan A. Mohrman, "Reward Innovations in *Fortune* 1,000 Companies," *Compensation and Benefits Review,* April 1995, p. 76; for the salary and commission data, see Gregory A. Patterson, "Distressed Shoppers, Disaffected Workers Prompt Stores to Alter Sales Commissions," the *Wall Street Journal,* July 1, 1992, p. B1; for the study of U.K. pay practices, see Stephen Wood, "High Commitment Management and Payment Systems," *Journal of Management Studies,* January 1996, p. 53.

3. For the Social Security Administration study, see Jone L. Pearce, William B. Stevenson, and James L. Perry, "Managerial Compensation Based on Organizational Performance: A Time Series Analysis of the Effects of Merit Pay," *Academy of Management Journal,* June 1985, p. 261; for the study of group-oriented compensation, see Larry Hatcher and Timothy L. Ross, "From Individual Incentives to an Organization-Wide Gain-sharing Plan: Effects on Teamwork and Product Quality," *Journal of Organizational Behavior,* May 1991, p. 169.

4. Gerald Marwell, "Altruism and the Problem of Collective Action," in V.J. Derlega and J. Grzelak, eds., *Cooperation and Helping Behavior: Theories and Research* (New York: Academic Press, 1982), p. 208.

# Overload

*Workers are stressed out and burned out from overwork.*
*Here's a fresh look at what's causing the problem and some*
*solutions for not overloading your workforce.*

## By Jennifer Laabs

Workloads never set out to hurt anybody. But doesn't it seem like over the past couple of years, someone named "Mr. Overload" muscled his way into all of our workplaces, sat down in our chairs and took over our lives? Both the increased speed and complexity of work these days is leaving everyone from the executive suite to the factory floor throbbing from a massive migraine just trying to get all their work done.

Why this has happened, and why no one seems to be talking about it intelligently, let alone doing something constructive about it—is even more puzzling. Overwork is a human resources management issue, and WORKFORCE is taking a close look at the problem, how we got here and what you can do about it.

### What's causing overwork and why is it a problem?

You guessed it. Most employees don't just sign up to get overworked because they enjoy it. Economic, technological and business factors such as downsizing, the skills shortage and low unemployment have forced those American workers who were left sitting in the hot seat to give 150 percent (or more) just to stay on top of their workloads. Now, U.S. business leaders have come to expect and rely on this accelerated pace. What were once considered crises-mode workloads have now become business as usual. After all, the more people get done, the more our companies profit, right? True, the United States certainly *is* enjoying economic nirvana, but at what price? Collective burnout? Of course, burnout isn't new, but what *is* new is the way in which job overload—causing burnout—has-elbowed its way into most of our work lives, sometimes without our even realizing it's a problem.

*Jennifer Laabs is the associate managing editor for WORK-FORCE. E-mail laabsj@workforcemag.com to comment.*

Take Jennifer Johnson, for instance. Johnson, who's now the principal strategist for Johnson & Co. in Santa Cruz, California, is a classic example of a fast-tracker who was headed for burnout, but jumped off the train before she crashed. "I was a corporate warrior for about 15 years," says Johnson. "When I first left college, I immediately began working 80-hour weeks in my first job at Novell in Provo, Utah." As a 22-year-old editor, she turned the company's in-house newsletter into an international consumer magazine that Novell sold three years later to The McGraw-Hill Companies for $10 million. She recalls nights when she'd stay at the office until 2 a.m., and was back in the office by 8 o'clock the next morning. "I realized it was the dues-paying time of my life and I actually thrived on the fast pace," Johnson admits.

After she took a job in advertising at another firm, got married and had kids, the pace became dizzying. She vividly remembers her breaking point 19 months ago when life and work clashed in the extreme. "My husband Scott, who headed the marketing function for one of 3Com's international-business units, was returning from a trip to Japan. The plan was for me to hand off the kids to him at the airport, and then I was going to catch a plane for the East Coast." It turns out her husband's plane was 20 minutes late. The moment he arrived, she threw the kids to him and sprinted to her own plane, luggage in tow.

In flight and exhausted, Johnson found herself writing a resignation letter. "I was laughing out loud as I wrote it because it was so obviously what I needed to do," she says. Johnson then started her own company—a virtual marketing organization that teams 17 contractors, mostly women, from across the country. Many of them were as desperate to balance their lives as she was. "I saw a lot of women who were forced to make the choice of either working or taking care of their families because their companies wouldn't be flexible," says Johnson. "I'm now seeing a world in which employees, after being downsized and rightsized, are turning the tables and they're *my-sizing* their jobs."

Workers who feel trapped in jobs in which they're powerless to do something about it tend to burn out faster. Ironically, those employees who are in fast-track careers are often the first ones to crash and burn, according to Beverly Potter, a workplace consultant and author of *Overcoming Job Burnout: How to Renew Enthusiasm for Work* (Ronin Publishing, 1998).

Although Johnson admits when she was a 22-year-old she actually liked being what she calls a "fast burner," it wore her out after a while. Right before she left Novell the second time (she returned there after the ad agency job), she asked to be able to telecommute two days a week. "It really surprised me that they were unwilling to let me do that, even though they're a technology company," says Johnson. She found during her second maternity leave that she often got a lot more done working at home than when she was in the office—and having to contend with meetings, interruptions and mountains of extraneous information. "If HR and business line managers could start thinking outside the box about what *really* needs to get done, I think it would help relieve a lot of people's workloads."

## Keeping pace, productivity and priorities.

Sure. Johnson is a poignant example of work overload. But the problem is that the Jennifer Johnsons of the world are becoming the norm, not the exception. The pace of work could be compared to an insidious weight problem. Like extra pounds, the extra minutes at work turn into extra hours, until one day you realize you never see daylight—or your waistline. Work consumes your life. It's always a challenge for companies to get the right balance between expectations, performance and productivity, and workers feeling like they're contributing and challenged, but not sucked dry.

*"Overload" is the first article in a series this year in which WORKFORCE will look closely at work overload, its impact on the workforce and the role of HR in finding solutions. If you have comments on this topic, or if you want to share anecdotes or solutions, please e-mail laabsj@workforcemag.com*

Lonnie Golden, a labor economist at Pennsylvania State University, located in Media, Pennsylvania, notes that recent research shows that weekly work hours are, indeed, on the rise—but the increase is unevenly distributed among manufacturing workers as opposed to service-sector workers. For example, overtime in U.S. manufacturing industries averages about 4.7 hours per week, and it's more than five hours in durable goods industries. Those figures, the same for 1996 and 1997, were all-time highs since such things began being recorded in 1956.

And the trend toward making fewer workers do more work continues most notably in unionized environments. "Employers are attempting to force more labor out of their current employees rather than creating new jobs. That's the bottom line," said Jim Grossfeld, a labor consultant, in an *Associated Press* article in November 1998. Union leaders cast mandatory overtime as a family values issue, arguing that it robs parents of time with their children and strains marriages. With workers already complaining during relatively rosy economic times, there's concern that the problem could grow worse during an economic downturn. For example, late last August when 35,000 members of the Communications Workers of America struck U.S. West Communications, based in Englewood, Colorado, their complaints included forced overtime that frequently meant 60-hour workweeks. The settlement included a cap on mandatory overtime at 16 hours per week in 1999, and eight hours per week beginning in 2001.

It's interesting to note that U.S. labor law doesn't limit the number of work hours as long as companies pay overtime for hours worked. But, by the way, we all know that means we have to compensate nonexempt workers for overtime. Exempt workers are on their own when it comes to negotiating higher pay for higher productivity or stronger business performance.

If we can call it the bright side, all this overtime is helping push the recent surge in American workers' productivity. After growing at a brisk 2.9 percent annual rate in the 1960s and early 1970s, productivity slowed to a miniscule 1 percent from 1974 through 1995. Since then, it has been growing at around a 2 percent rate. That growth has led some economists to speculate that the economy has embarked on a new era of productivity growth, driven by computers and other high-tech innovations.

With the influx of technology, such as cellular phones and the Internet, workers are wired to the office 24 hours a day and are expected to achieve mind-boggling workloads. The *Associated Press* reported last May that the average business manager receives 190 messages per day. "Many incoming messages today, unlike 20 years ago, demand a response," says Dan Wiljanen, vice president of human resources at furniture maker Steelcase, based in Grand Rapids, Michigan. "Today, you have to answer that voice mail or e-mail, so there's added pressure." (See "Information Overload: A Growing Problem.")

Overtime in other sectors, such as the service industry, can't reliably be tracked because part-time workers skew the numbers. For example, a November 2, 1998 article in *The New York Times* describes how part-time work is often now considered 35 to 40 hours a week. According to a 1997 study conducted by the Families and Work Institute, a nonprofit research group in New York City, the average workweek for a professional has stretched in the last 20 years to almost 48 hours from 45. "The complicated issue is: If a full week is 60 to 80 hours, what is part time?" Ellen Galinsky, president of the institute, was quoted asking. Indeed, our idea of a workweek has become blurred over the years.

WORKFORCE reported in "Working Smarter" (June 1993) that 95 percent of employees were working more than 40 hours a week, and our advice to HR execs back then was that they ought to start rethinking overflow and prioritizing tasks to boost productivity and morale. Those are still good solutions. The problem is few companies implemented them. Now the overwork problem has spiraled further out of control, threatening to suck the life out of workers, and workers themselves out of the workforce. Hundreds are quitting Corporate America daily because they're tired of the empty promises about companies helping them "balance their lives." The HR questions are: Have jobs grown too big for most workers? And what are companies really doing about it?

## Reengineering jobs to fit employees.

One of the running jokes at Redmond, Washington-based Microsoft Corp. is you can work any 18 hours a day you want. Although it's well known that Microsoft employees reap hefty rewards for their intense productivity in terms of comp, benefits, stock options and the like,

making overwork the corporate requirement can have its drawbacks. Many companies recognize the problem, and many think they've already solved it. But they should take another look at their solutions.

According to Terry Alan Beehr, professor of psychology at Central Michigan University in Mount Pleasant, Michigan, and an authority on organizational psychology, job stress is too often treated with medication or counseling rather than by making changes in the workplace and in workloads. Managers often are guilty of throwing work/life programs at workers or sending them to an Employee Assistance Program (EAP). In *Psychological Stress in the Workplace* (Routledge, 1995), Beehr says managers make the mistake of resisting organizational change instead of altering the source of job stress, such as long workdays, technological advances, work overload and role conflict—having two or more tasks that are incompatible.

William Bridges, founder and principal strategist at William Bridges & Associates, a Mill Valley, California-based consulting firm that provides resources to organizations and individuals in transition, purports that jobs as we know them are going away. Bridges, who's the author of *JobShift: How to Prosper in a Workplace Without Jobs*[R] (Addison Wesley, 1994), notes that we're already in what he calls the throes of having a "dejobbed" work environment in which the lines between jobs have become blurred. "In the old days when people had very clear jobs,

JENNIFER JOHNSON

*Jennifer Johnson now works from home so she can spend more time with her sons, Jamison (seated) and Truman.*

work—to get into your in-box—had to fall squarely into the category of your job description," Bridges explains.]

Not so any longer. At Job Boss Software in Minneapolis, the company's CEO, Ed Booth, has been quoted saying their workers "are like a volleyball team because it takes three hits to get the ball over the net, and it doesn't matter who hits it." Now, as companies move away from traditional job descriptions to having more flexible, cross-functional teams and employing more free agents, it gets less clear whose work any given project or task really is. "Because if it isn't clear whose work something is, it can be given to anybody, including the people who already are overworked," says Bridges. "People can't fend off work as easily anymore. And the fact that it 'isn't your job' just doesn't cut it."

Companies need to take stock of where they're really at with their workloads and how those workloads piled up to where they are today. "This is a time when work needs to be trimmed just as firmly as the workforce has been trimmed," says Bridges. He explains that companies have cut people out of the workforce (downsized) with razor-sharp accuracy, but haven't trimmed the workloads of the people who've remained with the same vigor. As a consultant, he has noticed there's a great deal of unnecessary work being done in U.S. companies. "Justifying work is very important," Bridges adds. It's a matter of figuring out what work is necessary and what isn't. It's es-

> ■ "People can't fend off work as easily anymore. And the fact that it 'isn't your job' just doesn't cut it," says Bridges. Companies need to take stock of where they're at with workloads. ■

sentially reengineering workloads. "I know that reengineering has a bad name," says Bridges, "but we need to take a close look at what we're making workers do." However, unlike reengineering, he says this is something workers themselves have to be very involved in.

For example, the HR leaders at Merck & Co., the giant pharmaceutical company based in Whitehouse Station, New Jersey, realized after hearing worker's complaints about overwork, inadequate training, schedule changes, poor new-hire screening and lack of communication, among other things, that they needed to respond—quickly. In a major work redesign effort, Merck's management team assigned employees to teams that were devoted to solving these problems. Work was analyzed, dissected and reorganized so that workers felt like they had more control

STEELCASE

*At Steelcase's headquarters in Grand Rapids, Michigan, new open work space models are helping make jobs less stressful.*

over their workloads and schedules. "We focused on the things that are really important to our customers," says Michelle Peterson, senior director of work/life flexibility, who oversaw the effort.

In one area of the company, payroll employees weren't happy with the large amount of overtime they had to put in. During a series of meetings, team leaders realized that most of their work was more critical earlier in the week than toward the end of the week. Solutions included reducing peoples' commute time by allowing them to work at home more often, and giving them compressed work weeks. They provided technology so payroll workers could input data at home. Solutions to the most difficult problems were implemented within three months and turnover slowed from 45 percent to 32 percent, and is still dropping. In addition, overtime costs and absenteeism plummeted. And for the employees, overtime and commute time were slashed.

HR managers should also be willing to suggest that managers outsource tasks that are unnecessary, or could be done more effectively by a third party. "Who should do the work?" is the question every manager should ask about every bit of work. "And you may find some of the work could go outside, and you readjust what's left so it isn't so overwhelming," says Bridges.

Dell Computer Corp.'s direct-to-customer business model, for example, takes outsourcing to a new level. The firm doesn't just outsource a few tasks; it actually turns over three-quarters of its work to non-employees, particularly field service and manufacturing. Still, the firm employs 20,800 people in 42 countries. "So Dell isn't just outsourcing in the sense they're having trouble with a certain process so they got rid of it," explains Bridges. "They've designed a new kind of organization in which the majority of the work is done by people who work for other companies." It's the concept of work distribution.

Dell started the company organizing work this way. However, it's more difficult for older companies to follow this model because it can mean layoffs or downsizing. Instead, some companies are beginning to look at how they organize jobs and roles throughout their organizations. Many are moving toward putting jobs into job families or roles.

For example, the Massachusetts Housing Finance Agency (MHFA), located in Boston, recently embarked on a comprehensive, strategic planning process to see whether the services they're providing to their customers are still relevant. They discovered during the process that they needed a new overall HR strategy that would result in a flatter, more flexible system. Previously, they had 400 employees and about 390 job descriptions. We're also victims of fewer people and increasingly more work to do," says Frank Creedon, MHFA's director of corporate planning and development. They didn't get rid of job descriptions, but did come up with five roles or "impact groups" throughout the company (such as business leaders and individual contributors) and eight core competencies

MERICK & CO.

*Merck & Co. underwent a major work redesign in which employees' schedules were reorganized for more flexibility.*

they see as most significant that those people need to accomplish. By focusing on what's important, they're starting to eliminate extraneous work.

## Focus on what's most important.

According to an article in the *Salt Lake Observer* in October 1998 called "The Zen of Managing Transition," one expert reminds us that you get what you focus on. Nancy Garbett, president of Transition Management Inc. of Salt Lake City, tells us this age-old idea has roots in quantum physics and cybernetics. "It's actually been proven in physics that what you focus on is what you get," Garbett says. "What happens with the brain is that once there's a compelling image of a desired outcome, the brain will give constant and corrective feedback—automatically and unconsciously—to keep us on track to that outcome." The idea is: Don't have just a flashlight on the goal, put a floodlight on it.

Bridges has observed that there are leaders and managers who take advantage of their powerful positions by telling workers to do things that really don't make sense. "It's the *Dilbert*™ *syndrome*, in which a manager says, 'Do this,' and the workers know it's ridiculous," Bridges quips. These days, in a 24-hour-a-day, global marketplace that moves faster than the speed of e-mail, it's important for HR managers to help their firms' management groups figure out what's most important to get done.

For example, this strategy has been a big focus at San Francisco-based AirTouch Communications Inc. this year. Tracey Borst, who heads the firm's HR team, says although she hears rumblings about overwork from time to time, the "noise level" about it hasn't gotten in the way lately. To nip the problem in the bud, the senior management team has been trying to get better at prioritizing work

# Information Overload: A Growing Problem

It's no wonder we're on information overload. Look at these facts, figures and observations to get an idea of how technology and other factors have changed the nature of work.

One-third of managers are victims of "Information Fatigue Syndrome." 49 percent said they're unable to handle the vast amounts of information received. 62 percent admitted their business relationships suffer. 43 percent of managers think that important decisions are delayed and their ability to make decisions is affected as a result of having too much information.

—*Reuters "Dying for Business" report, 1996*

More information has been produced in the last 30 years than the previous 5,000. The total quantity of all printed material is doubling every five years, and accelerating.

—*Reuters Business Information, 1996*

In the last seven months of 1996, the number of documents on the Web grew at more than a 100 percent rate—from 50 million in May to 80 million in December.

—*"How Much is Too Much?" Mercury Center*

Having too much information can be as dangerous as having too little. It can lead to a paralysis of analysis, making it harder to find the right solutions or make decisions.

—*Psychologist David Lewis, quoted in a CNN report*

The English language has grown by 65,000 words to 70,000 words since the mid-1960s.

—*Jeff Davidson, author of* Handling Information Overload]

A common response by managers is that "By the time you check your e-mail, voice mail, faxes and database, it's already time to go home."

—*Report from a business economic summit in Davos, Switzerland*

The World Wide Web contains an estimated 320 million pages of information.

—*NEC Research Institute, Princeton, New Jersey*

Information anxiety is a chronic malaise, a pervasive fear that we're about to be overwhelmed by the very material we need to master in order to function in this world.

—*Richard Saul Wurman, author of* Information Anxiety

Two-thirds of Americans don't get the recommended eight hours of sleep.

—*National Sleep Foundation, Washington, D.C.*

Source: Compiled by Enfish Technology Inc., Pasadena, California

---

throughout the company by letting employees know which company goals are most important. "Even if we had all the money in the world, we still wouldn't have enough people and would have to let some things fall by the wayside," says Borst. "There's a limited number of resources to maintain customers and to create new products, so you have to focus on what's most important and create balance."

According to predictions about what will be important in 1999, Flexible Resources, Inc., an employment and consulting firm based in Bloomfield, Connecticut, that specializes in providing flexible staffing solutions at the professional level, predicts employers will focus less on head count and more on employee output. To get more out of people, they predict managers will have to invest their resources in making sure employees get the most out of existing technology. Where appropriate, they'll redistribute workstations or components to ensure they're used to their full potential. Next, they'll step up efforts to boost productivity by using technology in new ways, such as equipping their remote workforces with laptop computers and cell phones.

These are things some top companies have already done. Says John Sullivan, head of San Francisco State University's HR management program, "I know of the overstressed world, but I don't find it in the top HR departments anymore." Sullivan says the better firms with world-class HR like Hewlett Packard (HP), Sun Microsys-

tems, Cisco Systems and Intel have already overcome much of that "do more with less" stress. "Much of it was overcome in the reengineering cycle we all went through two to four years ago, and the rest is being done through the use of technology that allows us to 'do more with less.' Sure, people still work long hours, but the stress levels have been reduced by using intelligent HR practices combined with technology. Turnover rates at the top firms (HP being the leader) are below 7 percent, even in the highly competitive Silicon Valley," he notes.

Still, even with all the tweaking of processes and technological advances, why is it that companies are scrupulous about maintaining their inert equipment, but don't pay as much attention to giving their human assets workload tune-ups? Machines regularly get oiled, cleaned and tuned. But when it comes to workers, we just expect they'll handle ever-increasing amounts of work without regard to regular check-ups. The human person is capable of a lot—probably much more than we can even imagine. But it seems we need to consider some age-old rules about human capacity along with some enlightened new ideas about how to work—and how *not* to work—in order to produce at the top of our game.

## Think "balance."

"Back some time ago, we used to say that some of our job roles here weren't unlike taking a drink from a fire hose. They were just overwhelming," quips Wiljanen, Steelcase's top HR leader. "The question is: How do we go about coping with the stress?" Last year, when Wiljanen's HR team sent out its first-ever, 18-question employee survey, it asked to what extent workers feel there's balance between their work and family lives. Wiljanen says the survey got a middle-of-the-road score that told him workers could really use more balance. "So we know that's an issue, and it may become more of an issue down the road. We want to think proactively about what we can do to relieve some of the stress and strain," says Wiljanen.

---

## ■ These ideas aren't just nice ideas to help workers feel not so stressed out. We're talking about boosting productivity through scheduled breaks in the work schedule. ■

---

The HR team is continuing to experiment with workspace design that addresses how to get work done in a less stressful way. The company is experimenting with an open plan with no private offices. It has a rule that no one can schedule meetings between 8 and 9 o'clock. "The idea is to keep that hour open so people can talk and catch up," says Wiljanen. The furniture is more like what you'd find at home and almost invites relaxation. There's even a large fishtank in the common area that workers like to congregate around. "We put things in the environment to almost cause people to take a deep breath and recognize there's more to business than meeting after meeting," he adds.

And the top management team at Steelcase has just embarked on another two-year experiment called "Fit for Life" to see the impact of fitness and health on executives' performance and feelings of well-being. "We're starting at the top because we think the top managers need to model these behaviors, and we're trying to change the norms around the organization. The idea is to give people permission to take a break in the middle of the day, or at the beginning or at the end of the day, two to three times a week," he explains. The company wants to make it part of the natural workweek to go to a local fitness center or to jog. "And we think that will have an impact on the stress people feel," Wiljanen adds. Steelcase seems like it's on the right track to a kinder, gentler—and perhaps more civilized—way of working.

"What we need most of all is a way of living and working that offers real solutions to the do-more-with-less, do-

less-with-less, do-more-with-more conundrum," says Let Davidson, in his book *Wisdom at Work: The Awakening of Consciousness in the Workplace* (Larson Publications, 1998). Davidson is a global corporate consultant and leads seminars on empowerment, stress, change management, and personal and spiritual development.

"This is a dilemma that can't be fully resolved by day planners, working smarter, better computers, more bandwidth, elaborate networking or even 30-hour workweeks." He offers the more spiritual approach of being and doing called "flow." We've all heard of "going with the flow." This is much like that. It's when people are "fully present, inwardly quiet and absorbed in the work." The idea is that instead of loading ourselves up with details and massive amounts of input, we need to step back and allow our inherent potential and creativity to be released so we can make our full contribution in our work and to one another.

Easier said than done? Perhaps. But Ron Rosenberg, president of Quality Talk, a Raleigh, North Carolina organization devoted to helping companies successfully implement change to improve performance and effectiveness, has ideas about how to get more balance in our work and personal lives. These ideas aren't just nice ideas to help workers not feel so stressed out. They're necessary solutions for employees who'll reach a breaking point from overwork if the problem isn't addressed sooner rather than later. We're talking about boosting productivity through scheduled breaks in the work schedules, not just giving people more downtime. Just as there's an ebb and flow to life and cycles in nature, there should be cycles to people's workloads.

Here are Rosenberg's suggestions:

- Vary the workloads of each individual.
- Rotate people on assignments.
- Set a time for individual and group rejuvenation.
- Give people a time out—both on the job and off the job (i.e. vacation).
- Give sabbaticals after five years or so.

"The concept is active inactivity," says Rosenberg. "Take time to just sit on the porch and watch the grass grow." People tend to get their best ideas (read: solutions to problems, including those at work) when they're not even consciously thinking about it.

When you come right down to it, perhaps we can't prevent "Mr. Overload" from coming to our offices altogether. But we can learn to work with him more consciously and intelligently. There are some new tools and ideas HR professionals can use to alleviate the work overload problem. Recognizing the problem exists and that it can be destructive is a good first step.

# Dealing with the
# Dark
# Side

*Several potentially dangerous brain conditions can be
controlled with medication—but only if employees take them.*

## By Dominic Bencivenga

A normally cheerful employee begins an emotional tailspin. Over the course of several weeks she becomes increasingly aggressive and threatening to her coworkers. You know she suffers from a condition that affects the brain—such as schizophrenia, bipolar disorder or depression, among others—but you also know that she has been taking medication to control this condition.

Now you begin to wonder if her recent mood swings are related to her condition—and if she will become violent. It's not an impossible prospect: Such conditions can result in dangerously aggressive behavior if they are not carefully managed. And in some cases, individuals have decided of their own volition to stop taking their medication.

Has your employee made a similar, risky decision? Could she become dangerous? What should you do?

She is most likely protected by the Americans With Disabilities Act (ADA), so one of your concerns is staying on the right side of the law. But another concern is ensuring that the employee's co-workers are not exposed to needless danger.

"There are tremendous concerns in the employer community as to how to deal with this issue," says Garry Mathiason, an attorney with Littler Mendelson in San Francisco.

The range of issues facing employers begins with finding the best way to approach the employee for a discussion or behavioral evaluation. It moves to whether an employer should require a psychiatric examination or drug testing to ensure the employee is taking medication, and then to the types of improper behavior that trigger discipline or firing.

## Gauging Your Reaction

Some experts say employer fear may be overstated. For example, schizophrenia—which is twice as common as bipolar disorder—affects only four out of every 1,000 persons. What's more, workers with schizophrenia who are able to work full time are unlikely to pose problems in the workplace.

"If they are able to get a job, they will, by definition, almost certainly fall into the 50 percent of people with schizophrenia who recognize they are sick and need medication," says Dr. E. Fuller Torrey, a research psychiatrist and executive director of the Stanley Foundation Research Programs in Bethesda, Md. "(Those workers) are much less likely to stop taking medication once they have a job."

But even if the risks are slight, the potential costs can be enormous. In 1998 alone, shooting sprees by mentally ill employees in Connecticut, South Carolina, Florida, Wisconsin and California left more than a dozen people dead or injured.

And last June, an Ohio bank paid at least $200,000 to settle a lawsuit brought by victims of a 1995 attack by a mentally ill former bank employee. That assault left four dead and two injured, according to published reports.

## Warning Signs

To prevent such tragedies, human resource managers or supervisors who believe an employee poses a threat should take quick action. The warning signs for employees with schizophrenia, bipolar disorder or severe depression include significant changes in behavior or interaction with others, such as the following:

- Screaming.
- Explosive outbursts over minor disagreements.
- Making off-color remarks.
- Crying.
- Decreased energy or focus.
- Deteriorating work performance and personal appearance.
- Becoming reclusive.

An employer's radar should go up if employees start becoming overly suspicious—suspecting that co-workers are trying to

# An employer's radar should go up if employees start becoming overly suspicious.

harm them or are sneaking into their computers to change information, Torrey says. "That person has a greater potential for danger than a person who is quietly psychotic but doesn't think people are sneaking in and doing things."

The behavior change, however, must be unique to the individual to raise concern. "There are some people who are antagonistic by their nature," says Larry Anderson, the Postal Service's manager of safety and workplace assistance in Washington, D.C. "That's the way they act. If all of a sudden they become withdrawn, and not antagonistic, that indicates something is different."

## Stepping In

Approaching an employee who is disrupting the work environment and who may be mentally ill requires some finesse. The most useful approach begins, experts say, with the employee's supervisor, members of the HR staff or workplace safety consultant. They typically meet informally with the employee, co-workers or even the employee's family to determine if there are any life-altering events—such as death, family crisis or financial problems—that could explain the change in behavior.

Employers should avoid any reference to mental or medical illness. But if an employee discloses a condition, the employer will need to allow the worker time to go to a doctor, take medication on the job or return home to retrieve the medication.

Company representatives may recommend that the employee voluntarily contact an employee assistance program (EAP). In some situations, employees can be referred to mandatory evaluations by psychologists or psychiatrists.

Some organizations offer specific training programs to help managers deal with the difficult task of approaching potentially dangerous employees. For example, over the past two years the U.S. Postal Service has trained more than 60,000 managers, supervisors and union stewards to identify unusual, threatening or combative behavior and to refer workers to the EAP.

The Postal Service can require employees to take psychiatric exams to determine their fitness for duty. The psychiatrists or clinical psychologists conducting the emergency fitness exams are directed by Postal Service officials to determine if there is an identifiable target and whether the employee is capable of being supervised by a current supervisor or other supervisors.

"We've found over the years that with many fitness for duty exams, particularly with psychiatrists, we'd get great reports—but they didn't answer some of those questions required by management to make an administrative decision," says Dr. David Reid, the Postal Service medical director. "They didn't tell whether that person should be working or not, or very specifically, the ability of that person to perform the duty he or she is asked to perform."

Reid adds, "You never can guarantee that a person is not going to fall off the wagon. That's something no psychiatrist can say. Even if people are being treated, there's nothing to say that one particular thing might not set them off, regardless of what medication they are being given."

## Firing and Discipline

Although employees with serious medical and mental conditions are protected by the ADA, you still have the right to fire them for valid work-related reasons. "If they fail to take their medication, the first time you have to make an accommodation. The second time, that's it," Mathiason says. "If they fail to take their medication, they are not giving reasonable accommodation to the

## Tackling Aggression: A Case Study

In the summer of 1997, U.S. Postal Service officials in a North Carolina district office were scrambling to resolve a personnel problem that was on the verge of exploding into violence.

A postal employee had threatened his co-workers and was removed from the workplace. He applied for a mental disability retirement, but his application was stalled. As the delay increased, he became more and more irate. Postal officials believed the employee was capable of returning to work to carry out his previous threats, so they contacted postal inspectors.

The postal inspectors took what was then a new approach. Rather than taking legal or disciplinary action against the employee—or leaving him to struggle with the application process alone—the inspectors spent several months calming

the man's anxieties and shepherding his application through the process until it was approved.

By taking an active, nonconfrontational approach, the inspectors averted what was "almost a certain critical (violent) incident," says Larry Anderson, the Postal Service's manager of safety and workplace assistance in Washington, D.C. "They were certain that this individual was a danger and—left on his own to become frustrated by a bureaucracy that isn't particularly sympathetic—they were concerned that he could have come back and (created) a critical incident."

Ignoring the threats or firing the employee outright were not considered because doing so would not have eliminated the danger; in fact, it might have made things worse. In some cases, postal employees who threaten co-workers "have been separated properly and have come back and acted violently," Anderson says.

# Accommodate employees until the behavior or performance violates workplace rules.

employer. Our advice is that is grounds for ending the relationship."

David Fram, director of EEO and ADA Services at the National Employment Law Institute in Washington, D.C., says employers could ask employees to take periodic tests to ensure they are taking the necessary medication, much as they would with workers who have drug or alcohol problems. But others say testing might be impossible in states like California, which has strict privacy laws.

When mentally disabled employees fail to take their medication or follow an employer's guidelines, Joseph A. Kinney, executive director of the National Safe Workplace Institute in Charlotte, N.C., says, "The issue no longer rests in accommodation; it rests upon disruption of the workplace and violation of workplace practices. If employees are not complying with the employer's rules or common practices, it's appropriate to terminate them."

The key, workplace safety experts say, is to accommodate employees until the behavior or performance violates workplace rules.

Then, "Focus on performance; do not focus on the mental disability," says Fram. "If the employee has stopped taking his medication and has threatened violence in the workplace, then employers should treat that person the same way they treat anybody else who has threatened violence in the workplace," he says. "If that includes discipline or termination, that's what they should do for somebody with a disability."

Firing an employee who poses a threat to others, or himself, is not a violation of the ADA. The guidelines to the ADA, published by the Equal Employment Opportunity Commission in 1997, make it clear that the law allows employers to fire mentally disabled employees if they pose a direct threat or a "significant risk of substantial harm" that cannot be eliminated by a reasonable accommodation.

Reasonable accommodation may include time off from work or a modified work schedule to obtain treatment. Employees must adhere to those accommodations and must comply with workplace behavior and conduct standards.

## Court Decisions

For the most part, the U.S. Court of Appeals has upheld decisions to fire disabled employees based on performance or behavior.

In a leading 1997 case, *Palmer v. Circuit Court of Cook County, Ill.* (No. 95-3659), the U.S. Court of Appeals for the 7th Circuit upheld the firing of a social service caseworker who suffered from depression and paranoid delusion disorder and threatened to kill her supervisor. The court wrote that the worker was fired for the threats, rather than her illness, and that the ADA "does not require an employer to retain a potentially violent employee."

The court declined to place employers "in jeopardy of violating the act if it fired such an employee, yet in jeopardy of being deemed negligent if it retained him and he hurt someone."

In March of 1998, the 5th Circuit used similar reasoning in *Hamilton v. Southwestern Bell* (No. 97-10352) and refused to reinstate the lawsuit of an employee who suffered from post-traumatic stress syndrome and was fired after yelling at and striking another employee.

There are limits, however, and employers must ensure they have a proper basis for their actions and ensure an accommodation is not unreasonably restrictive. In January 1998, the 7th Circuit held in *Duda v. Board of Education of Franklin Park* (No. 97-2457) that a school janitor with bipolar disorder could pursue ADA claims against his school district employer. The court found it was unreasonable for district officials to order that the janitor not talk to anyone at a school where he worked and to refuse to consider him for another job before firing him.

The *Duda* case shows that the discipline or termination process must be handled carefully because if a mentally disabled employee sues, a court will closely evaluate the process the employer uses. "The more comprehensive the process, the more people you talk to, the more the decisions stand up," Bobbi Lambert, president of Confidante Inc., a San Francisco Bay-area consulting firm that handles threat management, says.

As a result, employers are well-advised to develop clear, detailed policies for dealing with mentally ill workers, as well as an approach that will withstand the scrutiny of a jury if a disabled employee decides to file a federal discrimination suit.

In cases where the potential for violence means a troubled employee must be removed from the workplace immediately, an employer can consider "a suspension with pay for a few days to calm the situation," says Libby Roth, partner at General Coun-

## Fear in the Office

Often, the threat of violence alone is enough to terrorize. A decade ago, Bonnie Jones was the human resource director at a small medical equipment manufacturer in the San Francisco Bay area when she took a call from a psychiatrist treating a former employee. The ex-worker had been threatening to kill some of his former colleagues, and the psychiatrist felt violence might be imminent. The company hired private detectives to guard the building.

Within a month, the psychiatrist called back to say the threat had passed. But 10 years later, the memory is still vivid.

"It was very chilling," says Jones, who is now HR director at Mercury Interactive in Sunnyvale, Calif. The former employee was "blaming a lot of what happened to him on the company and a few specific people he had worked with, and he was going to harm those people," she says. "I had to figure out what to do, and how I was going to keep those people safe."

sel Associates in Mountain View, Calif. "It doesn't legally change the employer-employee relationship, and the employee can't argue that getting away from the workplace while still getting the salary is terribly damaging. That usually will be seen as a fair thing to do by an outside observer."

Because a jury "might be looking over a company's shoulder two or three years from now, it's important to slow down the analysis and to make (the process) as fair as it can be under the circumstances," Roth says.

## Reasons Not To Fire

Although employers have the legal right to fire employees who present a serious danger that cannot be overcome with accommodation, doing so is not always the right choice.

Kinney says employers have an obligation to resolve behavioral problems and obtain treatment for employees with mental illnesses. Otherwise, they risk pushing a problem worker into a new workplace,

where tragedy may occur. "Failing to deal with someone who is screaming or with some behavior problems exposes another employer unwittingly to a problem," he says.

Lambert agrees that terminations are not always the best solution. "One reason to not terminate an employee is you have someone out there with no evaluation, no idea of what they are going to do and they are really angry," she says.

Perhaps even more important, firing a potentially troubled worker may cost you a valuable employee—something most employers can't afford to lose.

Case in point: A company hired Lambert to deal with an employee who threatened a union shop steward. "There was a very real threat of violence," she says. "There had been direct threats, physical altercations and the person had weapons in his car."

Rather than firing the employee, Lambert recommended his suspension. Company security staff took the employee directly to a psychiatrist to begin mandatory treatment. After two months—during

which time the employee's medication was corrected and he attended a series of anger management classes and psychiatric sessions—he received medical permission to return to work.

"He's been a great employee ever since," she says.

---

*Editor's Note:* Are employees who can control a condition with medication protected by the Americans With Disabilities Act? To find out, see Article 7, page 43 "ADA: The Law Meets Medicine," from *HR Magazine*, January 1999.

*Dominic Bencivenga, a New York-based writer who has been covering HR issues for seven years, has been contributing to HR Magazine for three years. Previously, he worked as a business columnist and reporter with the* Sarasota Herald-Tribune *in Florida, where he specialized in reporting on workplace issues and legal affairs. His articles have appeared in the* New York Times *and* Newsday, *among others.*

# They Want More Support—Inside and Outside of Work

*The new word from employees is that their commitment hinges on employers helping them integrate their personal lives with their work lives.*

**By Jennifer Laabs**

Fifty years ago, if you used the term "work/life balance," most businesspeople would have looked at you funny. Back then, there was no such phrase—let alone a concept. No one acknowledged the fact that people had life issues to balance. If you worked, there was an unwritten rule that you didn't let your home life interfere with your work life. After all, what did employees' personal lives have to do with work, anyway?

Fast forward to 1998, and it's obvious the thinking on the work/life issue has changed dramatically. Or has it? That's the question thousands of employees across America are asking these days. And the answer, at least according to employees, is that although the bigger question of work/life balance has been addressed, they're now saying that businesses can still do a better job of addressing the work/life question in an everyday context.

According to the 1998 America @ Work℠ study conducted by Aon Consulting Worldwide Inc., an HR consulting firm based in Chicago, today's employee commitment is most strongly correlated with management's recognition of the importance of personal and family life, and the effects of work on workers' personal lives. In general, employees are crying out for more appreciation of their extra effort on the job, and how that often impacts the rest of their lives.

---

*Jennifer Laabs is the associate managing editor at WORK-FORCE. E-mail laabsj@workforcemag.com to comment.*

**Workers want more supportive workplaces.**

In Aon Consulting's workforce commitment study, the biggest driver of employee loyalty is having managers recognize their need to balance work with home life. But employees also value their co-workers' support of their personal lives in relationship to their work lives. Additionally, people want balance within their jobs, too.

Correlating the results of Aon's 1995 "Survey of Life-stage Needs" with its current study, we see that the amount of time workers are losing from their jobs because of personal distractions appears to be increasing. For example, in 1995, workers missed 13.6 days a year because of personal matters, but now lose an average of 15.1 (a 10 percent increase) because of the same types of distractions—which include everything from stress to caring for elderly dependents. Not surprisingly, many of the employees who miss time for one personal reason, also miss time for other personal reasons. This is especially true for time off due to stress. More than 80 percent of the employees who missed time due to stress also missed time because they had no elder-care provider or for other personal matters. And while the average time missed for stress has increased 36 percent since 1995, the percentage of employees who reported often feeling burned out by personal stress in their lives is virtually unchanged. However, the percentage of employees who report often feeling burned out by *job* stress has increased from 39 percent to 53 percent in 1998.

And here's the part where HR people need to perk up their ears: Increased time at work may play a part in this

## Tips from Female Employees to Encourage Loyalty

What do female employees say they want in exchange for loyalty? According to a small study conducted this summer of 30 professional business women who ranged in age from under 25 to 55, some interesting issues come to light.

- Say what you mean, mean what you say—there's no time for twisted communication
- Create recognition programs for top performers—offer more than money
- Develop procedures and follow up for improving performance of poor performers
- Develop a feeling of ownership through communication and involvement in decisions
- Have ongoing career discussions and learn employee interests
- Train and mentor managers to manage people and not just budgets
- Reward accomplishments and results versus hours spent at the office
- Realize that different things motivate each person
- Emphasize team building
- You can't communicate too much
- Recognition, recognition, recognition

## What Employees Say Discourages Loyalty

What do female employees say prevents them from being loyal? The respondents of the same study that yielded the above suggestions of ways to encourage loyalty were also asked what actions discouraged loyalty to their companies.

- Showing favoritism—lack of equity
- Not handling problems on a timely basis
- Secrecy
- Paying below market rates
- "Spin" communication
- Not recognizing and rewarding contributions
- Unclear policies about promotions and raises
- Frequent reorganizations

—Deb McCusker and Ilene Wolfman

additional stress for workers. In 1998, 23 percent of employees reported working an average of more than 50 hours per week, compared with 13 percent of the 1995 respondents. Remember how the new employee commitment deal involves employees working harder? Well, they are, and here's the effect: Though Aon's study finds there's no correlation between missed time and employee commitment (both committed and non-committed employees have to deal with personal issues), there is a correlation between job stress and employee commitment. The 53 percent of respondents whose job stress often causes them

to feel burned out are much less committed to their employers. The 28 percent of the workforce whose personal stress often causes them to feel burned out are also less committed to their employers. And the "1998 Business Work-Life Study" from the Families and Work Institute in New York City found that the better the quality of a person's job, the more committed he or she will be.

Employee-commitment studies find that as workplace supportiveness increases, so does loyalty. And now that some of the bigger support issues—such as flextime, telecommuting and onsite daycare—are being addressed by HR, employees are clamoring for employers to help with some of the smaller things that make their day-to-day lives easier, like finding a local fitness club, a pharmacy that delivers or a dry cleaner who makes house calls to the workplace. "I think anything that companies can do to inject that 'personal touch' is going to make employees feel more committed to that specific organization," says John Place, president of the Dependent Care Connection (DCC), a global provider of employee and EAP assistance services, based in Westport, Connecticut. "The more you recognize and address the balancing act that employees go through, the more committed those employees are going to be." Place says his HR clients tell him when they now go to college campuses to recruit, they're being asked straight up by prospective employees: "What are you going to do to help me balance work and life?" Ten years ago, that question never came up. But answering the question is the tricky part. Give them what they need for balance, but tie those benefits to tangible performance.

### Link work/life initiatives to performance.

Work/life initiatives are very important to employees. All the newest employee commitment studies make that clear. However, continuing to add one work/life initiative after another could be a problem down the line if workers start to see all the extra help and flexibility as simply another entitlement. For HR, it's a delicate balance. Give them what they want and need, but don't break the company bank in doing so.

Richard Federico, VP and National Practice Leader in the Work/life Practice at The Segal Company, an HR consulting firm based in New York City, has some excellent suggestions. "To my mind, the best way to foster commitment is to link work/life initiatives to performance as much as you can," says Federico. What he means is, use the work/life benefits arena as a strategic advantage to both attract high-performers to your company (who'll tend to stay because of your high-quality benefits) and as a reward for the high performance of the people you employ.

On the recruitment side, if you don't offer high-quality work/life benefits, you may not attract the right people. "They're never even going to come knocking on your Web site if you don't," quips Federico. He concedes that people may spend a minute or two on your Web site, but once they find out you're not offering what they want, they'll go elsewhere. And remember, people are the competitive advantage these days, so attracting them is a big deal. Federico points out that what's making the difference between winning companies and losing ones these days is that winners replace people who leave with high performers. "Losing companies replace people with mediocrity," he adds.

Once people are employed with your firm, work/life initiatives can also work for you if you play the cards right. If you give a menu of benefits from which employees choose, even the more personal-services type benefits, then they get what they want. And if you offer an increase of those benefits based on their good performance, you'll sustain good work. However, if employees start to perform poorly, you take some of those benefits away. It's that simple. Remember that the new employee-employer commitment is more of a give-and-take. When both sides give more, both parties get more. But the opposite is also true. If employees aren't holding up their end of the bargain, they shouldn't expect to stay on the gravy train.

"With quality of life predicted to be the controlling workforce issue of the 21st century, work/life is quickly taking center stage as a significant driver of employee commitment," explains Ann Vincola, senior partner with Corporate Work/Life Consulting, a division of Boston-based Children's Discovery Centers. A pioneer in the work/life arena, Vincola has provided consulting services to corporations for nearly 20 years. "In their efforts to attract and retain a diverse workforce, progressive companies are realizing that work and life are inextricably intertwined—when they're out of synch, both employees and organizations alike will suffer."

## HR responds to the cry for work/life help with balance.

In October, *Working Mother* magazine published its annual list of the 100 best companies for working moms. For the first time, the magazine considered whether companies give work/life training to managers and whether managers' pay is linked to their effectiveness in dealing with such issues. The magazine also gave closer scrutiny to whether work/family programs are well-used, in addition to considering its other usual criteria, such as pay, child-care benefits and flexibility.

Dallas-based Texas Instruments, which is on this year's list, is revising a seminar on flexible work arrangements to emphasize how to make them succeed. They'll also be making managers take classes on making decisions based not only on business needs, but on workers' needs, as

well. And at Allstate Insurance, based in Northbrook, Illinois, every new manager gets three days of training on how to foster a supportive work environment. Allstate's managers' merit raises are also partly based on employee surveys that since last year have included a question on whether managers promote a family-friendly atmosphere.

Then there's E.I. du Pont de Nemours and Co., the chemical giant based in Wilmington, Delaware, where managers are evaluated on whether they support work/life goals, and some departmental managers must take a mandatory course on using flexibility as a business tool. At drug maker Hoffman-La Roche, based in Nutley, New Jersey, the firm holds decision makers accountable for helping women advance by identifying talent. Executives must report quarterly on their efforts.

These efforts are notable, given the fact that a landmark study called "The 1998 Business Work/Life Study" published this summer by the nonprofit Families and Work Institute, based in New York City, found that only 44 percent of companies hold supervisors accountable for sensitivity to employees' work/family needs. And the same study found that nearly 40 percent of HR representatives said their companies didn't make a "real and ongoing" effort to tell employees of available work/family programs. Says Ellen Galinsky, president of the Families and Work Institute: "Traditionally, we've thought that pay and benefits were the motivators that really affected the decision about whether employees will stay or whether they'll give their all." But this doesn't prove to be true. "What really differs is the quality of jobs and how supportive the workplace is to the individual, both in terms of getting the work done and having a life outside the job. It's not like work/life is the magic bullet—but it's a fundamental part of having a workplace that's supportive."

## HR's role in helping employees achieve balance.

When people believe that managers and co-workers recognize their lives outside work are important, commitment skyrockets. Don't treat people like robots, and they won't act like them. Treat people as you'd want to be treated. As one work/life expert says, you want people to feel like they're working *with* you, not just *for* you.

And Aon Consulting's experts suggest that HR leaders evaluate plans and proposals for work/life-balance initiatives carefully before rolling them out because what you think is a priority, might not be a priority with your workforce. Establish a high level of employee interest and desire for such programs. Then give 'em what they want, but attach a price tag: high performance.

# Health Care on the

# Home Front

HR professionals increasingly are adding home health-care to their benefits plans. Employees can get back to work faster after a disabling event, and HR lowers its overall health-care costs.

## By Nancy Jackson

**W**hether an employee seeks medical care because of a nasty roller-blading spill or needs an emergency quadruple bypass operation, any time an employee is admitted to a hospital is cause for employer concern. According to the Washington, D-C.-based American Hospital Association, one inpatient day of eight hours or less in the hospital costs an average of $1,968, and one 24-hour stay costs approximately $9,228. Add to that additional medical care, lost time, monitoring for re-

turn-to-work, replacement workers and the overall impact on health-insurance premiums, and employers are motivated to help employees recover from illness or injury as quickly as possible.

As human resources professionals struggle to control skyrocketing health-care costs, many are finding a key strategy is decreasing hospitalization with the use of home health-care services. Home health-care companies employ health-care professionals and other trained personnel who work with patients and their families at home to help patients achieve their maximum level of health. Although home health-care encompasses a broad range of services from skilled nursing care to home medical-equipment repair, its main advantage is bringing necessary hospital services home to the patient—rather than allowing the patient to linger in the hospital.

Home health-care is the fastest growing segment of the health-care industry, and for good reason. Patients are finding that home health-care helps them heal in their home environments, teaches them to manage their injuries or illnesses and educates family members on how to be caregivers.

According to the Congressional Budget Office, national expenditures for all home health-care services were estimated at $36 billion in 1996 and are expected to grow an average of 13 percent per year through the year 2005. The Washington, D.C.-based National Association for Home Care, the largest home health-care industry group, reports that the number of home-health agencies in the United States grew from 1,100 in 1963 to more than 17,500 in 1995. The U.S. Labor Department expects home health-care to grow at the fastest rate of any industry through 2002.

The benefits of home health-care aside, the rise in its utilization is largely due to the increased use of managed care. In 1996, 77 percent of employees who have health insurance through their work were covered by a managed-care plan, according to William M. Mercer, a health-care benefits consulting firm based in New York City. Managed care falls into the categories of health maintenance organizations (HMOs), preferred provider organizations (PPOs) and point-of-service (POS) plans.

Approximately 27 percent of employees in 1996 were covered by HMOs, which restrict services to health-care providers chosen by the HMO; 31 percent were covered by PPOs, which provide discounted health-care services if the employee chooses health-care providers from the PPO network; and 19 percent were covered by POS plans, which allow employees to choose out-of-network providers at a higher out-of-pocket cost.

Managed-care organizations restrain health-care costs by scrutinizing treatment through utilization review and case management, assuring employers that pay for health insurance that employees receive only those services that are medically necessary. In short, the rise in managed care has led to the rise in home health-care providers, who either provide services as subcontractors to managed-care companies or directly to employers who buy the services home health-care companies provide and offer them to their employees, retirees and other dependents. As the purchaser of health-care services, either directly or indirectly, HR managers should be savvy about the benefits of home health-care and incorporate such care into their health-care strategies through their insurance contracts where warranted.

**Contracting with home health-care providers.** Managed-care organizations contract with home health-care providers to coordinate services delivered to patients in their homes. Contractual arrangements vary. Pacificare Health Systems Inc., a large HMO based in Cypress, California, contracts directly with individual home health-care agencies and home medical-equipment providers to deliver services to employees and dependents enrolled in the health plan.

Oakland, California-based Kaiser Permanente, the nation's largest HMO, for example, contracts with Apria Healthcare, a large provider of home health-care products and services with 350 branches in 50 states, covering more than one million patients. Thirty-five percent of Apria's business comes from managed-care organizations, 22 percent from patients covered either by traditional indemnity insurance or paying out-of-pocket, and 43 percent from Medicare and Medicaid.

Mario LaCute, president of CareLink and president of Seeley Medical of Andover, Ohio, a home health-care provider, says, "Home health-care is the most cost-effective component of health care today on a dollar-for-dollar basis when compared with hospital or skilled-nursing home health-care. Ultimately that translates to the employer as a lower cost per insured employee per month."

Representatives of home health-care companies work with physicians, discharge planners, nurses, social workers, therapists and other health-care professionals to select and provide the services patients need. They also set up and educate patients on equipment use. Generally, primary-care physicians who coordinate care for patients enrolled in an HMO file for the appropriate approvals for home health-care. Other managed-care plans follow a wide variety of procedures for authorizing payment for home health-care services, but the responsibility lies with the patient to verify coverage. Just because the patient's doctor recommends certain services doesn't necessarily mean the patient's insurance covers those services. Many home health-care providers help patients and their families verify their insurance to be sure requested services are covered *before* they're discharged from the hospital. They also may help patients monitor care usage if their insurance coverage has a dollar limit on home health-care services.

Some home health-care providers offer a broad spectrum of services. Others fall into the two categories of home-health agencies and home medical-equipment suppliers.

Home-health agencies provide nursing, occupational, speech and respiratory therapies, and personal services that include home-health aides who provide assistance with bathing, cooking and other daily living activities. Home medical-equipment suppliers provide equipment, services, education and caregiver training necessary for the successful use of home medical equipment. They also provide follow-up services and equipment repair and maintenance as part of the covered service.

Jim Liken, president of Liken Home Medical of Pittsburgh, a home medical-equipment provider, says, "Home health-care providers deal directly with the patient and the family at home. [Our staff] can make a significant impact by helping people understand what positive things they can do for their health and help them learn to manage their diseases."

Specific home health-care services may include oxygen and respiratory programs, home nursing care, physical therapy, infusion therapy, medical supplies, hospice care, home diagnostic and pediatric moni-

# Home Health-care: How Well Are Your Employees Covered?

Home health-care services generally are rolled into a company's overall health-insurance benefits package, but specific coverage can be negotiated. When you're ready to renew your policy you might be smart to ask these questions:

1. *How does the managed-care organization check accreditation of home health-care providers?*

Federal and state rules that govern care in nursing homes don't apply in private homes. The Joint Commission on Accreditation of Healthcare Organizations based in Oakbrook Terrace, Illinois (www.jcaho.org) accredits home health-care providers, but accreditation is voluntary. Many managed-care organizations are now pressuring home health-care providers to provide accreditation and other credentials.

2. *What home health-care services are provided?*

Many policies cover skilled nursing care. Find out if your policy also covers such services as physical, occupational, speech and respiratory therapies, home-health aides, and such medical equipment as wheelchairs, adjustable beds and traction devices.

3. *Are there limits to the amount of services a patient can receive?*

Some policies have dollar limits per episode or per year.

4. *What are the grievance procedures?*

Representatives of the organization should provide satisfactory responses to patients and patient advocates concerning coverage of home health-care services.

—NJ

toring, and disease-management programs. Although these processes and therapies can be complicated to administer and maintain at home, many factors are pushing home-care benefits for the patients who need them and the employers that pay for them.

**The use of home health-care services is growing.** The growth of home health-care services is being driven by a combination of demographic, technological, economic and consumer trends. Demographic considerations include the aging of the U.S. population, the increase in opportunities for Americans with disabilities and higher survival rates for premature and low birth-weight infants.

Advances in medical technology have reduced hospital lengths of stay and have enabled physicians to perform more surgery in outpatient settings. Manufacturers of home medical equipment continue to invest significant research and development resources to improve or develop devices and products to help those who have a condition that requires home health-care or special equipment. Many products once found only in hospitals and skilled nursing facilities are now miniaturized, portable and less expensive, allowing for equipment to be installed in the home. Among other devices, these include portable oxygen cylinders, home infusion therapy equipment and prosthetics.

Home health-care services are often more cost-effective than institutional care while providing a high level of satisfaction among employee patients. A 1991 study by Aetna Life & Casualty Co. found that home health-care resulted in a savings of approximately $20,000 per patient per month for AIDS patients and approximately $40,000 per patient per month for infants with breathing problems, over the same care provided in a hospital. A study conducted in 1991 and commissioned by the National Association of Medical Equipment Suppliers, an organization of home medical-equipment suppliers based in Alexandria, Virginia, compared home health-care with hospital care for three conditions responsive to home medical care. The potential cost savings of home health-care compared with institutional care for a hip fracture, for example, was $2,300 per episode. Multiplied by the 250,000 diagnoses of hip fractures in America each year, the annual potential savings amounts to $575 million a year.

Pat Alba, director of risk management for the City of Corpus Christi, Texas, is responsible for health plans that cover 3,200 employees and 8,000 insured lives, including dependents and retirees. Until March 1996, the city was self-insured and contracted home health-care agencies directly when an employee or dependent needed home health-care.

"That required hands-on management for us," Alba says. "We talked to the doctors and hired a case-management nurse to coordinate home health-care. Then we switched to Humana Health Plans, with the home health-care benefits rolled into the managed-care package. When we negotiated the health coverage, we told them we wanted to duplicate the plan we had because we cover our police force and firefighters as well as civilian workers. Now we leave it up to [Humana managers] if they feel that home health-care is more appropriate than staying longer in the hospital or going to a nursing home. We rarely get complaints that employees weren't provided with what they need." Educating employees about their health-care options and coverage goes a long way toward improving their quality of life. It also helps HR manage the health-care delivery process.

**Managing home health-care.** Quality of life is the driving force behind many Americans' preference for home health-care. The purpose of home health-care is to bring a sense of independence to patients who would otherwise be challenged beyond their capacity. Most people prefer to remain in their homes, surrounded by their families, possessions and pets. A study conducted in 1991 by the American Association of Retired Persons, a Washington-based national organization of Americans over age 50, indicated that 72 percent of people prefer to recuperate at home from a serious accident or illness.

Home health-care offers a care plan that can be tailored to the patient's needs and

---

A 1991 study by AARP says 72 percent of people over age 50 prefer to recuperate at home from a serious accident or illness.

---

provides the ability to control health-care options. Along with educational programs through physicians and medical groups, home health-care helps patients self-manage and prevent or minimize potential health crises such as debilitating episodes requiring hospitalization for those managing diabetes or respiratory illnesses.

Stamford, Connecticut-based GTE provides health coverage for about 83,000 domestic employees and 58,000 retirees, totaling about 250,000 covered lives, including dependents. Mark Bush, a regional health-care manager based in Stamford who's responsible for GTE's northeast region says, "GTE spends a significant amount of time and corporate resources in selecting and evaluating the quality of the health coverage we offer our employees. We look at health plans that aren't just

managing costs, but managing care through appropriate case management."

Case managers employed by the managed-care organization look at each case separately to assess the nature of the illness or injury and what support the patient needs at home. Bush says, "Provided appropriate care can be delivered in the home, anyone who can get out of the hospital and go home to be with his or her family is definitely better for it. This, and the corresponding cost differential between treatment at home and treatment at the hospital, are the driving forces in the rise in our use of home health-care. When we select a managed-care company, we expect it to manage the delivery of care to our employees to provide the highest quality, [most] cost-effective care available. A component of that care-management strategy is home health-care."

Although home health-care services are far less expensive than hospitalization or nursing-home care, they still can be expensive, especially for chronic illnesses or in caring for the senior population. Through the increased use of managed care and case management, employers gain control over proper utilization of home health-care benefits. When appropriately managed, home health-care can effectively help employees return to work as quickly as possible while meeting the challenge of delivering high-quality, cost-effective health care.

---

*Nancy Jackson is a free-lance writer based in Los Angeles. E-mail laabsj@workforcemag. com to forward comments to the editor.*

# Hands-On

## Health Care Benefits

*By Forrest Briscoe and James Maxwell*

*Orlando-area employers' partnerships with health care plans and providers have lowered costs and boosted quality.*

In the mid-1990s, the rapid spread of managed care appeared to clamp the lid on soaring health care costs, providing employers with much-needed relief.

In the late 1990s, however, things aren't quite as rosy. Further dramatic health care cost savings may be impossible: Corporate benefits departments have already steered the majority of employees into more affordable managed care plans, according to a 1997 KPMG Peat Marwick study. And recent data indicate that premiums have resumed significant increases.

As a result, the latest trend in health benefits is to cut—cut benefit components, cut health plan options or cut company contributions to premiums.

Should your HR policy follow suit? Not necessarily. There is a compelling reason to continue offering employees health benefits: the tightest labor market in 25 years.

Health benefits are a key ingredient in hiring and retaining the best employees available. Having downsized through the early and mid-1990s, many large firms are not keen to lose their prized employees to firms with better benefits.

Paying for relatively generous health care coverage may well be worth the cost.

But how can employers overcome the trade-offs between health benefit costs and labor market advantages?

## Lessons from a Fast-Growing Region

Some innovative ideas have emerged from Orlando, Fla., where the labor market during the past 10 years has presaged what much of the rest of the nation is now facing.

Orlando's employment grew a remarkable 28 percent during the decade preceding 1995. That year, the region's unemployment rate was estimated at approximately 4 percent, compared with 6 percent nationally. (Recent figures were 2.9 percent and 4.4 percent, respectively.) An HR official at one regional firm says, "We have 24-hour job hotlines and massive job fairs, and we still can't fill our hiring needs fast enough."

Becky Cherney, director of the Central Florida Health Care Coalition, predicts, "The labor shortage now is nothing compared to what it will be in four or five years."

The coalition of Orlando employers tries to provide generous health benefits—instead of cutting them—while simultaneously pushing to improve value in the health care system itself. These employers have taken an active interest in the cost and

> 'Improving the health care delivery system is the only way to contain costs in health benefits.'
> -Becky Cherney

quality of service provided by the region's health insurers, hospitals and physician groups.

In so doing, they have discovered opportunities to lower health care costs and raise quality. Since they pay the lion's share of their employees' health benefits, these efforts are reflected in their bottom lines.

As Cherney points out, "Improving the health care delivery system is the only way to contain costs in health benefits. Discounts, increased co-pays and so on merely shift the costs without changing the delivery system—and may come back to haunt you."

## Partnering To Improve Value

By instigating data collection and analysis at the health plan, hospital, group practice and physician levels, Orlando employers found opportunities to increase the value of their health care services.

The cost savings added up to millions of dollars; the improvements in the quality of care are priceless.

The Central Florida Health Care Coalition, which includes Disney World and other large employers, used quality data to drive changes in the health care delivery system. Concentrating on the two hospital systems used by its employees, the coalition collected data on diverse quality measures—such as rates of cesarean section, cardiac catheterization and blood pressure screenings.

Staff from the hospital systems and the employer coalition worked together on the project. Using data analysis software, they looked for variations in quality and utilization, identifying averages, benchmarks and unusual costs. The results were reported to hospital system officials, prompting greater awareness and often resulting in remedying action.

The benefits director of one participating employer was amazed at the changes made by a hospital system, "simply as a result of sharing our results with them." HR staff at Disney believe quality has im-

proved substantially. Excessive use of many procedures dropped dramatically. Cesarean section rates dropped from 36 percent to 21 percent in one year. Wasteful practices were identified and stopped, such as sterilizing and assembling 10 obsolete hysterectomy tools for each operation when surgeons used only one.

One large coalition participant, Orange County Public Schools (OCPS), pushed this idea further by encouraging data collection and analysis at the individual physician level. It helped develop quality performance criteria used to examine physician practices. This pioneering physician-level focus represents an investment of resources that many health plans do not have incentives to engage in without the joint interest of an active purchaser.

OCPS looked first at the doctors within its health plan hospitals and discovered big differences in physicians' practices—which resulted in wide variations in cost and quality. The results were shared with providers, individual physicians and other coalition employers.

Sharing the data led to measurable voluntary improvements. Poor-performing physicians and even those with average performance both improved.

Much of the initial investment required to start data collection was borne by the health plans and hospitals themselves; these costs would have been reflected in higher employer premium costs had the program not saved money. But the savings did materialize—quickly. As a direct result of the program, one participating hospital system saved $12 million in annual Medicare expenditures within two years.

Skeptical HR directors may fear that improvements paid for by their companies will be enjoyed by other regional employers at no cost to them. But this misses a crucial point: The major employers in any given region will draw on that community for labor over the long haul, so a short-term approach to a community's health may backfire in the not-too-distant future. "Employee turnover shouldn't be an excuse to avoid implementing prevention programs," says Cherney.

Partnering may be a particularly good idea if workers don't usually migrate out of your region. "People change jobs but rarely do they leave central Florida," says Cherney, "so every employer must work toward a healthier workforce."

## The HR Advantage of Partnering

The results of the efforts in Orlando are impressive. Turnover at Disney is a third of the service sector average of 100 percent per year, and absenteeism is well below that

of competitors. Further, healthier and more satisfied workers exhibit higher morale—a key ingredient in Disney's customer service and business success.

Other coalition participants report similar results. Darden Restaurants, owner of Red Lobster and The Olive Garden, provides generous health benefits in an industry that typically offers few benefits. John Reiker, Darden's benefits director, believes this generosity results in better recruitment and in reduced turnover and absenteeism, which are typically high in the restaurant industry.

Through the partnership approach, coalition participants are able to demonstrate that they are actively working in their employees' interest. When employees express concern over changes in their health care, employers are able to work out compromises through partnerships that would otherwise not have been possible. Disney, for example, was able to include an additional hospital system in its HMO offering and restore several of employees' regular physicians to their point-of-service plan option.

## How To Partner

Following the Orlando example by the book would be unwise for most employers. Labor needs vary by industry and firm; health care systems vary greatly by region. Nonetheless, any employer squeezed between labor market trends and health care costs can benefit from the following partnering advice.

**Capture the strategic value of your health benefits.** Develop a strategy that links your health benefits to your broader business goals, then communicate this vision to senior management.

Start by asking yourself, "Why do we offer health benefits?" As demonstrated in Orlando, one answer may be to attract and retain productive workers. Or you may find that health benefits can help your firm achieve specific business goals. For example, lower back strain may be a special concern for your workers, or other disability or absenteeism problems should be addressed through health benefits.

Of course, you should factor in changes in your health benefit goals as a result of company restructuring or reengineering of other HR policies.

Developing and sharing a health benefits strategy across the firm will help combat the notion that health benefits are "costs" that need to be minimized. It is important to remind senior managers of the value of health benefits. The short-term savings from scaling them back may be tempting, but the risks of a lower-caliber workforce, higher turnover, less healthy workers and less enthusiastic customer service must be considered.

# To **Join** or not to **Join**?

Health care conditions already exist in many regions of the country. How do you know if it is a good idea to join a local coalition?

Before joining, compare your health benefits goals with those of the other organizations involved. The fact that coalition members are in different industries may not be important. Widely different organizations have found common health benefits goals and worked together successfully in coalitions.

Make sure the broad goals of the coalition match up with your needs. Coalition goals can vary greatly. For example, some coalitions focus on improving the quality of health care provided by members' health plans but do not try to exercise their combined purchasing power.

Just as individual organizations should clarify their health benefit goals before embarking on a partnership, employer health care coalitions should consider their joint goals—both in terms of providing benefits to workers in the community and in specific clinical terms. For instance, the Central Florida Health Care Coalition has focused with its partner health plans on improving the diagnosis and treatment of depression and ulcers because it believes these to be key issues in its members' employee populations.

For more information on starting or joining a business coalition of health plan sponsors contact the National Business Coalition on Health at (202) 775-9300 or visit its web site at http://www.nbch.org.

---

**Understand your managed care market(s).** To capture the value of your health benefits strategy, you need to understand the managed care markets where your firm is located. Managed care markets are in flux, so you should examine health plans' financial stability, reputation among other employers and benefit features.

To determine the quality of a health plan, look for accreditation by national certification organizations, such as the National Committee for Quality Assurance, and for high ratings under the Health Plan Employer Data and Information Set. In addition, look at the quality ratings of individual hospitals and physicians that serve large numbers of your employees.

Understanding your managed care market may require expertise that your staff does not possess. If so, consider adding an expert to your staff, contracting with managed care consultants or pooling resources in a purchasers' coalition. Coalitions, which already exist in many regions, often retain consulting services. (For more on joining a coalition, *see box*, "To Join or Not to Join.")

If you choose to hire consultants, you'll find no shortage of approaches. Some large benefits consultants now focus on health plan "partnerships." A few work with firms to help them determine, quantitatively, the effect of their health care benefits on productivity, service and profits.

**Work to build health plan partnership(s).** Partnering means forging a common understanding and developing trust. You will need to stick with health plans for a few years while you work jointly to improve value and quality. Switching plans each year to save a few dollars makes it difficult to implement substantive changes or develop trust and a shared vision.

Ideally, both sides will invest time and resources in the partnership and both sides will reap the rewards of higher quality and lower cost.

To develop a strong partnership, you need to clearly articulate your health benefits strategy. For instance, you may believe that retaining employees' access to their current physicians is crucial. But health plans often restructure their provider networks. A viable partnership can provide early warning of such changes and effective ways to address them. (For example, OCPS learned that one of its health plans was going to drop a dozen physicians from its network. It quickly intervened to preserve its enrollees' access to them.)

Formulating your priorities and communicating them to the health plan from the outset will make it easier to negotiate mutually agreeable solutions when difficulties inevitably arise. You'll waste less time and energy, and employees will enjoy better outcomes.

Your partnership will involve quality measurement, continuous quality improvement and rewards for quality performance. This will require you to examine hospital and physician practices.

In Orlando, measuring hospital and physician quality incurred administrative costs, some of which were borne by employers. However, the rewards were huge. Physicians changed their practices after seeing how they compared to their colleagues'. Quality rose as costs dropped.

Quality measurement can be a daunting task, but you can analytically monitor quality of care through clinical tracking systems and software packages.

Remember that your goal is monitoring progress—not finding poor performance. You should be sharing data with physicians

so you can provide constructive information on the differences between them.

In the early years of data collection, make sure to keep an open dialogue on the meaning of the results. Many factors can affect interpretation of such data, including the overall health of the community and each physician's patient population. After an initial round of data collection, however,

> *Switching health plans each year to save a few dollars makes it difficult to implement substantive changes or develop trust and a shared vision.*

the focus will be on continuous quality improvement.

After working out a measurement plan, follow up with the joint process of continuous quality improvement. With your partner(s), set goals and target dates for priority areas and overall improvements. Prevention and chronic disease management are often priorities for improvement. In Orlando, cesarean section rates were higher than national averages, so they became a focus for improvement.

Structuring rewards based on quality performance is an important component of many successful partnerships. Health plans, hospitals and physicians all can have financial or other rewards linked to performance on quality measures. Health plans and hospitals often have a portion of total payments (3 percent, for example) put "at risk," contingent on a specified improvement in selected components or overall quality. Some employers link this reward to results of employee satisfaction surveys as well as more traditional quality performance components.

Quality improvement can also go beyond the traditional methods relied on in the health care delivery system. Based on your organization's health benefits goals, you can work with health plan partners to focus on the specific needs of your employee population. These needs may relate to absenteeism, workplace productivity, disability claims, mental health, family issues, etc.

Again, early communication of your strategic interests will enable you to work in continual partnership to address these specific needs and improve overall clinical quality. The result should be a tangible contribution to your corporate goals through a healthy and productive workforce. This focus on productivity and corporate goals is new to health benefits and is sure to grow in importance as strategic thinking spreads through the HR ranks.

## Conclusion

Experts predict that the current labor shortage will continue for many years. In this context, it will be important for HR departments to leverage health benefits as a tool for attracting, retaining and maximizing an effective workforce.

To get the most out of your health benefits, develop and communicate a health benefits strategy. Then get the expertise you need to understand your relevant managed care markets.

For some employers, it will make sense to create and leverage health plan partnerships to improve quality and cut costs in the region's health care systems. As Orlando-area employers have shown, such efforts may require some out-of-the-box thinking, but they can pay huge dividends for employers.

*Forrest Briscoe was project manager at John Snow Inc., a Boston-based health care consulting firm, for research on how U.S. companies purchased health care benefits. He is now a doctoral student in HR at the MIT Sloan School of Management. James Maxwell is director of health policy and management at John Snow, where he studies corporate health benefits.*

# Unit 6

## Key Points to Consider

❖ What trends do you see emerging from collective bargaining between organized labor and management in the next 5 to 10 years? Discuss the possibility that some concessions won by management may have to be given back to workers.

❖ Taking disciplinary action is often one of the most difficult and unpleasant activities that a manager must do. If you were a manager, how would you take disciplinary action? If you were the employee being disciplined, what would you do? What conflicts do you see in your responses to these two questions?

❖ What are some of the advantages of hiring temporary employees? How would you feel about being one? For how long would you agree to temporary status?

❖ Are corporations equally responsible for a situation where bribery exists? Why or why not?

 **Links**   **www.dushkin.com/online/**

These sites are annotated on pages 4 and 5.

The American labor movement has a long history dating back to the start of the industrial revolution. That history has been marked by turmoil and violence as workers sought to press their demands on business owners, whether represented by managers or entrepreneurs. The American labor movement exists because working conditions, pay, and benefits were very poor during the early years of the industrial revolution in both the United States and the rest of the world. It should be remembered that the American labor movement is only a small part of a broader, worldwide labor movement that includes most Western European societies. The working conditions under which the first American industrial workers labored would be unacceptable today. Child labor was common. There are documented instances of 6- and 7-year-old children, chained to machines for 12 hours a day, 6 days a week, who threw themselves into the machines—choosing death over life in the dehumanized and mechanized existence of the early factory. Conditions in some factories in the North prior to the Civil War were so infamous that Southern congressmen used them as a justification for the institution of slavery. Slaves sometimes lived in better conditions than the factory workers of New England and many other Northern states.

Unions exist because workers sought a better working environment and a better standard of living. Companies often took advantage of employees, and the government sided with management and the owners, frequently quelling strikes and other forms of labor protest initiated by the workers. Such incidents as the Pullman Strike, the Haymarket Square Riot, and the Homestead Strike exemplify the struggle of the American labor movement to achieve recognition and success in the attempt to improve the lives of all workers, whether unionized or not. The victories of labor have been hard-fought and hard-won. During the past hundred years, the fortunes of the American labor movement have varied. Today, its fortunes are in decline, but unions are trying to make a comeback by unionizing workers in industries that have not been unionized in the past.

Unions have been able to achieve their gains through the mechanism of collective bargaining. The individual has very little bargaining power when compared to a company, especially huge companies such as General Motors or AT&T. Collective bargaining allows workers to pool their collective resources and power to bargain with the corporation on a more equal footing. Unfortunately for the unions, many of the industries in which they are strongest are in decline. New leadership is necessary if the American labor movement is to survive and rebound in the next century, and if it is to serve as a useful organ of society.

A union's ultimate weapon in contract negotiations, the strike, represents a complete breakdown of discipline from management's perspective. Disciplinary situations are almost always unpleasant, and today they can often lead to court cases, with all of the attendant legal questions and problems. A key to effective disciplinary action is documentation of employees' actions and the steps that were taken to correct them. Management needs to trust its employees; if it does not, the work environment becomes untenable for both labor and management. Discipline in any organization needs to be based on the values of the organization and on the law. Organizations that do not do this are going to have a difficult time enforcing discipline.

During the past 15 years, primarily as a result of the dislocations in the job market, temporary workers became available to organizations. While there were certain advantages to this situation for the employer, times have now changed and the number of temporary workers is in decline. How companies who have depended on these workers will deal with this new situation remains to be seen as well as how temporary employee firms are going to find additional temporary workers to fill job openings.

Finally, there is the issue of ethics. How companies treat their employees and their customers is going to be of increasing concern in the future. Ethical behavior will be at a premium, especially in the international environment where questionable practices, by American standards, have often been employed as a matter of course. Bribery as a way of doing business is going to be less tolerated in the future than has been the case in the past.

# Fostering Employee/Management Relationships

# UNIONS: New Activism or Old Adversarial Approach?

Organized labor is back to an old-style adversarial relationship with management that damages U.S. competitiveness in the global market, says management attorney Steve Cabot. But the head of the AFL-CIO's Center for Workplace Democracy says what labor is undergoing is a renewed activism designed to ensure that workers get their fair share of what they contribute to their employers' success.

Cabot, chairman of the labor relations and employment law department of Harvey, Pennington, Cabot, Griffith & Renneisen in Philadelphia and author of *Everybody Wins* (Excalibur Business Press, 1998), cites these events as evidence of an adversarial approach:

- Strikes last year at Northwest Airlines, General Motors Corp. and Bell Atlantic represent the biggest surge in walkouts in years. This year pilots at American Airlines staged a 10-day "sick-out" that forced the airline to cancel more than 6,600 flights.
- In February Saturn employees voted out of office all local union leaders who had made Saturn one of the country's most prominent experiments in labor relations. They voted in United Auto Worker leaders who advocated a more traditional relationship with management. The new leaders have said Saturn should stop linking pay to productivity and should adopt many of the work rules that are in place at other GM factories.
- Union membership remains only about 14 percent of the U.S. population, but under President John J. Sweeney the AFL-CIO has allocated $20 million a year for organizing, up from $2.5 million annually before he was elected in 1995. In February the Service Employees International Union won labor's biggest organizing drive in 60 years when

74,000 Los Angeles home care workers voted to join the union.

Cabot believes what is occurring is all part of a master plan by the AFL-CIO. "There was a period of time where leaders of the AFL espoused cooperation a la Saturn. But leaders saw that membership was declining and the union movement needed to do different things to revitalize itself. So the labor movement is going back to the old way.

"Why did Saturn workers do what they did? Why was there a strike at UPS, which was futile and silly and had no winner? Why did they have the strike at General Motors? Why was there the futile and stupid strike at American Airlines? Because, from the perspective of organized labor, they needed a tougher position at the bargaining table to get higher visibility for organizing purposes. A tougher stance and highly vis-

ible stikes get the labor movement to the forefront," he says.

## SPREADING THE WORD

Labor organizers today are better trained and organizing campaigns are more targeted, Cabot says, citing the successful health care workers organizing drive that was begun by Sweeney when he was head of SEIU. The union is now focusing on 50,000 home health care workers in New York City.

"The AFL would like to see unionism spread to virtually every industry, to every unorganized worker in America. It's scary. Janitors and law firms and doctors are joining unions. There is growth, or strong potential for growth, for a broader spectrum of employees [to be represented]. In spite of the good economy, employees can get disgruntled."

## AVOIDING THE UNION LABEL

Find out directly from employees what they need and what they think and they won't be interested in joining a union, says management attorney Steve Cabot. "The most powerful word in a proactive vocabulary is a very tiny one—ask."

Your company's strategy should be predicated on asking people how they feel about what is going on in the company, Cabot says. He recommends at least twice a year asking employees a short series of questions about their views. The answers not only give you important information, the process itself is motivating for employees.

By asking, you can test your perception of whether your communication efforts are effective. Ask about morale—do employees enjoy coming to work? Do they trust upper management? Do they perceive supervisory practices to be evenhanded? Do they feel everyone is working toward the same goal? Do employees believe they are receiving the training they need? Do they see management trying to help them be the best employees they can be?

In the area of pay and benefits, don't ask if employees want more, ask "to what extent do you feel your pay and benefits are comparable to what other people in the area make?"

Don't just have a survey program, Cabot adds. "Be sure to have feedback. Make it a link in the chain, a part of the process."

It's management that is dropping the ball, says Cabot, who travels around the country speaking to employer groups. "An employer who gets a union deserves one."

Management needs to combat unionism if the United States is to sustain its current prosperity, he believes, because if companies get bogged down by labor strife it will hurt morale and productivity. To avoid that, "companies need to demonstrate to employees that they are indeed the most important resource.

talks about, says Nancy Mills, director of the AFL-CIO's Center for Workplace Democracy. "If employers can't succeed, then our members can't succeed."

## PAVING THE HIGH ROAD

The center was created two years ago to "assist unions to assist employers to pave the high road to economic competitiveness. We want our employers to be successful, but we want them to take the high road. We want them not just to

current labor law, according to Mills. "There are 10,000 workers who get fired illegally for organizing, and people wonder why we're adversarial. We're trying to assert workers' right to have a voice that most companies want to deny."

Once organized, the labor/management relationship doesn't have to remain adversarial, but she admits, "it takes a while to establish a different way." The vast majority of contract disputes are settled peacefully. "A strike is a sign that the balance has broken down between workers and management."

## FOCUS ON PARTNERSHIP

Mills believes more attention should be paid to the many labor/management partnerships that are working—the ones that help companies succeed and make sure workers get their fair share.

But when workers are not able to have a say in the decision making, she says, it's no wonder they don't want their compensation tied to the outcome of those decisions. "When we have huge fights it is because management is not making decisions that will keep the company well, or because we think management can afford to treat workers better."

For example, although workers at Saturn decided to go back to what has been called a traditional agreement, "it looks nothing like what most people think of as traditional. The struggle between the union and the company was over a difference of opinion of how resources should be spent—whether resources should be spent on marketing or on research or development. The union was on the side of research and development because it believed that to stay competitive the company had to develop new products. Most Americans don't think unions even get into that kind of debate."

The AFL-CIO new leadership team is committed to this new kind of activism that has paid off in the political and organizing arena, Mills says. "For the first time in 10 years we had a significant organizing win and we are winning more elections and doing more organizing. Workers are asserting their needs, but that is not the same as saying we are anti-employer."

---

# MEMBERSHIP STATISTICS:

In 1998 there were 16.2 million union members in the United States.

The share of wage and salary workers who were union members averaged 13.9 percent in 1998, compared with 14.1 percent a year earlier. In 1983, the first year for which comparable data are available, union membership was 20.1 percent.

In 1998 government workers continued to have a much higher unionization rate than their private sector counterparts, 37.5 percent versus 9.5 percent.

Median weekly earnings for union members who work full time were about a third higher than the median for nonunion workers.

# WORK STOPPAGES:

All measures of major work stoppage activity (including both strikes and lockouts by employers) rose in 1998, although they were low by historical standards.

Thirty-four major work stoppages began during 1998, idling 387,000 workers. In 1997 there were 29 stoppages and 339,000 workers idled.

The 1998 stoppage involving the most workers was between General Motors Corp. and the United Automobile Workers, representing 152,000 workers, most of whom were out for more than four weeks. Another large stoppage was between Bell Atlantic Corp. and the Communication Workers of America; it involved 73,000 workers and lasted three days.

At the beginning of 1999 the Allied Pilots Association launched a protest against American Airlines over American's acquisition of Reno Air.

*(Source: The U.S. Department of Labor's Bureau of Labor Statistics.)*

---

Words must be matched by actions. We spend a great amount of time developing business plans, but over 98 percent of companies do not have a formal labor relations plan, with responsibility and accountability built in."

Employees today want to be involved in the process, he says. "They say 'ask us how we feel. Don't treat us like children—lead us. Don't treat us like mushrooms; we have opinions,' " he says. If companies ask employees for input and listen to their responses, in turn employees will ask themselves, "What do I need a labor union for?"

Unions are not trying to hurt companies, but are trying to make sure employees are part of the process Cabot

succeed at any cost, but to invest in the workforce and to create high quality goods and services."

The creation of her department shows "a new activism, not a new adversarialism. It shows that working people don't want to be taken for granted anymore. It's not saber rattling. It equates with our commitment to represent the needs of working families in America."

Labor management relations have always had adversarial and cooperative aspects, Mills says. "It's always adversarial when you're figuring out how to divvy up the gains. It's always going to be cooperative when you've signed an agreement."

Organizing drives in the United States have to be adversarial because of

---

*STEPHENIE OVERMAN* is a New York business writer who has a masters' degree in labor studies.

# Workers Are Not The Usual Suspects

*When employees stand accused of crimes outside the workplace, employers must be careful in deciding how to handle them.*

*By Janine S. Pouliot*

**W**hat would you do if one of your employees were arrested for shoplifting or charged with an even more serious crime?

Let's say that you fire the worker on the strength of the charge and that the employee is acquitted. Now you're the one on the legal hot spot. Your former employee could sue you for wrongful termination. And legal experts say the former worker would have a very strong case.

Because the U.S. judicial system presumes innocence until guilt is proved, employers must be careful how they handle employees accused of crimes. Jeffrey G. Allen, a Beverly Hills, Calif., employment attorney, says a company should have a policy that's fair to everyone.

Consider these steps:

**Confer with an attorney on the law in your state.** Laws on termination resulting from arrest vary widely, says Allen. For example, California requires that there be a felony conviction before an employer has grounds to terminate. Laws in Georgia, New York, Pennsylvania, and Washington dictate that an employer notify a worker before seeking information related to an arrest, he says.

**Evaluate your options.** Firing is not your only choice when a worker has been arrested. You can take no action, of course. Or you can suspend a worker with pay pending the outcome of judicial proceedings. If you suspend without pay, you would need a solid basis for doing so, and you might have to provide back pay if the person is acquitted.

**Analyze your motives for wanting to fire someone accused of a crime outside the workplace.** If the offense is unrelated to job performance, you probably have weak grounds for firing. "This is an issue of discrimination, just like any other violation of protective legislation," says Allen. "It's really no different than if you let someone go because of their religion or gender. It's unrelated information."

On the other hand, some offenses automatically place the employee under suspicion at work. "If your controller is arrested for embezzling funds from his church group, it's as related a crime as I can think of," says Allen. In such a case, an employer would have the right to begin an internal investigation into the charges.

**Ask lots of questions.** Do your homework on the charges brought against your employee, says employment attorney Rita Risser, principal at Fair Measures Management Law Consulting Group in Santa Cruz, Calif., and the author of *Stay Out of Court! The Managers Guide to Preventing Employee Lawsuits* (Prentice Hall, $19.95).

"An investigation is necessary because otherwise the information is hearsay," says Risser. "Talk to witnesses and the arresting officer, review any documentation, look at all the evidence. But the most important step is to interview the accused."

That's the step that employers typically skip, sometimes to their regret, Risser says. "Often the evidence seems overwhelmingly against the accused," she says. The employer presumes that an interview would be unnecessary because the employee would simply deny the charges. But unless the investigation is completely unbiased—and the interview can help support such a claim—a termination decision may not be upheld by the courts.

**Ensure unbiased treatment.** Be careful not to take action that discriminates on the basis of race, sex, religion, age, or any other areas covered by Title VII of the Civil Rights Act of 1964 as amended, says Paul Tobias, founder of the National Employment Lawyers Association and co-author of *Job Rights & Survival Strategies* (NERI, $19.95).

"If, for example, a black male is charged with a crime, you can't treat him any differently than you would a white male charged with the same crime. The identical policies must apply across the board," says Tobias.

**Tread softly.** Never do anything that would tarnish the employee's reputation in or out of the workplace. Otherwise you could face a defamation-of-character lawsuit. Don't tell other employees that the accused worker was fired for committing a crime if the worker hasn't been found guilty.

And don't humiliate the accused worker publicly. Says Gary Simpson, an employment attorney in Bethesda, Md.: "Don't walk the person out of your company accompanied by armed guards. Try calling him at home to discuss the issue. Why go out of your way to injure his pride and dignity?"

**Protect other workers.** Though you must safeguard the rights of the accused and shield the person from harassment by other workers, you also must protect the safety of other employees. If a worker has been charged with a violent crime, you may have reason to fear for the well-being of your staff while the worker is out on bail.

"It may be prudent during your investigation to suspend the employee with pay to separate [him or her] from your workplace," suggests Risser. "Sometimes it's absolutely critical that the accused be barred from the premises." Moreover, she adds, it's well within your rights to do so.

---

*Janine S. Pouliot is a free-lance writer in Green Bay, Wis.*

# Values-Based
# Discipline

## Gregg Guetschow

*Ignoring a directive from his department head,
a supervisor hires an additional staff member.*

*A police officer is charged with a felony for an
off-duty assault.*

*A secretary uses confidential information to assist
a family member.*

*An employee is arrested for selling drugs from
city property.*

*A subordinate accuses a department head of sexual
harassment.*

**D**espite local government managers' best efforts in the recruitment, training, and supervision of employees, incidents like these do occur. Resolution of cases involving serious misconduct requires knowledge of the proper application of sometimes-conflicting court decisions covering immunity, due process, property and liberty interests, defamation, and other issues. Further complicating matters is the increasing likelihood that disciplinary proceedings that end in termination will be challenged in court.

There is an understandable tendency to approach serious discipline cases with an eye toward minimizing legal challenges. Avoiding litigation is an inadequate measure of success, however, when applied to the whole human resources picture. It is at least as important to establish and use practices that foster a productive work environment. Resolving a discipline case while advancing the long-term interests of the organization demands a broader perspective than is typically applied in examining one discipline case

Reprinted with permission from the May 1999 issue of *Public Management* magazine, pp. 16-19. Published by the International City/County Management Association, Washington, DC.

alone. As manager of the city of Owosso, Michigan, I believe that a more constructive approach involves ensuring that the organization's labor relations practices harmonize with its values.

It is beyond the scope of this article to examine in depth the various laws and court cases with an impact on disciplinary investigations in my locality. But it will help us to consider the framework that Owosso has established within which to apply the city's values beyond service delivery into that most challenging area, employee relations.

## Organizational Culture And Values

Discovering an organization's values does not call for the skills of a cultural anthropologist. But it is important to set aside any preconceptions about what those values should be. Those of us who have been involved in local government for a few years might be excused for believing that efficiency should motivate almost all of our actions; I suspect that in many organizations the values that foster pride in accomplishing meaningful outcomes take precedence over those oriented toward saving taxpayers' money.

The discovery of an organization's values requires an understanding of its history, work processes, leadership styles, and staff interactions. Interestingly, the investigation of incidents in which outcomes differ from expectations can offer subtle clues to matters of great importance in this regard. Because problems highlight conflicts between perceived and actual values, they can serve to provide a clearer understanding of an organization's culture.

An examination of Owosso's culture has led to our identifying four primary values that traditionally have guided service delivery but that are equally relevant to the practice of employee relations. These four values are:

1. Dependability: reliably meeting expected levels of service quality and adhering to established standards of conduct.
2. Fairness: impartial treatment of citizens and employees.
3. Professionalism: applying all relevant knowledge and skills to the provision of service or to the administration of labor relations.
4. Efficiency: the most effective use of limited financial, physical, and human resources.

The application of these four values, in this order of importance, directs our procedures for addressing violations of city policies and work rules by our employees. The most serious infractions are likely to involve the use of all of the following measures.

> **I believe that a more constructive approach involves ensuring that the organization's labor relations practices harmonize with its values.**

## Confidentiality

One of the unfortunate consequences of working in the public sector is the loss of privacy. News media, complainants, citizens attending council meetings, and employees can all be expected to show curiosity over disciplinary cases involving public officials. As city manager, I expect to sacrifice a degree of privacy about employment matters that affect me personally. I do not agree that the same expectation applies to all public employees.

It is particularly important to avoid public statements that could prejudice an investigation or defame an employee. After all, we are aware that an employee might well continue in our employ. I can recall several "open-and-shut" cases involving serious misconduct that collapsed during the investigation phase. Self-serving comments made in response to the pressures of addressing a challenging situation in a public arena are inconsistent with the values that promote employee morale and teamwork.

Fairness to the employee demands applying the highest level of confidentiality to all aspects of the disciplinary case. As a result, few people apart from those directly involved in an investigation will know about the actions being taken. While we might answer questions from the media about the duty status of an employee subject to an investigation, we never report the results of the investigation. If discipline results from a citizen complaint against an employee, we inform the citizen that appropriate action has been taken but not what that action was.

## Suspension with Pay

While not all rule infractions result in a suspension with pay, those that are judged to be most serious and that could potentially result in termination of employment generally do arrive at this point. A suspension with

pay removes an employee from a work environment where his or her continued presence could disrupt the workplace and impede the timely completion of an investigation. A suspension also permits the employer to take a more thoughtful approach to the investigation because the pressure to complete it and to discipline the working employee or minimize back pay has been relieved.

To pay an employee not to work can easily be misperceived by the council, public, and other employees. And there is no question that a suspension can be costly. One especially complicated investigation that I conducted took several months to complete, and the employee involved was suspended with pay for that entire time. Such an action might be inconsistent with efficient use of public resources, particularly as unpaid suspensions are acceptable in some instances. Fairness, however, still requires suspension with pay until the investigation has been completed and discipline administered. Organizational values that favor fair treatment of employees over saving taxpayers' money must govern a procedure that, in its early stages, has not yet established guilt.

## Investigation

The investigation phase of a discipline case highlights the first three of Owosso's principal values. Complainants and other employees must be assured that all allegations of rule violations will be investigated and that the investigation will be handled fairly in an attempt to discern the truth. Professionalism requires that all assumptions about guilt or innocence, even in light of past experience with the same employee, be set aside in favor of impartiality. Further, the investigation must be done as quickly and as rigorously as possible.

A professional investigation involves a decision about who is the most appropriate individual to conduct it. One of the first considerations is whether some or all of the task should be handled internally. Because of actual or perceived bias, the absence of the skills needed to complete a thorough investigation, or the lack of time to devote to completing it quickly, fair and professional treatment of the employee might require the use of outside investigators.

Even if an investigation is conducted internally, a decision must be made about who is most qualified to conduct it. Lower-level supervisors or department heads probably can handle minor rule infractions, but more serious matters require persons higher in the organization. In one of our cases, the employee relations director and I spent a month on an investigation that required interviewing every full- and part-time employee in a department. In another case, I was the only individual qualified to conduct an investigation that proceeded over several months. To devote such time makes the completion of other work tasks difficult. Organizational efficiency, however, comes behind other values when conducting this phase of the disciplinary process.

## Hearing

The Supreme Court's decision in *Cleveland Board of Education v. Loudermill* granted employees subject to suspension or termination for misconduct the right to a hearing on pending charges. The rigor that such a procedure requires is an important step in obtaining all information relevant to an investigation before dealing out discipline. Thus, Owosso has begun using the hearing in some cases not expected to result in a suspension or termination of employment.

When properly used, the elements of the hearing process – a written statement of pending charges, a reference to the rules violated, a description of possible discipline, the opportunity to present evidence – serve to advance the cause of a fair and professional investigation. If our purpose in conducting an investigation was to avoid legal challenges, this step in the process could become a rather perfunctory one. Our experience in Owosso, however, has demonstrated that concentrating on fairness and professionalism at this step has proven invaluable.

Information that we have received during our hearings has resulted in dropping some or all charges in certain cases, or in instituting discipline that was much milder than originally anticipated. While these outcomes have served the purpose of avoiding litigation, they also have helped to give a more favorable impression of the overall discipline process. An attorney representing an employee in one such hearing later commented to a colleague on the fairness of the city in handling disciplinary investigations.

## Discipline

Once a hearing has been conducted, a decision is made as to what discipline, if any, is warranted. While most cases for which we have used these procedures have appeared at first blush to warrant termination, only one employee has in fact been fired. In other cases, discipline has ranged from no action at all to suspension without pay for 30 days.

To value dependability is to assure that inappropriate conduct will generally result in discipline. Fairness requires that the punishment fit the crime and that, whenever possible, the discipline be an appropriate means of restoring the employee to work. In most cases in which we have focused on these values, discipline has gone unchallenged. In one instance, the spouse of an employee who received a lengthy unpaid suspension thanked me for my handling of the case.

Fairness and professionalism also require that we resist the temptation to use excessive discipline in an effort to satisfy complainants or the public or to set an example. In one recent case involving possible criminal activities by an employee, a law enforcement official from another jurisdiction requested information about our disciplinary proceedings and encouraged our termination of the employee. While cooperating with the investigation so as to achieve a felony conviction might have served the aim of resolving the employment issues we faced, it was contrary to everything we believed important about the way in which we handle personnel issues. We insisted on a subpoena for our disciplinary investigation file (it was never produced), and we resisted all attempts at influencing our decision. The employee was found innocent of the most serious charges against him and remains on our staff.

## Grievance Arbitration

While we might wish that using a values-based disciplinary approach would yield perfect harmony in labor relations, the reality is that conflicts between individual and organizational values and legitimate differences of opinion still give rise to disputes. It is at the final step of the disciplinary process that we see a marriage of fairness and efficiency.

Not having a dispute resolution process available in cases of employment termination increasingly means having to defend an action in court. To address such an eventuality, we in Owosso have adopted arbitration as the sole and exclusive remedy for employment disputes that might lead to termination for nonrepresented employees–mirroring the rights accorded to union members.

While arbitration is not without significant costs, it still is less expensive than relying on the courts. The setting for arbitration is less adversarial and can proceed faster toward a conclusion. Moreover, the use of a professional in the decision-making role lends a greater measure of fairness toward both parties in the dispute. All of these factors contribute to our seeing arbitration as a better fit with our values than the courts.

## Value for Citizens

Using these procedures in the manner described can demand a lot of management time and resources. For Owosso, though, these approaches are consistent with an organizational culture that sustains, and is sustained by, a well-qualified and highly motivated workforce. Most important, the practice of these beliefs produces value for citizens, in the form of high-quality public services.

Clearly, all organizations will not adopt as their values the four principles that we have articulated. Nor should they. The values of an organization must reflect the unique culture of that organization. Otherwise, statements of values will be seen as little more than window dressing, and their application will fail to produce the desired results.

But if current values do not contribute to a work environment that respects employees, and if they fail to produce work quality of which employees are proud, then a locality might consider turning its efforts toward changing the culture of its organization. The disciplinary process could be a good place to start.

---

*Gregg Guetschow is city manager of Owosso, Michigan.*

# Temp Firms Turn Up The Heat On Hiring

Today's labor shortage is forcing contingent staffing firms to recruit more creatively, focus on target groups and improve employee benefits.

## By Brenda Paik Sunoo

**R**afi Musher is part of the new breed of staffing firm executives.

As founder of Boston based Stax Research Inc., he's watched his firm grow in five years—primarily by word-of-mouth. Through his network of friends at Harvard Business School in Cambridge, Massachusetts, he's capitalized on the ready-made pool of young intellectuals pressured to pay back their college loans and furnish their low-rent apartments.

On the corporate side, he also knows employers are desperately seeking product managers, financial analysts, IT professionals and operations experts. His business venture, therefore, has been a match made in contingent heaven. "We have a way to bring starving talent to those finding it tough to recruit them," says Musher. Stax's clients, he adds, range from $40 million sporting-goods companies to billion-dollar technology firms.

These professionals are in demand, but with less time to find them, HR increasingly relies on contingent staffing firms to deliver the talent needed ASAP. Today, there are approximately 7,000 temporary staffing firms that have been in business for more than one year. Between them, they run more than 17,000 establishments throughout the nation, says Steve Berchem of the National Association of Temporary and Staffing Services (NATSS) in Alexandria, Virginia.

---

*Brenda Paik Sunoo is the senior editor for* WORKFORCE. *E-mail sunoob@workforcemag.com to comment.*

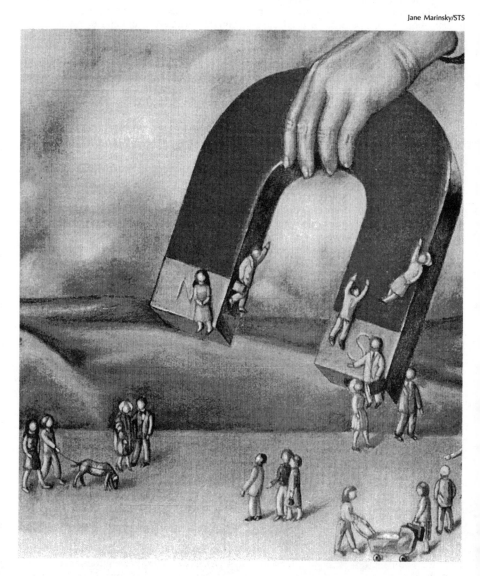

Jane Marinsky/STS

The good news is that despite the tight labor market, third quarter 1998 temporary-help revenues and employment were up, according to the NATSS quarterly survey of industry performance. In fact, revenues increased to $15 billion, up 16.3 percent from the third quarter of 1997. Meanwhile, employment grew to an average 2.9 million temporary employees per day in the third quarter of 1998, 9 percent more than in the same period in 1997.

"Job opportunities with staffing firms abound in nearly every area," says Richard A. Wahlquist, NATSS executive vice president in Alexandria, Virginia. Also, the Employment Outlook Survey, conducted quarterly by Milwaukee-based Manpower Inc., projected nationwide hiring prospects to remain essentially unchanged this opening quarter, when adjusted for seasonal variation, from the same quarter a year ago and the final quarter of 1998. Demand is particularly strong for accountants, financial analysts, commodity managers and information technology specialists.

Given the temporary staffing industry's fierce competition, HR can be more selective. Contingent staffing firms have been forced to recruit more creatively, focus on neglected target groups and provide more standard benefits, including training.

All of these efforts—topped with aggressive marketing campaigns—clearly work in your favor by increasing confidence in your vendors, guaranteeing greater diversity and lowering employee benefits and training costs. So reassess your current partnerships. Benchmark them against those successfully responding to the tight labor shortage.

## Creativity sparks recruitment strategies.

Today's labor market certainly is a double-edged sword for temporary staffing services, says Berchem. On one hand, overworked HR professionals are turning more and more to staffing firms. Approximately 90 percent of companies surveyed by NATSS say they increasingly rely on temp firms to help fill job vacancies. On the other hand, a 4.3 percent unemployment rate doesn't leave employers with a big pool of qualified applicants. "We're all trying different things," he says. "Our agencies tell us that recruitment is their number one problem."

That's why Burt Slatas, director of marketing services at Olsten Staffing Services, believes that *creativity* is an important component of one's strategy. It's not just a matter of defining *who* you're trying to recruit that's important, but *how* you intend to reach them.

For example, the Melville, New York-based agency has placed advertisements not only on the Internet, but on pizza boxes, place mats in food diners and cafeterias. Some recruiters even attend PTA meetings to entice the unemployed or dissatisfied parent professional.

And imagine a busload of urban commuters, startled by the outburst of an Olsten recruiter, who performs his or her *schtick* before the next bus stop? After getting the commuters' attention, the recruiter then hands out Olsten calling cards to facilitate the follow-up. In addition, Olsten's recruiters have handed out dummy checks on college campuses, announcing the types of benefits accrued by those who sign up with the firm. With such aggressive marketing strategies, Olsten recruiters have become more visible to the unemployed.

## You don't have to make a scene to reach the right market.

But one needn't always be in your face, so to speak. There are subtle and convenient methods of reaching the same audience. Adecco Job Shop is one example.

Last year, Adecco supplied more than 65,000 U.S. businesses with qualified personnel in a market that had record low unemployment. *Job Shop* is a first-of-its-kind interactive kiosk that reaches the public by using touch-screen technology to link job seekers with Adecco's network of employment opportunities.

Since last May, Adecco operates 65 Job Shop kiosks in 22 states, but the firm's goal is to have kiosks in 33 states by this spring. At the end of December last year, 659,600 people "touched" the Job Shop kiosks, producing 29,000 qualified applicants and placing 12,100 candidates, says Linda Tucker, national manager.

And that's just in the United States. Globally, Job Shop is located in 80 locations throughout Europe with plans to open in Australia with the Adecco/Olympics 2000 contract. "Whoever gets the recruit leads this market. It's definitely an employee-driven market," she says.

In one example, she recalls, an HR manager from Wells Fargo Bank—an existing Adecco client—was walking in the mall when she stumbled upon a Job Shop kiosk. In need of employees to work at retail banking stations (such as those found at grocery stores), she keyed in the locations, the job descriptions and other pertinent data. Within moments, the information was connected to Adecco's microsite on Monster.com, whereupon a list of possible recruits was identified for the bank.

Adecco's microsite with Monster.com, Tucker says, is called WorkFlex. It's a new

agreement between the temp firm and the Web-driven career development specialists. Basically, all the job profiles in a Job Shop kiosk are automatically downloaded onto the WorkFlex site—thereby allowing Monster.com (http://www.monster.com) visitors immediate and direct access to Adecco's job openings. One also can chat and hyperlink to other Web sites from WorkFlex. "We're taking advantage of those more highly skilled on the Web."

However, marketing one's recruiting strategy doesn't overshadow the importance of defining who you're trying to reach. Many temporary staffing firms, including Adecco and Olsten, are successfully reaching out to previously underrepresented groups of potential recruits.

## Staffing firms target underrepresented groups.

Given today's tight labor market, many temporary staffing firms are casting their nets far and wide. Says Susan V. Breen, CEO of GFI Professional Staffing Services in Keene, New Hampshire: "Recruitment is extremely frustrating, so we've been working very hard on retaining longer-term employees who prefer flexible work styles."

GFI's target segment, she says, has become broader. The cultural shift toward flexibility has given the temporary staffing industry a more positive glow. Years ago, employers primarily sought temps for clerical and administrative positions. Today, HR is seeking contingents for all rungs of the corporate ladder.

Temp firms also are diversifying the workforce by reaching out to seniors, minorities, welfare-to-work candidates, MBA moms—and the military. Both Adecco and Olsten, in particular, have established special programs to target the latter because of the information technology shortage.

Under Adecco's *Skills 2000* program, military personnel leaving the armed forces can turn to Adecco TAD (Technical Aid Design) for their next step in civilian careers. Through a special agreement with Redmond, Washington-based Microsoft Corp., transitioning service members will be able to be trained and recruited for jobs in the IT industry.

Similarly, Olsten Staffing Services and IMI Systems Inc. (the firm's IT division) will provide job placement services to help former military personnel through the transition toward a second career. In addition, they'll provide onsite and remote computer-based training, as well as career guidance to assist service members and their families in launching and developing IT careers. More than 650,000 individuals come out of the military each year, so programs such as Skills 2000 is a promising way of addressing the IT shortage.

Senior citizens, Slatas says, are another reliable pool of temporary workers. "Many seniors have retired early, but they still need supplementary income." Moreover, seniors are living longer, and contribute a positive work ethic and experience to today's chaotic workplace.

The key to recruiting and retaining this sector, Slatas says, is by continuing to upgrade their skill levels. Indeed, as HR professionals increasingly rely on temporary services for personnel, they're also relying on these firms to provide more benefits and to assume more training responsibilities—thus relieving employers of such costs.

## Rely on vendors who provide benefits and training.

At a time when companies are still downsizing and have less available resources, temp firms that provide benefits and training will be more competitive. Once candidates are hired, what's to prevent them from turning down the next best offer? "In order to retain people, we have to stretch and provide them with what's important to them, [such as] benefits and training" says Slatas.

Olsten and other temporary staffing firms continue to provide and upgrade their employee benefits, such as medical, holiday and vacation pay. Some have even offered retirement plans. "It's very critical," says Slatas. Whereas in the past, contin-

gents weren't given standard benefits, it's becoming more of the norm in the staffing services industry today. In addition to substantive wages and benefits, contingents also are looking for firms that provide free employee training.

Therefore, many firms are meeting that demand as well. In fact, NATSS reported that staffing companies are spending more than ever to enhance the skills of their temporary workers. In 1997, the industry spent an estimated $866 million training temporary employees, two and a half times more than the $335 million spent in 1995.

Ninety percent of staffing companies provided training at no cost to their temporary employees, according to NATSS' quarterly survey. In 1997, an estimated 4.8 million temporary workers received specific training in a wide variety of career-building skills. While much of the instruction occurred in training centers, classrooms or personal tutorials, the majority of companies also supplied computer tutorials.

Most offered training on data entry and basic computer skills. Staffing companies also helped workers with education in math, reading, English as a second language, résumé and cover-letter writing, interviewing skills, telephone etiquette, dressing for success, stress management, Internet applications, bookkeeping, collections, sales and customer service. "When staffing companies invest in upgrading the skills of their temporary employees, everybody wins," says Wahlquist.

To keep their temp employees working, many staffing firms also have employment

counselors to provide career pathing for their contingents. Slatas says Olsten recruiters thus find it easier to "bottomfill"— that is, to find people with lower level skills and then upgrade them to higher positions. As employers hire these temporary workers, they're able to observe their performance and see how they'd fit in with the corporate culture long-term.

Such mutual arrangements have apparently been very successful. According to industry experts, approximately one-third of all contingent jobs have moved from temp-to-hire, which is a positive trend for employers seeking a stable workforce.

So remember, those in the temporary staffing services industry are scrambling to become your vendor of choice. As you reassess the ones you have, HR might even consider the notion of *vendor consolidation*. In other words, instead of getting your contingents from several temporary staffing services, you may want to consider working with only one; the advantage being that the arrangement would simplify record-keeping, relationship building, communication and negotiating rates.

After all, when it comes to contracting with a temporary staffing agency, what you're looking for is a reliable partner. One that views itself as working alongside HR, respects your company's culture and understands your business goals and needs. So rather than worrying about today's tight labor market, transfer the heat onto your staffing services vendors. Let them find temps-to-go.

# Cutting Off The Supply Side Of Bribes

## BEING AGAINST CORRUPTION
## IS MORE DIFFICULT THAN YOU THINK

Address by RON BERENBEIM, *Director, Conference Board's Working Group on Global Business Ethics Principles*

*Delivered to the OECD Washington Conference on Corruption, Washington, D.C., February 23, 1999*

It is a pleasure to have this opportunity to speak to the OECD's Washington Conference on Corruption on corporate efforts to limit or cut off the "supply side" of bribes. Meeting with people around the world and doing the research for The Conference Board Working Group's report on Global Business Ethics practices has convinced me of the urgent need for effective corporate anti-corruption strategies and programs.

What is critical for companies to recognize in this regard is that corruption's victims are beginning to blame companies as the primary cause of its harmful consequences. A recent Cameroon survey is a case in point. People who live in Cameroon have an unmatched expertise on corruption issues which they have obtained the hard way—Transparency International named Cameroon as the most "corrupt" country (an assessment that was shared by 77 percent of the 616 Cameroon survey respondents). Significantly, for purposes of our discussion, the Cameroon sample suggests that long-suffering citizens in corrupt countries now view bribe givers as the moral equals of bribe takers. Fifty-three percent said that corrupt officials were primarily to blame for Cameroon's difficulties and 47 percent assigned primary blame to company failure to resist. These data demonstrate that

"supply side" accountability is no longer one of several alternative strategies; it is essential and, increasingly, it is likely to be demanded by host country public opinion.

We need to acknowledge that we confront formidable obstacles in implementing effective corporate anti-corruption systems. These barriers are best illustrated by an anecdote involving Calvin Coolidge, our most laconic President. Upon returning from church one Sunday, his wife asked him about the subject of the minister's sermon. "Sin" was the answer. "What did he say?" asked the First Lady. "He was against it," replied the President. It does not take a great deal of theological sophistication to realize that Coolidge's recollection leaves a good deal to be desired. Opposition to sin was probably not the minister's subject; it is more likely that he focused on the challenge of being against something that takes many forms—not all of them instantly recognizable as evil.

Just as Coolidge said of his minister, we can say, and North and South American, Asian and European Conference Board Working Group participants have said, that they are against corruption and that they regard its marginalization as, perhaps, the most important global business priority. Such a declaration is easy. What is more difficult is to acknowledge the beliefs and customs—

From *Vital Speeches of the Day*, April 15, 1999, pp. 408-410. © 1999 by City News Publishing Company, Inc. Reprinted by permission.

many of them good and none self-evidently bad—that constitute formidable barriers to combating corruption.

For example, tolerance is a word that has very positive associations. As befitting citizens of the continent with perhaps the greatest cultural diversity in the smallest space, Europeans are justly proud of their openness to other customs and cultures. Owing to the relative youth of their civilization and conscious of their country's wealth and power, Americans are also acutely sensitive to and respectful of practices in other parts of the world. Unfortunate memories of imperialism and gunboat diplomacy are additional reasons why European and American businesses are reluctant to impose their values when doing business in other parts of the world.

In his presentation to The Conference Board's Global Business Ethics Working Group's Paris meeting, INSEAD professor Henri-Claude de Bettignies provided vivid descriptions of "tolerance's" different rationales for corruption: (1) "Refusal to bribe is a Western hang-up." (2) "Bribery is a parallel distribution system. Everyone does it." (3) "It is the traditional way of doing business in this culture."

Let us be frank about these kinds of justification for bribery—opposing corruption may require a fair measure of intolerance. Bribes may be a deeply ingrained part of the cultural fabric. And, of course, bribes are not always labeled as such. Distinguishing between a customary but exceptionally lavish gift and a bribe may require an exercise of what some would call cultural imperialism.

Still, when confronting bribery situations, we should not be unduly concerned about the sensitivities of extortionists. There are better ways than bribery to show appreciation for an ancient culture. In fact, it is not difficult to argue that permissive attitudes toward corrupt behavior show a complete lack of respect.

Loyalty is the second admirable quality that can interfere with the effective implementation of corporate anti-corruption methods. Employees need confidential and reliable advice regarding the advisability of potentially questionable activities and an early warning system regarding potential misconduct can be a critical corporate tool in deterring it. Encouraged in part by the compliance system incentives in the Revised Organizational Sentencing Guidelines (1991), many U.S. companies have instituted hotlines or, as they are sometimes called, "helplines" for employees to get advice and report suspected activities.

While U.S. companies and operations report that "helplines" have achieved some degree of acceptance and have proven to be useful, comments at Working Group sessions in Paris, Rio de Janeiro, and New Delhi suggest that management and employee attitudes outside the United States are not so positive. The one exception to this generally negative view was Japan. Despite widespread survey participant comment that "helplines" would encounter resistance in Japan, 40 percent of the 15 participating Japanese companies said that they had such a program and none of them reported serious opposition.

The greatest hostility to helplines was found in Europe. One European company received 47 minutes of calls over a twelve month period. Another participant had two calls in three years. Commentators attributed this dislike to the unhappy legacy of governmental and occupation forces use of informers.

The consensus at the Brazil meeting was only slightly more positive. Still, two major obstacles were cited. First, many Latin American employees have little or no access to or experience with using a telephone in the workplace. Second, discussants said that in the region's rigidly hierarchical societies it is difficult for people to report problems to company headquarters that may reflect poorly on the boss.

The New Delhi Working Group participants had the most optimistic assessment. They argued that a helpline could succeed if the users could have complete confidence in the confidentiality of their disclosures. In this regard, the most important factor in confidentiality is the identity of the person who hears the complaint. Ideally, the listener should be the CEO—though participants recognized the impracticality of that suggestion, the comment underscores the need for the complaint recipient to be publicly identified and to command great respect within the organization.

The New Delhi participants also drew an important distinction between confidentiality and anonymity. Disclosure confidentiality they said was essential to the preservation of workplace morale; while anonymity offered employees a dangerous temptation to make malicious and irresponsible accusations.

The Conference Board Working Group discussions and survey data suggest that the same cohesiveness and group loyalty that companies encourage in the design, production, and sale of products and services can be a barrier to effective implementation of compliance systems. Anti-corruption policies cannot be enforced voluntarily. Indeed, if that were the case, there would be no need for them. By the same token, no rules can effectively deter if there is not a willingness on the part of community members to report the infractions of others.

Commitment to and belief in product quality is the third desirable sentiment that can complicate effective implementation of corporate anti-corruption measures. Suppose, for example, you were a project manager bidding on a local governmental contract to build a bridge. You know that a bribe is necessary for your proposal to even receive serious consideration. Other companies that you believe do inferior work will not hesitate to pay the bribe. Should you sacrifice the lives and safety of a country's innocent citizens because of your company's unwillingness to accede to deeply ingrained cultural and political practices? No act of yours will put an end to this practice; the only consequence will be death and injury to those who use the bridge.

The project manager's dilemma illustrates how difficult it can be to refuse to pay a bribe when utilitarian analysis tells the decision-maker that the bribe will be paid in any event and that the only consequences will be that the ultimate consumer will get an inferior product at a higher price. In this case, we can sympathize; faulty bridges are a very serious threat to life and safety. Still, a few nagging questions remain. How can the manager be certain that his company's bridge is sufficiently superior to justify the bribe? If we allow the justification for bridge bidding, what others must we also permit? Should those who believe themselves to be purveyors of other higher quality, lower cost products be allowed similar flexibility?

The bridge contract bid example shows that the firmer the conviction in the desirability of the ends, the easier it is to rationalize the means. Consumers have derived immeasurable benefits from the fierce corporate commitment to quality. Still, it is important to recognize that the missionary zeal that drives the pursuit of excellence is also capable of constructing a moral universe in which bribery can be justified.

In closing, The Conference Board's Global Working Group discussions and survey affirm that ethical decision-making seldom confronts us with a choice between good and evil. More often the necessary task is to limit the scope that we give to our better impulses in order to achieve a greater good. Tolerance of diverse cultures and customs, loyalty to colleagues and company, commitment to product quality are all essential to the success of a global enterprise. Yet if we are serious about cutting off the "supply side" of corruption, we are going to have to recognize the danger that making these values absolute can justify its continuation. Being against corruption may be more difficult than we thought.

## Unit Selections

## Key Points to Consider

❖ How does the smaller world affect the practice of human resource management?

❖ What is the impact of foreign workers, both at home and abroad, on the human resource practices of the organization?

❖ What are some considerations of transnational firms in the human resource area?

❖ How would you expect organizations in the future to view the market for potential employees?

 **Links**   **www.dushkin.com/online/**

These sites are annotated on pages 4 and 5.

The world is changing and getting smaller all the time. At the beginning of the twentieth century, the Wright brothers flew at Kitty Hawk, and some 25 years later, Charles Lindbergh flew from New York to Paris alone, nonstop. In 1969 the spacecraft *Eagle One* landed on the Moon, and Neil Armstrong said, "One small step for man, one giant leap for mankind."

Indeed, the giant leaps have become smaller. The world has shrunk due to transportation and communication. Communication is virtually instantaneous—not as it was during the early part of the 1800s, when the Battle of New Orleans was fought several weeks after the peace treaty for the War of 1812 had been signed. For centuries, travel was limited to the speed of a horse or a ship. During the nineteenth century, however, speeds of 60 or even 100 miles an hour were achieved by railroad trains. Before the twentieth century was half over, the speed of sound had been exceeded, and in the 15 years that followed, humans circled the globe in 90 minutes. Less than 10 years later, human beings broke free from Earth's gravity and walked on the Moon. The exotic became commonplace. Societies and cultures that had been remote from each other are now close, and people must now live with a diversity unknown in the past. A key problem that will face organizations in the future will be not only dealing with American employees abroad but with employees from abroad in their home country.

A shrinking world also means an expanding economy, a global economy, because producers and their raw materials and markets are now much closer to each other than they once were. People, and the organizations they represent, often do business all over the world, and their representatives are often members of foreign societies and cultures. Human resource management in just the domestic arena is an extremely difficult task; when the rest of the world is added to the effort, it becomes a monumental undertaking.

Workers in the United States are competing directly with workers in other parts of the world. Companies often hold out for the lowest bidder in a competition for wage rates. This often forces the wage rates down for higher-paying countries, while only marginally bringing up the wages of the lower-paying societies—a development that is bound to have a direct impact on the standard of living in all of the developed countries of the world.

As more firms become involved in world trade, they must begin to hire foreign workers. Some of these people are going to stay with the firm and become members of the corporate cadre. In the global economy, it is not uncommon for Indian employees to find themselves working for American or European multinational corporations in, say, Saudi Arabia. This presents the human resource professional with a problem of blending the three cultures into a successful mix. In this example, the ingredients are a well-educated Asian, working in a highly traditional Middle Eastern society, for a representative of Western technology and culture. The situation involves three different sets of values, three different points of view, and three different sets of expectations on how people should act and be treated.

American industry does not have a monopoly on new ideas in human resources. Other societies have successfully dealt with many of the same problems. While U.S. firms certainly will not adopt every idea (lifetime employment as practiced in Japan seems the most obvious noncandidate), they can learn much from organizations outside the United States.

Faster and better communication and transportation are leading to a more closely knit social, cultural, and economic world, where people's global abilities can make the difference between the success or failure of an organization.

# The Impact of 'Inpats'

## *Stay on top of legal and cultural considerations when sponsoring foreign nationals.*

### BY CARLA JOINSON

In an era of low unemployment and merciless jockeying for skilled employees, HR professionals are grabbing at any opportunity they can find to access additional labor pools. For some, the recent increase in the H-1B visa cap has been good news, but it has simultaneously opened other areas of concern, such as legal compliance issues and employee assimilation and adjustment. Fortunately, any company with an "inpat" population can make these hires more successful by identifying typical concerns and addressing them with sensitivity and speed.

## Welcome to the United States

Put yourself in your inpat's shoes: You've moved to a foreign country, started a new job and now must pay for medical benefits that were free in your own country. On top of that, you can't understand American slang. How would you want an HR person to assist you and your family?

"You can't assume there won't be problems simply because your employees want to come here and will get paid well," says Peggy Love, president of Full Circle International Relocations Inc. in McLean, Va.

"These families want to put a down payment on a house, but the employee can't open a bank account because he doesn't have a Social Security card. Or, they may need to register a child for school but don't understand U.S. immunization requirements."

Several years ago, Fujitsu Network Communications Inc. in Richardson, Texas, began hiring workers from abroad when it became difficult to find technical employees in the United States. "Here, every employee already has cross-cultural training on how to work in a Japanese environment," says Fredda Walters, manager of relocation and temporary services at Fujitsu. "Additionally, inpats can receive language training and cross-cultural training for the U.S., as well as settling-in services.

"The biggest problem people have, though, is assimilating into the non-workplace environment," Walters says. One foreign national employee e-mailed her for help when his spouse needed to get a driver's license.

The procedure for a sponsored employee's spouse is to go to the Social Security office with a passport and visa, get a non-work designated Social Security number, then go to the Department of Motor Vehicles to get a driver's license. Then the spouse must return to the Social Security office to get a tax ID card. "This may involve hours of waiting in line and can be such a frustrating experience," Walters notes. She says the company earned that employee's gratitude by picking up his spouse and accompanying her to the necessary destinations.

Companies also help inpats by making arrangements with banks or credit unions to smooth procedures for establishing bank accounts and credit, as well as by setting up programs with preferred vendors for other employee necessities, such as vehicles. Fujitsu's

> # One of the myths about inpat assimilation is that it will be a simple process because the United States offers so many choices.

U.S. cross-cultural training covers such items as medical systems and wills, so that employees can make informed decisions. The company also has an on-site relocation support group, which family members can attend.

One of the myths about inpat assimilation is that it will be a simple process because the United States offers so many choices, says Love. "Actually, that's very stressful," she says. "How does the family decide which medical plan, which brand of soap or which phone company to choose? Later on, when they're comfortable, they're very pleased that they have choices and can make changes; however, it's very difficult at first."

Her advice is to plan well and to try and figure out every component that works into the relocation, including the family's needs. "There can be several groups helping with a move, such as attorneys, accountants, movers, trainers or consultants, and the transferee can get confused," says Love. "From the start, HR should explain to the employee who is doing what and reassure the person that everyone is working on his behalf."

## Fitting In

As one might expect, language can be a big problem for workers coming into the United States, says Linda Stokes, president of PRISM International Inc., an assessment, consulting and training firm in Sanford, Fla. "After that, it really is the culture."

American workers often don't realize the strength of the workplace culture because they are accustomed to it. "One barrier to acceptance for international employees is the failure to follow U.S. workplace culture," says Stokes. "For instance, in a brainstorming or solution-oriented meeting, it is our way to jump in, talk and solve the problem. However, folks from other cultures may feel this is a waste of time because we haven't thought it all through and are throwing out various solutions that may not work.

"We then say, 'What's wrong with them? Why don't they speak up?' Then, there's a domino effect: They get invited to meetings less and less."

Interviewing techniques also need to account for cultural differences. "A Vietnamese candidate will say, 'I will do my best,' instead of, 'Of course I can do the job,' the way an American would." Or, the candidate may avoid eye contact. In many cultures, candidates who get a job offer will want to go home and think about it or discuss it with family members for several days—not give an immediate answer, which the interviewer may expect, she adds.

When Omaha-based Inacom Corp. recruited Chinese IT workers for computer configuration and networking jobs, it found that they didn't jump in as fast as U.S. workers. "They were waiting to be told what to do," says Eva Fujan, vice president of technical recruiting. "But once they understood the different situation they were in—and the self-motivation behind it—they loved it and really took off."

The company also has found that candidates who speak fluent English don't necessarily speak "business English" or "technical English." Inacom is considering contracting with a professor at the University of Nebraska to offer an English class specifically for the high tech industry.

## The Benefits Gap

Most people know that some countries offer more paid time off than do U.S. companies, such as the four-week vacations employees receive after their first year on the job in Germany. But international employees value lesser perks as well. Workers accustomed to two-hour lunches in France or the Middle East may be shocked at the thought of eating a sandwich at their desks. The cost of cafeteria meals in France and the United Kingdom often are based on the employee's salary or may be subsidized. In Europe, employers may pay half of an employee's commuting costs.

U.S. employers can counter these perceived losses with the benefits they do offer, or they can explain why certain benefits are not offered. A commuting subsidy, for example, may not apply in the United States because gas is less expensive here.

Walters seeks compromise on vacation issues. "Our Canadian competitors give three weeks of vacation, and we try to be sensitive to that. We let employees 'borrow' vacation time from future accruals or purchase it through paycheck deductions." Sign-on bonuses can help equalize disparate benefits as well, she adds.

"Employees used to social maintenance systems that pay their dental and medical bills can have problems with the U.S. system of private care and deductions," says Tom Murrill, vice president of HR at Royal Caribbean Cruises Ltd. in Miami. "You have to be right up front with candidates and explain it thoroughly."

He finds that the most complex issues involve taxes and retirement plans. "Will employees from countries with very high taxes have to pay taxes in both countries? Some employees will have to pay into two [pension] systems if they want to keep their retirement plans, while others can pay in the U.S. and receive credit in their home country." Murrill advises HR to work with an accounting firm with international experience or an HR consultant to define the procedures.

Most U.S. companies do not make elaborate benefits changes to meet international expectations, although most will make reasonable accommodations. Murrill and Fujan have found that the opportunities open to workers in the United States generally compensate for any benefits the employee loses through relocation. "Employee expectations are going to vary from culture to culture," says Stokes. "Just be very clear about what you do offer."

## Navigating Red Tape

After making a job offer, employers that sponsor candidates must file an H-1B petition with the Immigration and Naturalization Service (INS) and pay a $110 application fee and a newly instituted $500 fee, which goes into an account for American workforce training. Companies also must fill out a labor condition application (LCA) with the Department of Labor (DOL). The process may seem simple, but experienced HR professionals usually seek outside expertise with all phases of it.

"There are a lot of traps for the unwary," says Lesley Amano, an attorney specializing in immigration issues at the Law Offices of Sheela Murthy in Baltimore. "The LCA you file says that you will pay the prevailing wage to your H-1B employees, but how do you determine prevailing wage? Unless you use a determination from the state labor office, which many employers don't feel accurately reflects wages, what other source can you use? Will that survey be acceptable in its geographical area or statistical sampling? You must get these points right, or you may violate this particular provision."

Murrill, whose company frequently hires international superintendents and nautical officers who are highly skilled on the technical aspects of running a ship, stresses that HR professionals should thoroughly understand the candidate's background and skills. "You have to demonstrate that a U.S. person with that skill isn't readily available," he warns.

Furthermore, poor or improper documentation of that skill can cause delays. "If you hire someone from Scandinavia who has a degree written in Swedish, you need to type an explanation or perhaps even have it translated so there won't be any confusion," he advises.

As long as the candidate has a degree, the INS will accept work experience in lieu of a degree in a particular field, but the consulate examining the accompanying paperwork and explanation will make the final call. "The more degrees and more technical expertise someone has, the easier it is to get that person in the country," says Murrill.

Amano agrees that there can be problems when a candidate's experience fails to reflect his degree. "Lately," she adds, "the INS has asked more questions about detail than they ever did in the past. Consulates may ask [companies] for building leases, organizational charts, W-2 forms or contracts. Much of this request for evidence occurs when they don't actually believe the company exists. That can be very hard on a new company, which can't necessarily show profits until they get these people in as employees."

## Paying for Mistakes

"One HR person making an honest mistake is not going to get a terrific fine," says Eyleen Schmidt, an INS spokesperson in Washington, D.C. She says that one incident of an employee with the wrong kind of visa would probably result in a written warning. "However, a construction company that said it was hiring structural engineers but was really hiring laborers recently got hit with a $1 million fine. This had occurred with multiple workers over a number of years."

HR managers must also understand the provisions of the American Competitiveness and Workforce Improvement Act of 1998 (ACWIA). Remedies against improper recruiting and failure to meet LCA requirements include a $1,000 (per violation) civil money penalty (CMP) and debarment for one year from the H-1B program. Once the DOL implements ACWIA's regulations, it may authorize additional penalties of up to $35,000 (per violation) and debarment for five years if a company fails to comply with wage, working condition, notification and hiring attestations, and that failure displaces an American worker. The act also forbids U.S. companies from passing on any fees and costs of the H-1B program to the employee.

The DOL assessed a $1,000 CMP and $24,000 in back wages against a Los Angeles restaurant that failed to pay a prevailing wage to an accountant. In Orlando, a computer manufacturer hired an employee it claimed would be a systems engineer who did janitorial work instead. Additionally, the company failed to post information about the job in the workplace and, consequently, faced $2,250 in fines. Generally, the DOL investigates these kinds of violations based on complaints it receives, often from other employees at the affected workplace.

Although employing international workers involves effort on the part of the company—especially the HR department—it still remains a good source of manpower for hard-to-fill positions. Companies that do a good job of accommodating diversity and are willing to locate and use specialized expertise find that the addition of international workers adds to their success.

*Carla Joinson, a contributing editor to* HR Magazine, *is based in San Antonio. She specializes in writing about business and management issues.*

# Don't Get Burned By Hot New Markets

## Be ready to do your part in evaluating proposed new locations.

By Charlene Marmer Solomon

The numbers practically sizzle off the page. Just look at this: U.S. direct investment abroad sky-rocketed from $467.8 billion in 1991 to more than $796 billion in 1996, according to the U.S. Department of Commerce. U.S. corporations have invested more than $10 billion in China alone, another $23.6 billion in Brazil, $16 billion in Thailand and $12.5 billion in Indonesia. Many of these hot markets are growing at a robust GDP (gross domestic product) of 7 percent, or 8 percent a year.

One after another, American companies seek—and seize—new opportunities in rapidly growing yet unfamiliar markets. China, India, Brazil, Russia and many others offer untold opportunities with their megamillion populations and growing consumer classes. And U.S. firms are right there, offering everything from light bulbs to power plants and selling their expertise about manufacturing, marketing and managing global operations.

The ventures into these new territories can be profitable. But they also can be risky. New entrants must navigate gingerly over a hotbed of coals that will singe those who are unprepared for myriad laws and regulations, unfamiliar political and social structures, and unpredictable infrastructures, all of which manifest themselves in workforce issues. That's why HR's role is central to strategizing, planning and ultimately helping to choose new business destinations.

It's clear that the critical issues to success in new markets often revolve around typical HR concerns: hiring, training, compensating and managing people—but in a multiplicity of environments and a maze of legal and political circumstances. These are complex and multilayered

business issues, to be sure, but they are, nonetheless, issues that require understanding and thorough business, labor, legal and social analysis through an HR perspective.

**HR must participate in a business analysis of proposed locations.** "We increasingly see whole new industries going out—information technology, telecommunications, specialized pharmaceuticals, agriculture, insurance—and we're also seeing companies that have been established internationally for many years going into new markets," says Bill Sheridan, director of international compensation services at the New York City-based National Foreign Trade Council.

Sure, there's money to be made. But what makes global executives choose certain destinations as most receptive or at least worthy of the difficulties firms must surmount? The decision must always begin with the business objectives.

"Before we venture into new markets, we now start with a detailed strategic market analysis. We look at our markets over the next five to 10 years and try to determine where we need to be in four or five years' time," says Patrick Morgan, human resources manager, Latin America Region for San Francisco-based Bechtel Corp., the construction giant. "It's important to actually think through what it is you're going to do, where your market is, what your relative chances are of being successful, and then begin to prioritize where you want to go after that."

Morgan is always a key member of the management team that assesses the big picture. The cost-benefit analysis factors in: the position of competitors, infrastructure as it relates to personnel (such as telecommunications), regulatory and trade barriers, and the tax situation (both cor-

# 15 Top Emerging Markets

The "Global Relocation Trends 1996 Survey Report," containing research collected by the National Foreign Trade Council and Windham International (both in New York City), identifies the 15 countries presented in the next four pages as emerging destinations for international assignments. These countries were chosen most often by the 192 respondents (representing

| Country or Region [1] | Type of Government [2] | GDP Per Capita (US$) [2] | Inflation Rate [2] | Native Languages [2] | Travel Per Diem (US$) [3] | Entry Requirements [4] | Standard Workweek [4] | Labor Law Snapshot [4] |
|---|---|---|---|---|---|---|---|---|
| **People's Republic of China (PRC)** (*Zhonghua Renmin Gongheguo*) | Communist state | $2,900 | 10.1% | Standard Chinese or Mandarin, Yue (Cantonese), Wu, Minbei, Minnan, Xiang, Gan, Hakka dialects, minority languages. | Range: $119 – 226 | U.S. citizens must have a passport and visa. Most business visitors on initial visits enter on tourist visas, which don't require a letter of invitation. | Mon. through Fri., 08:00 – noon and 13:00 (or 14:00) – 17:00. | Rules for hiring Chinese nationals depend on the type of establishment: wholly-owned, joint venture or representative office. |
| **Republic of India** | Federal republic | $1,500 | 9% | English is important for national, political and commercial communication. Hindi is the primary tongue of 30% of the people. | Range: $186 – 306 | A passport and visa are required. Also: evidence of yellow fever immunization if the traveler is arriving from an infected area. | Most offices: Mon. through Fri. Some offices: Mon. through Sat. | Less than 2% of the total workforce is unionized. Worker days lost to strikes and lockouts have declined since 1991. |
| **Federative Republic of Brazil** (*Republica Federativa do Brasil*) | Federal republic | $6,100 | 23% | Official language: Portuguese. Also Spanish, English and French. | Range: $56 – 252 | Travelers must have a temporary business visa (valid for 90 days) if they plan to transact business. | Mon. through Fri., 08:30 or 09:00 – 17:30 or 18:00 with a one- to two-hour lunch. Some factories: half-days on Sat. | Labor unions, especially in the most skilled sectors, tend to be well-organized and aggressive in defending wages and conditions. |
| **Russian Federation** (*Rossiyskaya Federatsiya*) | Federation | $5,300 | 7% | Primary language: Russian. | Range: $191 – 319 | U.S. citizens must have a passport and visa. Visas are issued based on support from a sponsor: a Russian individual or organization. | 40 hours per week. | Local labor mobility within Russia is limited by housing shortages and difficulties in obtaining government-required residence permits. |
| **United Mexican States** (*Estados Unidos Mexicanos*) | Federal republic operating under a centralized government | $7,700 | 52% | Spanish and various Mayan dialects. | Range: $61 – 255 | U.S. citizens can apply for a business visa for up to 30 days on arrival in Mexico. Longer stays require a FM-3 visa. | 48 hours, including one paid day of rest. | For overtime, workers must be paid twice their normal rate – and three times their hourly rate when more than nine hours per week of overtime. |
| **Republic of Singapore** | Republic within a commonwealth | $22,900 | 1.7% | National language: Malay. Other official languages: Chinese, Tamil and English. | $211 | Passports are required. Visas aren't necessary for U.S.-based travelers. | 44 hours: Mon. through Fri., 08:30 – 17:30 and Sat., 08:30 – 13:00. | The government places a ceiling on the % of foreign workers various industries may employ and a monthly levy for each foreign worker. |
| **Hong Kong** | Territory of China as of July 1997 | $27,500 | 8.4% | Chinese (Cantonese) and English. | $344 | Visas allowing residence and local employment for expats are granted on the basis of simple procedures. | Mon. through Fri., 09:00 – 17:00. Sat. was traditionally a half-day, but many companies now advertise 5-day workweeks. | Minimal labor relations difficulties. The average number of days lost due to industrial conflicts is one of the lowest in the world. |

46,900 expats) as among the three countries they see emerging as assignment locations for their organizations. The countries are listed in rank order beginning with China, chosen by 27 percent of companies—down through Australia, chosen by 4 percent. The corresponding data fields included in this table were compiled from a variety of sources to delineate some of the HR-related concerns companies should have as they evaluate international assignment locations.

[1-8]Please refer to "Heading Notes" on the next 2 pages for additional details about each of the categories below

| Labor Force [2] | Unemployment Rate [2] | Literacy Rate [2] | Telephone System [2] | Health & Medical Care [4] | International Schools [5] | Corruption Rating [6] | Hardship Premium [7] | Direct Investment (US$) [4] | U.S. Companies [4] | Embassy Information [8] |
|---|---|---|---|---|---|---|---|---|---|---|
| 583.6 million (1991) | 5.2% (1995) | 81.5% (1995) | Domestic and international services are increasingly available for private use. Unevenly distributed system. | Co. insurance should cover emergency evacuations. Serious cases are often handled in Hong Kong. | 9 schools in 6 cities | 2 | 15 – 25% | Foreign investment (including U.S.): $38 billion in 1995. | Information not available. | **Embassy of the PRC** 2300 Connecticut Ave. NW Washington, D.C. 20008 Tel: 202 / 328-2500 E-mail: webmaster@china-embassy.org URL: www.china-embassy.org/ |
| 314.751 million (1990) | Info not available. | 52% (1995) | Probably the least adequate system of the industrializing countries. Slows industrial and commercial growth. | Adequate care is available in population centers. Doctors and hospitals often expect payment in cash. | 6 schools in 6 cities | 2 | 10 – 20% | U.S. investment: $192 million in 1995. | CMS Generation Coca-Cola General Motors Guardian J. Makowski Williams Corp. | **Embassy of India** 2107 Massachusetts Ave. NW Washington, D.C. 20008 Tel: 202 / 939-7000 URL: www.indiaserver.com/embusa/ |
| 57 million (1989) | 5% (1995) | 83.3% (1995) | Good working system. | Information not available. | 12 schools in 10 cities | 3 | 0 – 10% | U.S. investment: $23.6 billion by end of 1995. | Alcoa Caterpillar Dow Chemical Ford IBM Xerox | **Embassy of Brazil** 3006 Massachusetts Ave. NW Washington, D.C. 20008 Tel: 202 / 745-2700 E-mail: scitech@brasil.emb.nw.dc.us URL: www.brasil.emb.nw.dc.us/ |
| 85 million (1993) | 8.2% (1995) | 98% (1989) | Enlisting foreign help to speed up modernization. A severe handicap to the economy. | Far below Western standards with severe shortages of basic supplies. | 3 schools in 3 cities | 2 | 10 – 25% | Foreign investment (including U.S.): $2.1 billion in 1996. | Information not available. | **Embassy of the Russian Federation** 2650 Wisconsin Ave. NW Washington, D.C. 20007 Tel: 202 / 298-5700 URL: www.russianembassy.org |
| 33.6 million (1994) | 10% (1995) | 89.6% (1995) | Adequate domestic service for business and gov't, but the public is poorly served. | Dependable in the principal cities. Most private doctors have U.S. training. | 15 schools in 10 cities | 2 | 0 – 5% | Information not available. | Information not available. | **Embassy of Mexico** 1911 Pennsylvania Ave. NW Washington, D.C. 20006 Tel: 202 / 728-1600 |
| 1.649 million (1994) | 2.6% (1995) | 91.1% (1995) | Good domestic facilities and international service. | Information not available. | 7 schools in a small country (3X the size of Wash., D.C.) | 8 | 0% | Foreign investment (including U.S.) in manufacturing: $4.1 billion in 1996. | Approximately 1,300 U.S.-based firms. | **Embassy of the Republic of Singapore** 1824 R St. NW Washington, D.C. 20009 Tel: 202 / 537-3100 |
| 2.915 million (1994) | 3.5% (1995) | 92.2% (Age 15+ had some school; 1995) | Modern facilities provide excellent domestic and international service. | Information not available. | 11 schools in a small region (6X the size of Wash., D.C.) | 7 | 0% | U.S. investment: $13.8 billion by the end of 1995. | More than 1,100 U.S.-based businesses. | **Embassy of the PRC** 2300 Connecticut Ave. NW Washington, D.C. 20008 Tel: 202 / 328-2500 E-mail: webmaster@china-embassy.org URL: www.china-embassy.org/ |

| Country or Region [1] | Type of Government [2] | GDP Per Capita (US$) [2] | Inflation Rate [2] | Native Languages [2] | Travel Per Diem (US$) [3] | Entry Requirements [4] | Standard Workweek [4] | Labor Law Snapshot [4] |
|---|---|---|---|---|---|---|---|---|
| **Republic of Idonesia** (*Republik Indonesia*) | Republic | $3,500 | 8.6% | Official language: Bahasa Indonesia (modified form of Malay). Also English, Dutch and local dialects. | Range: $110 – 305 | Business visitors from the U.S. may obtain a 60-day short visit pass on arrival. Temporary residence visas may be obtained from the embassy. | Mon. through Fri., 08:00 – 16:00 and Sat. 08:00 – 13:00. Moslems are released for prayers every Fri. 11:00 – 12:00. | The government sets minimum wages by region. The minimum wage in Jakarta and West Java as of April 1997 is approx. US$ 2.40/day. |
| **United Kingdom of Great Britain and Northern Ireland (U.K.)** | Constitutional monarchy | $19,500 | 3.1% | English, Welsh, Scottish form of Gaelic. | Range: $150 – 294 | Employees of British subsidiaries of U.S. firms encounter little difficulty in obtaining permission to enter and remain in the U.K. | Mon. through Fri. 09:00 – 17:30. | Information not available. |
| **Argentine Republic** (*Republica Argentina*) | Republic | $8,100 | 1.7% | Official language: Spanish. Also English, Italian, German and French. | Range: $120 – 223 | Visas are no longer required for U.S. citizens traveling to Argentina. Passport holders are granted a 90-day visa on entry. | Mon. through Fri. | The labor code traditionally has been a disincentive in hiring. New regulations that allow greater flexibility in personnel mgmt. will help job growth. |
| **Kingdom of Thailand** | Constitutional monarchy | $6,900 | 5.8% | Primary language: Thai. English is the secondary language. Also, regional dialects. | Range: $80 – 167 | Passports and onward/return tickets are required. Visas aren't needed for stays of up to one month. | Mon. through Fri., 54 hours for commercial workers and 48 for industrial workers. | All employers must determine the terms of employment for their staff. Those with 10 or more employees must specify working regulations. |
| **Malaysia** | Constitutional monarchy | $9,800 | 5.3% | Official language: Malay. Also English, Chinese dialects, Tamil and numerous tribal dialects. | Range: $121 – 165 | U.S. business visitors don't need visas unless coming for employment purposes. Instead, they'll be given passes at the point of entry. | Mon. through Thurs. 08:00 – 12:45 and 14:00 – 16:45. Fri. 08:00 – 12:15 and 14:45 – 16:15. Sat. 08:00 – 12:45. | There are a number of national unions, but the government prohibits the formation of a national union in the electronics industry. |
| **Republic of Venezuela** (*Republica de Venezuela*) | Republic | $9,300 | 57% | Official language: Spanish. Also native dialects spoken by 200,000 Amerindians in the interior. | $184 | To obtain a business visa, contact the nearest consulate. | 40 hours per week maximum (non-manual labor). Offices: 08:30 – 12:30 and 14:30 – 18:00. | Law places restrictions on the employment decisions made by foreign investors; e.g., foreigners may not exceed 10% of employees. |
| **Socialist Republic of Vietnam** (*Cong Hoa Chu Nghia Viet Nam*) | Communist state | $1,300 | 14% | Official language: Vietnamese. Also French, Chinese, English, Khmer and tribal languages. | $244 | Passports and visas are required. Any Vietnamese embassy can process visas. | Mon. through Fri., 08:00 – 17:00 and Sat. 08:00 – 11:30. | Labor is becoming more regulated. Foreign employers must pay income taxes for their employees, including steep rates for middle managers. |
| **Commonwealth of Australia** | Federal parliamentary state | $22,100 | 4.75% | Official language: English. Also native languages. | Range: $107 – 283 | A passport and either a visa or an electronic travel authority are required for Americans traveling for business. | Mon. through Fri., 38 hours. | The negotiation of contracts covering wages and working conditions is gradually shifting away from the centralized system. |

**Heading Notes 1 – 4:**

1: Source: Countries or regions were selected for this table because they were identified as emerging destinations for international assignments in "Global Relocation Trends 1996 Survey Report" put together by the National Foreign Trade Council and Windham International, both in New York City.

2: Source: The CIA World Factbook (www.odci.gov/cia/publications/nsolo/factbook). *GDP Per Capita* and *Inflation Rates* are 1995 estimates. *Literacy Rates* pertain to the percentage of the population aged 15 and over that can read and write, unless otherwise stated.

3: Source: The U.S. Department of State (www.state.gov/www/perdiems/9709/perdiems.html). Numbers are recommended per diem allowances for foreign travel.

4: Source: STAT-USA, U.S. Department of Commerce (www.stat-usa.gov). *Entry Requirements* and *Labor Law Snapshot* are short excerpts from the source and shouldn't be perceived as complete information. Some *Direct Investment* figures are "cumulative to date" and others are "annual." Some are "U.S." and others are "foreign."

| Labor Force [2] | Unemployment Rate [2] | Literacy Rate [2] | Telephone System [2] | Health & Medical Care [4] | International Schools [5] | Corruption Rating [6] | Hardship Premium [7] | Direct Investment (US$) [4] | U.S. Companies [4] | Embassy Information [8] |
|---|---|---|---|---|---|---|---|---|---|---|
| 67 million (1985) | 3% (1994) (under-employment: 40%) | 83.8% (1995) | Domestic service is fair; international service is good | There are a few modern clinics in Jakarta, but expats generally fly to Singapore for treatment of serious illnesses. | 23 schools in 20 cities | 2 | 10–15% | Approved U.S. investment since 1967: $12.5 billion. | Arco Freeport McMoRan General Electric General Motors Mobil NYNEX | **Embassy of the Republic of Indonesia** 2020 Massachusetts Ave. NW Washington, D.C. 20036 Tel: 202 / 775-5200 |
| 28.048 million (1992) | 8% (1995) | 99% (age 15+ finished 5 years of school; 1978) | Technologically advanced domestic and international systems. | Information not available. | 12 schools in 9 cities | 8 | 0% | U.S. investment: $4.314 billion 1994 – 1995. | Information not available. | **Embassy of the United Kingdom of Great Britain and Northern Ireland** 3100 Massachusetts Ave. NW Washington, D.C. 20008 Tel: 202 / 588-6500 |
| 10.9 million (1985) | 16% (1995) | 96.2% (1995) | Modern system, but few private phones. System often goes out in rainstorms. | There are many competent doctors, dentists and specialists available in Buenos Aires. | 6 schools in 1 city | 2 | 0% | U.S. investment totals $10 billion by mid-1996. | Information not available. | **Embassy of the Argentine Republic** 1600 New Hampshire Ave. NW Washington, D.C. 20009 Tel: 202 / 939-6400 URL: athea.ar/cwash/homepage/ |
| 32.153 million (1993) | 2.7% (1995) | 93.8% (1995) | Service to the general public is inadequate. | Medical care, especially in Bangkok, is adequate. Doctors often expect immediate cash payment. | 10 schools in 4 cities | 3 | 10–15% | U.S. investment exceeded $16 billion in 1997. | Ford General Motors IBM Kellogg | **Royal Thai Embassy** 1024 Wisconsin Ave. NW, Suite 401 Washington, D.C. 20007 Tel: 202 / 944-3600 E-mail: thai.wsn@thaiembdc.org URL: www.thaiembdc.org/ |
| 7.627 million (1993) | 2.8% (1995) | 83.5% (1995) | Adequate or good domestic service, depending on location. Good international service. | Information not available. | 4 schools in 2 cities | 5 | 0% | Based on approvals, U.S. projects valued at $1.2 billion in 1996. | Baxter International Exxon Intel Mattel Mobil Motorola | **Embassy of Malaysia** 2401 Massachusetts Ave. NW Washington, D.C. 20008 Tel: 202 / 328-2700 |
| 7.6 million (1993) | 11.7% (1995) | 91.1% (1995) | Modern and expanding. | Information not available. | 6 schools in 5 cities | 2 | 5% | Information not available. | Avon BellSouth Black & Decker Citibank Colgate-Palmolive Ralston Purina | **Embassy of the Republic of Venezuela** 1099 30th St. NW Washington, D.C. 20007 Tel: 202 / 342-2214 |
| 32.7 million (1990) | 25% (1995) | 93.7% (1995) | Considerable progress in some areas, far behind in others. | Most medical facilities don't meet international hygiene standards and lack qualified doctors and supplies. | 3 schools in 2 cities | 2 | 25% | Licensed capital for U.S. projects: $773 million in 1996. | Information not available. | **Embassy of the Socialist Republic of Vietnam** 1233 20th St. NW, Suite 400 Washington, D.C. 20037 Tel: 202 / 861-0737 E-mail: vietnamembassy@msn.com URL: www.vietnamembassy-usa.org/ |
| 8.63 million (1991) | 8.1% (1995) | 100% (1980) | Good domestic and international service. | Medical and dental services and all types of health facilities are comparable to those in the United States. | 2 schools in 2 cities | 8 | 0% | Information not available. | American Express Campbell Soup Coca-Cola Microsoft Philip Morris Toys 'R' Us | **Embassy of Australia** 1601 Massachusetts Ave. NW Washington, D.C. 20036 Tel: 202 / 797-3255 URL: www.aust.emb.nw.dc.us/ |

**Heading Notes 5 – 8:**

5: Source: "The ISS Directory of Overseas Schools 1997 – 1998" compiled by International Schools Services Inc. in Princeton, NJ (www.iss.edu).

6: Source: The 1997 TI-Corruption Ranking is a joint initiative of Göttingen University in Germany and Transparency International. The index uses seven survey sources and measures the perception of corruption by business professionals, risk analysts and the general public. Scores range from 0 (highly corrupt) to 10 (totally clean). (www.gwdg.de/~uwvw/rank-97.htm)

7: Source: Rochester, Wisconsin-based Runzheimer offers these U.S. State Department percentages as a general indicator of the appropriate salary increase that should be offered to an expatriate for accepting an assignment in these locations. Runzheimer cautions that it's best to seek customized data relating to your specific company.

8: Source: Contact information for all embassies was provided by The Electronic Embassy Site (www.embassy.org).

Research was conducted by Valerie Frazee, special projects editor for WORKFORCE and GLOBAL WORKFORCE. E-mail frazeev@globalworkforce.com to comment.

## Tips To Get You Started

Planning and becoming educated about new destinations is fundamental to the success of your endeavor. Follow these easy but crucial tips as you begin your exploration of new marketplaces.
- Network with colleagues who are already doing business successfully in the country.
- Ask about cross-cultural differences.
- Conduct a review of the local environment in the context of your specific kind of business.
- Evaluate two or three destinations.
- Examine existing educational and training opportunities—either at local universities or available through other businesses.

—CMS

porate and individual). Ideally, the new market would be a country where there's an untapped need for your products or services; a quality, skilled labor pool capable of manufacturing the products; and a welcoming environment (governmental and physical).

Are there such countries? Indeed, each has its pluses and minuses (see "15 Top Emerging Markets"). While Singapore has an educated, English-speaking labor force, basks in political stability and encourages foreign investment, it has a small population. While Mexico shines as an excellent example of a country that has aggressively lowered its income tax rates (from 60 percent in 1988 to 35 percent today) and attempts to alleviate other governmental hurdles in an effort to attract foreign investment, it has severe pollution. Many countries in Eastern Europe possess an eager, hungry-to-learn labor pool, but their infrastructures create difficulties. And, while India holds enormous promise, conducting business there is complex and difficult.

India's promise lays in its attributes. According to "Venturing in India: Opportunities and Challenges," a 1996 Conference Board report, India's impressive economic reforms have made it quite attractive for corporate investors. Because of its British roots, it has a strong legal system, developed technology and a growing financial sector. Known for its well-educated workforce, world-class scientific, engineering and management talent, and business schools that churn out excellent job candidates, India offers a labor pool that values education.

These positive attributes can be outweighed by potentially negative ones, however. India has an inadequate infrastructure, for example, with problems such as frequent power outages and crowded, unpaved roadways. And most daunting is India's political environment and highly bureaucratic and protectionist government that stir the flames of anxiety among multinational business leaders. For HR, the Indian business environment requires adroit management of people amid mountains of regulations.

For instance, the government wrought havoc with Houston-based Enron Development Corp. for five years.

Enron (along with Bechtel and General Electric Co., both of which had been successful in India with other projects) was in the midst of building a $2.8 billion power plant. It was the first foreign-owned power plant in India and one of the largest foreign investments ever. When a new regional government was elected, officials shut down construction of the plant and entangled the company in a judicial quagmire of 24 law-suits for 16 months. Knowing situations such as these are probable, HR must determine which issues (staffing vs. regulations) are more compelling.

**Consider the quality and availability of the local labor force.** The greatest challenge in entering a new market is often the work-force, specifically senior management. "After you determine that you have a marketplace that's going to utilize what you're producing, you need to see if there is the capability and talent in the local workforce to support the endeavor," says Richard Bahner, human resources head at New York City-based Citicorp. "You really need to do a total balanced evaluation. Some of these places offer less-expensive labor, but if they don't have the capabilities you're looking for, it may not be a savings because you'll have to supplement it with a large amount of computer support, training or expatriates."

The extent of the staffing challenges depends on your industry. "If you're distributing Pepsi™, you can manufacture it locally and teach people how to sell it easily enough, but if you're in global banking, you've got a lot more restrictions," Bahner explains.

Citibank has experienced this in the Asia-Pacific region. With relationships in China and Hong Kong for almost a century, it had an advantage when it looked to expand into Indonesia and Thailand. But it was hampered by the need for an educated workforce. Citibank developed the market in Indonesia and taught the people about electronic banking—eventually generating millions of Citibank Visa cardholders. But the HR issues were daunting.

"The biggest problem is the dearth of qualified locals," says Bill Fontana, formerly of Citibank in Indonesia and now vice president of international HR for the National Foreign Trade Council. It's a big, big problem. There are so few qualified people who can take senior positions (among 200 million Indonesians), that other U.S. companies will bid for this unique individual. "It jacks up the cost of your senior local person, and then you begin to pirate people away from other companies because they speak English, they've worked at another multinational organization, and therefore, you would pay almost anything to get them onto your payroll. It leads to spiraling inflation in the workforce."

As an example, Fontana was recruiting for a treasury head at Citibank in Indonesia. The position was staffed with an expat, and he wanted to fill it with a local. It took more than one year to identify a qualified person. Citibank offered the man $150,000 and a guaranteed base of $100,000. "He turned me down," says Fontana. "He told me that the Bank of Bali was offering him more money! And the expatriate was only making about $115,000."

The situation is similar in other parts of the region. Experienced, multilingual Thais and Taiwanese can look to their talented colleagues in Hong Kong and China for ways to bid-up their going wages. As these countries develop, the competition for talent is becoming ferocious. Local companies are vying with foreign firms for the same employees.

One obvious solution is education. In addition to the traditional training that internationally experienced firms such as Motorola, Coca-Cola and McDonald's have conducted for years, there are now joint ventures between universities and businesses. For instance, Baltimore-based Johns Hopkins University has paired with Nanjing University in China. Based in the city of Nanjing, 100 students each year participate in a bicultural business program and living experience (a Chinese and an American student are roommates) that prepares them for senior-level management positions.

The receptivity to education varies by location. Eastern Europe is different from Asia-Pacific. "The work ethic is very strong, and equally important, there's a strong interest in learning," says Fontana. "When we went into Eastern Europe, the question [from employees] was, 'When do I get my next training course?' The thirst for training and knowledge is staggering." Training can rarely keep pace with need.

**Evaluate laws and regulations.** The next thing you need to think about is whether the government has created an environment receptive to foreign businesses. The question is: Do the laws enhance or inhibit the chance of success?

No matter where in the world your company ventures, as economies develop and competition increases, local companies become stronger, and they often exert pressure on local governments to tighten regulations regarding foreign firms. For example, work permits for expats aren't as easy to obtain in many parts of the world as they once were. Mandated workforce practices can either aid or decrease your company's opportunities. Labor law and its effect on compensation and benefits requires research and comprehensive understanding.

One of the first questions must be: How restrictive is the labor law? "As an example, generally, in countries where the British flag has flown, the labor code is simple, straightforward and employer-friendly. Where the Napoleanic code has predominated, you find labor legislation that's complete, complex, confusing and expensive," says John de Leon, regional director of international HR consulting services for Deloitte & Touche LLP, based in Wilton, Connecticut. "In Asia-Pacific, generally speaking, labor law (although very different from the U.S.) isn't as restrictive and permits companies greater freedom to make decisions."

These restrictions refer to the presence of work councils that get involved in activities Americans would consider purely management decisions. They may restrict part-time and temporary employees. They will have provisions that affect termination. For example, in the United Kingdom, although there's a cost associated with terminating employment, it's far less expensive and less complicated to calculate than in most parts of Latin America.

You can't assume you're operating with a U.S. frame of reference. In many countries, the labor code includes a concept called *acquired rights.* The code says you can't take away anything from an individual. So, for example, job content, responsibilities, pay and benefits must remain constant. Another concern is strong labor unions. And, still another difficulty is that many rapidly growing countries spur growth by being less restrictive when a company enters the country to set up business. "It's at the back end where you get a lot of intervention," says Fontana. "I let go of nine people in Indonesia at a cost of $1.2 million in severance pay.

And then there's compensation and benefits. Social costs, medical-care costs, pension and social security costs differ greatly from one country to another. And often, the ways in which salaries are quoted and designed are significantly different. "Until recently, India capped the base salary for executives at a pretty low level in hard currency because of the socialist mindset," says Sheridan. "So, firms offered myriad allowances—cars, drivers, servants, clothing. American companies saunter in and want to roll it all into one basic salary, and they aren't seeing the other factors involved."

In other words, if you aren't discerning, country-specific labor laws and regulations can begin to eat severely into profits. Or, if you're not careful, you may get burned because you've unwittingly trespassed legal boundaries.

**Ask yourself, "How hospitable is this country to the business?"** Beyond the more narrowly defined and obvious HR issues, receptivity and overall friendliness to foreign business are major factors in selecting a destination country. How protectionist is the environment? What types of bureaucratic, regulatory and economic constraints exist? Is there political tension or security risk? Corruption? A workable legal system? Economic stability?

All of these issues complicate the ability to staff your operations. For instance, if your company faces political security risks, how will that affect the expatriation of employees? If it's a highly bureaucratic and regulated country, what will that do to your ability to hire and fire employees? If there's gross corruption in the local business environment, how will you train your staff to handle the situation?

How do all these elements interact? Latin America, for example has always ranked prominently in international operations for Farmington, Connecticut-based Otis Elevator Co. Worldwide. The company had maintained escalator factories throughout Latin America at one time, and then it consolidated most of the operations in Brazil (as well as small operations in Argentina and Uruguay). "Even though the business climate was kind of 'iffy' because of the hyperinflation (at the time), we chose Brazil because we were still making money. We had invested in a factory: we had a good relationship with the government so we could repatriate funds, and the labor market was good," says Jim Defau, director of compensation and benefits for the firm. "Overall, it's a conducive environment for doing business."

Defau explains that a receptive government provides a foundation from which to start the assessment of the business climate. The intangible quality of hospitality is a mixture of distinct factors. Is the legal and ethical environment one that your company can handle? Is the location a place that will attract or repel managers and workers from other countries? Will the government help or hinder your day-to-day concerns? Overall, is the country a place where all the factors combine so you'll be able to help your employees do the best job for the company and where your company can thrive?

Success depends on so many elements. It requires more skillful management of every aspect of the organization when you edge into new markets. There are so many hot spots and fumaroles, and the unprepared will surely get burned. HR is part of the holistic picture. "The functional silos that once existed are no longer in place. We're all business partners—HR, legal, finance, engineering, and, every aspect of the business affects every other aspect," says Defau.

If ever HR was core to business success, it has never been more obvious than in the pursuit of these active, hot markets.

_Charlene Marmer Solomon is a contributing editor for_ WORKFORCE _and_ GLOBAL WORKFORCE. _E-mail charsol @aol.com to comment._

**BY CARLA JOINSON**

# Why HR Managers Need To Think

# G L O B A L L Y

*Don't have any international operations?*
*Better learn about them before you do.*

American businesses are sending their employees to foreign locations in record numbers, largely because of international mergers, start-ups, acquisitions and joint ventures. The way human resource executives handle international issues can make or break an expatriate assignment, as well as affect a company's success in foreign markets. For many in HR, though, international responsibilities can come with little or no warning. Acquiring a global outlook now can help domestic HR staff more easily assume international duties later.

## Global marketplace drives international assignments

The National Foreign Trade Council (NFTC) estimates that 300,000 U.S. expatriates are on assignment at any given time. *The Global Relocation Trends 1996 Survey Report*, sponsored by Windham International and the NFTC, shows a solid trend toward more international assignments by responding companies, with 64 percent expecting expatriate growth. Additionally, 81 percent of participants in Arthur Andersen's 1997 *Global Best in Class* study of international human resource programs ex-

pected expansion into new regions in the world.

Even when businesses try to reduce their expatriate population by transferring their responsibilities to local nationals, expatriate growth continues. According to the *Global Relocation Trends* survey, a growing dependence on global sales has actually stepped up the demand for expatriates. Companies responding to the survey generate 43 percent of their revenues outside their headquarters country. Consequently, they need expatriates who can support their expansion through both technical expertise and cultural understanding.

Telecommunications, aerospace, engineering and information technologies, as well as banking and financial services, are prime fields for continued global expansion. Even small companies trying to expand their markets may need to send two or three people overseas.

Heidi O'Gorman, a manager of international HR consulting services at Arthur Andersen, says that all business these days is global. "A mid-sized business may get components from one company and sell to another company—either of which may be outside the U.S.," she explains. "Or that same company may suddenly find itself with a labor force in another country if it's part of a merger."

## Surprises for HR

Many HR managers with international responsibilities enjoy their jobs but admit that there can be surprises along the way. HR software based on U.S. needs might be inadequate in another country. Recruiting may involve caste systems and nepotism, while productivity during holidays such as the month-long Ramadan may lag because employees are fasting. No one can know everything about another country, but "business as usual" may be difficult if you're not prepared for an international spin.

"Try to remove the assumption you have that 'this will happen because I asked them to do it,'" says Olivier Maudiere, international HR manager at Walt Disney World. "Remove the assumption that once you put something in place, it will work. Follow-up, follow-up, follow-up."

"It's a totally different job from domestic HR," he continues. "And because you generally have more than one country you're responsible for, you can't rely on just one system or way of doing things. You have to be open to all the different problems."

It's important for HR staff to upgrade any weak areas such as negotiation skills, then quickly acquire country- or regional-specific knowledge and skills about laws and the political system. "Otherwise, you'll be perceived as woefully incompetent," says Scott Russell, senior vice president for human resources at Cendant Mobility in Danbury, Conn.

Experts say other surprises most often occur in the following areas:

**Communications.** Jerry Torma, director of international human resources and compensation at Nordson Corp. in Amherst, Ohio, says it's easy to take communication—in terms of time, distance, language and culture—for granted. That is, until geography makes it difficult.

"It's so much easier to communicate across four time zones in the United States than across 24 time zones around the world," he explains. "You can't decide to talk to people only when you're in the office.

"If you're communicating with someone in the Middle East, for example, you have four days of the week in which it will be hard to catch people in the office: Thursday and Friday for them, and Saturday and Sunday for you. This can be extremely frustrating, though e-mail can help."

**Physical demands.** "You need physical stamina for this job," says Russell. "Someone calling on his lunch hour with a gripe may be waking you up at midnight, or you may get a call about a business issue at 3 a.m."

Travel also can be demanding. "HR people need to travel to the countries they support, or they'll miss out on a lot of issues," says Maudiere. "It's like trying to use the Internet in place of face-to-face relationships; you must know what your subsidiaries need, or you'll fail to be their ambassador when you get back."

**Involvement with employees.** "One thing that surprised me," says Jeanne Dennison, director of HR for International Telecommunications Group at Bell Atlantic in White Plains, N.Y., "is how involved you get with an employee's family and personal life.

"Employees will often look to HR to know all about things that affect their families," Dennison explains, "and you can get involved at a level unheard of with domestic generalists."

**Cross-cultural gaps.** The differences between cultures can surprise both HR and the expatriates on assignment. Without cross-cultural training, anyone involved in the assignment can have trouble. "HR spends untold hours teaching people how to manage here in the U.S.," says Russell. "But they'll send someone to China without any training on how to manage the local workforce." He tells of an American company in Japan that charged its Japanese HR manager with reducing the workforce. "He studied the issue but couldn't find a solution within cultural Japanese parameters," says Russell. "So when he came back to the Americans, he reduced the workforce by resigning—which was not what they wanted."

Texas A&M International University professor Paul Herbig, author of the *Handbook of Cross-Cultural Marketing* (Hayworth, 1997), notes that these kinds of management mistakes happen all the time. "A sales manager in Brazil recruited 30 college graduates and gave them a week's training," he says. "Then he told them they would be selling door to door, and they all quit right in front of him. In Brazil, college graduates don't do that kind of work."

# Where
# **in the world**
# to get help

Though a single clearinghouse for international HR information isn't available, newcomers can still find plenty of help. Advice from experts includes the following:

1. Network within your own company or contact a counterpart in the host country.

2. Contact professional associations, such as the Society for Human Resource Management's Institute for International Human Resources (800-283-7476), the American Compensation Association (602-922-2020) or the International Personnel Association (203-358-9799).

3. Turn to domestic advisers such as tax or employment attorneys, if they have international expertise.

4. Hire international HR consultants, especially to help you lay the groundwork when you first start your program.

5. The two Arthur Andersen stud[ie]s mentioned in this article are available free of charge from Arthur Andersen LLP, Mailstop 05-40, 33 W. Monroe, Chicago, IL 60603.

6. National Foreign Trade Council Inc. (1270 Avenue of the Americas, New York, NY 10020-1700; (212) 399-7128) will send you its *1998 Directory of International Service and Information Providers.*

A manager in England saw workers making their own hot tea during breaks and thought he'd introduce some break-room efficiencies. "He took away their teapots and replaced them with an American vending machine selling iced tea," says Herbig, "and then he had a revolt on his hands."

Bill Sheridan, director of international compensation services at the NFTC, believes Americans often encourage behavior that is not appropriate to another culture. "In many countries, people are risk averse or don't want to stand out in a crowd. We tell them, 'be the best you can be' or try to motivate them within an American framework, and we just make them very uncomfortable."

O'Gorman notes that HR managers suddenly thrust into an international situation can be frustrated by the amount of time it takes to get things done. "Our fast-paced way of life isn't shared by other cultures," she says, "and you have physical and time boundaries you have to work around. For example, trying to collect compensation data for expats can be difficult," she continues. "Form W-2s need to come to you by the end of January, but that's an American institution. April 15th doesn't mean much in other cultures."

Torma warns HR people that their positions may not always generate respect. "Outside the United States, countries have 'personnel' or 'industrial relations,' which are several layers below HR," he says. "You need to be a businessperson first, then a practitioner. Interface with line people as much as possible, and learn as much as you can about your customers' products."

He, too, advises international HR staff to travel to the areas they support. "E-mail is not enough. With the possible exception of third-world countries, your customers will want you to go to them." He stresses that HR people should "try to get invited up-front to all the possible strategic planning sessions, so you can be proactive instead of reactive."

## The HR learning curve

"Things are hard enough to do in your own culture," says Rita Bennett, managing partner of Bennett Associates. "Companies underestimate the competency and skills, and the unbelievable demands, required of HR when they're given international responsibilities."

One of the most crucial skills a newcomer to international HR has to acquire is cultural sensitivity. "Even if a compensation specialist never leaves New Jersey, she'll still interact cross-culturally and will need to know how to communicate and deal with the other culture," says Bennett. She, and others, can rattle off a list of practical matters that need handling: visas, work permits and currency; housing, schools and medical care; language and cross-cultural training; avenues of communication; evacuation insurance, taxes and compensation. These factors, along with things such as host country recruiting and management, have to be juggled across cultural, economic and political systems that may be very different from one other.

The first thing HR must do, however, is to provide policy and guidance for these issues. "You don't want to be writing your international HR policy when the first guy's already on the plane," says Jo-Anne Vaughn, a consultant with Global Human Resource Services Ltd. of Bethesda, Md. Realistically, however, she finds that most companies won't put a plan together unless they do think they're getting ready to send someone overseas.

A study by Arthur Andersen, *Exploring International Assignees' Viewpoints*, shows clearly that few employees will accept an assignment if their families object or are unable to accompany them. The backbone of your international HR policy should be expatriate support, tempered by your company's corporate culture, needs and growth. Flexibility is key, since an assignment in the United Kingdom differs from one in Saudi Arabia or Zimbabwe. "If someone is living in a difficult area, you need to help them," says Vaughn. "An employee in Jakarta might be given a week of R&R in Singapore, where the family can also take care of medical needs."

Bell Atlantic's Dennison believes compensation is one of the key areas in which HR needs to come up to speed very quickly. "Some of the issues are quite varied and unique, such as the impact of hyperinflation or deflation. Many of the elements of compensation are far removed from base pay: COLA, housing, mobility premiums and the like."

Money matters also are close to the expatriate's heart. Retirement benefits, tax equalization and host country tax law, spousal lost-income compensation, and social security issues can have many ramifications for the expatriate. HR must develop policies to ensure that the expatriate isn't hurt financially by accepting an assignment, and then make certain that he or she understands all the options and responsibilities.

Legal issues and host country laws can also be areas of difficulty. "There's an idea of life-long employment in many countries," says Herbig. "In Japan, for instance, it can be hard to fire someone. Then it can be hard to hire other Japanese when they see this implied agreement broken." Sheridan echoes this concern. "Many countries have very pro-employee laws," he says. "Termination may

---

## COMMON CONCERNS

# What expatriates are worried about

The most important concerns of expatriates have been identified as follows:

### FAMILY NEEDS

The first consideration is for the trailing spouse's job, and the second is for their children's education.

### SAFETY

Arthur Andersen's *Exploring International Assignees' Viewpoints* study indicates that employees are less concerned about cultural or religious differences than they are about political stability and threats to their safety. Assignments in the Mid/Near East and Africa are least likely to be accepted.

### NEED FOR CROSS-CULTURAL TRAINING

In Arthur Andersen's *Global Best in Class* study, respondents rated this training as very important for success, yet it was only the third most frequently offered support program. Many experts cite a wish for more cross-cultural training as the No. 1 comment made by expatriates after their return.

### CAREER PLANNING

Only 46 percent of responding companies in the *Global Relocation Trends* survey, conducted by Windham International and the National Foreign Trade Council, formally address long-term career planning with their expatriates. Among the companies that do, 42 percent limit it to pre-assignment planning.

### DISENGAGEMENT FROM THE COMPANY

Many expats report a sense of alienation or a feeling of being forgotten by the home office. Giving expats a contact and keeping them up-to-date on changes and news within the company can counteract these feelings.

### REPATRIATION

Almost 60 percent of respondents to Arthur Andersen's *Exploring International Assignees' Viewpoints* study said they were not guaranteed a job upon completion of their assignments. Combined with a general lack of career counseling and few formal repatriation programs, companies often have significant attrition rates for returning employees.

mean very high monetary compensation, and some of these laws apply to expats, too."

Vaughn says HR should be aware that U.S. law doesn't necessarily follow the expat overseas. "Sexual harassment issues may be ignored or poorly enforced," she says. "Your U.S. employees can also evade things like child support or other domestic litigation," she continues. "This can be very hard on HR—they may know nothing about the problem until they get a court order demanding information."

## Trends in global HR

"Companies of all sizes are continuing to expand internationally," says Sheridan. "Suddenly, U.S. companies have a lot of expertise and capital that are needed in other countries. Enough barriers are coming down so that even businesses that traditionally didn't go overseas, such as insurance, are now able to expand. It's a push from U.S. business to find new markets, and a pull by host countries for our expertise."

Additionally, many companies are recruiting overseas for technical workers, and inpatriate HR responsibilities require the same cultural sensitivity and HR skills as expat management. "We send out 15 expats but bring in 80 to 100 inpatriates," says Monica Crone, an international HR generalist with British Aerospace N.A. Inc. in Chantilly, Va. "A lot of things we take for granted, our inpats know nothing about, such as how to open a bank account or get a driver's license in the United States."

Crone expects more intercompany transfers within the aerospace industry, and more joint ventures and global collaboration in general. Other experts see trends toward shorter, unaccompanied assignments where that's feasible, or where the location is less desirable. The Windham International/NFTC study shows that China and India are the top "emerging" destinations, but are perceived as the most challenging destinations and may require greater support from HR.

Disney's Maudiere believes today's expats have a new mindset. "It used to be only for the money," he says. "Now people are viewing expat assignments as something to put on their resumes." One last trend is within HR itself. Nordson's Torma sees more bilingual and bicultural people coming into HR, and even non-HR employees taking on these international responsibilities.

Experts agree that the effort HR gives to formulating policy and acting as advocates for expatriates is key to any international assignment's success. HR support of an expatriate's personal and family needs, training requirements, career development and repatriation may be the crucial factor in earning a return from the company's three-year, $1 million investment.

---

*Carla Joinson is a San Antonio freelance writer who specializes in business and management issues.*

# Interviewing in Japan

## BY BROCK STOUT

Not all of us are comfortable with the new global economy, but we may not be able to avoid it. If your company is not now exporting to Japan, it may be soon. As part of your firm's Japan market-entry strategy, you should start preparing to open and staff an office in Japan.

Japan is similar to North America in many ways, but the HR systems and philosophies are very different. I have seen many North American companies make very costly HR mistakes in Japan.

Fortunately, you can profit from their experiences.

The main thing to consider is how to recruit good managers in Japan. Here are three general suggestions I offer from my experience as a recruiting consultant who has interviewed hundreds of Japanese applicants in Tokyo.

## SUGGESTION #1: DON'T JUDGE BY ENGLISH ABILITY ALONE

I have worked with many international recruiters who are fooled by English-language facility. Last year, for example, a large American beverage company was hiring for top management-track positions in its Tokyo office. The company chose a young woman who had recently earned an MBA from a U.S. university and who was the most convincingly intelligent of any applicant.

She was hired, along with three other candidates, but was given a salary that exceeded those of the other new hires by $20,000 per year.

One month later the company realized that she lacked the basic skills for the job. Although the other candidates had not presented themselves as well—because their English was not

as polished—they were actually better qualified to work in the Japanese market than their more highly paid colleague.

The story ended happily—the employee was moved around between several departments until a good fit was found—but a lot of money and energy were wasted. This could have been avoided with better screening in the first stages of the process.

This problem is all too common. One of the biggest weaknesses of personnel policies in foreign companies is the tendency to choose applicants based on how well they speak English, observed the Japan Institute of Labor, a Tokyo-based think tank. And this weakness is not limited to North American organizations: Many companies from France and other European nations also place too high a priority on English language ability.

Ironically, facility in English may mean that a candidate is actually *less* qualified. (He or she may have spent too much time on homework for English class at the expense of other subjects.) Or it could mean that the candidate relates well with English speakers but is not able to relate as well to Japanese people. I have seen many such cases.

You will avoid problems by asking yourself at the end of each interview, "Do I like this candidate because his or her communication style made me feel comfortable?" Don't be ashamed if you answer "yes." After a few days in a country where it seems that only people at the hotel speak English, you may be excited to hear someone who articulates more than basic greetings without struggling.

## Nonbank Foreign Affiliates of U.S. Companies, 1995

| Country | No. of affiliates | No. of employees (thousands) | Total assets (millions of dollars) |
|---|---|---|---|
| *United Kingdom* | 2,393 | 928.8 | $641,348 |
| *Canada* | 2,023 | 918.1 | 246,242 |
| *Germany* | 1,358 | 596.3 | 219,538 |
| *France* | 1,226 | 413.9 | 135,906 |
| *Japan* | 1,006 | 414.9 | 280,164 |
| *Netherlands* | 999 | 138.8 | 139,078 |
| *Australia* | 855 | 258.7 | 81,055 |
| *Mexico* | 823 | 743.6 | 59,115 |
| *Italy* | 757 | 198.7 | 59,468 |
| *Switzerland* | 505 | 50.6 | 132,464 |
| *Africa* | 502 | 126.5 | 22,604 |
| *Brazil* | 400 | 299.9 | 48,477 |

**Source: U.S. Multinational Companies: Operations in 1995, in the October 1997** *Survey of Current Business*

## SUGGESTION #2: HEED CULTURAL DIFFERENCES

It seems trite to say that it is important to take cultural differences into account when judging people of other cultures. But if the idea is truly such a basic exercise in common sense then why do so few people remember to do it?

Here are some issues to consider.

**Views of teamwork.** I have interviewed many Japanese middle managers who have described the amazing work they did in executing new programs. Sometimes it was increasing sales in a region by 300 percent; sometimes it was reducing company costs by 25 percent. "I've finally found Superman," I thought.

But on several occasions, I happened to interview someone else from the same company who made the same claims.

I finally figured out that these projects were executed by teams, or were perhaps companywide. So it was actually 20 salespeople who increased sales, not just Mr. Suzuki's single-handed efforts.

The lesson for HR professionals: Always find out whether candidates have relied on teams to carry them.

**Views on authority.** Japan's sense of hierarchical structure is high. Japanese culture teaches submissiveness to elders and authority. So the person sitting across the desk from you may be unwilling to answer your questions directly.

(This trait is also found in other cultures. A person from Indonesia, for example, is more likely than someone from Europe to exhibit such behavior; within Europe, Italians believe in the importance of hierarchy more than Swedes do.)

In the democratic mind-set generally held by North Americans, informality is valued. But Japanese workers dislike questioning those in authority. Hence, many Japanese workers will claim to understand what an interviewer says even when they do not. You may be viewed as an authority figure and not someone to whom an applicant should admit ignorance.

**The value of Japanese universities.** I worked with a U.S.-based securities brokerage that insisted on Japanese locals who were also U.S. Ivy League graduates. They didn't recognize that each country has its own "Ivy-League-class" schools.

As an HR professional, you must do more than merely accept the value of Japanese schools. You must learn *why* Japanese schools have good reputations. (Is it academic standards or strong old boy networks?)

Japan's most prestigious public school is undoubtedly the University of Tokyo. Waseda and Keio are rivals for the rank of top private school. Hitsotsubashi is known for strong alumni networks. Sophia and International Christian University produce more bilingual graduates.

Top universities generally do not specialize in a certain discipline as North American schools do, with one school excelling in medicine, another in business or computer science. Japanese schools are designed to develop students with overall knowledge. Then the employer trains the new recruit in a discipline, such as computer programming, after the recruit joins the company. For this reason, you may want to hire mid-career people until your subsidiary is well established.

**Confidence.** Not all cultures teach individuals to appear self-assured. Most, including Europeans, don't encourage it as much as North Americans do.

Japanese culture trains people to intentionally demean themselves as a form of politeness. So if an interviewee appears overly meek, don't assume a lack of self-esteem.

**Risk aversion.** "Playing hard to get" may have helped to get dates in high school, but it turns off most potential employers. So it was with a Boston-based computer firm that sought a marketing manager in Japan.

In this case, I interviewed a woman from a competitor. The applicant had experienced broken promises with her current employer so she was understandably gun-shy. Her fears made her appear aloof and suspicious when the company made an offer in the final meeting. They were not able to understand and address her fears, so they lost out on a great manager and ended up with a second-choice candidate.

## SUGGESTION #3: COMMUNICATE FOR UNDERSTANDING

Personal space is very important. Have you ever watched two Europeans embrace and kiss on the street, even if they are only friends? You probably have not seen two Japanese people do so.

Every culture assigns a certain distance that surrounds each person; it is not acceptable for others to enter that space. Japanese have a large space requirement. Even mothers don't hug and kiss their own children very much. So don't stand or sit too close to an interviewee because it may cause discomfort.

To avoid intruding on personal space, plan the room layout ahead of time.

Another simple warning: Non-native English speakers will have a harder time expressing themselves and a harder time understanding you. Expect to make extra efforts to facilitate good communication. Here are some tips to bear in mind.

**Give large amounts of information in writing.** Let applicants read through the long explanations about the company and the position instead of presenting such information in a 10-minute speech. Listening to a foreign language can be taxing and can take all of the applicant's concentration, leaving little energy for the core parts of the interview. Use diagrams to explain concepts: Flowcharts are a good way to make processes easier to understand.

**Use examples and case studies.** This is helpful in any interviewing situation but is vital for cross-cultural interviewing. Allowing candidates to compare and contrast situations discourages them from seeking the "right answer" and will help you understand answers in the cultural context.

Here are some examples of the type of questions that will elicit better information about candidates:

- "You are working on a project for Mr. Smith. What would you do?" This is a much better question than "Do you think you are a team player?"
- "What would be the best way to handle this situation in Japan? How would it differ from the way it is best done in the U.S.?" (This shows the candidate's awareness of cultural differences and how to address them in a multicultural organization.)
- "You must tell Mr. Tanaka that he has been fired. How would you do this as a Japanese manager? How would you do it if you were both Westerners?

**Don't interview in Japanese unless you are fully fluent.** Twelve years ago I made the mistake of interviewing candidates in Japanese—after studying the language for only a year. In one interview a young woman admitted to having an adulterous affair—even though this was not even close to the topic I was inquiring about—because of my unskilled use of the language.

**Speak slowly.** We all forget this point more often than we should.

Four other hints: (1) enunciate clearly; (2) avoid slang, jargon, colloquialisms and other difficult phraseology; (3) repeat often; and (4) avoid long sentences.

**Listen well and confirm what you have heard.** Communicating well with an interviewee obviously includes listening. A key to understanding is to clarify without prompting, to avoid having the candidate change a statement because he or she thinks you disagree with it.

As any experienced interviewer knows, rephrasing can lead the interviewee. A good way is to say, "Do you mean X or Y?" That way you are less likely to prompt for correct answers.

If you say, "Did you really mean to say X?" then the applicant will assume X is the "correct" answer. A better way is to mention a third answer that is not likely to be thought "correct" by the interviewee. If he or she says, "I can relocate to anywhere in the world," ask something like, "How about Afghanistan?" Then you may get a reply such as, "I mean anywhere in North America or Europe."

Most people become nervous in an interview situation, and many people revert to their native languages when they become nervous. So you may hear sentences with non-English words or incorrect words thrown in. If this makes the sentence unclear to you, it is important to ask what is meant. Simply saying you don't understand will frustrate the applicant, so

you should rephrase what was said and ask for confirmation.

**Encourage interviewees to speak up.** Here are some tips:

- Be patient. Don't finish sentences for candidates. And allow them time to construct sentences in their own words. After all, candidates may be translating the answers to your questions into English after composing the answers in their heads in Japanese.
- Minimize meeting interruptions. What someone of another culture considers to be annoying may vary, so limit interview interruptions as much as possible.

## CONCLUSION

Because of cultural differences, it can be easy to hire the wrong person in Japan. The road to becoming a successful screener of Japanese job candidates is long, but you can do it. Following these suggestions will steer you around the major potholes.

---

*Brock M. Stout, principal of Japan Management Solutions, spends half of his time in Tokyo and half in the United States. He can best be reached at—HYPERLINK mailto: career@ Japan-mail.com.*

We encourage you to photocopy and use this page as a tool to assess how the articles in **Annual Editions** expand on the information in your textbook. By reflecting on the articles you will gain enhanced text information. You can also access this useful form on a product's book support Web site at **http://www.dushkin.com/ online/.**

NAME: _____     DATE: _____

TITLE AND NUMBER OF ARTICLE: _____

BRIEFLY STATE THE MAIN IDEA OF THIS ARTICLE: _____

LIST THREE IMPORTANT FACTS THAT THE AUTHOR USES TO SUPPORT THE MAIN IDEA:




WHAT INFORMATION OR IDEAS DISCUSSED IN THIS ARTICLE ARE ALSO DISCUSSED IN YOUR TEXTBOOK OR OTHER READINGS THAT YOU HAVE DONE? LIST THE TEXTBOOK CHAPTERS AND PAGE NUMBERS:




LIST ANY EXAMPLES OF BIAS OR FAULTY REASONING THAT YOU FOUND IN THE ARTICLE:




LIST ANY NEW TERMS/CONCEPTS THAT WERE DISCUSSED IN THE ARTICLE, AND WRITE A SHORT DEFINITION: